RENDEZVOUS WITH ADA:
A Programmer's Introduction

Robert
Chotticks

RENDEZVOUS WITH ADA:
A Programmer's Introduction

David Naiditch

JOHN WILEY & SONS
New York • *Chichester* • *Brisbane* • *Toronto* • *Singapore*

Copyright © 1989 by David Naiditch.

All rights reserved. Published simultaneously in Canada.

Reproduction or translation of any part of this work beyond that permitted by Section 107 or 108 of the 1976 United States Copyright Act without the permission of the copyright owner is unlawful. Requests for permission or further information should be addressed to the Permissions Department, John Wiley & Sons, Inc.

Library of Congress Cataloging in Publication Data:
Naiditch, David.
   Rendezvous with Ada: a programmer's introduction / David Naiditch.
     p. cm.
   Bibliography: p.
   Includes index.
   ISBN 0-471-61654-0
   1. Ada (Computer program language)   I. Title.
QA76.73.A35N35   1989   88-7929
005.13'3--dc19   CIP

To my grandmother, Regina Schachter

Contents

Acknowledgments	xiii
Preface	xv

1. Introduction — 1

    Development of Ada — 2
    Features of Ada — 4
    Current Uses of Ada — 5
    Exercises — 6

2. Overview — 7

    A Sample Program — 7
        Line-by_Line Analysis of Program — 10
        With Clause — 14
        Use Clause — 15
    Additional Features of Ada — 16
        Features of Ada Typical
            of High-Level Languages — 16
        Unusual Features of Ada — 18
    Exercises — 21

3. Basics of Ada   23

    Lexical Elements   23
        Identifiers   23
        Delimiters   25
        Literals   26
        Comments   30
    Scalar Types   30
        Integer Type   32
        Floating Point Type   35
        User-Defined Enumeration Types   36
        Character Type   37
        Boolean Type   38
    Subtypes   42
    Attributes   46
    Type Conversion   49
    Order of Operations   50
    Exercises   53

4. Control Structures   57

    The If Statement   57
    The Case Statement   65
    Loop Statements   72
        The Simple Loop   72
        The While Loop   73
        The For Loop   76
    The Goto Statement   84
    Exercises   86

5. Arrays   91

    One-Dimensional Arrays   92
    Two-Dimensional Arrays   99
    Anonymous Array Types   103
    Dynamic Arrays   105
    Unconstrained Array Types   106
    Strings   107
    Boolean Vectors   113
    Array of Arrays   114
    Array Attributes   115
    Operations on Arrays   119
    Exercises   122

6.	**Records**	**129**
	Record Types without Discriminants	130
	Record Types with Discriminants	136
	Variant Records	136
	Records with Different Sized Components	147
	Two Other Uses of Discriminated Records	149
	Exercises	150
7.	**Blocks, Procedures, and Functions**	**157**
	Blocks	158
	Procedures	162
	Functions	164
	Features of Procedures and Functions	167
	Parameter Modes	167
	Positional and Named Notation	171
	Default Parameter Values	172
	Subunits	174
	Subprogram Library Units	177
	Overloading	178
	Returning Composite Values	183
	Recursive Subprograms	184
	Exercises	187
8.	**Packages**	**195**
	Package Specifications	196
	Package Bodies	198
	Examples of Packages with Specifications and Bodies	198
	Designing in Ada	205
	The With Clause and Use Clause	206
	When to Employ the Use Clause	210
	Embedded Packages	214
	Private Types	218
	Limited Private Types	224
	Exercises	228
9.	**Generics**	**235**
	Generic Functions	236
	Generic Procedures	241
	Generic Packages	245
	Generic Subprogram Parameters	250
	Exercises	260

10. Compilation Units — 263

    Primary Units and Secondary Units — 264
    Compilation Dependencies — 267
    Compilation Order — 268
    Recompiling Dependent Units — 270
    Compiling an Entire Ada Program — 272
    Developing Ada Programs — 272
    Exercises — 274

11. Exceptions — 277

    Predefined Exceptions — 278
    User-Defined Exceptions — 281
    Propagation of Exceptions — 283
    Suppressing Exceptions — 291
    Exercises — 293

12. Access Types — 299

    Pointers — 300
    Linked Lists — 309
    Exercises — 326

13. More About Types — 329

    Universal Types — 329
    Derived Types — 334
    Fixed Point Types — 339
    Implicit Conversion of Universal Types — 341
    Exercises — 343

14. Input/Output — 347

    TEXT_IO Package — 348
        Formatting I/O — 349
        File I/O — 360
    SEQUENTIAL_IO Package — 368
    DIRECT_IO Package — 371
    IO_EXCEPTIONS Package — 375
    Referencing Unprintable Characters — 377
    Exercises — 378

15. Tasking — 381

- Tasks That Do Not Interface — 382
- Tasks That Interface Without Transferring Data — 385
- Tasks That Interface and Transfer Data — 391
- The Selective Wait — 394
- Conditional Entry Calls and Timed Entry Calls — 400
- Task Attributes — 401
- Entry Families — 402
- Pragma Priority — 403
- Task Types — 404
- Task Interference — 405
- Dynamically Created Tasks — 408
- Real-World Example — 409
- Exercises — 415

16. Low-Level Programming — 421

- Representation Attributes — 423
  - *Attribute ADDRESS* — 423
  - *Attribute SIZE* — 423
  - *Attribute STORAGE_SIZE* — 424
  - *Attributes POSITION, FIRST_BIT, and LAST_BIT* — 424
- Representation Clauses — 425
  - *Length Clauses* — 425
  - *Enumeration Clauses* — 426
  - *Record Representation Clauses* — 429
  - *Address Clauses* — 433
- Pragma PACK — 435
- Unchecked Conversion — 436
- Language Interfaces — 437
- Exercises — 438

Appendixes — 441

- A. Predefined Language Attributes — 441
- B. Predefined Language Pragmas — 449
- C. STANDARD Package — 451
- D. SYSTEM Package — 455
- E. TEXT_IO Package — 457
- F. SEQUENTIAL_IO Package — 461
- G. DIRECT_IO Package — 463
- H. Keywords — 465

Index — 467

Acknowledgments

I would like to thank my wife, Jacqueline Naiditch, who was the technical editor for this book. Ms. Naiditch did extensive rewriting, research, and consulting with me to ensure clarity and conciseness. In addition, Ms. Naiditch wrote the introduction and drew all the figures. Her writing and editing skills, conscientiousness, and commitment contributed immeasurably to the book.

I would also like to thank Erik Magnuson, who reviewed the text for technical accuracy and completeness, compiled all the programs, and supplied a choice program sample for the packages, generics, and tasking chapters.

Finally, I would like to thank Diane Cerra, editor, Scientific and Technical Division, John Wiley & Sons. Ms. Cerra coordinated this entire project with great efficiency and obvious expertise. She also took the time to answer all of my questions with patience and good humor.

Preface

When I first started learning Ada, I was rather unhappy with the Ada books on the market. They were either too advanced or too superficial. In almost all cases, the books were poorly written. The complexity of the Ada language remained obscured by the complexity of the English language used to write the book.

Years later, when I began teaching Ada, these difficulties became especially evident as I searched for an appropriate textbook. As a result, I developed my own material for teaching that combined clear writing with many code examples. Whenever possible, I used humor to make the material more palatable.

This book is based on the techniques that I have successfully used in teaching the Ada language. The goal of the book is to be clear and direct yet technically accurate, to give concrete form to abstract concepts in numerous code examples, to help the reader retain what is learned by including many exercises, and, through it all, to make the reader smile at least once per chapter.

The book is especially geared toward beginning Ada programmers learning the language on their own and toward students desiring a clearly written textbook. In either case, previous knowledge of at least one other high-level programming language is advisable.

The more advanced programmer is not ignored. Technical accuracy and completeness are not sacrificed for the sake of simplicity. Entire chapters are devoted to advanced topics. In addition, all readers will benefit from the warnings of common Ada "pitfalls." These pitfalls have been gleaned from repeated mistakes made by students and professional programmers as they learn the language.

Since the book is especially geared toward the beginner, it is structured to introduce the reader gradually to the complexities of the Ada language. The beginning chapters cover the more basic aspects of the language and provide a solid foundation for the subsequent, more advanced chapters.

Each chapter is clearly organized. First, an introduction explains topics that will be covered in the chapter. Each topic is then discussed, in the order mentioned in the introduction. The chapter concludes with exercises to help reinforce key points. In the classroom, of course, these exercises can be used as homework or for tests.

Ada is one of the most powerful programming languages ever to be developed. I hope that this book will enable a broad spectrum of programmers to take advantage of its many innovative features.

David Naiditch
Los Angeles, California

RENDEZVOUS WITH ADA:
A Programmer's Introduction

Chapter 1

INTRODUCTION

In the early 1970s, there was a full-blown software crisis. Department of Defense (DOD) funds were being rapidly drained by exorbitant software costs. In 1973, software costs constituted $3 billion of the $7.5 billion spent by the DOD on computer systems. These costs were primarily caused by a plethora of programming languages and the "primitive" nature of these languages.

The huge number of languages—more than 450—was created by defense agencies and system project offices, which kept spawning new languages from existing ones in order to meet project requirements. With numerous languages came numerous problems. For instance, languages were largely incompatible; they could not easily "talk" to each other. This computer "Tower of Babel" resulted in many costly mistakes. In one situation, an attempt was made to develop a tactical operations system that would use computers to help battlefield commanders make decisions. When the system was tied to other systems using different computer languages, translation was slow and full of errors. The entire program was halted after $100 million was spent. Another problem with numerous languages was that software was not portable: It could not be easily transported to different computers or projects. Similarly, software engineers could not transfer their skills across a broad spectrum of projects; rather, they they had to become highly specialized. The many languages also resulted in minimal software being available for each language, as well as restricted competition in the maintenance and enhancement phases of projects. Competition was restricted because a competitor had to bear the initial investment associated with a new language—including support software and programmer training—already made by the developer of a language.

In addition to the overabundance of computer languages, the existing languages were inadequate because they were obsolete—they did not support modern software engineering principles. Thus, code was difficult to write and maintain, because it was hard to read and understand. The code lacked clear structure and contained low-level details that would have been hidden by a more modern language. The obsolete languages also resulted in software that was hard to reuse, because units of code were so interdependent. Modules often could not be extracted and used in different programs. This interdependency also made it difficult to modify code without introducing unwelcome side effects.

All of the problems mentioned were especially severe in embedded systems. An embedded system is one in which a computer is part of a larger system, such as computerized radar used in aircraft. Embedded systems are typically complex real-time systems that contain many lines of code, are long lived, and are continually being modified. Because of the size, complexity, lifespan, and volatility of these systems, they were responsible for 56% of DOD software costs in 1973.

The software crisis, then, included problems such as software being excessively expensive, not portable, difficult to maintain, and not reusable. All of these problems were exacerbated in embedded systems. Clearly, something had to be done to help address this crisis. The "something" was Ada. In this chapter, we will explore the development of the Ada programming language, the features of the language, and its current uses.

DEVELOPMENT OF ADA

In 1975, the DOD acted to reverse the trend of proliferating computer languages. Instead of hundreds of languages, only one computer language would be used. To determine which language would become the new standard, a requirements document was written for a high-level language appropriate for embedded computer systems.

The requirements document, called Strawman, was sent to interested civilians and military personnel. These people reviewed the document and sent their comments to the joint-service High Order Language Working Group (HOLWG), which had been organized to write the requirements document and to evaluate existing programming languages.

A revised version of the requirements document, called Woodenman, was written in 1975. This document was widely circulated for comments. Based on the comments received, a third version, Tinman, was issued in 1976. By this time, through this unprecedented method of soliciting comments and refining requirements, HOLWG had a good idea of the needs of the software community. A language was needed that would support modern software engineering principles such as modularity, strong typing, data abstraction, and information hiding.

During 1976, 23 existing programming languages were evaluated against the requirements in Tinman. None of the languages met all the requirements. However, ALGOL 68, Pascal, and PL/1 were recommended as a starting point for development of a new language.

A fourth set of requirements, called Ironman, was then written. Ironman contained a description of a new programming language, which served as the basis for an international design competition. There were 15 bidders who entered the competition. In 1977, these 15 bidders were narrowed down to 4. The remaining 4 bidders were contracted to design the new language. The best-designed language would be selected as the official language of the DOD. In order for each design to be judged in an unbiased manner, each design document submitted was only identified by a color: blue, green, red, and yellow. The four designs were evaluated by specific groups commissioned by each branch of the military and were also reviewed by interested civilians. All four languages developed were based philosophically on Pascal.

In 1978, two of the four languages were selected for further development: "red," which was Intermetrics, Boston; and "green," which was Cii-Honeywell Bull, France. These two teams were instructed to base further development on a new, final set of requirements, Steelman, which was published in 1978. The two final designs were reviewed by experts from 15 nations, and the winner was selected: Cii-Honeywell Bull.

In 1979, the winning language was named Ada, in honor of Ada, the Countess of Lovelace and daughter of Lord Byron. Ada Lovelace lived in the early 1800s, was a mathematician, and is often given the honor of being considered the first computer "programmer." Her programs were written for a computer designed by Charles Babbage. The computer, called the Analytical Engine, was never built because the technology was not sophisticated enough to manufacture gears and levers of the required precision. Development of such a computer had to await the age of electronics.

The language now had a name but was still called "Preliminary Ada." Before being standardized, Ada went through an extremely rigorous test and evaluation phase, again unprecedented by any other language. Approximately 80 teams of programmers reviewed the language and suggested changes. In October 1979, a workshop was held, with presentations and discussions. The resulting 900 comments were analyzed by a company contracted by the DOD and by a group of language experts called the "distinguished reviewers." As always, comments were solicited from people in diverse fields: academia, industry, DOD, and consulting firms. Finally, in February 1983, Ada was published as a standard: ANSI/MIL-STD-1815A.

Ada offers many advantages over other programming languages. For instance, since no subsets or supersets are allowed, Ada source code may be ported between different Ada compiler systems, with minimal changes. In addition to code portability, people portability is enhanced. Programmers can move from project to project without having to learn new languages. Ada also helps manage the complexity and improve the maintainability of software by supporting modern software engineering principles. Finally, Ada source code is easy to read.

All of these advantages resulted because of the tremendous input from the software community. Before Ada was standardized, approximately 7000 comments from 15 different countries were reviewed. Therefore, the final version of Ada contains features that reflect the needs of a vast community of software engineers.

FEATURES OF ADA

Ada supports principles of modern software engineering, such as modularity, strong typing, data abstraction, information hiding, overloading, exception handling, and structured control statements. Modularity means that code consisting of many modules can be written. Instead of being overwhelmed by a complex mass of code, the programmer can deal with manageable units of code. Also, a complex problem, through successive refinement, can be reduced to a set of simple problems that are trivial to implement as modules.

The principle of strong typing mandates that every data object belong to a type and have a clearly defined set of possible values and operations. Objects belonging to different types cannot be confused with one another, because they cannot be assigned or compared to one another.

Data abstraction enables the programmer to extract essential properties while omitting nonessential details. Information hiding helps enforce data abstraction. Irrelevant details can be made inaccessible by being hidden. Thus, reliability is improved, because coding strategies cannot be based on these hidden details. In addition, information hiding can be used for security purposes, to prevent outsiders from accessing "sensitive" portions of code.

Overloading is the ability to use one name to mean more than one thing; exception handling allows programmers to intercept runtime errors and take appropriate remedial action; and structured control statements enable programmers to write well-structured code that avoids the use of GOTO statements.

CURRENT USES OF ADA

In 1980, the Ada Joint Program Office (AJPO) was established within the office of the Secretary of Defense. AJPO is responsible for Ada policy in the DOD and for the recognition, acceptance, and standardization of Ada as the official computer programming language of the DOD. Before March 1987, many companies working on DOD contracts were able to obtain waivers from the DOD and avoid the use of Ada. However, on March 30, 1987, the DOD issued much stricter regulations requiring Ada to be the single, common high-order programming language.

The DOD has mandated that Ada be used in the Advanced Tactical Fighter (ATF) program. In addition to its use by the DOD, Ada will be used by the National Aeronautics and Space Administration (NASA) for the space station, and by the Federal Aviation Administration (FAA) for air traffic control.

Furthermore, Ada is employed in the private commercial sector. For instance, Boeing is using Ada for the 7J7 aircraft program. Also, several computer firms, such as Computer Corporation of America (CCA) and CRI, Inc., have written database management systems in Ada. Ada is even being used in business activities such as payroll.

Ada is not just reaching government and civilian markets in the United States; it is also widely accepted in Europe. This is not surprising, considering the Ada design team included four times as many Europeans as Americans. In Europe, Ada enjoys widespread use in finance and communications.

In finance, British banks will be using Ada, largely for security reasons. Ada makes computer crime difficult because implementation details can be hidden and the use of data structures can be controlled. Two leading Finnish banks have rewritten much of their business software in Ada. In communications, National Public Telephone and Telegraph of Belgium, Nippon Telephone and Telegraph of Japan, and Ericsson, a Swedish PBX manufacturer, will use Ada.

In addition, the Spanish government is using Ada for an air traffic control system. Also, the North Atlantic Treaty Organization (NATO) has selected Ada for its command, control, and information systems.

Because Ada is enjoying such widespread use in the international community, the International Standards Organization wants to establish Ada as an international standard. Another reflection of international popularity is the list of countries with members that belong to SIGAda (Special Interest Group on Ada), which is sponsored by the Association for Computing Machinery, Inc., New York. The many countries represented in SIGAda include Argentina, Costa Rica, Denmark, Egypt, Korea, Malaysia, Norway, Portugal, Taiwan, and Yugoslavia.

In addition to SIGAda, there are numerous other Ada working groups, such as AdaJUG (Ada-JOVIAL Users Group), PIWG (Performance Issues Working Group), SDSAWG (Software Development Standards and Ada Working Group), Ada-Europe, and Ada-Sweden. These groups are increasing their membership as Ada becomes more popular.

With this increased popularity, Ada has inspired the creation of companies whose sole business is Ada technology and support. These companies manufacture Ada compilers, Ada support tools, educational material, and dedicated Ada workstations. A few of these companies have written inexpensive Ada compilers that can be run on personal computers.

Thus, the language that began as a solution to the DOD software crisis has ended by addressing the needs of a much broader community. Ada has indeed become the wave of the future in both the military and civilian sectors.

This chapter provided an introduction to the development, features, and use of Ada. The next chapter is an overview of the Ada language.

EXERCISES

1. What problems constituted the software crisis?

2. How was Ada developed?

3. What are some of the advantages of Ada over other programming languages?

4. Describe three modern software engineering principles supported by Ada.

5. Describe one use of Ada in the private commercial sector.

6. Explain why some British banks will be using Ada.

7. What is an embedded system, and what are its characteristics?

Chapter 2

OVERVIEW

This chapter presents an overview of Ada. When learning a large, complex language such as Ada, there is a risk of initially focusing too much on the details and not seeing the overall structure of the language. Since this chapter is an overview, concepts and features of the language are introduced that will not be fully explored until later in the book. Read this chapter, then, without expecting to fully understand everything; concentrate on getting a feel for the Ada language.

This overview consists of two sections. The first section is a detailed examination of a complete Ada program. This sample program, although simple, uses many of Ada's features. These features will be discussed as they are encountered in the code. The second section covers features of Ada that are not illustrated in the sample program. The discussion at this point will be quite general. Full details about each feature will follow in the succeeding chapters of this book.

A SAMPLE PROGRAM

Let us begin the overview by examining an Ada program that, despite its simplicity, illustrates many important features of Ada. These features include control structures, the context specification, procedures, packages, generic instantiation, input/output operations, the TEXT_IO package, overloading, default parameter values, and the Ada library.

8   Rendezvous with ADA: A Programmer's Introduction

```ada
with TEXT_IO;  use TEXT_IO;      -- context specification
procedure TOTEM_POLE is          -- procedure specification
                                 -- (excluding the keyword is)
   -- declarative part
   TOTEMS : INTEGER := 1;
   package INT_IO is new INTEGER_IO (INTEGER);
   use INT_IO;
begin
   -- statement part
   PUT_LINE ("How many faces in the Totem Pole?");
   GET (TOTEMS);
   NEW_LINE;                              -- advances 1 line on screen
   PUT ("Here is a Totem Pole with ");    -- outputs a string
   PUT (TOTEMS);                          -- outputs an integer
   PUT (" faces:");                       -- outputs a string
   NEW_LINE (2);
   for FACES in 1..TOTEMS loop            -- for loop
      PUT_LINE ("\\\\\\\\");
      PUT_LINE ("| (*) | (*) |");
      PUT_LINE ("|   o    |");
      PUT_LINE ("_____/");
   end loop;
end TOTEM_POLE;
```

If you have access to an Ada compiler, try compiling and running this program. A sample run of the program follows:

```
How many faces in the Totem Pole?
> 3
Here is a Totem Pole with 3 faces:

\\\\\\\\
| (*) | (*) |
|   o    |
_____/
\\\\\\\\
| (*) | (*) |
|   o    |
_____/
\\\\\\\\
| (*) | (*) |
|   o    |
_____/
```

The user is first prompted for the number of faces to be placed in the totem pole. The user's response is entered after the prompt, >. In this sample run, the user enters the number 3. The user is then informed that a totem pole consisting of 3 faces follows, and the totem pole is output.

We will begin our discussion of this program with a few general comments. We will then explain the program line by line. When you look at the code, the first thing you might notice is that words are written three different ways: in lowercase bold letters, in uppercase and lowercase letters, and in all uppercase letters.

The words in lowercase bold letters, called keywords or reserved words, are those that have special meaning in the Ada language. These words are printed in boldface letters to help flag them out to the reader. The keywords used in our example are **with**, **use**, **procedure**, **is**, **package**, **new**, **begin**, **for**, **in**, **loop**, and **end**. For a complete list of keywords, see appendix H.

Words that appear in uppercase and lowercase letters are used in strings and comments. Strings consist of text that appears within quotes. In strings, Ada distinguishes between uppercase and lowercase letters. Comments consist of text that follows a double hyphen, --.

Finally, identifiers (names) of items such as variables, constants, types, procedures, and packages, are written in all uppercase letters.

This use of uppercase, lowercase, and boldface letters follows the conventions used in the *Reference Manual for the Ada Programming Language* (hereafter referred to as the Ada Language Reference Manual). How closely you follow these conventions is up to you. Use uppercase or lowercase letters as desired. As far as Ada is concerned, uppercase letters are indistinguishable from lowercase letters. Just be consistent and make your code as easy to read as possible.

In the sample program, you may have also noticed the use of semicolons. Unlike languages such as Pascal where the semicolon is used as a separator, in Ada the semicolon is used as a terminator. Every complete Ada statement must end with a semicolon. This does not mean that every line of code must end with a semicolon. The following line of code does not end with a semicolon because it is not a complete statement:

for FACES **in** 1..TOTEMS **loop**

This **for** loop statement is not complete because it does not end with the keyword **loop**. Rather, it ends with the keywords **end loop** several lines later in the code. The terminating semicolon therefore appears after **end loop**.

Statements like this **for loop** not only may extend through many lines of code; they may contain other statements within them. In our example, the **for** loop statement extends through six lines of code and contains four PUT_LINE statements. The PUT_LINE statements embedded within the **for** loop are indented several spaces to the right. Even though the Ada compiler does not care how you indent your code, people who read your code do care. When embedded statements are indented, the structure of the code can easily be seen.

10   Rendezvous with ADA: A Programmer's Introduction

The layout of Ada programs, then, has an impact of how easily code can be read. This layout can vary, depending on the programmer. Again, this book closely follows the layout style presented in the Ada Language Reference Manual. It is recommended that you follow a similar style. However, as just mentioned, the Ada compiler is not concerned about indentation of code or other matters of layout. The compiler even accepts the following unsightly layout:

```
-- acceptable to compilers but not to humans
with TEXT_IO; use TEXT_IO; procedure TOTEM_POLE is TOTEMS:
INTEGER := 1; package INT_IO is new INTEGER_IO (INTEGER); use
INT_IO; begin PUT_LINE ("How many faces in the Totem Pole?"); -- etc.
```

Line-by-Line Analysis of Program

Let us now examine the preceding program, TOTEM_POLE, one line at a time. The first line of this program consists of two statements, which form the context specification. These statements contain the keywords **with** and **use**:

```
with TEXT_IO;  use TEXT_IO;  -- context specification
```

These two statements are often placed on the same line because they are frequently used together. A context specification defines the context or environment in which an Ada program exists. Context specifications play a key role in Ada. We will therefore return to this topic after we finish our line-by-line discussion of this program.

The two hyphens that appear at the end of the context specification denote the beginning of a comment. The comment extends to the end of the line. Comments are ignored by the compiler; they are provided for the benefit of humans who read the code.

The next line in the program begins with the keyword **procedure**. In Ada, the main program is almost always a procedure. Other program units making up a program may also be procedures. Following the keyword **procedure** is a user-supplied procedure name. In this case, the procedure name is TOTEM_POLE. In Ada, a name can be of any length (as long as it fits on a single line) and can consist of upper- and lowercase letters and embedded underscores. The procedure name is followed by the keyword **is**. A semicolon is not placed after **is**. Even though **is** appears at the end of a line of code, it does not terminate this procedure. The procedure terminates with the last line of the program:

```
end TOTEM_POLE;
```

In this last line, the procedure name, TOTEM_POLE, is placed between the keyword **end** and the semicolon. Repeating the procedure name at the end of a procedure is optional, but highly recommended, because it makes code easier to read and understand. If the procedure name is supplied, then the compiler will check to make sure that the name is correct.

The keyword **procedure,** followed by the procedure name, is known as the procedure specification. The procedure specification defines this unit of code as a procedure with the name TOTEM_POLE. The remainder of the code is known as the procedure body. The body contains the implementation of the procedure and has two parts: the declarative part and the executable statement part. The declarative part lies between the keywords **is** and **begin**. The executable statement part lies between the keywords **begin** and **end**. In the declarative part, items such as types, variables, and constants are declared. In the executable statement part, processing is performed. At runtime (as the program is executing), declarations are elaborated and executable statements are executed. The elaboration of declarations brings objects into existence, and the execution of statements manipulates or processes objects.

In the TOTEM_POLE example, the first declaration defines a variable, TOTEMS, to be of type INTEGER:

TOTEMS: INTEGER := 1;

A variable is an object that can assume different values as the program executes. An initial value may be given to a variable when it is declared. The symbol, :=, assigns the value on the right of the symbol to the variable on the left. In this example, TOTEMS is given the initial integer value of 1. An integer is a whole number that has no decimal point.

The next declaration in TOTEM_POLE is an instantiation of the generic package INTEGER_IO:

package INT_IO **is new** INTEGER_IO (INTEGER);

Such an instantiation of the INTEGER_IO package is required whenever integers need to be input or output. The INTEGER_IO package is a generic unit, which means that it serves as a template from which actual packages are created. The effect of this instantiation is to create an "instance" of the INTEGER_IO package, called INT_IO. Once created, the INT_IO package can be used to input or output integers. Thus, even the simplest of programs often requires generic packages. However, the topic of generic packages is advanced and cannot be fully explained until Chapter 9.

The next line of code in TOTEM_POLE makes the package INT_IO directly visible (directly available) to the programmer:

use INT_IO;

The **use** clause will be discussed later in this chapter.

Now that we have covered all the declarations in TOTEM_POLE, we will discuss the executable statements of this procedure. Before we do so, note that the order in which declarations and executable statements are placed in a program is critical. Declarations are elaborated, and statements are executed, in the order listed in the code. As a consequence, an object must be declared before the point in the code where it is used. In our example, this requirement is satisfied since the variable TOTEMS is declared before it is used in the **for** loop.

Now let us consider the first seven executable statements in the example. These are procedure invocations, also known as procedure calls. These statements call procedures that exist outside the main procedure TOTEM_POLE. To call a procedure means to activate it. Unlike some computer languages, however, no keyword **call** is used.

The first of these seven procedure calls prompts users of the program to enter the number of faces that they wish to appear on the totem pole:

PUT_LINE ("How many faces in the Totem Pole?");

This procedure call is a PUT_LINE statement. A PUT_LINE statement outputs a string to the standard output device, which we will assume is a video screen, and then automatically advances to the next line. As previously mentioned, a string consists of text within quotes. The text appears on the screen exactly as written because, within strings, Ada distinguishes between upper- and lowercase letters.

The next procedure call is a GET statement:

GET (TOTEMS);

A GET statement gets input from the user at runtime and assigns it to the variable placed in parentheses. If the user of our program, for example, enters the integer 3, then the value of the variable TOTEMS will be set to 3. Even though TOTEMS is initialized to 1 when it is declared, because it is a variable, this initial value may be replaced with a new value. Initializing TOTEMS to 1, therefore, serves no purpose in this program; it is only done for illustrative purposes.

Ada is a strongly typed language. Objects belonging to different types may not mix. In our example, since TOTEMS is declared to be an integer variable, it can only be assigned integer values. If the user enters a value of some other type, such as the real number 3.5, then a type mismatch is reported and the program aborts. (A real number is one that contains a decimal point.)

The next executable statement is a procedure call:

NEW_LINE;

When this procedure is called, the program advances to the next line on the screen.

The next three statements output a message explaining that a totem pole follows with the number of faces previously specified by the user:

```
PUT ("Here is a Totem Pole with ");    -- outputs a string
PUT (TOTEMS);                          -- outputs an integer
PUT (" faces:");                       -- outputs a string
```

The first and third of these PUT statements output strings. The second PUT statement, however, outputs the value of TOTEMS. TOTEMS does not appear in quotes since we are not outputting the name TOTEMS but rather the value of the variable called TOTEMS. The same procedure, PUT, thus appears to be capable of outputting both strings and integer values. But this is not the case. We are actually invoking two different PUT procedures, one that outputs strings, the other that outputs integer values. Two different procedures with the same name are said to be overloaded.

A question that naturally arises is, how does the compiler know which overloaded version of the PUT procedure is being invoked? The answer is, by examining the item that is being output. If the output item is a string, the compiler selects the PUT procedure that outputs strings. If the item is an integer, the compiler selects the PUT procedure that outputs integers. Other languages besides Ada support overloading. What is unusual about Ada, however, is that the programmer can do the overloading. That is, the programmer may assign the same name to different procedures. As we shall show in Chapter 7, a programmer may even overload operators such as + or > !

Returning to the PUT statements in the code, even though three separate PUT statements are used, only one line of output is displayed on the screen. Unlike the PUT_LINE statement, these PUT statements, in other words, do not advance to the next line after outputting data to the screen. Three separate PUT statements must be used, because a PUT statement can only output a single value. A statement such as the following is illegal:

```
PUT ("Here is a Totem Pole with ", TOTEMS, " faces:"); -- illegal
```

After the third PUT statement, another call to NEW_LINE is made. Whereas NEW_LINE was first called without any parameter (a value in parentheses following the procedure name), this time it is called with a parameter value of 2. Whenever NEW_LINE is invoked without a parameter, the default of 1 is assumed, and the program advances 1 line on the screen. If NEW_LINE is called with a parameter, such as 2, then this value overrides the default of 1, and 2 lines are advanced. Most other programming languages do not support default values.

The next statement is a control structure called a **for** loop, which is like the **for** loop of Pascal and the **DO** loop of FORTRAN. A **for** loop is used to execute a group of statements repeatedly. Within this **for** loop are four PUT_LINE statements that output a "face" by printing the special symbols inside the quotes.

Let us examine the **for** loop more closely. Following the keyword **for** is the user-supplied name of the loop counter (loop index). In our example, the loop counter is named FACES. The loop counter steps through (i.e., gets assigned, in turn) each value in the range 1 .. TOTEMS, which appears after the keyword **in**. Since TOTEMS was assigned the value 3, the range becomes 1 .. 3 (1 to 3). For each value assigned to the loop counter—first 1, then 2, then 3—the group of statements within the loop is executed. Thus, three faces are output on the totem pole, one for each time through the loop.

The astute reader may have noticed that the loop counter, FACES, is used without ever having been explicitly declared. This seems to violate the rule that objects must be declared before they can be used. In general, this rule is true. However, loop counters are not explicitly declared. Rather, the compiler infers their type from the range of values that the counters assume. For instance, by examining the range 1 .. TOTEMS, the compiler can determine that FACES is an object that can assume integer values from 1 to TOTEMS. (More details about the **for** loop will be given in Chapter 4.) After the **for** loop is exited, the program ends.

With Clause

Now that we have gone over the code line by line, let us consider some issues that have been sidestepped. Throughout our program, such procedures as PUT and PUT_LINE are called. But where do these procedures exist? The answer can be found by reconsidering the first clause in our context specification:

with TEXT_IO;

This specification makes the resources of the TEXT_IO package, which comes with every Ada compiler, available to the TOTEM_POLE program. Among these resources are the procedures called by the TOTEM_POLE program to perform input and output (I/O) operations. PUT and PUT_LINE are therefore not keywords that are built into the Ada language to allow us to perform I/O. Rather, these are procedures that need to be imported from an external package. Without the **with** clause, the compiler would complain that it could not find these procedures.

In general, packages are used to bundle together related resources. These resources can include items such as procedures, functions, and other packages; and declarations of types, variables, and constants. In addition to predefined packages, such as TEXT_IO, programmers may define their own packages. In either case, the resources of these packages can easily be made available by employing a **with** clause and, optionally, a **use** clause.

The TEXT_IO package, as well as other program units that can be accessed by the **with** clause, is contained in the Ada library. (Program units, also called compilation units, are units of code that are separately compiled.) Although our sample program is very short, Ada was designed with embedded systems in mind. The software for embedded systems typically consists of many thousands of lines of code. Such large Ada programs may consist of many different compilation units. To manage all these units (a job nasty enough to give any software configuration manager conniptions), an Ada library is provided. The Ada library contains information about each compilation unit. This information is used to check that compilation units are correctly referenced by each other. Whenever a compilation unit such as TEXT_IO is mentioned in a **with** clause, the Ada library is searched. If this compilation unit is found, it is made available. A check is made that the TEXT_IO package contains all the procedures, such as PUT, that are used within the program TOTEM_POLE. In addition, a check is made that these procedures are properly used—that they are called with the correct number and types of parameters.

Use Clause

Whereas the **with** clause makes the resources of the TEXT_IO package available to the program, the **use** clause makes these resources directly visible. By directly visible, we mean that a resource, such as a procedure, can be called simply by using its name, such as NEW_LINE and PUT_LINE. If we omit the **use** clause, these procedures can only be called by placing the name TEXT_IO before the procedure name, as follows: TEXT_IO.NEW_LINE, TEXT_IO.PUT_LINE, or TEXT_IO.PUT. This "dot notation" tells the compiler from which library package to import the procedure.

Not all of the procedures in TOTEM_POLE come from the TEXT_IO package. Procedures such as GET and PUT, which handle input and output of integer values, come from the INT_IO package. The resources of this package are not made available through a **with** clause, like the resources of the TEXT_IO package. Rather, these resources are made available when the INT_IO package is created by generically instantiating the INTEGER_IO package contained within the TEXT_IO package.

As with the TEXT_IO package, a **use** clause is needed to make the resources of the INT_IO package directly visible. Without this **use** clause, the procedures provided by this package can only be called using dot notation, as follows: INT_IO.GET and INT_IO.PUT.

The procedure INT_IO.PUT must be used when outputting integer values, whereas TEXT_IO.PUT must be used when outputting strings. Thus, without the **use** clauses, the three lines in our program that inform the user about the Totem Pole would appear as follows:

```
TEXT_IO.PUT ("Here is Totem Pole with");   -- PUT from TEXT_IO package
INT_IO.PUT (TOTEMS);                       -- PUT from INT_IO package
TEXT_IO.PUT (" faces:");                   -- PUT from TEXT_IO package
```

Recall from our discussion on overloading that there are two procedures with the name PUT: one for outputting strings, the other for outputting integer values. As we have just seen, these two procedures are contained in different packages. The PUT procedure that outputs strings is imported from the TEXT_IO package. The PUT procedure that outputs integer values is imported from the INT_IO package.

Our sample program has been used to guide us through a number of Ada topics. The main topics covered have been **for** loops, **with** and **use** clauses, procedures, generics, input/output, the Ada library, overloaded procedures, and packages. The next section discusses features not shown or not sufficiently covered in the sample program.

ADDITIONAL FEATURES OF ADA

This section is divided into two parts: features of Ada that are commonly provided by modern high-level languages and features of Ada that are unusual or handled in a unique manner.

Features of Ada Typical of High-Level Languages

Ada supports certain features that are typical of high-level languages. These features include control structures, arrays and records, subprograms, access types, and types.

Control Structures

Ada supports a variety of control structures: the **if** statement, the **case** statement, the **goto** statement, and three kinds of loop statements. Control structures control the program's path of execution. Instead of sequentially executing one statement after another, control structures allow code to be executed along different paths. For instance, an **if** statement or **case** statement selects one group of statements to execute instead of alternative groups.

The **goto** statement jumps over a section of code and continues execution elsewhere. In Ada, the **goto** statement is rarely necessary and should be avoided. The **goto** statement is mainly used when translating code from languages such as FORTRAN (that rely on **goto** statements) to Ada.

A loop is used to execute a group of statements repeatedly. There are three varieties of loops: the simple loop, which loops forever (unless another statement stops the looping); the **while** loop, which keeps looping while a certain condition is satisfied; and the **for** loop, which loops each time its loop counter advances to the next value. We have already seen an example of the **for** loop in the TOTEM_POLE program.

Ada does not support the **repeat until** loop that is supported by other languages such as Pascal. In Ada, however, an equivalent control structure is easily created using the **exit** statement. The **exit** statement is used to exit a loop when a specified condition is met.

Arrays and Records

Ada supports two kinds of composite objects—that is, objects consisting of components: arrays and records. Individual components of these composite objects can be referenced, or the entire set of components may be referenced and manipulated as a whole. For example, an array called RAINBOW might be used to store all the colors of a rainbow. Each color may be referenced individually, or the set of colors may be referenced as a whole, using the identifier RAINBOW.

Although arrays and records are to be found in most modern high-level languages, Ada adds a few new twists. For example, in a single assignment statement, an array may be given an entire set of specified values. Perhaps even more surprising is that, in Ada, arrays belonging to the same type may differ in size.

Subprograms

Subprograms come in two varieties: procedures and functions. (Some languages, such as FORTRAN, refer to procedures as subroutines.) In the sample program, TOTEM_POLE, we have seen calls to procedures PUT, PUT_LINE, GET, and NEW_LINE. In addition, the TOTEM_POLE program is itself a procedure. There is nothing about a main program that, by itself, distinguishes it from other procedures. We have not yet seen any examples of functions. The main difference between a procedure and a function is that a procedure is invoked as a statement and returns values (if any) through its parameters:

```
CIRCLE_AREA (AREA, 1.0); -- procedure
```

The value 1.0 is passed to the procedure, CIRCLE_AREA, which calculates the area of a circle and returns the result through the parameter, AREA.

A function is invoked as an expression and returns a single value through the function name. Consider, for example, the following function call:

```
AREA := CIRCLE_AREA (1.0); -- function
```

The function, CIRCLE_AREA, appears on the right side of the assignment operator because it is an expression that yields a result. This function calculates the area of a circle with a radius of 1.0. The result is returned through the function identifier CIRCLE_AREA. This result is then assigned to the variable AREA.

Access Types

Many modern languages provide pointers that are used to point to objects. Ada has its own version of pointers called access values (values of access types), which access objects. Due to Ada's strong typing, however, pointers may only point to objects of a specified type. Thus, a character pointer may only point to characters, and an integer pointer may only point to integers.

Types

In Ada, every object belongs to some type. Ada provides a variety of predefined types. For instance, there are integer types, floating point types, Boolean types, and character types. In addition, a programmer is allowed to create new types. For example, a programmer can create a type called MONTHS consisting of the values JANUARY, FEBRUARY, MARCH, APRIL, and so on, or a type called SHAPE consisting of the values CIRCLE, RECTANGLE, and TRIANGLE. The values—CIRCLE, RECTANGLE, and TRIANGLE—are to be thought of as actual values of type SHAPE. We do not have to worry about how these values are numerically represented within the computer.

Unusual Features of Ada

Ada supports various language features that are unusual or handled in unique ways. These features include attributes, packages, generics, exceptions, tasking, and low-level programming.

Attributes

Ada supports 49 different predefined attributes (see Appendix A). Attributes yield various characteristics of items. In other languages, programmers often have to search through code or documents to find these characteristics. For example, in most computer languages, if one wants to know the largest integer value available with a particular compiler, one must read the compiler's reference manual. In Ada, however, such an integer attribute can be referenced from within the program by writing INTEGER'LAST. On a 16-bit machine, this expression often yields the value 32,767; on other machines, this value will probably be different. By using attributes like INTEGER'LAST, code is made more general and portable, and the use of "magic numbers" such as 32,767 may be avoided.

Packages

As previously mentioned, a package (which is often a compilation unit) bundles together related resources. Packages usually consist of two parts: a specification and a body. The specification contains interface information that is available to the users of the package. This information includes everything users need to know in order to use the resources of the package. The package body, however, contains the underlying implementation of the resources defined in the corresponding package specification. The contents of the package body are unavailable to users of the package. Users of a package do not need to know how the resources of a package are implemented any more than the users of a radio need to know how radio waves are propagated, received, and converted into sound. By hiding the code that implements the resources, users of a package cannot abuse or corrupt this code or base their design on irrelevant details contained in this code.

Generics

One of the most unusual features of Ada is generic units. Generic units serve as templates from which procedures, functions, and packages can be created. We have already seen, in our sample program, how an instance of the INTEGER_IO package is created by a method known as generic instantiation. By using generic units, code duplication can be greatly reduced because, from a given template, many copies can be created that only differ in specific ways. For instance, a generic package can be written that sorts objects. The code within this package that does the sorting need only be written once. From this generic package, many copies (instances) can be created that only differ in the types of objects that can be sorted. Thus, the generic sort package can be used to create packages that sort integers, strings, characters, and so on. Without generics, each type of item to be sorted would require that another version of the sort package be written.

Exceptions

As anyone with even a modicum of programming experience can attest, large programs, even those that have been successfully running for years, may unexpectedly encounter an error. In such unexpected situations, different responses are required, depending on the kind of error that is encountered. At one extreme, an error is fatal, and the program is required to halt as soon as possible. At the other extreme, the error is simple to rectify, and processing continues after perhaps a friendly warning message is issued.

Ada provides a special mechanism for handling runtime errors (errors that occur as a program is executing rather than as a program is compiling). In Ada, runtime errors are called exceptions, and the mechanism for handling these exceptions is called the exception handler. Exception handlers intercept exceptions, identify the type of exception that was raised, and then follow a specified course of action depending on the nature of the exception.

Exceptions are identified with either predefined names or user-defined names. Predefined exceptions, such as CONSTRAINT_ERROR, are automatically raised whenever a value such as an array index goes out of range. This should be welcome news to, for instance, FORTRAN programmers. Instead of spending hours attempting to debug a program where data are being clobbered by a wayward array index, Ada will announce the error as soon as it is encountered.

In addition to predefined exceptions, programmers may define their own exceptions. The programmer names the exception and then explicitly raises this exception, by name, whenever warranted.

Tasking

In certain applications, various activities need to be performed during the same period of time. In Ada, each activity can be concurrently executed by a unit of code known as a task. Tasks may be used to model events in the real world that occur at the same time. Tasks may also be used to increase execution speed, especially when the computer has multiple processors.

Tasks may meet each other and exchange information. Such a meeting of tasks is called a rendezvous. As we shall see in Chapter 15, tasking and the rendezvous are two of the more innovative features of Ada.

Low-Level Programming

Since Ada was designed with embedded systems in mind, Ada supports low-level programming. Low-level programming means getting down to the "bare iron" of the machine. This means dealing with bits and bytes, hardware interrupts, machine specific instructions, addresses, and so on.

Now that we have an overview of the Ada language, we are ready to delve into the details. The next chapter, therefore, covers the basics of Ada.

EXERCISES

1. Modify the TOTEM_POLE program to output the integer numbers from 1 to the value of TOTEMS.

2. What happens if you try to declare the loop counter FACES?

3. Try outputting the value of FACES after the **for** loop (after keywords **end loop**). Can you explain the problem?

4. What happens when the TOTEM_POLE program is executed with a request to output 0 faces? What about a request to output a negative number of faces?

5. Give an example of an application where Ada tasks might be used.

6. Give an example of an application where low-level programming might be used.

7. Compare the general features of Ada with those of any other high-level language with which you are familiar (e.g., Pascal, FORTRAN, C).

Chapter 3

BASICS OF ADA

The last chapter provided an overview of the Ada language. This chapter focuses on the details of the language. The chapter begins with a discussion of the basic components of Ada, called lexical elements. Lexical elements are identifiers, delimiters, literals, and comments. We will then explore scalar types, which are the integer, floating point, and user-defined enumeration types; character types; and Boolean types. Next, we will cover subtypes and some of the commonly used attributes. A discussion of type conversion then follows. We conclude the chapter with an explanation of the order in which arithmetic, relational, and logical operations are performed.

LEXICAL ELEMENTS

Lexical elements, the basic language components of Ada, are identifiers, delimiters, literals, and comments.

Identifiers

Ada identifiers are names that identify various Ada objects, such as variables, constants, procedures, functions, and so on. The following are examples of Ada identifiers:

```
AGE
NUMBER_OF_NEAR_MISSES
P23
```

Identifiers should be descriptive and easy to interpret. For instance, avoid identifiers such as RECNUM and instead write RECORD_NUMBER.

There are seven rules to follow when constructing Ada identifiers:

1. Identifiers can only contain letters, numbers, and underscores.
2. Identifiers can be of any length, as long as the entire identifier appears within a single line.
3. In identifiers, Ada does not distinguish between upper- and lowercase letters.
4. Identifiers cannot have the same name as a keyword.
5. Identifiers must begin with a letter.
6. Identifiers cannot have underscores at the beginning, end, or side by side.
7. Underscores in identifiers are significant.

Rule 1 states that identifiers can only contain letters, numbers, and underscores. This means that special symbols, such as * or &, cannot appear in an identifier. The following identifiers are therefore illegal:

```
SPIN-OFF               -- illegal symbol: -
Brightness&Sunshine    -- illegal symbol: &
Mobius Strip           -- illegal embedded blank
```

Rule 2 states that identifiers can be of any length, as long as the entire identifier appears within a single line. The following identifier is therefore legal:

```
THIS_IS_A_VERY_LONG_IDENTIFIER
```

Rule 3 states that, in identifiers, Ada does not distinguish between upper- and lowercase letters. In this book, identifiers are written in uppercase letters for better contrast with keywords, which are written in bold lowercase letters. However, as far as Ada is concerned, the following four identifiers are the same:

```
CONTINUE   -- these four identifiers are considered to be the same
Continue
continue
CoNtInUe
```

Rule 4 states that identifiers cannot have the same name as a keyword. A keyword, such as **procedure**, has a predefined meaning and cannot be redefined by the programmer. Thus, a syntax error will occur if an attempt is made to use an identifier name such as PROCEDURE, BEGIN, or LOOP. However, the name of a keyword can appear as part of an identifier:

```
REM                    -- illegal identifier; REM is a keyword
REMARKABLE             -- OK
```

Rule 5 states that identifiers must begin with a letter. The following identifier is therefore illegal:

```
2_BY_4      -- illegal; begins with a number
```

Rule 6 states that identifiers cannot have underscores at the beginning, end, or side by side. The following identifiers are therefore illegal:

```
_ETC              -- illegal; underscore at beginning
CONTINUE_         -- illegal; underscore at end
A_B__C            -- illegal; two underscores between B and C
```

Rule 7 states that underscores in identifiers are significant. The following three identifiers are therefore considered to be distinct:

```
One_And_A_Two     -- each of these identifiers is distinct
One_AndA_Two
OneAndATwo
```

Delimiters

Delimiters are symbols that have special meaning within Ada. These symbols are used, for instance, as operators and statement terminators. There are single delimiters, which consist of only one symbol, and double delimiters, which consist of two symbols:

Single Delimiters:

+	Addition or positive
-	Subtraction or negative
*	Multiplication
/	Division
=	Equality
<	Less than
>	Greater than
&	Concatenator
|	Vertical bar
;	Terminator
#	Enclosing based literals
(	Left parenthesis
)	Right parenthesis
.	Dot notation
:	Separates data object from its type
"	Double quote
'	Single quote or tick mark

Double Delimiters:

**	Exponentiation
/=	Inequality
<=	Less than or equal
>=	Greater than or equal
:=	Assignment
<>	Box
=>	Arrow
<<	Left label bracket
>>	Right label bracket
..	Range

The preceding lists only give a basic idea of how these delimiters are used. Detailed descriptions will be given as the delimiters are introduced in this book.

One of these delimiters, however, deserves special consideration in this chapter, because it is so frequently encountered. This is the assignment operator, :=. We have seen this operator used in the TOTEM_POLE program in chapter 2:

TOTEMS: INTEGER := 1;

When TOTEMS is declared as an integer variable, it is also assigned a default value of 1.

In addition to appearing in declarations, the assignment operator may appear in assignment statements:

TOTEMS := 8;

In this assignment statement, TOTEMS is assigned the value of 8.

The value to the right of the assignment operator may also be an expression:

TOTEMS := 5 + 4 - 3;

The expression 5 + 4 - 3 is evaluated to 6. The result, 6, is then placed in the variable TOTEMS. Any previous value TOTEMS may have had is replaced by this new value.

Literals

A literal is a particular value of a type that is explicitly written and not represented by an identifier. In this section, we will discuss integer literals, such as 7; real literals, such as 7.2; character literals, such as 'c'; string literals, such as "Ada"; and Boolean literals, such as TRUE.

Let us begin by considering integer literals. Integer literals are whole numbers that do not contain a decimal point:

0,   187,   2546

(Negative integers are not integer literals, but expressions. The negative sign, in other words, is an operator that operates on a single integer value.)

Large integer literals, such as 5737639019, can be difficult to read if they are not separated into groups. Normally, we would write such large integers using commas: 5,737,639,019. However, in Ada, commas cannot be embedded within an integer literal. Underscores, though, are allowed. Unlike the underscores in identifiers, underscores in integer literals have no significance; they are ignored by the compiler. These underscores are only used to make numbers easier for humans to read. Therefore, the previous integer literal might be written as 5_737_639_019. As with identifiers, underscores can appear anywhere within an integer literal except at the beginning, end, or side by side.

In addition to underscores, integer literals may use scientific notation (also known as exponential notation), as follows:

2E3,   12E+15

The E, which can be written in upper- or lowercase, means "times ten to the power of." Thus, 2E3 means 2 times 10 to the power of 3, or 2×10^3, which evaluates to 2000. Note that, in effect, the exponent to the right of the E indicates how many zeros follow the integer to the left of the E. Thus, 12E+15 is simply 12 followed by 15 zeros. The optional plus sign is used to explicitly state that the exponent 15 is a positive number. When the plus sign is omitted, the compiler assumes that a positive exponent is intended.

Not only can integer literals be written using scientific notation; they can be written in bases other than base 10. In everyday life, we use base 10 numbers, which are composed of the ten digits 0, 1, 2, 3, 4, 5, 6, 7, 8, and 9. Base 10 integers are written as a sequence of these digits. The place value of a digit is determined by its position in the sequence. Thus, in the number 2754, the rightmost digit, 4, is in the ones position, and the place value increases by a factor of 10 as one advances from right to left. The 5 is in the tens position, 7 is in the hundreds position, and 2 is in the thousands position.

There is nothing special about base 10 numbers. We write numbers in base 10 probably because we are equipped with a counting device consisting of 10 "digits" that we always carry with us, namely, our fingers. If we ever meet an intelligent extraterrestrial who has 12 digits, chances are that this creature will use base 12 numbers. Ada is designed to accommodate extraterrestrials possessing from 2 to 16 digits. In other words, integer literals can be written in any base from 2 to 16. For computer scientists, the most commonly used bases (besides base 10) are bases 2, 8, and 16. This is not because computer scientists have a different number of fingers from the rest of humanity, but because digital computers operate in base 2, and base 2 numbers are conveniently represented in base 8 or base 16.

Based numbers should be familiar to you from a mathematics class or an introductory computer class. The following explanation of based literals is therefore meant as a review.

Base 2 numbers, called binary numbers, are composed of the two digits 0 and 1. Base 2 integers are written as a sequence of these digits. In the binary number 1101, the rightmost digit is in the ones position, and the place value increases by a factor of 2 as one advances from right to left. The 0 is in the twos position, the 1 to the left of the 0 is in the fours position, and the leftmost 1 is in the eights position.

Base 8 numbers, called octal numbers, are composed of the eight digits 0, 1, 2, 3, 4, 5, 6, and 7. Base 8 integers are written as a sequence of these digits. In the octal number 1247, the rightmost digit, 7, is in the ones position, and the place value increases by a factor of 8 as one advances from right to left. The 4 is in the eights position, the 2 is in the 64s position, and the 1 is in the 512s position.

Base 16 numbers, called hexadecimal numbers, are composed of the 16 digits 0, 1, 2, 3, 4, 5, 6, 7, 8, 9, A, B, C, D, E, and F. Note that since there are only 10 digits in our number system, letters are used to represent the other 6 digits: A is 10, B is 11, C is 12, and so on. Base 16 integers are written as a sequence of these digits. In the hexadecimal number 3A4F, the rightmost digit, F, is in the ones position, and the place value increases by a factor of 16 as one advances from right to left. The 4 is in the 16s position, the A is in the 256s position, and the 3 is in the 4096s position.

In Ada, a based literal is enclosed within the pound sign symbols, #, and is preceded by the number that indicates the base. The binary number 1101, for example, is written as 2#1101#. The octal number 1247 is written as 8#1247#. The hexadecimal number 3A4F is written as 16#3A4F#.

Based literals can be written using scientific notation, such as 2#11#E3. But be careful. Because this is a binary number, the E3 does not mean 10^3 but 2^3. In the hexadecimal number 16#F#E2, the E2 means 16^2.

This concludes our discussion of integer literals. Now let us consider real literals. Real literals have a decimal point (fractional part):

0.0,   127.021,   4728.1

Real literals must have a digit on each side of the decimal point. The literal .5, for example, is illegal; it must be written as 0.5.

Just as integer literals can use underscores, so can real literals. Thus, 4129345.01 can be written as 4_129_345.01. (An underscore, however, cannot be placed beside the decimal point. Therefore, 4_129_345_.01 is illegal.)

Also, like integer literals, real literals can use scientific notation. Thus, 1.2345E3 means 1.2345 x 10^3, which evaluates to 1234.5. Note that, in effect, the exponent to the right of the E indicates how many places the decimal point is shifted to the right. When an exponent is negative, a left shift is required instead of a right shift.

Just as integer literals can be written as based literals, so can real literals be written as based literals. Note that, in base 10, the place values decrease by a factor of 10 from left to right. In the base 10 number 0.754, for example, 0 is in the ones position, 7 is in the tenths position, 5 is in the hundredths position, and 4 is in the thousandths position.

Similarly, for real binary literals, the place values decrease by a factor of 2 from left to right. For instance, in the binary number 0.101, the 1 to the right of the radix point is in the one-halves position, the 0 to the right of this 1 is in the one-fourths position, and the rightmost 1 is in the one-eights position. The term "radix point" is used instead of "decimal point" because, strictly speaking, decimal point implies a decimal (base 10) number. In Ada, the binary number 0.101 is written as 2#0.101#. Octal and hexadecimal real literals are handled similarly.

As with integer based literals, real based literals can be written using scientific notation, such as 2#11.0111#E3. Again, be careful. The E3 means 2^3, not 10^3. This based literal may therefore be written without the scientific notation by shifting the radix point three places to the right: 2#11011.1#.

Now that we have discussed integer and real literals, let us consider character literals. Character literals consist of individual characters, placed within a pair of single quotes, as follows:

'A', 'a', '*', '8'

As shown, character literals include uppercase letters, lowercase letters, special symbols, and numerals written as text. (Although Ada is case insensitive, it does distinguish between upper- and lowercase character literals.) Note that the character literal '8' is not the same as the integer literal 8. The character literal '8', unlike the integer literal 8, cannot be used in arithmetic calculations.

Whereas character literals are single characters that are placed within a pair of single quotes, string literals consist of a sequence of printable characters that are placed within a pair of double quotes:

"This is a string literal!"

In string literals, as with character literals, upper- and lowercase letters are distinguished from one another.

Let us consider one more kind of literal: Boolean literals. Boolean literals consist of the values FALSE and TRUE. These values should not be thought of as strings. FALSE and TRUE are explicit Boolean values, just as 7 is an explicit integer value.

Comments

In Ada and other programming languages, comments are placed within code to describe its purpose, use, and implementation. Comments are also used at the beginning of a unit of code to give header information, such as the name of the programmer, the date, and the name of the project. Comments are provided for human readers and are ignored by compilers.

In Ada, comments are line oriented; they begin with a double hyphen (--) and extend to the end of the line. Text consisting of any printable characters or symbols may follow the double hyphen.

```
-- comments may take up a full line
-- or several lines
X := 2#1010#; -- comments may be placed after code
Y := -- even the placement of this comment is OK
    100;
```

SCALAR TYPES

In Ada, every object belongs to a type. Just as collie belongs to type DOG and plum belongs to type FRUIT, the literal 'A' belongs to type CHARACTER, and the literal FALSE belongs to type BOOLEAN. In Ada, types come in as many bewildering varieties as the life forms that inhabit the dense jungles of the Amazon. And just when you think you have encountered every variety, a new and even more exotic one greets you. The classification of types is depicted in Figure 3.1.

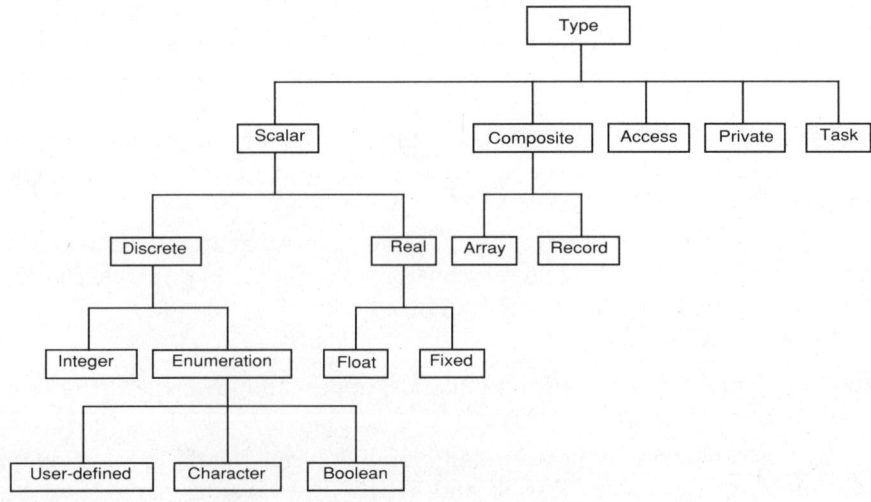

Figure 3.1 Classification of types

Scalar types are included in this chapter because they are basic to Ada and are frequently used in Ada programs. The other types are more specialized and will be covered in later chapters.

Scalar types are types that do not have any internal components or structure. Unlike scalar types, composite types do have an internal structure. The two varieties of composite types, arrays and records, will be covered in Chapters 5 and 6. Access types act as pointers to objects. Access types will be discussed in Chapter 12. Private types are used to hide the internal structure of a type and to limit the kinds of operations that can be performed on objects of that type. Private types will be explored in Chapter 8. Task types are used to declare units of code that can run concurrently. Task types will be covered in Chapter 15.

Scalar types consist of discrete types and real types. A discrete type is composed of objects that have immediate successors and predecessors. A real type is composed of numbers that form a continuum and that, from a mathematical perspective, have no immediate successors or predecessors.

As shown in Figure 3.1, discrete types also come in two varieties: integer types and enumeration types. Integer types consist of integers, which are numbers that have no fractional part. Enumeration types are types that are defined by explicitly enumerating their values. For example, the enumeration type BOOLEAN is defined by the list of values FALSE and TRUE. Enumeration types consist of user-defined enumeration types, as well as the predefined enumeration types: CHARACTER and BOOLEAN.

Figure 3.1 also shows that real types come in two varieties: float and fixed. Float numbers are real numbers whose decimal point is not fixed at a particular location but is free to move around. Thus, these numbers are known as floating point numbers. Fixed numbers are real numbers whose decimal point is fixed at a particular location. Thus, these numbers are known as fixed point numbers.

Scalar types are either predefined or user defined. The predefined scalar types are defined in the package called STANDARD, which is included with every Ada compiler. These predefined types are INTEGER, FLOAT, CHARACTER, and BOOLEAN. The package STANDARD is unique because its resources are always available; one cannot mention this package in a **with** or **use** clause. Programmers can therefore always use these predefined types.

In the following subsections, we will discuss the two predefined numeric types: integer types and floating point types. We will then describe user-defined enumeration types, followed by the predefined enumeration types: character and Boolean types. Fixed point types, which must be defined by the programmer, are a more advanced topic that will be discussed in Chapter 13.

Integer Type

This section covers integer variables, integer constants, and integer expressions. We will first discuss integer variables and constants. An integer variable is an identifier that can assume different integer values during the execution of a program. An integer constant is an identifier with a value that cannot change during the execution of the program. As the following example shows, integer variables and integer constants are declared using the predefined type INTEGER:

```
declare
    -- declarative part
    NUMBER_OF_NEAR_MISSES: INTEGER;
    A, B, C: INTEGER;
    SUM: INTEGER := 0;
    FIRST_SCORE, SECOND_SCORE: INTEGER := 25;
    TOTAL_SCORE: INTEGER := FIRST_SCORE + SECOND_SCORE;
    DOZEN: constant INTEGER := 12;
begin
    -- executable statement part
    null;    -- at least one executable statement is needed;
             -- the null statement satisfies this requirement
end;
```

Before discussing these variables and constants, let us briefly explain the structure of the code. There are two parts to this code: the declarative part and the executable statement part, which we will refer to as the statement part. The declarative part contains declarations, which are placed between the keywords **declare** and **begin**. The statement part contains one or more executable statements, which are placed between the keywords **begin** and **end**. At least one executable statement is required, even if it is only the "do-nothing" **null** statement. This entire structure is called a block statement and will be covered in detail in Chapter 7. Block statements will be used in many examples, because they are the simplest Ada constructs that contain a declarative part and a statement part.

During runtime, statements are executed, and declarations are elaborated. When a statement is executed, some action is performed; when a declaration is elaborated, the declared object is created.

The first declaration in the preceding code defines the object, NUMBER_OF_NEAR_MISSES, to be an integer variable. Note that the word "variable" does not appear in the code. No initial value is assigned to this variable, and, in Ada, no default value is given. If a value is not assigned to this variable before it is read, then erroneous code results. Erroneous code is code that contains an error that may or may not be caught by the compiler. A compiler that fully meets Ada standards is under no obligation to detect such an error.

The second declaration defines the objects A, B, and C to be integer variables. Once again, no initial values are assigned.

The third declaration defines the object SUM to be an integer variable and uses the assignment operator, :=, to initialize SUM to 0. Since SUM is an integer variable, it can only be initialized to an integer value, such as 0. Attempting to initialize SUM to, for instance, a real value, will result in an error. Also, note that since SUM is a variable, its initial value of 0 can later be overridden.

The fourth declaration defines the objects FIRST_SCORE and SECOND_SCORE to be integer variables. With a single assignment operator, both of these integer variables are initialized to 25. Initializing more than one variable at a time is only allowed in declarations, not in assignment statements, such as the following:

```
A, B := 5; -- illegal
```

The fifth declaration defines the object TOTAL_SCORE to be an integer variable and initializes this variable to FIRST_SCORE plus SECOND_SCORE. This can be done since FIRST_SCORE and SECOND_SCORE have already been declared and initialized to 25. TOTAL_SCORE is thus initialized to 50.

The last declaration defines the object DOZEN to be an integer constant with the value of 12. Since DOZEN is declared to be a constant, it must be given an initial value. (In Chapter 8, we will see an exception to this rule.) Since DOZEN is a constant, if an attempt is made to alter its value, the compiler will report an error.

So far, we have discussed integer variables, integer constants, and, in the previous section, integer literals. Next, we will consider integer expressions, in which operations on these integer variables, constants, and literals are performed. An integer expression is an expression that, no matter how complex, always resolves to a single integer result. Integer expressions may contain the following arithmetic operators:

+	Addition, positive
-	Subtraction, negative
*	Multiplication
/	Division
**	Exponentiation
mod	Modulus
rem	Remainder
abs	Absolute value

The following code demonstrates how these operators can be used in integer expressions:

```
with TEXT_IO; use TEXT_IO;
procedure INTEGER_EXPRESSIONS is
```

```
        package INT_IO is new INTEGER_IO (INTEGER);
        use INT_IO;
        A, B: INTEGER := 7;
        C: INTEGER := 2;
        D: constant INTEGER := -1;
     begin  -- INTEGER_EXPRESSIONS
        PUT (3 + C);             -- outputs 5
        PUT (+A);                -- outputs 7
        PUT (A - C);             -- outputs 5
        PUT (-A);                -- outputs -7
        PUT (3 * D);             -- outputs -3
        PUT (7 / 4);             -- outputs 1
        PUT (2 ** 5);            -- outputs 32
        PUT (17 rem 9);          -- outputs 8
        PUT (17 mod 9);          -- outputs 8
        PUT (abs D);             -- outputs 1
        PUT (2#1011# + 8#12#);   -- outputs 21
     end INTEGER_EXPRESSIONS;
```

Note that the operators + and - can be used in two different ways. As unary operators (operators that operate on a single object), + indicates that an integer is positive, and - indicates that an integer is negative. As binary operators (operators that operate on two objects), + adds one integer to another, and - subtracts one integer from another.

There are a few pitfalls to avoid when using integer expressions. Be careful when dividing integers. The fractional part of the result, if there is one, is discarded. For instance, 7/4 yields 1, since the fractional part, .75, is discarded. Also be careful not to place two arithmetic operators side by side. The integer expression 2 * -4, for instance, is illegal because the two operators, * and -, are placed next to each other. In such cases, parentheses are required: 2 * (-4). In addition, be careful when using exponents. Ada standards forbid the use of a negative exponent with an integer number. For example, 2 ** (-3) will result in a runtime error. Also, when using exponents, remember that any number with an exponent of 0 yields 1; even 0 ** 0 yields 1.

The remainder operator, rem, and the modulus operator, mod, are very similar to each other. Both these operators give the remainder of integer division. The integer expressions 5 rem 3 and 5 mod 3, for example, both yield the value 2, because 2 is the remainder when 5 is divided by 3. The operators rem and mod yield the same result except when one operand (the object being operated on) is a positive integer and the other operand is a negative integer. In such cases, rem and mod yield different results, as shown in the following chart. Note that mod yields a result that has the same sign as its right operand, and rem yields a result that has the same sign as its left operand.

J	K	J mod K	J rem K
-5	-5	0	0
-4	-5	-4	-4
-3	-5	-3	-3
-2	-5	-2	-2
-1	-5	-1	-1
0	-5	0	0
1	-5	-4	1
2	-5	-3	2
3	-5	-2	3
4	-5	-1	4
5	-5	0	0
-5	5	0	0
-4	5	1	-4
-3	5	2	-3
-2	5	3	-2
-1	5	4	-1
0	5	0	0
1	5	1	1
2	5	2	2
3	5	3	3
4	5	4	4
5	5	0	0

The **abs** operator returns the absolute value of a number. The absolute value of an integer is the magnitude of the integer, which is positive, regardless of whether the integer itself is positive or negative. Thus, **abs** 3 and **abs** (-3) both yield the value of 3.

The last PUT statement of the program INTEGER_EXPRESSION adds the binary integer 2#1011# to the octal integer 8#12#. The result is output as a decimal number. (In Chapter 14, we will see how to output numeric values in other bases.)

Floating Point Type

As shown in Figure 3.1, there are two types of real numbers: float (floating point) numbers and fixed (fixed point) numbers. This chapter only discusses floating point numbers. (As mentioned, fixed point numbers will be discussed in Chapter 13.) As the following code illustrates, objects can be declared to be floating point variables and constants by using the predefined type FLOAT:

```
declare
    X, Y, Z: FLOAT;
    INCHES: FLOAT := 8_532.19;
    YARDS: FLOAT := INCHES / 36.0;
    PI: constant FLOAT := 3.1415927;
```

```
begin
    null;
end;
```

In this code, the first declaration defines the objects X, Y, and Z to be floating point variables. The second declaration defines the object INCHES to be a floating point variable and initializes it to 8_532.19. The third declaration converts the value of INCHES into yards. The last declaration defines the object PI to be a floating point constant with the value of 3.1415927. Since PI is a constant, its value cannot be changed.

So far we have discussed real variables, real constants, and, in the previous section, real literals. Next, we will consider real expressions (expressions that yield a real result), in which operations on these real literals, variables, and constants are performed.

Real expressions may contain the following arithmetic operators: +, -, *, /, **, and **abs**. These operators were already covered when we discussed integer operations, but a few differences should be noted. For instance, when division is performed on real numbers, the fractional part of the result is not truncated, as with integer division. Thus, 14.0/5.0 yields 2.8, not 2. Also, unlike integers, real numbers may have a negative exponent. For example, 4.0 ** (-2) yields the real number 0.0625. (However, neither integers nor real numbers may have a real exponent.) Finally, **mod** and **rem** can only take integer operands, but **abs** can take an integer or real operand.

User-Defined Enumeration Types

An enumeration type is defined by enumerating the values that belong to the type. Some enumeration types are predefined and reside in the package STANDARD. Enumeration types may also be defined by the user (programmer). We will begin our discussion with user-defined enumeration types.

Suppose that a program developed for a psychiatric institute needs a type that consists of the different kinds of personalities. Such a type may be declared as follows:

type PERSONALITY **is** (LOVING, CUTE, LOATHSOME, OBNOXIOUS,
        BLAND, VOLATILE, FUN_TO_PINCH);

The enumeration type PERSONALITY is defined by enumerating the values that belong to the type: LOVING, CUTE, LOATHSOME, and so on. These values are placed in parentheses. Each value is not a string but an enumeration literal. For instance, the literal, CUTE, is an explicit value of type PERSONALITY, just as the literal, 7, is an explicit value of type INTEGER.

The order in which enumeration literals are listed is significant. The compiler assumes that enumeration literals are listed in ascending order, from left to right. This topic will be discussed when we cover Boolean expressions later in this chapter.

Once type PERSONALITY is defined, variables and constants of this type can be declared. This is done in the same manner that variables and constants of integer and real types are declared:

```
TYPICAL_PERSONALITY: PERSONALITY := BLAND;
MY_TYPE_OF_PERSON: constant PERSONALITY := FUN_TO_PINCH;
```

The first declaration defines the object TYPICAL_PERSONALITY to be a variable of type PERSONALITY that is initialized to BLAND. The second declaration defines the object MY_TYPE_OF_PERSON to be a constant of type PERSONALITY that is initialized to FUN_TO_PINCH.

In addition to user-defined enumeration types, there are two predefined enumeration types. These two types, contained in the package STANDARD, are the character type and the Boolean type. We will cover these types in the next two sections of this chapter.

Character Type

The character type is defined in the package STANDARD as follows:

type CHARACTER **is** (*nul*,...,'1',...,'9',...,'A',...,'Z',...,'a',...,'z',...,*del*);

The character type contains all of the 128 characters that make up the character set of the American Standard Code for Information Interchange (ASCII). Only a few of the characters are shown in the preceding type declaration. A complete list can be found in the package STANDARD, which is listed in Appendix C.

Note that printable character literals appear within a pair of single quotes. (Pairs of double quotes are used for string literals.) The characters denoted by *del* and *nul* are unprintable ASCII characters. Unprintable characters include the control characters that perform a carriage return, line feed, and so on. In Chapter 14, we will describe how these unprintable characters can be made available.

Character variables and constants can be declared as follows:

```
FIRST_INITIAL, LAST_INITIAL: CHARACTER;
KEY: CHARACTER := 'A';
PERIOD: constant CHARACTER := '.';
SINGLE_QUOTE: constant CHARACTER := '''';
```

The first declaration defines the objects FIRST_INITIAL and LAST_INITIAL to be character variables. The second declaration defines the object KEY to be a character variable and initializes it to an uppercase A. The third and fourth declarations define the objects PERIOD and SINGLE_QUOTE to be character constants and initialize them to a period and a single quote.

Boolean Type

The Boolean type is defined in the package STANDARD as follows:

```
type BOOLEAN is (FALSE, TRUE);
```

The Boolean type, then, is just a predefined enumeration type that contains two values (Boolean literals): FALSE and TRUE.

Boolean variables and constants can be declared as follows:

```
POLITICALLY_CORRECT: BOOLEAN;
MALE_CHAUVINIST_PIG: BOOLEAN := TRUE;
T: constant BOOLEAN := TRUE;
```

The first declaration defines POLITICALLY_CORRECT to be a Boolean variable. The second declaration defines MALE_CHAUVINIST_PIG to be a Boolean variable and initializes it to TRUE. The third declaration defines T to be a Boolean constant and initializes it to TRUE. Once this Boolean constant is declared, it can be used in place of the Boolean literal TRUE.

Now that we have discussed Boolean variables, constants, and literals, let us discuss Boolean expressions. Boolean expressions are those that yield Boolean results. Even though these expressions yield Boolean results, they may contain operations on objects that belong to non-Boolean types, such as integer, floating point, or character types.

Boolean expressions may use the following relational operators: <, >, <=, >=, =, /=. These operators, which are defined in the section of this chapter on delimiters, can be used to compare operands belonging to any of the scalar types. Consider, for example, the following program:

```
with TEXT_IO; use TEXT_IO;
procedure RELATIONAL_OPERATORS is
    package BOOLEAN_IO is new ENUMERATION_IO (BOOLEAN);
    use BOOLEAN_IO;
    type DIALECTIC is (THESIS, ANTITHESIS, SYNTHESIS);
    FIRST_STEP: constant DIALECTIC := THESIS;
    DOZEN: constant INTEGER := 12;
    HIGHEST_GRADE: CHARACTER := 'B';
begin -- RELATIONAL_OPERATORS
    PUT ( 3 /= 5 );                     -- outputs TRUE
    NEW_LINE;
```

```
        PUT ( 8.1 < 1.1 + 1.2 );              -- outputs FALSE
        NEW_LINE;
        PUT ( TRUE > FALSE );                 -- outputs TRUE
        NEW_LINE;
        PUT (DOZEN = 6 * 2);                  -- outputs TRUE
        NEW_LINE;
        PUT ( THESIS <= SYNTHESIS );          -- outputs TRUE
        NEW_LINE;
        PUT ( FIRST_STEP = THESIS );          -- outputs TRUE
        NEW_LINE;
        PUT ( 'C' >= 'P' );                   -- outputs FALSE
        NEW_LINE;
        PUT ( HIGHEST_GRADE = 'A' );          -- outputs FALSE
    end RELATIONAL_OPERATORS;
```

No matter what type of objects these relational operators are comparing, the result is a Boolean value of either TRUE or FALSE. Note that FALSE < TRUE and that THESIS < SYNTHESIS. This is due to the order in which these enumeration literals are listed in their type declarations. As already mentioned, the compiler assumes that enumeration literals are listed in ascending order, from left to right. For example, FALSE < TRUE because, in the package STANDARD, type BOOLEAN is defined with FALSE preceding TRUE.

In addition to relational operators, Boolean expressions may use logical operators. Whereas relational operators can operate on operands of any scalar type, logical operators can operate only on Boolean operands. Logical operators include **and, or, xor, not**, and the special "short circuit" forms **and then** and **or else**. All of these operators are binary operators except for **not**, which is a unary operator. The behavior of these logical operators, excluding the short circuit forms, is shown in Table 3.1.

Table 3.1 Truth table

A	B	A **and** B	A **or** B	A **xor** B	**not** A
True	True	True	True	False	False
True	False	False	True	True	False
False	True	False	True	True	True
False	False	False	False	False	True

As shown in this "truth table," the **and** operator returns the value TRUE only if both operands are true; otherwise, the value FALSE is returned. The **or** operator returns the value FALSE only if both operands are false; otherwise, the value true is returned. The **xor** operator is called the *exclusive or*. This operator returns the value TRUE if the operands have opposite values, that is, if one of the operands is TRUE and the other is FALSE; otherwise, the value FALSE is returned.

Two different forms of *or* are used in the English language as well as in computer science. Whereas in computer science, these two forms—*or* and *exclusive or*—are distinguished by two different operators (**or** and **xor**), in the English language, these two forms are both indicated by the word *or*. Consider the following sentence: "To be admitted to this university, you need a GPA greater than 3.0 or an SAT score greater than 600." Obviously a person is not denied admission if he or she has both a GPA greater than 3.0 and an SAT score greater than 600. This sentence, therefore, uses the nonexclusive *or*. The following sentence, however, uses the *exclusive or*: "Charles will either rendezvous with Ada or attend a poetry reading with Lord Byron." The *exclusive or* is used because Charles will engage in one of these activities *or* the other but not both. Note the use of the word *either*, which, in conjunction with *or*, indicates that an *exclusive or* is being used.

The **not** operator is a unary operator that returns a value that is opposite its operand: **not** TRUE is FALSE and **not** FALSE is TRUE.

The following program demonstrates how the logical operators can be used in Boolean expressions:

```
with TEXT_IO; use TEXT_IO;
procedure LOGICAL_OPERATORS is
    package BOOLEAN_IO is new ENUMERATION_IO (BOOLEAN);
    use BOOLEAN_IO;
    type OUTPUT_DEVICE is (DISK, PRINTER, SCREEN);
    DEFAULT_OUTPUT: constant OUTPUT_DEVICE := SCREEN;
begin  -- LOGICAL_OPERATORS
    PUT ( TRUE or FALSE );                          -- outputs TRUE
    NEW_LINE;
    PUT ( 2 < 5 and 2 + 3 = 5 );                    -- outputs TRUE
    NEW_LINE;
    PUT ( TRUE xor TRUE );                          -- outputs FALSE
    NEW_LINE;
    PUT ( not TRUE);                                -- outputs FALSE
    NEW_LINE;
    PUT ( not ( DEFAULT_OUTPUT = PRINTER) );        -- outputs TRUE
    NEW_LINE;
    PUT ( DISK < SCREEN and 'P' < 'B' );            -- outputs FALSE
    NEW_LINE;
    PUT ( TRUE xor ( 3.2 /= 1.1 and 1+1 /= 3) );    -- outputs FALSE
end LOGICAL_OPERATORS;
```

In addition to the logical operators used in this program, there are two additional forms that are variations of the **and** and **or** operators: the short circuit forms **and then** and **or else**. Whenever possible, these forms short circuit the evaluation process by only evaluating the first operand, not the second operand.

Consider the following expression that uses the short circuit **and then**:

X **and then** Y -- evaluates Y only if X is true

In this expression, assume that X and Y are Boolean operands. The operand X is evaluated first. The second operand, Y, is only evaluated if X is true. When X is false, there is no need to evaluate Y, because the entire expression is false regardless of the value of Y. By using the short circuit form **and then,** processing time may be saved because the second operand is not evaluated unless necessary. More important, the short circuit **and then** may be used to avoid erroneous code. The following erroneous expression uses the standard **and** operator:

A /= 0 **and** B / A > C   -- erroneous code

The problem with this expression is that, when A = 0, an illegal mathematical operation is performed: dividing a number, B, by zero. When this happens, the compiler raises a runtime error. (Both A/= 0 and B/A > C are evaluated, but the order of their evaluation is unspecified.)

To avoid the risk of dividing a number by zero, we can use the short circuit form **and then**:

A /= 0 **and then** B / A > C -- evaluates B / A > C only if A /= 0

In this example, B /A > C is only evaluated when A /= 0.

Ada also has the short circuit form **or else**:

X **or else** Y   -- evaluates Y only if X is false

Again, in this expression, X and Y are assumed to be Boolean operands. X is evaluated before Y, and Y is evaluated only if X is false. If X is true, then Y is ignored, because the entire compound expression, X **or else** Y, must be true regardless of the value of Y.

In addition to using the operators just discussed, a Boolean expression may use the keyword **in** to perform a membership test. A membership test determines whether an object falls within a particular range of scalar values. Consider the following membership test:

NUMBER **in** 1..5

Assume that NUMBER is an integer variable or constant. This Boolean expression is TRUE if the value of NUMBER is in the range 1 to 5; otherwise, this Boolean expression is FALSE. Note that NUMBER must belong to the same scalar type as the range.

Membership tests provide a concise notation. Without using the membership test, we would have to write

NUMBER = 1 **or** NUMBER = 2 **or** NUMBER = 3 **or** NUMBER = 4 **or** NUMBER = 5

or an expression such as

NUMBER >= 1 **and** NUMBER <= 5

There is a variation of the membership test, which uses the keyword **not**. For instance, to determine whether NUMBER is not in the range 1 to 5, we could write

NUMBER **not in** 1..5

In this case, the Boolean expression yields the value TRUE if NUMBER is less than 1 or greater than 5; otherwise, it yields the value FALSE.

SUBTYPES

A subtype consists of a subset of values of a type. A subtype does not define a new type but defines a constraint upon an existing type.

When an object does not need to assume all the values of a type, a subtype should be introduced. For example, a variable should rarely be declared as an integer, because a variable rarely needs to assume all the integer values. By using subtypes to restrict the range of values that an object can legitimately assume, errors that might be difficult for programmers to detect are raised as constraint errors. A constraint error is raised when an object is given a value that is out of range.

In the following subtype, PERSONS_AGE is constrained (restricted) to numbers of type FLOAT from 0.0 to 120. 0:

subtype PERSONS_AGE **is** FLOAT **range** 0.0 .. 120.0; -- age in years

To declare a subtype, the keyword **subtype** is followed by a user-supplied subtype name. This name is then followed by the keyword **is** and the name of the subtype's base type (the type on which the subtype is based). This base type is then followed by an optional constraint, consisting of the keyword **range** followed by a range constraint. In the previous example, constraining the range from 0.0 to 120.0 makes sense if we are measuring a person's age in years.

Given the subtype PERSONS_AGE, we can then declare objects of this subtype:

```
AGE: PERSONS_AGE;
DRINKING_AGE: constant PERSONS_AGE := 21.0;
```

In the first declaration, AGE is defined as a variable that belongs to the subtype PERSONS_AGE. Therefore, AGE is restricted to floating point values in the range of 0.0 to 120.0. If an attempt is made to assign a value to AGE that is outside of this range, then a constraint error is raised:

```
AGE := 121.0;  -- constraint error is raised; AGE is out of bounds
```

The second declaration shows that constants can also belong to a subtype. DRINKING_AGE is defined to be a constant of subtype PERSONS_AGE and is given the value 21.0.

Since range constraints are optional, a subtype may be declared that has the same range of values as its base type:

```
subtype LOGICAL is BOOLEAN;
```

In this case, LOGICAL is simply another name for type BOOLEAN.

Let us consider a few more examples:

```
subtype HOURS_IN_DAY is INTEGER range 0 .. 23;
subtype UPPER_CASE is CHARACTER range 'A' .. 'Z';
HOUR: HOURS_IN_DAY;
UPPER: UPPER_CASE;
```

In the first declaration, HOURS_IN_DAY is defined to be a subtype of integers from 0 to 23. In the second declaration, UPPER_CASE is defined to be a subtype of characters from 'A' to 'Z'.

There are two forms of subtypes: explicit subtypes and implicit subtypes. Explicit subtypes have names; implicit subtypes do not have names. In the previous declarations, the variables HOUR and UPPER belong to the explicit subtypes HOURS_IN_DAY and UPPER_CASE, respectively. We could declare HOUR and UPPER to belong to implicit subtypes, which do not have names:

```
HOUR: INTEGER range 0 .. 23;
UPPER: CHARACTER range 'A' .. 'Z';
```

Once again, the variable HOUR is constrained to integers from 0 to 23, and the variable UPPER is constrained to characters from 'A' to 'Z'.

Since explicit subtypes, unlike implicit subtypes, have names, explicit subtypes can be used to reflect our hierarchical view of the world. Light, for example, is part of the electromagnetic spectrum that includes visible light as well as "invisible" light—infrared and ultraviolet light. This hierarchical relationship between these parts of the electromagnetic spectrum is reflected in the following declarations:

```
type    ELECTROMAGNETIC_SPECTRUM is (RADIO, TELEVISION,
        MICROWAVE, INFRARED, RED, ORANGE, YELLOW, GREEN,
        BLUE, INDIGO, VIOLET, ULTRAVIOLET, X_RAYS,
        GAMMA_RAYS);
        -- listed from longest to shortest wavelength

subtype LIGHT is ELECTROMAGNETIC_SPECTRUM
        range INFRARED .. ULTRAVIOLET;
subtype VISIBLE_LIGHT is LIGHT range RED..VIOLET;
        -- subtype of a subtype
```

Note that VISIBLE_LIGHT is a subtype of LIGHT, which is a subtype of the enumeration type ELECTROMAGNETIC_SPECTRUM.

The names of explicit subtypes may also be used to represent ranges, resulting in code that is more concise and general. Consider, for instance, the following explicit subtype:

```
subtype DIGIT is INTEGER range 0 .. 9;
```

Once this subtype is declared, the identifier DIGIT may be used to represent the range 0..9. For example, the following two membership tests are logically equivalent:

```
NUMBER in 0 .. 9     -- these two membership tests are equivalent
NUMBER in DIGIT      -- DIGIT represents the range 0..9
```

As a second example, consider the range 0..9 used in a **for** loop:

```
for NUMBER in 0 .. 9 loop . . .
```

Once again, we can represent this range with the name of the subtype:

```
for NUMBER in DIGIT loop . . .
```

We will continue this discussion of alternate ways to represent ranges in Chapter 4 on control structures.

Ada is a strongly typed language. Objects of different types cannot be assigned or compared to one another and cannot appear in the same expression. The illegal mixing of types is shown in the following code:

Basics of ADA   **45**

```
declare
    type MESOZOIC_ERA is (TRIASSIC, JURASSIC, CRETACEOUS);
    type CENOZOIC_ERA is (TERTIARY, QUATERNARY);
    AGE_OF_ARCHAEOPTERYX: MESOZOIC_ERA := JURASSIC;
    AGE_OF_NEANDERTHAL: CENOZOIC_ERA := QUATERNARY;
begin
    if (AGE_OF_ARCHAEOPTERYX < AGE_OF_NEANDERTHAL) and
        -- error; mixed types
        (AGE_OF_ARCHAEOPTERYX not in CENOZOIC_ERA)         then
        -- error; mixed types
        AGE_OF_NEANDERTHAL := AGE_OF_ARCHAEOPTERYX;
        -- error; mixed types
    end if;
end;
```

Since the variables AGE_OF_ARCHAEOPTERYX and AGE_OF_NEANDERTHAL belong to different types, they cannot be compared or assigned to one another. The membership test is also illegal since the member being tested belongs to a different type than the discrete range represented by the type CENOZOIC_ERA. (A discrete range is a range of values belonging to a discrete type.)

Whereas objects of different types cannot mix, objects of a subtype can mix with objects of its base type. Furthermore, objects of different subtypes can mix if these subtypes are descended from the same base type. This is as expected since, as mentioned previously, subtypes do not define new types. Consider, for instance, the following code:

```
declare
    type GEOLOGIC_PERIOD is (CAMBRIAN, ORDOVICIAN, SILURIAN,
        DEVONIAN, CARBONIFEROUS, PERMIAN, TRIASSIC, JURASSIC,
        CRETACEOUS, TERTIARY, QUATERNARY);

    subtype PALEOZOIC_ERA is GEOLOGIC_PERIOD range
        CAMBRIAN..PERMIAN;

    subtype MESOZOIC_ERA is GEOLOGIC_PERIOD range
        TRIASSIC..CRETACEOUS;

    subtype CENOZOIC_ERA is GEOLOGIC_PERIOD range
        TERTIARY..QUATERNARY;

    AGE_OF_TYRANNOSAURUS: MESOZOIC_ERA := CRETACEOUS;
    AGE_OF_TRILOBITE: PALEOZOIC_ERA := CAMBRIAN;
    AGE_OF_MASTODON, AGE_OF_HOMO_SAPIEN: GEOLOGIC_PERIOD;
```

```
begin
    if (AGE_OF_TYRANNOSAURUS in  CENOZOIC_ERA) or
       (AGE_OF_TRILOBITE < AGE_OF_TYRANNOSAURUS) then
        AGE_OF_MASTODON := QUATERNARY;
        AGE_OF_HOMO_SAPIEN := AGE_OF_MASTODON;
    end if;
end;
```

Since all the subtypes are descended from a common base type, GEOLOGIC_PERIOD, there is no problem of type mismatches. Also, since a subtype does not introduce a new type, operations such as <, which is allowed for objects of type GEOLOGIC_PERIOD, are also allowed for objects that belong to any of the subtypes of GEOLOGIC_PERIOD.

In addition to the user-defined subtypes just discussed, there are predefined subtypes. Two of these subtypes, POSITIVE and NATURAL, are defined as follows:

```
subtype POSITIVE is INTEGER range 1 .. INTEGER'LAST;
subtype NATURAL is INTEGER range 0 .. INTEGER'LAST;
```

These subtypes are defined in the package STANDARD and are therefore always available for use.

ATTRIBUTES

Attributes are characteristics of an object. For example, every computer has a largest integer value that it can support. This value is an attribute of the integer type. In most computer languages, attributes must be looked up in a computer manual or be found by examining code. In Ada, however, attributes are available within the language. In other words, the code can directly reference attributes. We shall discuss eight useful attributes that are frequently applied to scalar types: P'FIRST, P'LAST, P'POS, P'VAL, P'SUCC, P'PRED, P'IMAGE, and P'VALUE. (See Appendix A of this book for a complete list.) In all of these attributes, P stands for a type or subtype, which is followed by a tick mark, ', and the name of the attribute. With the exception of P'FIRST and P'LAST, all of these attributes require a parameter and apply only to scalar types that are discrete. To see how these attributes work, consider the following program:

```
with TEXT_IO;  use TEXT_IO;
procedure ATTRIBUTES is
```

Basics of ADA 47

```ada
type SOLAR_SYSTEM is (MERCURY, VENUS, EARTH, MARS, JUPITER,
    SATURN, URANUS, NEPTUNE, PLUTO);
subtype INNER_PLANETS is SOLAR_SYSTEM range MERCURY .. MARS;
subtype OUTER_PLANETS is SOLAR_SYSTEM range JUPITER..PLUTO;
subtype GAS_GIANTS is OUTER_PLANETS range JUPITER..NEPTUNE;

package BOOL_IO is new ENUMERATION_IO (BOOLEAN);
package ENUM_IO is new ENUMERATION_IO (SOLAR_SYSTEM);
package REAL_IO is new FLOAT_IO (FLOAT);
package INT_IO is new INTEGER_IO (INTEGER);
use ENUM_IO, REAL_IO, INT_IO, BOOL_IO;

begin -- ATTRIBUTES
    PUT ( INTEGER'FIRST );              -- outputs the
    NEW_LINE;                           -- smallest integer
    PUT ( INTEGER'LAST );               -- outputs the
    NEW_LINE;                           -- largest integer
    PUT ( INTEGER'SUCC (7) );           -- outputs 8
    NEW_LINE;
    PUT ( INTEGER'PRED (0) );           -- outputs -1
    NEW_LINE;
    PUT ( INTEGER'IMAGE(31) );          -- outputs 31
    NEW_LINE;                           -- (the string)
    PUT ( INTEGER'VALUE("31") );        -- outputs 31
    NEW_LINE;                           -- (the integer)

    PUT (FLOAT'LAST );                  -- outputs the largest
    NEW_LINE;                           -- FLOAT number

    PUT ( BOOLEAN'FIRST );              -- outputs FALSE
    NEW_LINE;
    PUT ( BOOLEAN'LAST );               -- outputs TRUE
    NEW_LINE;
    PUT ( BOOLEAN'IMAGE (FALSE) );      -- outputs FALSE
    NEW_LINE;                           -- (the string)
    PUT ( BOOLEAN'VALUE ("FALSE") );    -- outputs FALSE
    NEW_LINE;                           -- (the Boolean literal)

    PUT ( SOLAR_SYSTEM'FIRST );         -- outputs MERCURY
    NEW_LINE;
    PUT ( OUTER_PLANETS'FIRST );        -- outputs JUPITER
    NEW_LINE;
    PUT ( SOLAR_SYSTEM'LAST );          -- outputs PLUTO
    NEW_LINE;
    PUT ( INNER_PLANETS'LAST );         -- outputs MARS
    NEW_LINE;
    PUT ( GAS_GIANTS'LAST );            --outputs NEPTUNE
    NEW_LINE;
    PUT ( SOLAR_SYSTEM'POS (MERCURY) ); -- outputs 0
    NEW_LINE;
```

```
        PUT ( INTEGER'POS (-7) );                    -- outputs -7
        NEW_LINE;
        PUT ( SOLAR_SYSTEM'VAL (1) );                 -- outputs VENUS
        NEW_LINE;
        PUT ( OUTER_PLANETS'VAL (4) );                -- outputs JUPITER
        NEW_LINE;
        PUT ( SOLAR_SYSTEM'SUCC (EARTH) );            -- outputs MARS
        NEW_LINE;
        PUT ( SOLAR_SYSTEM'PRED (EARTH) );            -- outputs VENUS
        NEW_LINE;
        PUT ( SOLAR_SYSTEM'IMAGE (EARTH) );           -- outputs EARTH
        NEW_LINE;                                     -- (the string)
        PUT ( SOLAR_SYSTEM'VALUE ("EARTH") );         -- outputs EARTH
        NEW_LINE;
        PUT ( INNER_PLANET'PRED (INNER_PLANET'SUCC (MARS) ) );
            -- outputs MARS without raising an error, even though the
            -- intermediate result, INNER_PLANET'SUCC(MARS), is out of range

end ATTRIBUTES;
```

The first statement outputs INTEGER'FIRST, which yields the smallest integer value available on a particular computer. INTEGER'LAST yields the largest integer value available on a particular computer. On a standard 16-bit machine, INTEGER'FIRST might be equal to -32,768, and INTEGER'LAST might be equal to 32,767. The attributes FLOAT'FIRST and FLOAT'LAST yield the smallest and largest floating point numbers, respectively, available on a particular computer. When the attributes FIRST and LAST are applied to an enumeration type or subtype, they return the first and last literal of that type or subtype. Thus, SOLAR_SYSTEM'FIRST yields MERCURY, and GAS_GIANTS'FIRST yields JUPITER.

The attributes SUCC and PRED apply only to discrete types and yield the value of a SUCCessor and PREDecessor, respectively. Therefore, given the preceding declaration of type SOLAR_SYSTEM, SOLAR_SYSTEM'PRED (EARTH) yields the predecessor of EARTH, which is VENUS. The compiler knows that VENUS comes just before EARTH, not because the compiler is equipped with a basic understanding of astronomy, but because of the order in which the planets are listed in the enumeration type SOLAR_SYSTEM. Note that the attributes SUCC and PRED are inverse functions. (They perform opposite operations.) Thus, as the last statement in the example illustrates, the PRED of a SUCC of an object yields the original object.

When using the attributes PRED and SUCC, be careful not to go out of bounds. In other words, if PRED is used with the first value of a type or SUCC with the last value of a type, a constraint error is raised. There is no "wrap-around" feature that automatically brings us from one end of the list to the other. Therefore, SOLAR_SYSTEM'SUCC (PLUTO) generates an error. Since PLUTO is the last planet in the solar system, it has no successor.

However, as shown in the last statement in the code, a value of a subtype may temporarily go out of range if it is just an intermediate value in some calculation and if it lies within the range of the base type. In such cases, as long as the final value falls within the allowed range, no constraint error is raised.

Like PRED and SUCC, the attributes IMAGE and VALUE are inverse functions that apply only to discrete types. P'IMAGE converts an object of type P to a string representation. Thus, INTEGER'IMAGE (31) = " 31" (note the leading blank), and BOOLEAN'IMAGE (FALSE) = "FALSE". P'VALUE converts a string to a literal of type P. Thus, INTEGER'VALUE ("31") yields the integer literal 31, and BOOLEAN'IMAGE ("FALSE") yields the Boolean literal FALSE. The attribute IMAGE, of course, cannot be used to convert a string to a Boolean literal when the string does not match a Boolean literal. Therefore, BOOLEAN'IMAGE ("YES") is illegal.

The attributes POS and VAL are also inverse functions that apply only to discrete types. (Do not confuse the attributes VALUE and VAL; they are different.) P'POS yields the POSition of an object in a type. Therefore, SOLAR_SYSTEM'POS (MERCURY) yields 0, because MERCURY is the first literal listed in the declaration of the enumeration type SOLAR_SYSTEM. Note that the first position starts with the number 0, not 1. Thus, within the type SOLAR_SYSTEM, the position of the planets MERCURY, VENUS, EARTH, and MARS are 0, 1, 2, and 3, respectively. (These position numbers do not necessarily coincide with the way that enumeration literals are internally mapped to numbers within the computer.) P'VAL yields the VALue of an object of type P at the indicated position. Therefore, SOLAR_SYSTEM'VAL (1) yields VENUS. Again note that since position starts with 0, the planet at position 1 is the second planet represented in the type. Also note that POS and VAL do not operate on a subtype but on its base type. Thus, OUTER_PLANETS'VAL (4) yields JUPITER, not PLUTO. Finally, note that, with integers, the position starts with INTEGER'FIRST, not 0. Therefore, INTEGER'POS (-7) = -7. In general, for all integers N, INTEGER'POS (N) = N.

TYPE CONVERSION

Although Ada does not allow objects of different types to mix, there is a method for circumventing this restriction: type conversion. To convert an object from one type to another, use the name of the target type (or subtype) as a conversion operator. For example, if you wish to convert the integer 7 to a floating point number, write FLOAT(7). Consider the following example:

```
declare
    INT: INTEGER := 1;
    COUNTER: NATURAL := 0;
    REAL: FLOAT := 1.2;
    BOOL: BOOLEAN := FALSE;
    CHAR: CHARACTER := 'A';
begin
    INT := 3.8;                      -- illegal; mixed types
    INT := INTEGER ( 3.8 );          -- assigns the value 4
    INT := INTEGER (REAL);           -- assigns the value 1
    COUNTER := NATURAL (2.2);        -- assigns the value 2
    REAL := 6;                       -- illegal; mixed types
    REAL := FLOAT ( 6 );             -- assigns the value 6.0
    REAL := FLOAT (INT);             -- assigns the value 1.0
    INT := BOOL;                     -- illegal; mixed types
    INT := INTEGER (BOOL);           -- still illegal; cannot convert
    INT := INTEGER (CHAR);           -- also illegal; cannot convert
end;
```

As shown in this block statement, type conversion can only be used for numeric types. For instance, a real number can be converted to an integer number and vice versa, but a character cannot be converted to an integer, or vice versa. Also note that when a real number is converted to an integer (or to an integer subtype), the real number is rounded off, not truncated. Thus, INTEGER (3.8) yields the value 4, not 3. The Ada standards do not dictate what the compiler should do if the real number is midway between two integer values. In other words, INTEGER (3.5) could yield either 3 or 4, depending on the particular compiler.

ORDER OF OPERATIONS

In this section, we will first discuss the internal hierarchy of arithmetic, relational, and logical operations. We will then consider how these three kinds of operations are ordered in relation to each other.

In Figure 3.2, the arithmetic operators are listed in order of precedence, from top to bottom. Operations on the same level are performed from left to right. Consider the following expression:

-2 ** 5 + 2 * 3 ** 2

According to Figure 3.2, exponentiation is performed first, followed by multiplication, followed by negation (making a number negative), followed by addition. The preceding expression is thus evaluated as if parentheses were used as follows:

(- (2 ** 5)) + (2 * (3 ** 2))

Highest Precedence

**	abs		
*	/	mod	rem
+	− (unary)		
+	− (binary)		

Lowest Precedence

Figure 3.2   Hierarchy of arithmetic operators

This expression evaluates to -14.

It is recommended that parentheses be used whenever the order of operations is not obvious; fewer errors will be made, and readers of the code will have an easier time understanding the expression. Parentheses, of course, must be used when the precedence of the operations needs to be overridden.

Let us now consider the order of logical operators, shown in Figure 3.3. The logical operator **not** takes precedence over **and**, **or**, and **xor**, which are all on the same level. Consider the following compound expression, where P and Q are Boolean operands:

  not P **and** Q -- **not** takes precedence

Since **not** P is evaluated first, this expression is equivalent to the following:

  (**not** P) **and** Q

Highest Precedence

not
and, or, xor

Lowest Precedence

Figure 3.3   Hierarchy of logical operators

Unlike the arithmetic operators, even though the operators **and, or,** and **xor** are on the same level, order between these operators is undefined and must be provided by using parentheses. For instance, the following expression is illegal:

    P **and** Q **or** R   -- illegal; must use parentheses

However, parentheses are not required when the same operator is used multiple times:

    P **and** Q **and** R   -- legal; evaluated from left to right

In such cases, the expression is evaluated from left to right.

Unlike arithmetic and logical operators, the relational operators are all on the same level:

    <, >, <=, >=, =, /=

The order of these operators is undefined and must be provided by using parentheses:

    FALSE < 7 < 9   -- illegal; must use parentheses
    FALSE < (7 < 9)   -- OK; evaluates to TRUE

Be careful to avoid mixing types when using several relational operators in the same expression. In the preceding example, for instance, the following use of parentheses is illegal:

    (FALSE < 7) < 9   -- illegal; mixed types
                           -- FALSE is Boolean; 7 is integer

The next expression also illegally mixes Boolean and integer types:

    (3 < 5) < 9 -- illegal, mixed types; (3 < 5) is Boolean, 9 is integer

When arithmetic, logical, and relational operations are used in the same expression, the hierarchy shown in Figure 3.4 applies. Arithmetic operations have the highest precedence, and binary logical operators have the lowest precedence. By limiting the logical operators to binary operators, we are excluding the unary logical operator **not**. The operator **not** does not fit into this hierarchy since it has the highest precedence level, along with the arithmetic operators ** and **abs**.

Let us consider an example of an expression that uses arithmetic and relational operators, and a logical operator:

    1 + 2 > 0 **and** 3 - 2 = 1

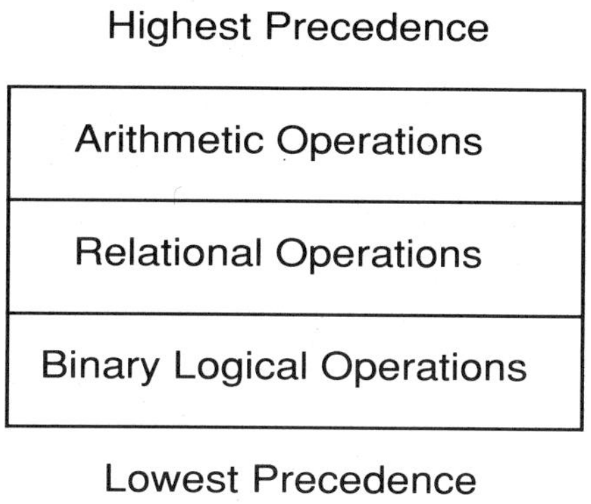

Highest Precedence

| Arithmetic Operations |
| Relational Operations |
| Binary Logical Operations |

Lowest Precedence

Figure 3.4 Hierarchy of operations

As shown in Figure 3.4, the arithmetic operations, + and -, are performed first. The relational operations, > and =, are then performed. Finally, the logical **and** operation is performed. The preceding expression is thus evaluated as if it contained these parentheses:

((1 + 2) > 0) **and** ((3 - 2) = 1)

This expression evaluates to TRUE.

This chapter has introduced basic features of Ada such as Boolean expressions, subtypes, and attributes. However, this chapter has not examined how these basic features are used. The Boolean expressions introduced in this chapter are frequently used in **if** statements and **while** loops. Subtype names and certain attributes are frequently used to represent discrete ranges in **for** loops and **case** statements. Constructs such as **if** statements, **case** statements, **while** loops, and **for** loops are known as control structures. Control structures are the topic of the next chapter.

EXERCISES

1. Which four of the following identifiers are illegal?
    a. 9W   b. W9   c. YES&NO
    d. Alpha_Beta_Gamma   e. _GO_   f. BEGIN

2. Evaluate each of the following expressions. Note that these expressions may be of type INTEGER, FLOAT, BOOLEAN, or CHARACTER. If the expression results in an error, then give the reason(s) for the error. (Hint: There are six errors.)

- a. 16#1#E3 = 1_000
- b. 13#BAD# = 2002
- c. 2#111_101_001# = 8#751#
- d. 2#1101_0011_1000# = 16#D38#
- e. 12#10# = 11#11#
- f. 15#BAD# = 14#D66#
- g. -1 + 3 * 2 ** 2 - 1
- h. -11 + 5 ** 2 - 5
- i. 7.0 ** 2 + 9.1 * 3.5 ** 3
- j. 0 ** 0
- k. **abs** ((8#5.0#e-1) - (5.0 / 8.0)) < 0.001
- l. 'A' < 'B' **and** 1 < 2 **or** FALSE
- m. 2#1010# = 10 **and** 8#10# < 10 **and** 16#10# = 16
- n. **not** TRUE **or** FALSE
- o. 0 < (5 **and** 2)
- p. (3 > 2) **or else** FALSE
- q. -2 **mod** (-9) = -2 **rem** (-9)
- r. -2 **mod** 9 = -2 **rem** 9
- s. 5.0 **rem** 2.5
- t. INTEGER (3.6)
- u. .5 <= FLOAT (1)
- v. FLOAT (5 / 3) = FLOAT (5) / FLOAT (3)
- w. CHARACTER'VAL (CHARACTER'POS ('X'))
- x. FLOAT'SUCC (2.0)
- y. BOOLEAN'LAST = TRUE
- z. BOOLEAN'IMAGE (TRUE) = "TRUE"

3. Evaluate each of the following expressions. If the expression results in an error, then give the reason(s) for the error. (Hint: There is one error.)

   Assumed Declarations:

   type MUSIC **is** (CLASSICAL, JAZZ, BLUES, BLUEGRASS, KLEZMER);
   subtype BACKGROUND_MUSIC **is** MUSIC **range** CLASSICAL..JAZZ;

   - a. (KLEZMER < JAZZ) **xor** (JAZZ < CLASSICAL)
   - b. MUSIC'POS (CLASSICAL)
   - c. MUSIC'SUCC (KLEZMER)
   - d. MUSIC'VAL (1)
   - e. BACKGROUND_MUSIC'VALUE ("CLASSICAL")
   - f. MUSIC'FIRST
   - g. BACKGROUND_MUSIC'LAST
   - h. BACKGROUND_MUSIC'FIRST = MUSIC'FIRST
   - i. BACKGROUND_MUSIC'IMAGE (JAZZ)
   - j. MUSIC'LAST = KLEZMER

k. BACKGROUND_MUSIC'POS (JAZZ)
l. BLUES **not in** BACKGROUND_MUSIC
m. MUSIC'SUCC (BLUES) = MUSIC'VAL (MUSIC'POS (BLUES) + 1)

4. Evaluate each of the following expressions. Note that these expressions may be of type INTEGER, FLOAT, or BOOLEAN. If the expression results in an error, then give the reason(s) for the error. (Hint: There are five errors.)

   Assumed Declarations:

   INT : INTEGER := 5;
   CONST : **constant** INTEGER := -10;
   FLT: FLOAT := 2.0;
   CHAR: CHARACTER := 'A';
   YES: **constant** BOOLEAN := TRUE;

   a. 6 + INT
   b. -INT
   c. INT / 3 = 1
   d. **abs** CONST
   e. INT **rem** 4
   f. (INT + 2#111#) < 16#E#
   g. (CHAR < 'D') **and** YES
   h. YES > FALSE
   i. YES **xor** (**not** YES)
   j. CHAR **in** 'A' .. 'Z'
   k. INT **not in** 1 .. 4
   l. FLT **not in** 1.0 .. 4.0
   m. INT ** (-1)
   n. INT ** FLT
   o. FLT ** CONST
   p. INT = 1_000.0
   q. INT * -CONST
   r. INT > 1 **and** CONST > (-2)
   s. INT < CONST < 10
   t. TRUE > (INT = CONST)

5. Which three of the following assignment statements will not compile due to mixed types?

   declare
      INT: INTEGER := 5;
      POS: POSITIVE := 6;
      FLT: FLOAT := 8.7;
      NEG: INTEGER := -5;
      CHAR: CHARACTER := 'P';

```
      begin
         INT := FLT;
         FLT := 5;
         INT := INTEGER (FLT);
         FLT := FLOAT (5);
         FLT := FLOAT (POS);
         INT := POS;
         CHAR := CHARACTER (INT);
         POS := NEG + POS;
      end;
```

6. Explain why it is often better to use attributes rather than just the particular literal values. For instance, why is it often better to write SOLAR_SYSTEM'LAST instead of PLUTO?

7. Write a program to calculate and output the area and the volume of a sphere whose radius, RADIUS, equals 72.52. Label each answer. Use the following formulas:

    AREA = 4 Π RADIUS^2

    VOLUME = 4 / 3 Π RADIUS^3

    where $\Pi \approx 3.14159$

8. Let   X = 12.6
           Y = 2.9
           Z = 1.5

    Write a program that calculates and outputs the values of the following expressions:

    $$2X - 5Y \qquad Z + Y \qquad \frac{Z}{2} - 2X^3$$

    $$2Z \qquad X - 1$$

    $$X^3 - 2.4X^2 + 3X - 1$$

    Explain what happens when the value of Z is 0.0 or the value of X is 1.0.

9. Rewrite the expression

    A /= 0 **and then** B / A > C

    replacing the **and then** with an **or else**. Make sure that the new expression is logically equivalent to the original expression and that it also avoids the possibility of dividing B by A when A is 0.

Chapter 4

CONTROL STRUCTURES

The kinds of Ada statements that we have studied thus far are executed sequentially. There is only one "path" through the code. Control structures provide alternative paths. A control structure might execute one group of statements instead of another group of statements, or execute a group of statements multiple times, or jump over a group of statements and resume execution elsewhere in the code. In all of these instances, instead of following a single path through the code, alternative paths may be selected.

In this chapter, we will examine four types of control structures: the **if** statement, the **case** statement, **loop** statements, and the **goto** statement.

THE IF STATEMENT

The **if** statement in Ada is very similar to the **if** statements of other languages. The **if** statement evaluates a Boolean expression, that is, an expression that yields the value of true or false. Based on whether the expression is true or false, the **if** statement decides which group of statements, if any, to execute.

The **if** statement starts with the keyword **if**, which is followed by a Boolean expression, the keyword **then**, and one or more executable statements. The **if** statement terminates with the keywords **end if**. Note the necessary space between the **end** and the **if**:

```
if Boolean expression then
    statements
end if;
```

A simple example of an **if** statement follows:

```
if MOOD = SOMBER then
    PUT_LINE ("Read Dostoevski");
    PUT_LINE ("Listen to Mahler");
end if;
```

This example is not a complete, compilable Ada program, and we are assuming that certain declarations and assignments have been made. For instance, we are assuming that the variable, MOOD, belongs to a user-defined enumeration type that includes various emotional states such as SOMBER, EUPHORIC, and ANXIOUS. (Recall that a user-defined enumeration type is a type whose members are enumerated by the programmer. See Chapter 3 for a more detailed explanation.) However, this assumption should be evident. By using fragments of code such as the preceding example, it is easy to focus on the relevant aspects of the code and not to get sidetracked. Therefore, code fragments are presented throughout this book, but complete programs are frequently presented to reinforce the reader's understanding of the overall structure of Ada programs.

Let us return to the preceding example. The Boolean expression, MOOD = SOMBER, is evaluated and resolves to either true or false, depending on whether one's mood is somber. If one's mood is somber, then the computer outputs "Read Dostoevski" and "Listen to Mahler" and proceeds to the statement (not shown) following the **end if**. If one's mood is not somber, then no action is taken, and the line of code following the **end if** is executed. Some languages have abbreviated forms of the **if** statement, where the keywords **then** and **end if** can be eliminated. Ada does not provide this option.

The **if** statement may include an **else** clause. The general form of this type of **if** statement follows:

```
if Boolean expression then
    statements
else
    statements
end if;
```

An example of an **if** statement with an **else** clause follows:

```
if ART = ABSTRACT or ART = NONOBJECTIVE then
    PUT_LINE ("Whine and complain");
    PUT_LINE ("Leave room");
else
```

```
        PUT_LINE ("Stay and enjoy");
    end if;
```

In this example, if the art is abstract or nonobjective, the computer outputs "Whine and complain" and "Leave room". If the art is neither abstract nor nonobjective, then the statements between the **else** and the **end if** are executed, and the computer outputs "Stay and enjoy". Note that the **else** clause always guarantees that a group of statements will be executed.

The **if** statement may also include an **elsif** clause. The general form of this type of **if** statement follows:

```
if Boolean expression then
    statements
elsif Boolean expression then
    statements
elsif Boolean expression then
    statements
    . . .
elsif Boolean expression then
    statements
else
    statements
end if;
```

The three dots indicate that additional **elsif** clauses may be used. Note that the keyword **elsif** does not contain an e between the s and the i. Note also that **elsif** clauses may be used without the **else** clause.

A complete Ada program containing an **if** statement that uses the **elsif** clause follows:

```
with TEXT_IO; use TEXT_IO;
procedure DAILY_ACTIVITY is

    type DAYS_OF_WEEK is (MONDAY, TUESDAY, WEDNESDAY,
        THURSDAY, FRIDAY, SATURDAY, SUNDAY);
    subtype DAYS_OFF is DAYS_OF_WEEK range SATURDAY .. SUNDAY;
    DAY: DAYS_OF_WEEK;
    package DAYS_IO is new ENUMERATION_IO (DAYS_OF_WEEK);
    use DAYS_IO;

begin -- DAILY_ACTIVITY

    PUT_LINE ("What day is it? (Fully type out the name of the day.)");
    GET (DAY);

    if DAY = FRIDAY then
        PUT_LINE ("Call in sick");
        PUT_LINE ("Play computer games");
    elsif DAY in DAYS_OFF then
        PUT_LINE ("Sleep");
    else
```

```
    else
        PUT_LINE ("Go to work");
    end if;
end DAILY_ACTIVITY;
```

There are three possible paths through this program. Each path results in a different group of statements being executed. One path results in the execution of the statements:

```
PUT_LINE ("Call in sick");
PUT_LINE ("Play computer games");
```

A second path results in the execution of the single statement:

```
PUT_LINE ("Sleep");
```

A third path results in the execution of the single statement:

```
PUT_LINE ("Go to work");
```

Consider, for instance, the following sample run of this program, which takes the first path through the **if** statement. The user's response follows the prompt, >:

```
What day is it? (Fully type out the name of the day.)
>FRIDAY
Call in sick
Play computer games
```

When the user enters FRIDAY, then only the two statements between **then** and **elsif** are executed: PUT_LINE ("Call in sick") and PUT_LINE ("Play computer games"). After these two statements are executed, the **if** statement is exited and the program ends.

Here is another sample run of this program, which takes the second path through the **if** statement:

```
What day is it? (Fully type out the name of the day.)
>SATURDAY
Sleep
```

When the user enters SATURDAY, then only the statement between **then** and **else** is executed: PUT_LINE ("Sleep"). After this statement is executed, the **if** statement is exited and the program ends. Note that we are using the membership test described in Chapter 3 to test whether the value of DAY, in this case SATURDAY, is a day off: DAY **in** DAYS_OFF. The discrete range SATURDAY to SUNDAY is represented by the subtype name DAYS_OFF. There are other ways to represent discrete ranges. The following alternatives are logically equivalent:

if DAY **in** SATURDAY .. SUNDAY **then** . . .
if DAY **in** DAYS_OF_WEEK **range** SATURDAY .. SUNDAY **then** . . .
if DAY **in** DAYS_OFF'FIRST .. DAYS_OFF'LAST **then** . . .
if DAY **in** DAYS_OFF **then** . . .

The first alternative uses the discrete range SATURDAY..SUNDAY. The Ada compiler knows that this range of values is taken from the base type DAYS_OF_WEEK.

The second alternative uses this discrete range: DAYS_OF_WEEK **range** SATURDAY..SUNDAY. This alternative is the same as the first alternative, except that the values used in the lower and upper bounds of the range, SATURDAY and SUNDAY, are explicitly indicated as belonging to the type DAYS_OF_WEEK. It is rarely necessary to indicate explicitly the type or subtype, except in ambiguous situations, which will be discussed later in this chapter. However, some programmers prefer this second form of discrete range to the first form, because it clarifies the code by documenting the type or subtype of the discrete range.

The third alternative uses the attributes FIRST and LAST. Recall that, when applied to a discrete type or subtype, the attributes FIRST and LAST yield the lower and upper bounds of the type or subtype. (A discrete type is either an integer type, a Boolean type, a character type, or a user-defined enumeration type.) DAYS_OFF'FIRST is the same as SATURDAY, and DAYS_OFF'LAST is the same as SUNDAY. The discrete range DAYS_OFF'FIRST..DAYS_OFF'LAST thus yields the range SATURDAY..SUNDAY.

The fourth alternative uses the name of the subtype, DAYS_OFF, to represent the discrete range SATURDAY to SUNDAY. This is the most concise way to represent a discrete range. However, use of the subtype (or type) name is only possible when the full range of values in the subtype (or type) is employed.

The advantage of the second two alternatives over the first two alternatives is that the code is easier to modify: when changes are made in one part of the code, additional changes do not have to be made in another part of the code. In other words, the goal is to write code where changes can be localized. For instance, consider the changes that are necessary if we decide to change the days listed in the subtype DAYS_OFF. If we add FRIDAY, then our new subtype appears as follows:

subtype DAYS_OFF **is** DAYS_OF_WEEK **range** FRIDAY..SUNDAY;

If we use either of the first two alternatives to represent a discrete range, then we have to search throughout our code and change all discrete ranges of the form SATURDAY..SUNDAY to FRIDAY..SUNDAY. However, if we use either of the second two alternatives, no changes are necessary. DAYS_OFF'FIRST automatically refers to FRIDAY, and the subtype name DAYS_OFF automatically refers to the range FRIDAY..SUNDAY.

There is a third path that can be followed in the preceding example, program DAILY_ACTIVITY. If the user enters a day from MONDAY to THURSDAY, then the statement in the **else** part of the code is executed. This is demonstrated in the following sample run:

What day is it? (Fully type out the name of the day.)
>**WEDNESDAY**
Go to work

So far we have only examined the **if** statement used by the program DAILY_ACTIVITY. Now let us briefly examine the rest of the code. In the declarative part of DAILY_ACTIVITY, which is the part of the code between the keywords **is** and **begin**, the enumeration type DAYS_OF_WEEK is defined, as well as the subtype DAYS_OFF. The subtype DAYS_OFF is defined as a subrange of values, SATURDAY to SUNDAY, of the base type DAYS_OF_WEEK. As we have seen, one of the advantages of subtypes is that the subtype name can be used to represent a discrete range concisely.

The declarative part of the program DAILY_ACTIVITY also contains a generic instantiation:

package DAYS_IO **is new** ENUMERATION_IO (DAYS_OF_WEEK);

This generic instantiation of the ENUMERATION_IO package, which will not be fully explained until the chapter on generics (Chapter 9), is needed to perform input or output on objects of the enumeration type DAYS_OF_WEEK. In this program, we need this instantiation because the user interactively inputs the value for DAY, which belongs to the type DAYS_OF_WEEK. In general, whenever nontextual information (information that does not consist of strings or characters) needs to be input or output, a generic instantiation must be performed. The following generic instantiations are needed for various kinds of input/output:

package INT_IO **is new** INTEGER_IO (INTEGER);
    -- needed when INTEGER input or output is performed
package REAL_IO **is new** FLOAT_IO (FLOAT);
    -- needed when FLOAT (real) input or output is performed
package BOOLEAN_IO **is new** ENUMERATION_IO (BOOLEAN);
    -- needed when BOOLEAN input or output is performed

The names INT_IO, REAL_IO, and BOOLEAN_IO are user-defined names. The names INTEGER_IO, FLOAT_IO, and ENUMERATION_IO, however, are not user-defined names. These are the names of the generic packages that are contained in the TEXT_IO package that comes with every Ada compiler. Because these generic packages are contained in the TEXT_IO package, the program that instantiates these packages must mention TEXT_IO in its **with** clause and optionally in a **use** clause.

Control Structures   63

We have seen how the program DAILY_ACTIVITY uses the **elsif** clause. When possible, use this clause instead of placing **if** statements within **if** statements, as follows:

```
--poor coding style
if JULIUS_SQUEEZER = BOA_CONSTRICTOR then
    PUT ("Feed it a plump rabbit");
else
    if JULIUS_SQUEEZER = RAT_SNAKE then
        PUT ("Feed it a live mouse");
    else
        if JULIUS_SQUEEZER = KING_SNAKE then
            PUT ("Feed it a lizard");
        else
            PUT ("No information on this snake");
        end if;
    end if;
end if;
```

There is nothing illegal about this code, but it is hard to read with all the nested **if** statements and the cascade of **end if**s at the end. Note that the indentation reflects the structure of the code. The **else** clause of the outermost **if** statement contains another **if** statement. The **else** clause of this other **if** statement contains yet another **if** statement. We thus have a double nesting of **if** statements: an innermost **if** statement within an **else** clause of an **if** statement, which is all placed within the **else** clause of an outermost **if** statement. In addition to being hard to read, the structure of the code is misleading because it seems to imply that JULIUS_SQUEEZER is more likely to be a Boa Constrictor than a Rat Snake or a King Snake. This may or may not be the case.

The following code is logically equivalent to the preceding code (it produces the same results) but is improved by use of the **elsif** clause:

```
if JULIUS_SQUEEZER = BOA_CONSTRICTOR then
    PUT ("Feed it a plump rabbit");
elsif JULIUS_SQUEEZER = RAT_SNAKE then
    PUT ("Feed it a live mouse");
elsif JULIUS_SQUEEZER = KING_SNAKE then
    PUT ("Feed it a lizard");
else
    PUT ("No information on this snake");
end if;
```

This second version of the code is easier to read and understand than the first version. Unlike the first version, the structure of the code is not misleading. We can see from the two versions that style is very important when writing code.

Consider another example of poor coding style:

```
--poor coding style
if TEMPERATURE > 950 then
    DANGER := TRUE;
else
    DANGER := FALSE;
end if;
    . . .
if DANGER = TRUE then
    PUT ("Sound the alarm!");
end if;
```

This coding style is poor because it does not fully take advantage of the fact that a Boolean variable is itself either true or false. As a result, the code is unnecessarily wordy and awkward. Consider the following logically equivalent alternative that, to use Daniel C. Dennett's phrase, is a "cure for the common code":

```
DANGER := TEMPERATURE > 950;
    . . .
if DANGER then
    PUT ("Sound the alarm!");
end if;
```

The first line of this code replaces the entire five-line **if** statement of the first version. The Boolean variable, DANGER, is assigned the result of the Boolean expression, TEMPERATURE > 950. For instance, if the temperature is 1000 degrees, then the expression TEMPERATURE > 950 is true, and the Boolean variable, DANGER, is assigned the value of true.

The **if** statement of the new, improved version of code replaces the last **if** statement of the original version. Instead of testing whether there is danger by stating

```
if DANGER = TRUE then . . .
```

we simply write

```
if DANGER then . . .
```

Because DANGER is a Boolean variable, we can directly use it in place of the Boolean expression, DANGER = TRUE.

Let us consider one more coding style issue, shown by the following nested **if** statements:

```
if A /= 0 then
    if B / A > C then
        -- statements
    end if;
end if;
```

To make this code easier to read, it can be restructured as follows:

```
if A /= 0 and then B / A > C then
    -- statements
end if;
```

Note that we are using the short circuit logical operator **and then**, which was discussed in Chapter 3. This short circuit form is needed so that we do not risk dividing B by zero. The expression A /= 0 is evaluated first. If this expression is true, then the next expression, B / A > C, is evaluated. However, if the first expression is false (A = 0), then the second expression is not evaluated, and we avoid dividing by zero.

THE CASE STATEMENT

The **case** statement is similar to the **if** statement because it selects a group of statements to execute. However, the **case** statement differs from the **if** statement because it uses a single **case** expression rather than one or more Boolean expressions. A **case** expression yields a value that belongs to a discrete type.

In order to compare **if** statements and **case** statements, consider this example of an **if** statement:

```
if FLOCK_OF_BIRDS = LARKS then
    PUT_LINE ("An exultation of larks");
elsif FLOCK_OF_BIRDS = PEACOCKS then
    PUT_LINE ("An ostentation of peacocks");
elsif FLOCK_OF_BIRDS = CROWS then
    PUT_LINE ("A murder of crows");
elsif FLOCK_OF_BIRDS = GEESE then
    PUT_LINE ("A gaggle of geese");
elsif FLOCK_OF_BIRDS = SPARROWS then
    PUT_LINE ("A host of sparrows");
elsif FLOCK_OF_BIRDS = MAGPIES then
    PUT_LINE ("A tiding of magpies");
elsif FLOCK_OF_BIRDS = PHEASANTS then
    PUT_LINE ("A bouquet of pheasants");
elsif FLOCK_OF_BIRDS = OWLS then
    PUT_LINE ("A parliament of owls");
elsif FLOCK_OF_BIRDS = STARLINGS then
    PUT_LINE ("A murmuration of starlings");
```

```
     elsif FLOCK_OF_BIRDS = PARTRIDGES then
         PUT_LINE ("A covey of partridges");
     elsif FLOCK_OF_BIRDS = NIGHTINGALES then
         PUT_LINE ("A watch of nightingales");
     elsif FLOCK_OF_BIRDS = WOODPECKERS then
         PUT_LINE ("A descent of woodpeckers");
     else
         PUT_LINE ("No special name");
     end if;
```

Note the 12 Boolean expressions. In each instance, we are testing whether the same variable, FLOCK_OF_BIRDS, is equal to one of 12 values: LARKS, PEACOCKS, CROWS, and so on. When a single variable, such as FLOCK_OF_BIRDS, is being tested more than once, Ada provides a special control structure known as the **case** statement. If we rewrite the preceding code using the **case** statement, we obtain the following result:

```
     case FLOCK_OF_BIRDS is
         when LARKS            => PUT_LINE ("An exultation of larks");
         when PEACOCKS         => PUT_LINE ("An ostentation of peacocks");
         when CROWS            => PUT_LINE ("A murder of crows");
         when GEESE            => PUT_LINE ("A gaggle of geese");
         when SPARROWS         => PUT_LINE ("A host of sparrows");
         when MAGPIES          => PUT_LINE ("A tiding of magpies");
         when PHEASANTS        => PUT_LINE ("A bouquet of pheasants");
         when OWLS             => PUT_LINE ("A parliament of owls");
         when STARLINGS        => PUT_LINE ("A murmuration of starlings");
         when PARTRIDGES       => PUT_LINE ("A covey of partridges");
         when NIGHTINGALES     => PUT_LINE ("A watch of nightingales");
         when WOODPECKERS      => PUT_LINE ("A descent of woodpeckers");
         when others           => PUT_LINE ("No special name");
     end case;
```

Case statements begin with the keyword **case**. The keyword is followed by a **case** expression, which is the variable FLOCK_OF_BIRDS in the example. (Usually the **case** expression just consists of a single variable.) The **case** expression is followed by the keyword **is**, which is followed by one or more **when** clauses. The value of the **case** expression determines which **when** clause is executed. For instance, if FLOCK_OF_BIRDS equals PEACOCKS, then the computer outputs "An ostentation of peacocks". The arrow, =>, separates the choice (LARKS, PEACOCKS, etc.) from the statements to be executed for that choice. (As we will see in later chapters, Ada uses the arrow, =>, in other contexts besides the **case** statement.) Any number of statements may be placed into a single **when** clause. Just place these statements before the next appearance of the keyword **when**.

The **when others** clause works similarly to the **else** clause in the **if** statement. In the preceding example, if the flock of birds is not one of the choices explicitly covered in a **when** clause, then the **when others** clause is selected, and the statement "No special name" is output.

The keywords **end case** must be used to terminate the **case** statement. These two keywords must be separated by one or more blanks.

The general form of a **case** statement, then, is

> **case** *case expression* **is**
>   **when** *choices* => *statements*
>   **when** *choices* => *statements*
>   . . .
>   **when** *choices* => *statements*
> **end case**;

Before we examine the rules governing **case** statements, let us consider a complete Ada program that uses the **case** statement:

```
with TEXT_IO; use TEXT_IO;
procedure CLASSIFICATION_OF_ELEMENTS is

    subtype ATOMIC_NUMBER_TYPE is INTEGER range 1 .. 105;
    ATOMIC_NUMBER: ATOMIC_NUMBER_TYPE;
    package INT_IO is new INTEGER_IO (INTEGER);
    use INT_IO;

begin -- CLASSIFICATION_OF_ELEMENTS

    PUT_LINE ("Enter the atomic number of an element, from 1 to 105");
    GET (ATOMIC_NUMBER);
    NEW_LINE;
    PUT ("The element with atomic number ");
    PUT (ATOMIC_NUMBER);
    PUT (" belongs to the group: ");

    case ATOMIC_NUMBER is
        when 1                        =>    PUT ("Hydrogen");
        when 2 | 10 | 18 | 36 | 54 | 86   =>    PUT ("Noble Gas");
        when 3 | 11 | 19 | 37 | 55 | 87   =>    PUT ("Alkali Metal");
        when 4 | 12 | 20 | 38 | 56 | 88   =>    PUT ("Alkaline Earth Metal");
        when 5 | 13 | 31 | 49 | 81        =>    PUT ("Aluminum Family");
        when 6 | 14 | 32 | 50 | 82        =>    PUT ("Carbon Family");
        when 7 | 15 | 33 | 51 | 83        =>    PUT ("Nitrogen Family");
        when 8 | 16 | 34 | 52 | 84        =>    PUT ("Chalcogen");
        when 9 | 17 | 35 | 53 | 85        =>    PUT ("Halogen");
        when 58 .. 71                 =>    PUT ("Rare Earth");
        when 90 .. 103                =>    PUT ("Actinide");
        when others                   =>    PUT ("Transition Metal");
    end case;
    NEW_LINE;

end CLASSIFICATION_OF_ELEMENTS;
```

This **case** statement uses numeric literals (1, 2, 3, 4, etc.) for the **case** statement choices. The vertical bar, |, sometimes called a selector operator, is used to handle multiple choices within the same **when** clause. For instance, when the atomic number is 2, 10, 18, 36, 54, or 86, then this **case** statement outputs "Noble Gas", and so on. Consider the following sample run:

```
Enter the atomic number of an element, from 1 to 105
>17
The element with atomic number 17 belongs to the group: Halogen
```

Note that the **when** clauses that are the second and third from the end of the **case** statement express choices using the discrete ranges 58..71 and 90..103. Also note that, because all the atomic numbers from 1 to 105 are not explicitly covered, we must use the **when others** clause at the end of the **case** statement to cover atomic numbers from 21 to 30, 39 to 48, 57, 72 to 80, 89, and 104 to 105.

Now that we have seen a complete program that uses the **case** statement, let us consider the rules that apply to **case** statements:

1. The **case** expression must be of a discrete type.
2. Every possible value of the **case** expression must be covered in one and only one **when** clause.
3. If the **when others** clause is used, it must appear as a single choice at the end of the **case** statement.
4. Choices in a **when** clause must be static.

Rule 1 states that the **case** expression must be of a discrete type. The following code has a **case** expression, RADIATION, that is of type LIGHT. This code follows rule 1 because LIGHT is a user-defined enumeration type, which is a discrete type.

```
declare
    type LIGHT is (INFRARED, RED, ORANGE, YELLOW, GREEN, BLUE,
        INDIGO,VIOLET, ULTRAVIOLET);
    subtype VISIBLE_LIGHT is LIGHT range RED..VIOLET;
    RADIATION: LIGHT := RED;
begin
    case RADIATION is
        when INFRARED =>
            PUT_LINE ("Detect as heat");
        when RED .. VIOLET =>
            PUT_LINE ("Detect with eyes");
        when ULTRAVIOLET =>
            PUT_LINE ("Detect as sunburn");
    end case;
end;
```

Control Structures   69

Note that within the second **when** clause, a choice is expressed using the discrete range RED..VIOLET. Other forms of discrete ranges are also permitted within the **when** clause. This **when** clause could be replaced by:

```
when VISIBLE_LIGHT'FIRST.. VISIBLE_LIGHT'LAST =>
    PUT_LINE ("Detect with eyes");
```

or

```
when VISIBLE_LIGHT =>
    PUT_LINE ("Detect with eyes");
```

Also note that an **others** clause is not needed, because all of the different kinds of light are covered.

The next example is illegal according to rule 1, because the **case** expression, AGE, is a real number belonging to the type FLOAT:

```
declare
    subtype AGE_TYPE is FLOAT range 0.0..19.0;
    AGE : AGE_TYPE := 13.0;
begin
    case AGE is -- illegal; AGE does not belong to a discrete type
        when 0.0..12.0 => PUT ("Child");
        when others => PUT ("Teeny-Bopper");
    end case;
end;
```

Rule 2 states that every possible value of the **case** expression must be covered in one and only one **when** clause. This rule can be violated in two different ways: a value of a **case** expression can exist that is not covered by a **when** clause, or a **case** value can exist that is covered by more than one **when** clause. The following code violates rule 2 in the first way:

```
declare
    RESPONSE : CHARACTER;
begin
    GET (RESPONSE);
    case RESPONSE is -- illegal
        when 'Y' | 'y' => PUT_LINE ("You are being positive");
        when 'N' | 'n' => PUT_LINE ("You are being negative");
    end case;
end;
```

This code is illegal because it does not account for all possible values of RESPONSE. Because the variable RESPONSE is declared to be of type CHARACTER, it can assume any value from the ASCII character set, not just upper- and lowercase Y and N. One method for correcting this code is to declare the variable RESPONSE to be of some type, such as:

```ada
type RESPONSE_TYPE is ('Y', 'y', 'N', 'n');
```

Another method for correcting this code is to use the **when others** clause to handle all inappropriate responses, as follows:

```ada
when others => PUT_LINE ("Your response is not recognized");
```

If no action needs to be taken after the preceding **when others** clause, then use the **null** statement as follows:

```ada
when others => null;
```

The **null** statement is a do-nothing statement that is used as a place holder when no action is needed. This statement is used because Ada syntax requires that some statement be placed after the =>.

The following code illustrates the second way that rule 2 can be violated:

```ada
declare
    RESPONSE : CHARACTER;
begin
    GET (RESPONSE);
    case RESPONSE is -- illegal
        when 'Y' | 'y' | 'N' | 'n' => PUT_LINE ("Legal entry");
        when 'Y' | 'y' => PUT_LINE ("You are being positive");
        when 'N' | 'n' => PUT_LINE ("You are being negative");
        when others => null;
    end case;
end;
```

This code is illegal because choices 'Y', 'y', 'N', and 'n' are each covered by more than one **when** clause.

Rule 3 states that if the **when others** clause is used, it must appear as a single choice at the end of the **case** statement. The following **when others** clause is illegal because it contains multiple choices:

```ada
when 'A' | others => null; -- illegal
```

Rule 4 states that the choices in a **when** clause must be static: they must be determined at compilation time and not at runtime. The following **case** statement violates rule 4:

```ada
declare
    subtype TEST_VALUE is INTEGER range 1 .. 100;
    VALUE: TEST_VALUE := 10;
    MAX: INTEGER;
begin
    GET (MAX);
```

```
        case VALUE is
            when 1.. MAX => PUT_LINE ("In range");   -- illegal; MAX is not
                                                     -- static
            when others => PUT_LINE ("Out of range");
        end case;
    end;
```

This **case** statement violates rule 4 because the value of the choice 1..MAX is determined at runtime. In other words, the value of the integer variable, MAX, is interactively input by the user when the program is running. Therefore, the compiler cannot possibly know in advance what value MAX will have.

What if we do not interactively input the value of MAX when the program is running? Instead, what if we initialize MAX to 5 as the variable is declared?

```
declare
    subtype TEST_VALUE is INTEGER range 1 .. 100;
    VALUE: TEST_VALUE := 10;
    MAX: INTEGER := 15;
begin
    case VALUE is
        when 1.. MAX => PUT_LINE ("In range");      -- illegal; MAX is not
                                                    -- static
        when others => PUT_LINE ("Out of range");
    end case;
end;
```

This **case** statement is also illegal. Since MAX is a variable whose value can change while the program is running, MAX is not static.

We can solve our problem by declaring MAX to be a constant. Constants are static: Their value is set at compilation time and is not permitted to change during program execution. See the following example:

```
declare
    subtype TEST_VALUE is INTEGER range 1 .. 100;
    VALUE: TEST_VALUE := 10;
    MAX: constant INTEGER := 15;
begin
    case VALUE is
        when 1.. MAX => PUT_LINE ("In range");    -- OK
        when others => PUT_LINE ("Out of range");
    end case;
end;
```

Whereas the **if** statement and the **case** statement select which group of statements to execute, the **loop** statement selects the number of times a group of statements is executed.

LOOP STATEMENTS

Loop statements are used to execute a group of statements multiple times. Ada has three forms of loop statements: the simple **loop**, the **while** loop, and the **for** loop. The similarities and differences between these loop statements can be seen below:

Simple **Loop**

> **loop** -- loop forever
>   *statements*
> **end loop**;

While Loop

> **While** *Boolean expression* **loop**
>   *statements*
>   -- loop until the Boolean expression becomes false
> **end loop**;

For Loop

> **for** *loop counter* **in** *discrete range* **loop**
>   *statements*
> **end loop**;

Note that each loop statement terminates with the keywords **end loop** and never with **end for** or **end while**.

The Simple Loop

The most basic form of the loop statement is the simple **loop**. This form begins with the keyword **loop** and terminates with the keywords **end loop**. Without a special statement inside the **loop** such as an **exit** statement, the **loop** continuously executes whatever statements are inside of it. Such infinite loops can be useful. For instance, a 24-hour automated teller machine infinitely loops, forever seeking customer requests to withdraw cash, pay bills, deposit checks, or transfer funds.

The usual way to exit an infinite **loop** is to use the **exit** statement:

```
loop
    -- executable statements
    if A = 0 then
        exit;
    end if;
    -- executable statements
end loop;
```

One or more **exit** statements may be placed anywhere within the loop. In the example, the loop is exited if A = 0. (We are assuming, of course, that some of the executable statements within this loop are modifying the value of A; otherwise, this **exit** statement would be pointless.) The preceding **if** statement that tests whether the loop should be exited has an alternative form that is more concise:

```
exit when A = 0;
```

Additional information on the **exit** statement will be presented in the subsection on the **for** loop.

Consider the following program that uses the simple **loop** and an **exit** statement:

```
with TEXT_IO; use TEXT_IO;
procedure ABUSE_THE_USER is

    HAD_ENOUGH: BOOLEAN;
    package BOOLEAN_IO is new ENUMERATION_IO (BOOLEAN);
    use BOOLEAN_IO;

begin -- ABUSE_THE_USER

    loop
        PUT_LINE ("Had enough? Answer true or false");
        GET (HAD_ENOUGH);
        exit when HAD_ENOUGH;
    end loop;

    PUT_LINE ("OK");
end ABUSE_THE_USER;
```

The While Loop

The following program uses the **while** loop and is logically equivalent to the preceding program that uses the simple **loop** with an **exit** statement:

```
with TEXT_IO; use TEXT_IO;
procedure ABUSE_THE_USER is

    HAD_ENOUGH: BOOLEAN := FALSE;
    package BOOLEAN_IO is new ENUMERATION_IO (BOOLEAN);
    use BOOLEAN_IO;

begin -- ABUSE_THE_USER

    while not HAD_ENOUGH loop
        PUT_LINE ("Had enough? Answer true or false");
        GET (HAD_ENOUGH);
    end loop;
    PUT_LINE ("OK");

end ABUSE_THE_USER;
```

As you can see, the logic is more straightforward in this **while** loop than in the previous simple **loop**, because the **while** loop is more descriptive of the action taking place. Also, there is no special **exit** construct embedded within the loop, so the loop is more concise. As the following sample run illustrates, the phrase "Had enough? Answer true or false" keeps being output to the screen until the fed-up user enters "true":

```
Had enough? Answer true or false
>FALSE
Had enough? Answer true or false
>FALSE
Had enough? Answer true or false
>FALSE
Had enough? Answer true or false
>TRUE
OK
```

The following is another example of a complete Ada program that uses the **while** loop.

```
with TEXT_IO; use TEXT_IO;
procedure SERIES_OF_NUMBERS is

    package INT_IO is new INTEGER_IO (INTEGER);
    NUMBER: POSITIVE;

    function EVEN (N: POSITIVE) return BOOLEAN is
    begin
        return N rem 2 = 0;
    end EVEN;

begin -- SERIES_OF_NUMBERS
    PUT_LINE ("Enter a positive integer");
    INT_IO.GET (NUMBER);
    NEW_LINE;
    INT_IO.PUT (NUMBER);
    NEW_LINE;

    while NUMBER /= 1 loop

        if EVEN (NUMBER) then
            NUMBER := NUMBER / 2;
        else -- odd number
            NUMBER := 3 * NUMBER + 1;
        end if;

        INT_IO.PUT (NUMBER);
        NEW_LINE;

    end loop;

end SERIES_OF_NUMBERS;
```

This program prompts the user for a positive number, outputs this number, and then outputs a sequence of numbers that are created within the **while** loop of this program. This **while** loop keeps executing until the number 1 is reached. The **if** statement within this **while** loop uses the EVEN function (to be discussed shortly) to check whether NUMBER is even. If NUMBER is even, then the value of NUMBER is replaced by NUMBER / 2, else NUMBER is replaced by 3 * NUMBER + 1. The updated value of NUMBER is then output.

For instance, let us assume that the user enters the number 7. Because 7 is odd, the next number generated is 7 * 3 + 1 or 22. The number 22 is even, so the next number generated is 22 / 2 or 11. Because 11 is odd, the next number generated is 11 * 3 + 1 or 34, and so on. The final series of numbers generated is as follows:

7 22 11 34 17 52 26 13 40 20 10 5 16 8 4 2 1

This program continues looping until the number 1 is reached. But, what guarantees that 1 will eventually be reached? Were we just lucky in this exercise? No. Computers have worked this problem, known as Ullam's conjecture, with many different numbers. Without exception, the number 1 is eventually reached. However, no one has yet been able to prove mathematically that the number 1 will always be reached. For our purposes, though, we should feel confident that this **while** loop will eventually terminate.

A few new features are introduced in the preceding example. One such feature is a function called EVEN, which is written within the declarative part of the main procedure, SERIES_OF_NUMBERS. Because the function EVEN is defined in the declarative part of the procedure, the executable statements of this procedure have access to the function. The function EVEN is invoked (activated) in the following **if** clause, taken from the preceding example:

    if EVEN (NUMBER) **then** . . .

When EVEN is invoked, the value of NUMBER is passed to the parameter N. The function EVEN then returns the result of the Boolean expression N **rem** 2 = 0. If N is an even number, then this expression is true because there is no remainder when N is divided by 2. Thus, when the function is invoked, it returns a Boolean value TRUE if its parameter, N, is even but FALSE if N is odd. (We will cover functions in detail in Chapter 7.)

As we have seen, the number of iterations through a **while** loop is determined by the Boolean expression at the beginning of the loop. Some languages, such as Pascal, have a special construct (usually called a **repeat until** loop) for situations where the Boolean expression comes at the end of the loop. Ada does not have any special loop structures to handle this situation, but such a structure can be created by placing an **exit when** in the last statement of a loop. (See, for example, the previous procedure, ABUSE_THE_USER, which uses the simple **loop**.)

The For Loop

One of the most useful constructs introduced by FORTRAN in the mid-1950s was the **DO** loop. Since then, practically every programming language has supplied a similar construct. In Ada (and in Pascal and BASIC), this loop is known as a **for** loop. **For** loops are used when the number of iterations through the loop is known in advance or can be determined by the compiler during runtime, before the **for** loop is entered. Conversely, **while** loops keep looping until some condition is met; the actual number of iterations may be unknown until the loop actually terminates, if it ever does terminate.

The **for** loop used in Ada is more abstract than the **DO** loop in FORTRAN. Whereas the **DO** loop can only loop over a range of numbers, the **for** loop can loop over any discrete range. A discrete range can be a range of integers or a range of any enumeration literals.

The following complete Ada program uses a **for** loop:

```
with TEXT_IO; use TEXT_IO;
procedure BLAST_OFF is
    type COUNT_DOWN is (TEN, NINE, EIGHT, SEVEN, SIX, FIVE, FOUR,
        THREE, TWO, ONE, BLAST_OFF);
    package COUNT_DOWN_IO is new ENUMERATION_IO
        (COUNT_DOWN);
    use COUNT_DOWN_IO;
begin -- BLAST_OFF
    for COUNTER in COUNT_DOWN loop
        PUT (COUNTER);
        NEW_LINE;
        delay 1.0; -- wait 1 second
    end loop;
end BLAST_OFF;
```

The loop counter, COUNTER, is not explicitly declared. Its type is implicitly determined from the type of its discrete range, TEN..BLAST_OFF. COUNTER "steps" through the enumeration literals from TEN to BLAST_OFF. Since there are 11 literals in the enumeration type COUNT_DOWN, this loop cycles 11 times. Each time through the loop, a successive enumeration literal of type COUNT_DOWN is output, and action is delayed 1 second. The final output generated by this program appears as follows:

```
TEN
NINE
EIGHT
SEVEN
SIX
FIVE
FOUR
THREE
TWO
ONE
BLAST_OFF
```

This example uses the **for** loop:

    for COUNTER **in** COUNT_DOWN **loop**...

Within this **for** loop, the discrete range is expressed by using the type name COUNT_DOWN. Other forms of discrete ranges are also permitted with the **for** loop. These other forms are shown in the following three **for** loops, which are logically equivalent to the preceding **for** loop:

    for COUNTER **in** TEN .. BLAST_OFF **loop** ...
    for COUNTER **in** COUNT_DOWN **range** TEN .. BLAST_OFF **loop** ...
    for COUNTER **in** COUNT_DOWN'FIRST .. COUNT_DOWN'LAST **loop** ...

In greater detail, here is what happens in procedure BLAST_OFF. COUNTER is initially assigned the first value, TEN, of the discrete range represented by the type name COUNT_DOWN. The program outputs this value to the screen and advances to the next line, and the **delay** statement delays execution 1 second. Note the value placed after the keyword **delay** is a real number that gives the number of seconds that the program is to delay execution. (The time delayed is only approximate; the time may be greater if the computer is busy with other activities.) The **for** loop counter, COUNTER, is then assigned the next value of the range, which is NINE. Again, the program outputs this value to the screen and advances to the next line, and the **delay** statement delays execution 1 second. This looping continues until the loop counter, COUNTER, is finally assigned its last value, BLAST_OFF. After BLAST_OFF is output to the screen, the program advances to the next line and delays execution 1 second. The **for** loop is then exited, and the program terminates.

Now that the structure of **for** loops is understood, let us consider some rules that apply to **for** loops.

1. The loop counter is not explicitly declared.
2. The loop counter's range is tested at the beginning of the loop, not at the end of the loop.
3. Inside the loop, the loop counter may be used but not altered.

4. The loop counter's discrete range may be dynamic.
5. The discrete range of the loop is evaluated before the **for** loop is first executed.
6. The loop counter only exists within the loop.
7. Within the loop, the loop counter hides identifiers that exist outside the loop and have the same name as the loop counter.
8. We may only loop over a discrete range.
9. **For** loops may step through the discrete range in reverse order.
10. An expression containing integer literals cannot appear as a bound of a discrete range.

Rule 1 states that the loop counter is not explicitly declared. The Ada compiler knows that the type of the loop counter must be the same as the type of the discrete range. The type of the discrete range is the type to which its upper and lower bounds belong:

for N in 1..3 **loop** . . .

In this clause, the compiler infers that the loop counter N is of type INTEGER and has a range from 1 to 3.

Rule 2 states that the loop counter's range is tested at the beginning of the loop, not at the end of the loop:

for VALUE in 5..1 **loop**
    PUT ("This sentence will never appear");
end loop;

In this **loop** statement, the counter's range, 5..1, is tested at the beginning of the loop. Because the initial value, 5, is greater than 1, the statements within the loop are not executed. Control passes to the statement following the loop (not shown in example).

Rule 3 states that, inside the loop, the loop counter may be used but not altered. Therefore, the following example is illegal:

for DO_NOT_CHANGE_ME **in** 1..5 **loop**
    DO_NOT_CHANGE_ME := 1; -- illegal
end loop;

During a particular iteration through the loop, the loop counter is treated like a constant insofar as its value cannot be changed.

Rule 4 states that the loop counter's discrete range may be dynamic. That is, the range of the loop may be determined at runtime rather than at compilation time, as follows:

Control Structures 79

```
GET (UPPER_BOUNDS);
for LIMIT in 1..UPPER_BOUNDS loop
    -- executable statements
end loop;
```

The value for UPPER_BOUNDS cannot be known until runtime, which is when the GET statement obtains the value input from the terminal. However, this code is perfectly legal.

When rule 4 states that the loop counter's discrete range may be dynamic, it does not mean that the bounds can be changed from <u>within</u> the loop. For instance, the following example, though legal, does not do what the programmer may have intended: to go through the loop 100 times.

```
LIMIT := 3;
for INDEX in 1..LIMIT loop
    LIMIT := 100;
end loop;
```

The behavior of this loop is explained by rule 5.

Rule 5 states that the discrete range of the loop is evaluated before the loop is executed. Therefore, in the preceding example, the value of the variable LIMIT used in the discrete range is established when the loop is first entered and is never reevaluated. Thus, when the value of LIMIT is set to 100 within the loop, the **for** loop still loops only three times. (However, when the loop is exited, the value of LIMIT is 100, not 3.)

Rule 6 states that the loop counter only exists within the loop. Therefore, the following code is illegal, because X does not exist after the loop is exited. X, in other words, is undefined. (We are assuming that a variable X is not defined before this loop.)

```
for X in 1..5 loop
    -- executable statements
end loop;
X := X - 1; -- illegal unless X is declared before the loop
```

Rule 7 states that within the loop, the loop counter "hides" identifiers that exist outside the loop and have the same name as the loop counter. In the following example, a variable N is declared in procedure P, and a variable N is used as a loop counter:

```
with TEXT_IO; use TEXT_IO;
procedure P is
    package INT_IO is new INTEGER_IO (INTEGER);
    package REAL_IO is new FLOAT_IO (FLOAT);
    use INT_IO, REAL_IO;
    N: FLOAT := 4.8;
```

```
begin
    -- the N of procedure P is visible here
    for N in 1..5 loop
        -- the loop counter N hides the N declared in procedure P
        PUT (N);     --outputs the integer N
        PUT (P.N);   --outputs the floating point number 4.8
    end loop;
    -- the N of procedure P is visible here
end P;
```

As shown in this example, within the loop, the loop counter N hides the outer N declared in procedure P. Within the loop, however, the outer N can be referenced by using the dot notation: P.N.

A loop counter may also hide outer loop counters that have the same name:

```
for N in 1..5 loop
    -- the integer N is visible here
    for N in MONDAY .. FRIDAY loop
        -- the day N is visible here
    end loop;
    -- the integer N is visible here
end loop;
```

Note that both the inner and outer **for** loops use a loop counter named N. In such situations, within the inner **for** loop, the N of the inner loop hides the N of the outer loop. In other words, if N is accessed within the inner loop, then the N that is the inner loop counter is accessed, not the N that is the outer loop counter.

But, what if, within the inner loop, we want to access the N of the outer loop? To do this, we assign an identifier to the outer loop. The identifier, which can be any valid Ada name, can then be used to reference hidden loop counters like the outer N. For instance, we can identify the outer loop as OUTER_LOOP by placing

```
OUTER_LOOP:
```

before the keyword **for.** The identifier OUTER_LOOP must also be placed at the end of the loop, after the keywords **end loop**. When an identifier, such as OUTER_LOOP, is given to the outer loop, then the outer loop counter, N, can be accessed within the inner loop through the use of dot notation: OUTER_LOOP.N. The following example shows how this is accomplished:

```
OUTER_LOOP :
for N in 1..5 loop
    for N in MONDAY..FRIDAY loop
```

```
        PUT (N); -- outputs the day N
        PUT (OUTER_LOOP.N); -- outputs the integer N
    end loop;
end loop OUTER_LOOP;
```

This example assumes that the appropriate instantiations of the INTEGER_IO package and the ENUMERATION_IO package have been made.

Remember the reason that we have to go through all this trouble to access the loop counter of the outer loop from within the inner loop: both loops use the same loop counter name. If each loop used a different name for its loop counter, there would be no such problem.

Loop identifiers can be assigned to any kind of loop, not just the **for** loop. Also, loop identifiers have other uses besides accessing hidden identifiers. Loop identifiers can also be used in conjunction with the **exit** statement to exit from various levels of nested loops. Normally, we exit the loop in which the **exit** statement lies. However, by using identifiers, we can exit an outer loop. In the following example, the **exit** statement lies in the inner loop; however, it is the outer loop that is exited:

```
OUTER_LOOP :
for J in 1..M loop
    . . .
    for K in 1..N loop
        . . .
        exit OUTER_LOOP when A = 0;
        . . .
    end loop;
    . . .
end loop OUTER_LOOP;
-- the exit statement inside the inner loop passes control here
```

Note that the loop identifier is used by the **exit** statement to specify which loop to exit. **Exit** statements can use loop identifiers to exit any type of loop: the simple **loop**, the **while** loop, or the **for** loop.

Rule 8 states that we can only loop over a discrete range. A range is discrete if its values belong to a discrete type. Thus, we cannot loop over real numbers:

```
for N in 0.0 .. 9.0 loop
    -- this is illegal
end loop;
```

The following example, however, is legal since it loops over the discrete range of Boolean values:

```
for N in BOOLEAN loop
    -- This code will loop twice
end loop;
```

82   Rendezvous with ADA: A Programmer's Introduction

Recall from Chapter 3 that the package STANDARD defines the Boolean type so that FALSE precedes TRUE:

type BOOLEAN **is** (FALSE, TRUE);

Therefore, in the preceding **for** loop, the loop counter, N, has the value of FALSE the first time through the loop and has the value of TRUE the second time through the loop.

The following complete program uses nested **for** loops that loop over the Boolean type:

```
with TEXT_IO; use TEXT_IO;
procedure TRUTH_TABLE is
      P, Q : BOOLEAN;
      package BOOLEAN_IO is new ENUMERATION_IO (BOOLEAN);
      use BOOLEAN_IO;
begin
      PUT ("  P      Q      P or Q    ");
      PUT ("P xor Q    P and Q");
      NEW_LINE (2);
      for P in BOOLEAN loop
        for Q in BOOLEAN loop
          PUT (P, 6);
          PUT (Q, 9);
          PUT (P or Q, 11);
          PUT (P xor Q, 11);
          PUT (P and Q, 5);
          NEW_LINE;
        end loop;
      end loop;
end TRUTH_TABLE;
```

This program outputs the following "truth table":

P	Q	P or Q	P xor Q	P and Q
FALSE	FALSE	FALSE	FALSE	FALSE
FALSE	TRUE	TRUE	TRUE	FALSE
TRUE	FALSE	TRUE	TRUE	FALSE
TRUE	TRUE	TRUE	FALSE	TRUE

The second parameter that appears in the PUT statements in the inner **for** loop is used to format the output so that the TRUE and FALSE values are aligned in columns. This parameter specifies the width of the output field. Formatted input/output will be discussed in detail in Chapter 14.

Rule 9 states that **for** loops may step through the discrete range in reverse order. This form of **for** loops uses the keyword **reverse**:

for N **in reverse** 1 .. 5 **loop**
   -- loop counter N is assigned the values 5, 4, 3, 2, 1
end loop;

Even though the range is traversed from 5 to 1, the discrete range is still written as 1..5. The range 5..1 is a null range, even if the keyword **reverse** is added.

Rule 10 states that an expression containing integer literals cannot appear as a bound of a discrete range. The following **for** loop is therefore illegal:

for K **in** 2-1..5 **loop** . . . --illegal; 2-1 is a literal expression

The problem is that 2-1 is a literal expression. Surprisingly, the following **for** loop is also illegal:

for K **in** -2..5 **loop** . . . --illegal; -2 is a literal expression

The problem is that -2 is a literal expression, not a literal. The value -2 is a literal expression because the minus sign is an operator that operates on the literal value 2. Such literal expressions cannot appear in a **for** loop unless the type is explicitly declared to be INTEGER. The following alternatives may therefore be used:

for K **in** INTEGER **range** -2..5 **loop** . . . -- OK

or

for K **in** INTEGER'(-2)..5 **loop** . . . -- OK

In the first alternative, the discrete range is explicitly declared to be an integer range. In the second alternative, the expression -2 is qualified to be of type INTEGER.

Unlike languages such as FORTRAN and BASIC, in Ada there are no step values that can be used in **for** loops. That is, there are no special forms of the **for** loop that permit us to step through the range, selecting every other value, or every third value, and so on.

Let us now consider a problem that occurs when the compiler cannot determine the loop counter's type by examining the loop counter's discrete range. Consider, for example, these two enumeration types:

type PHILOSOPHER **is** (PLATO, PYTHAGORAS, LEIBNIZ, PASCAL,
    DESCARTES, HUME, BERKELEY);
type MATHEMATICIAN **is** (EUCLID, PYTHAGORAS, LEIBNIZ, PASCAL,
    DESCARTES, GAUSS, RIEMANN, LOBATCHEWSKY);

Because many great philosophers were also great mathematicians, enumeration literals with the same name appear in both the preceding enumeration types. Such enumeration literals are said to be "overloaded." This overloading can lead to ambiguity, as in the following **for** loop clause:

for GREAT_THINKER **in** PYTHAGORAS .. DESCARTES **loop** -- ambiguous

Because the upper and lower bounds of the range PYTHAGORAS .. DESCARTES consist of literals PYTHAGORAS and DESCARTES that belong to both the philosopher type and the mathematician type, the compiler has no way of knowing which type is intended. (The compiler needs this information, since the enumeration literals from different types are distinct, even if they have the same name.) To solve this problem, we can qualify one or both of the literals forming the bounds of the discrete range:

for GREAT_THINKER **in** PHILOSOPHER'(PYTHAGORAS) .. DESCARTES
   loop
   -- qualification makes this unambiguous

In this case, only PYTHAGORAS is qualified, but this is sufficient to resolve the ambiguity. (DESCARTES could also be qualified, but this is not necessary.) The qualifier explicitly states the type to which the literal belongs. The qualifier consists of the name of the type to which the literal belongs, followed by a tick mark, ', followed by the literal enclosed in parentheses.

Another way of solving this problem of ambiguity is to state explicitly the type to which the discrete range belongs:

for GREAT_THINKER **in** PHILOSOPHER **range** PYTHAGORAS ..
   DESCARTES **loop**
   -- explicitly stating the type makes this unambiguous

Note that the following **for** loop clause is unambiguous:

for GREAT_THINKER **in** PLATO .. DESCARTES **loop**
   -- unambiguous

Although DESCARTES is overloaded, PLATO is not overloaded. Since PLATO is of type PHILOSOPHER, the compiler knows to loop over literals of that type.

THE GOTO STATEMENT

The **goto** statement often results in unstructured code that is difficult to understand and maintain. Why, then, does a modern, structured language like Ada have the **goto** statement? Primarily because the **goto** statement is useful when translating programs written in other languages into Ada. For instance, it would be very difficult to write an automatic FORTRAN-to-Ada translator program if Ada did not have the **goto** statement. However, when we write Ada code that has not been translated from another language, the **goto** statement can be avoided by using other Ada statements, such as the **exit** statement.

In the following example, a **goto** statement is used to jump to a point further down the code. This statement can also be used to jump to a prior point in the code.

```
goto THE_HEAD_OF_THE_CLASS;
   . . .
<< THE_HEAD_OF_THE_CLASS >>
```

When the **goto** statement is reached, the program branches to the label that is BRACKETED with << and >>. (Quality assurance personnel may have had a hand at making the Ada label so conspicuous.) The label inside the brackets is not declared:

```
<< THE_HEAD_OF_THE_CLASS >>
```

The Ada compiler recognizes that this is a label by the way in which it is bracketed.

There are certain restrictions on the use of the **goto** statement. For instance, we cannot jump into the code within an **if** statement, a **case** statement, or a **loop** statement. Neither can we jump between different groups of statements within an **if** statement or a **case** statement. The following code illustrates an illegal use of a **goto** statement:

```
if YOU_TRIED_IT then
    if YOU_LIKE_IT then
        PUT_LINE ("Enjoy it");
        goto CONTINUE;    -- this is illegal
    else
        PUT_LINE ("Go knock it");
    end if;
else
    << CONTINUE >>   -- cannot jump into an else clause
    PUT_LINE ("Don't knock it");
end if;
```

In this chapter, we have discussed the **if** statement, the **case** statement, the **loop** statement, and the **goto** statement. In the next chapter, we will discuss a composite data type known as an array.

EXERCISES

1. Which one of the following is true about **case** statements?
    a. The **when others** clause may appear anywhere in the case statement.
    b. The **case** expression may belong to any scalar type.
    c. Any **case** statement can be rewritten in a straightforward manner as an **if** statement.
    d. A value of a **case** expression may be covered by two or more **when** clauses.
    e. Any **if** statement can be rewritten in a straightforward manner as a **case** statement.

2. Which one of the following is false about the **for** loop counter?
    a. Within the loop, it can be referenced but not changed.
    b. It does not exist outside the loop.
    c. If it is an INTEGER type, then it cannot be incremented by values other than 1.
    d. Its type must be explicitly declared.

3. Translate the following **if** statements into **case** statements:

    a. **if** GOAL = DOCTOR **then**
         MAJOR := ANY_SCIENCE;
       elsif GOAL = ACCOUNTANT **then**
         MAJOR := BUSINESS;
       elsif GOAL = LAWYER **then**
         MAJOR := ANYTHING;
       else
         MAJOR := UNDEFINED;
       end if;

    b. **if** MONTH **in** APRIL..JUNE **then**
         PUT_LINE ("Do spring cleaning");
       elsif MONTH = JANUARY **or** MONTH = NOVEMBER **then**
         PUT_LINE ("Go skiing");
       elsif MONTH = JULY **then**
         PUT_LINE ("Go to Caribbean");
       else
         PUT_LINE ("Go to work");
       end if;

4. Translate the following **case** statements into **if** statements:

    a. **case** ANTAGONIST **is**
         when ME =>
           PUT_LINE ("I am firm");

```
      when YOU =>
        PUT_LINE ("You are stubborn");
      when others =>
        PUT_LINE ("He or she is pig headed");
    end case;
 b. case MONTH is
      when JANUARY | MARCH | NOVEMBER =>
        PUT_LINE ("Buy");
      when MAY | JUNE..AUGUST =>
        PUT_LINE ("Sell");
      when others =>
        PUT_LINE ("Do nothing");
    end case;
```

5. Write an **if** statement that outputs the grade of A, B, C, D, or F, depending on the value of TEST_SCORE. Values from 100 to 90 are an A, 89 to 80 a B, 79 to 70 a C, 69 to 60 a D, and 59 to 0 an F.

6. Rewrite the **if** statement in problem 5 as a **case** statement.

7. State whether the following code segment is correct. If incorrect, explain what is wrong.

```
    -- assume TEXT_IO is visible
    declare
      type DAYS_OF_WEEK is (MON, TUES, WED, THURS, FRI,
        SAT, SUN);
      package DAYS_IO is new
        TEXT_IO.ENUMERATION_IO (DAYS_OF_WEEK);
      use DAYS_IO;
      DAY : DAYS_OF_WEEK;
    begin
      GET (DAY);
      case DAY is
        when MON .. THURS => PUT_LINE ("Go to work.");
        when FRI => PUT_LINE ("Call in sick.");
      end case;
    end;
```

8. Modify the **procedure** DAILY_ACTIVITY, shown in this chapter, so that the days off are from Saturday to Monday.

9. Consider the following declarations:

```
    type DESTINATION is (FRANCE, YELLOWSTONE, LAS_VEGAS);
    subtype LONG_VACATION is INTEGER range 21..70; -- days
    subtype AVERAGE_VACATION is INTEGER range 7..20; -- days
    subtype SHORT_VACATION is INTEGER range 1..6; -- days
```

Write a program that prompts the user for the length of his or her vacation and then uses a **case** statement to determine where the person should take the vacation. The program should select France, Yellowstone, or Las Vegas, depending on whether the vacation is long, average, or short, respectively. Use the names of the subtypes—LONG_VACATION, AVERAGE_VACATION, and SHORT_VACATION—to express the discrete ranges within the **case** statement.

10. What values will the following program output? Is the X that is explicitly declared as an integer variable the same as the X used as a **for** loop counter?

    ```
    with TEXT_IO; use TEXT_IO;
    procedure P is
       X: INTEGER := -1;
       SUM: INTEGER := 0;
       package INT_IO is new INTEGER_IO (INTEGER);
       use INT_IO;
    begin
       for X in 1..5 loop
          SUM := SUM + X;
          PUT (SUM);
          NEW_LINE;
       end loop;
       PUT (X);
       NEW_LINE;
       PUT (SUM);
    end P;
    ```

11. Rewrite the following program using a **while** loop instead of a **for** loop. Then rewrite the program using a simple loop with an **exit** statement.

    ```
    with TEXT_IO; useTEXT_IO;
    procedure STRANGE_CLAIMS is
       type THINGS_TO_BE_SKEPTICAL_OF is
          (LOCH_NESS_MONSTER, UFOS, ESP, BIGFOOT,
           CLAIRVOYANCE, BURMUDA_TRIANGLE, DOWSING,
           GHOSTS, PALMISTRY, ASTROLOGY, CHANNELING,
           PSYCHIC_SURGERY);
       package PHENOMENON_IO is new
          ENUMERATION_IO (THINGS_TO_BE_SKEPTICAL_OF);
       use PHENOMENON_IO;
    begin
       PUT_LINE ("The following are things to be skeptical of:");
       NEW_LINE;
       for PHENOMENON in THINGS_TO_BE_SKEPTICAL_OF loop
          PUT (PHENOMENON);
          NEW_LINE;
       end loop;
    end STRANGE_CLAIMS;
    ```

Control Structures   **89**

12. Write a timer program that, every second, outputs the number of hours, minutes, and seconds that have elapsed since the program started executing. Use nested **for** loops and the **delay** statement.

13. Find the errors in this code:

    ```
    declare
        subtype ONE_TO_SEVEN is INTEGER range 1..7;
    begin
        for INDEX in ONE_TO_SEVEN loop;
            INDEX := INDEX + 1;
        end for;
        INDEX := INDEX -1; -- INDEX that is loop counter
    end;
    ```

14. Modify the program SERIES_OF_NUMBERS in the **while** loop section of this chapter to output the number of steps taken to reach the number 1. Starting with the number 341, how many steps does it take to reach 1? Starting with the number 27, how many steps does it take to reach 1?

15. Rewrite the following code so that all the **goto** statements are removed.

    a. ```
       if SUNNY then
           goto BEACH;
       end if;

       << MOVIE >>

       WATCH_MOVIE;

       if RAINING then
           goto MOVIE;
       end if;

       goto HOME;

       << BEACH >>

       if WINDY then
           FLY_KITE;
       else
           SWIM;
       end if;

       EAT;
       goto MOVIE;

       << HOME >>
       ```
       ```

b. << WEIGHT_CLINIC >>

if FAT **then**
   DIET;
   goto WEIGHT_CLINIC;
else
   goto PIG_OUT;
end if;

<< TRY_AGAIN >>

if THIN **then**
   goto PIG_OUT;
else
   goto EXIT_PROGRAM;
end if;

<< PIG_OUT >>

EAT;
goto TRY_AGAIN;

<< EXIT_PROGRAM >>

16. Write a program that outputs the daily deposit and the total amount of money in a piggy bank each day a deposit is made. Assume that 30 consecutive daily deposits are made and that the size of the deposit doubles each day: one cent the first day, two cents the second day, four cents the third day, and so on, for 30 days.

17. Write a program that converts and outputs the temperatures from 0 to 10 degrees Centigrade (Celsius) to Fahrenheit and Kelvin in increments of 1 degree. Use the formulas:

    FAHRENHEIT = 1.8 * CENTIGRADE + 32
    KELVIN = CENTIGRADE + 273.15

18. Write a program that finds and outputs the maximum and minimum values of Y, where

    $Y = -2X^2 + 4X - 2$, for $-2 \leq X \leq 2$.

    Test all values of X in this range in increments of 0.1.

19. Write a program that calculates and outputs the sum of all the odd integers from 1 to 199 that are not divisible by 7, 9, or 13.

Chapter 5

ARRAYS

An array is an object that consists of multiple components, each belonging to the same type. An entire array is referenced with a single identifier. An individual component of the array is referenced with the array identifier, followed by an index value placed in parentheses. Consider, for example, an array called RAINFALL, which represents the number of inches of rain for each month of the year. To reference a component of this array, we must supply an index value. Let the index assume the values JANUARY to DECEMBER. Thus, the array component RAINFALL (APRIL) represents the amount of rain for the month of April. If there are 75 inches of rain in April, we can assign this value to the array component, just as we can assign a value to a regular variable:

RAINFALL (APRIL) := 75;

The array named RAINFALL is a one-dimensional array because it is a list (row) of items. Only one index is needed to select an item in this list. A two-dimensional array can be thought of as a table or matrix. To reference an object in this table, two indexes are needed. The first index specifies the row (horizontal list) in which the item appears; the second index specifies the column (vertical list) in which the item appears. For example, a second index can be added to the RAINFALL array to represent years. Thus, the array component RAINFALL (JANUARY, 1989) represents the amount of rain during the month of January 1989.

A three-dimensional array can be thought of as pages of tables. To reference an item in a three-dimensional array, one needs three indexes. The first index specifies the row in which the item appears, the second index specifies the column in which the item appears, and the third index specifies the "page" on which the item appears. For example, a third index can be added to the previous RAINFALL array to represent locations. Thus, the array component RAINFALL (JANUARY,1989, LOS_ANGELES) represents the amount of rain that fell in Los Angeles during January 1989. Arrays of dimensions greater than three are possible but infrequently used. Be careful: as you increase the number of dimensions, computer memory is quickly consumed to store all of these additional array components. For example, a three-dimensional array whose dimensions are 100 by 100 by 100 consists of 100^3 or 1,000,000 components.

The following topics are included in this chapter: one-dimensional arrays, two-dimensional arrays, anonymous arrays, dynamic arrays, unconstrained arrays, strings, Boolean vectors, array of arrays, array attributes, and operations on arrays.

ONE-DIMENSIONAL ARRAYS

Let us consider how a one-dimensional array can be used. Suppose that a data structure is needed to store the various daily specials offered by a diner. Assume that the diner is open from Wednesday through Saturday and that a single daily special is provided on each of these days:

Day	Special
Wednesday	Spam
Thursday	Burger
Friday	Meat Loaf
Saturday	Hot Dog

Without arrays, this information could be stored using multiple variables:

```
WED_SPECIAL := SPAM;
THURS_SPECIAL := BURGER;
FRI_SPECIAL := MEAT_LOAF;
SAT_SPECIAL := HOT_DOG;
```

Such unstructured data are error prone and awkward to manipulate, especially if the number of variables proliferates into the hundreds. By using a one-dimensional array, however, these related variables may be grouped together under the same name, for instance, SPECIAL. SPECIAL, then, is the name of the array, and WED through SAT are its index values. A particular array component may be selected by using the name SPECIAL, followed by an index value—WED, THURS, FRI, or SAT—enclosed in parentheses. Thus, SPECIAL (WED), SPECIAL (THURS,) SPECIAL (FRI), and

SPECIAL (SAT) represent the daily specials for Wednesday through Saturday, respectively.

Before an array can be used, it must be declared (defined). The following code declares the SPECIAL array:

```
type FOOD is (BURGER, HOT_DOG, SPAM, MEAT_LOAF);
type DAYS_OPEN is (WED, THURS, FRI, SAT);
type DAILY_SPECIAL is array (DAYS_OPEN) of FOOD;
SPECIAL: DAILY_SPECIAL;
```

The first line declares the enumeration type FOOD, which contains the possible delicacies that can be served as daily specials. The second line declares the enumeration type DAYS_OPEN, which lists the days that the diner is open for business. The third line declares the array type DAILY_SPECIAL. Array type declarations have this form:

type *array name* **is array** *(index specification)* **of** *type*;

In our example, the keyword **type** is followed by the name of the array type, DAILY_SPECIAL, then the keywords **is array**, and the array index specification, enclosed in parentheses. The index specification defines a discrete range of possible values that the index can assume. In this example, the index specification consists of the type name DAYS_OPEN. This type name is used to represent the discrete range WED..SAT. This method of representing discrete ranges was presented in Chapter 4 when we used discrete ranges in **for** loops and **case** statements.

The index specification is followed by the keyword **of**, which is followed by the type to which every component of the array belongs. In our example, every component belongs to type FOOD. The fourth line declares the object SPECIAL to be an array of type DAILY_SPECIAL. Since the components of SPECIAL belong to the type FOOD, SPECIAL may be described as a FOOD array.

An array, then, is a composite object consisting of components, each belonging to the same type. Ada places no restrictions on the component type. Thus, a component type may be any scalar type, such as INTEGER, FLOAT, BOOLEAN, and CHARACTER; or a user-defined enumeration type, such as type FOOD. As we will see in the "Array of Arrays" section of this chapter and in the next chapter, a component type can even be a composite type. The result is an array of arrays or an array of records.

Once the array SPECIAL is declared, values can be assigned to its components just like any variable of type FOOD:

```
SPECIAL (WED) := SPAM;
SPECIAL (THURS) := BURGER;
SPECIAL (FRI) := MEAT_LOAF;
SPECIAL (SAT) := HOT_DOG;
```

Note again that each individual component of an array is referenced by the array name followed by an index value in the range WED..SAT, which is placed in parentheses. (This index may be a literal, a constant, a variable, or an expression.)

The components of an array can be of any type; however, index values must belong to a discrete type. In our example, the index type, DAYS_OPEN, is a user-defined enumeration type.

Just as literal expressions cannot appear in the discrete range of a **for** loop, they cannot appear in the discrete range of an index specification in an array type declaration:

type A **is array** (-2..5) **of** INTEGER; -- illegal

As mentioned in the previous two chapters, the value -2 is a literal expression because the minus sign is an operator that operates on the literal value 2. Such literal expressions cannot appear in an index specification unless the type is explicitly declared to be of type INTEGER. The following alternatives may therefore be used:

type A **is array** (INTEGER **range** -2..5) **of** INTEGER;   --OK

or

type A **is array** (INTEGER'(-2)..5) **of** INTEGER;   --OK

Another example of an array follows:

type BEANS **is** (LIMA, LENTIL, GARBANZO, PINTO, KIDNEY, BLACK, SOY, MUNG, JELLY);
type COUNT_TYPE **is array** (BEANS **range** PINTO..JELLY) **of** NATURAL;
BEAN_COUNT: COUNT_TYPE;

In this example, BEAN_COUNT is an array of natural numbers. (Recall that NATURAL is defined in the package STANDARD as an integer subtype whose range is from 0 to INTEGER'LAST.) The index is constrained to values in the range of PINTO to JELLY; LIMA, LENTIL, and GARBANZO are excluded from this range:

BEAN_COUNT (SOY) := 181;
BEAN_COUNT (JELLY) := 3_825;
BEAN_COUNT (LENTIL) := 24;   -- error, index out of bounds

The last statement is illegal because the index value LENTIL is out of bounds. The Ada compiler will catch this mistake and raise a constraint error. This should be good news to, for example, FORTRAN programmers. Practically every FORTRAN programmer has, at one time or another, written code where an array index accidently goes out of bounds. Standard FORTRAN does not catch this error, either at compilation time or at runtime. Therefore, programmers sometimes spend days debugging a program before catching this error. The philosophy behind Ada is to have the compiler detect as many errors as possible, thus reducing the time spent debugging code.

As we have seen, an array may be initialized by separately assigning a value to each of its components. In situations where every component of the array needs to be assigned the same value, the **for** loop may be used:

> **for** DAY **in** DAYS_OPEN **loop**
>   SPECIAL (DAY) := SPAM; -- special for every day is spam
> **end loop**;

Ada offers yet another alternative to array initialization. An entire array may be initialized by assigning it an array aggregate:

> SPECIAL := (SPAM, SPAM, SPAM, SPAM);
>   -- special for every day is spam

An array aggregate can be thought of as an array literal, that is, a particular set of values for an entire array. Note that by initializing an array to an aggregate, different values may just as easily be assigned to each array component:

> SPECIAL := (SPAM, MEAT_LOAF, HOT_DOG, BURGER);
>   -- positional notation

Each value in the aggregate is assigned to the array component in the corresponding position. The first value in the aggregate, SPAM, is assigned to the first component, SPECIAL (WED); the second value in the aggregate, MEAT_LOAF, is assigned to the second component, SPECIAL (THURS); and so on. The aggregate must be complete: it must assign a value to every component of the array. Incomplete aggregates are illegal.

Aggregates can be written using two different notations: named notation and positional notation. The preceding example uses positional notation: each value in the aggregate is assigned to the array component in the corresponding position. The following example uses named notation:

> SPECIAL := (WED => SPAM, THURS => MEAT_LOAF, FRI => HOT_DOG,
>   SAT => BURGER);
>   -- named notation

In named notation, the name of the index value to the left of the arrow is associated with the value to the right of the arrow. In the example, SPAM is assigned to the array component with the index value WED, MEAT_LOAF is assigned to the array component with the index value THURS, and so on.

Named notation has two advantages over positional notation. First, named notation clearly documents which values are assigned to which array components. For instance, at a glance, one can see that spam is the daily special for Wednesday and hot dogs for Friday. Second, the order of items in the aggregate does not matter. Thus, ordering errors are avoided. The preceding aggregate could therefore be written in this equivalent form:

```
SPECIAL := ( SAT => BURGER, WED => SPAM, FRI => HOT_DOG,
             THURS => MEAT_LOAF);
```

Array aggregates may use the **others** keyword to assign a value to array components that are not explicitly given a value. (Recall that the **others** keyword functions similarly in **case** statements.) Every component of the array SPECIAL may be assigned the same value, SPAM, as follows:

```
SPECIAL := (others => SPAM);
   -- special for every day is spam
```

Aggregates can be qualified. Recall that a qualifier removes ambiguity by explicitly stating the type to which an object belongs. First, one writes the name of the type to which the object belongs. The name is followed by a tick mark, ', followed by the object being qualified, in parentheses. The preceding aggregate can be written as

```
SPECIAL := DAILY_SPECIAL'(others => SPAM);
   -- qualified aggregate
```

This aggregate has the qualifier DAILY_SPECIAL appended to it. (The aggregate already contains parentheses, so we do not need to add an additional set of parentheses following the tick mark.) The qualifier helps the compiler determine what components need to be assigned the value SPAM. In this case, the qualifier is not needed. In other cases, typically where the keyword **others** is used, the qualifier may be needed. The rules that determine whether or not a qualifier is needed are complex and subtle. Therefore, the safe and easy approach is always to qualify an array aggregate when it uses the **others** keyword. (Array aggregates also must be qualified when they are used in expressions or as parameters to subprograms. In such cases, the type to which the aggregate belongs is not clear from its context.)

The following example uses named notation to assign BURGER to SPECIAL (WED) and MEAT_LOAF to SPECIAL (SAT). All other array components are assigned the value SPAM, as indicated by the keyword **others**:

```
SPECIAL := DAILY_SPECIAL'(WED => BURGER, SAT => MEAT_LOAF,
            others => SPAM);
   -- Wednesday special is burger; Saturday special is meat loaf
   -- for all other days, the special is spam
```

In the next example, BURGER is assigned to SPECIAL (WED) and MEAT_LOAF is assigned to SPECIAL (THURS) by positional notation. All other array components are assigned the value SPAM:

```
SPECIAL := DAILY_SPECIAL'(BURGER, MEAT_LOAF, others => SPAM);
    -- Wednesday special is burger; Thursday special is meat loaf
    -- for all other days, the special is spam
```

This is the only case where positional and named notation can be mixed in array aggregates. In other words, in mixed notation, only the named item **others** is allowed, and it must be placed at the end of the aggregate. The following mixed notation is therefore illegal:

```
SPECIAL := (BURGER, MEAT_LOAF, FRI => SPAM, SAT => SPAM);
    -- illegal; cannot mix positional and named notation
```

The keyword **others**, if used, must always appear at the end of the aggregate, even when named notation is used:

```
SPECIAL := DAILY_SPECIAL'(others => SPAM, WED => BURGER);
    -- illegal; others must be last item
```

Recall that, in Chapter 4, the vertical bar is used in **case** statements to select various choices. The vertical bar may also be used within an array aggregate, as follows:

```
SPECIAL := DAILY_SPECIAL'(THURS | SAT => BURGER,
    others => SPAM);
    -- on Thursday or Saturday, special is burger
    -- for other days, the special is spam
```

In this statement, if the day is Thursday or Saturday, then the special is BURGER; otherwise, the special is SPAM.

The vertical bar cannot be used to combine an index value with the keyword **others**:

```
SPECIAL := DAILY_SPECIAL'(WED | others => BURGER);
    -- illegal; others cannot be combined with index values
```

The vertical bar is particularly useful when the index values (such as THURS and SAT) are not contiguous. When the index values are contiguous, a discrete range may be used:

```
SPECIAL := DAILY_SPECIAL' (THURS..SAT => BURGER, others => SPAM);
    -- from Thursday to Saturday, special is burger
    -- for other days, special is spam
```

In this example, burgers are the daily special for all days from Thursday to Saturday. For all remaining days, in this case, Wednesday, the special is spam.

A discrete range can cover the entire range of index values:

```
SPECIAL := (WED..SAT => SPAM);
    -- special for every day is spam
```

In this example, the value of every component of the SPECIAL array is set to SPAM.

The vertical bar, the discrete range, and **others** can, of course, all be used in a single aggregate:

```
SPECIAL := DAILY_SPECIAL' (WED | FRI .. SAT => MEAT_LOAF,
                    others => SPAM);
    -- special for Wednesday, or for Friday to Saturday is meat loaf
    -- for other days, the special is spam
```

In this example, meat loaf is the daily special on Wednesday and on Friday through Saturday. Spam is the daily special on the remaining day, Thursday.

In Ada, objects may be initialized when they are declared. Arrays are no exception, as shown in the DIETARY_STATUS array in the following program:

```
with TEXT_IO; use TEXT_IO;
procedure YOU_ARE_WHAT_YOU_EAT is
    type EDIBLE_THINGS is (APPLE, ORANGE, CAKE, ICE_CREAM,
                    BURGER, FRIES);
    type FOOD_CATEGORY is (FATTENING, NONFATTENING);
    type FOOD_ARRAY is array (EDIBLE_THINGS) of FOOD_CATEGORY;
    package FOOD_IO is new ENUMERATION_IO (EDIBLE_THINGS);
    package INT_IO is new INTEGER_IO (INTEGER);
    use FOOD_IO, INT_IO;

    DIETARY_STATUS: constant FOOD_ARRAY := -- constant array
            ( APPLE           =>     NONFATTENING,
              ORANGE          =>     NONFATTENING,
              CAKE            =>     FATTENING,
              ICE_CREAM       =>     FATTENING,
              BURGER          =>     FATTENING,
              FRIES           =>     FATTENING);

    MORSEL: EDIBLE_THINGS;
    NUMBER_OF_SINS: NATURAL := 0;
begin
    for SAMPLE in 1..50 loop
        PUT_LINE ("What are you about to eat?");
        GET (MORSEL);
        NEW_LINE;
```

```
        if DIETARY_STATUS (MORSEL) = FATTENING then
            PUT_LINE ("Remove from your mouth immediately!");
            NUMBER_OF_SINS := NUMBER_OF_SINS + 1;
        else
            PUT_LINE ("Good for you");
        end if;
    end loop;

    PUT ("Number of times sinned is ");
    PUT (NUMBER_OF_SINS);
    NEW_LINE;

    if NUMBER_OF_SINS < 9 then
        PUT_LINE ("You did well");
    else
        PUT_LINE ("Failed again fatty");
    end if;
end YOU_ARE_WHAT_YOU_EAT;
```

After this user-unfriendly program finds out what morsel of food is about to be consumed, the "look-up table," which is the constant array DIETARY_STATUS, is used to check whether this particular morsel is fattening or nonfattening. (Since DIETARY_STATUS is a constant array, it must be initialized when it is declared, and its value cannot be changed.) If the morsel is fattening, then the message "Remove from your mouth immediately!" is output, and the counter NUMBER_OF_SINS is incremented by 1. If the morsel is nonfattening, then the message "Good for you!" is output. The program loops (prompts the user for the morsel and outputs the appropriate message) 50 times. When the program is done looping, it outputs the number of times that the person sinned. If this number is less than 9, then the message "You did well" appears; otherwise, "Failed again fatty" is output.

TWO-DIMENSIONAL ARRAYS

Let us modify our diner example so that three daily specials are served each day: one for breakfast, one for lunch, and one for dinner. Because breakfast is served, let us also add eggs to the list of possible specials:

	Breakfast	Lunch	Dinner
Wednesday	Spam	Hot Dog	Meat Loaf
Thursday	Eggs	Spam	Hot Dog
Friday	Spam	Spam	Burger
Saturday	Spam	Burger	Meat Loaf

To look up a particular special in the previous one-dimensional array example, all you have to know is the day of the week. Hence, only one index, or a one-dimensional array, is required. In this example, to look up a particular special, you have to know the day of the week and the meal. Hence, an array with two indexes, or a two-dimensional array, is needed.

The following declarations result in the definition of a two-dimensional array, SPECIAL, which can be used to store the daily special for each meal of each day that the diner is open:

```
type FOOD is (BURGER, HOT_DOG, SPAM, MEAT_LOAF, EGGS);
type DAYS_OPEN is (WED, THURS, FRI, SAT);
type MEAL_TYPE is (BREAKFAST, LUNCH, DINNER);
type DAILY_SPECIAL is array (DAYS_OPEN, MEAL_TYPE) of FOOD;
SPECIAL: DAILY_SPECIAL;
```

As can be seen, a two-dimensional array has two indexes; in this case, these indexes are of different types. The index for the first dimension is of type DAYS_OPEN and has the range WED..SAT. The index for the second dimension is of type MEAL_TYPE and has the range BREAKFAST..DINNER. The first index specifies the rows of the table. There is a Wednesday row of specials, a Thursday row of specials, and so on. The second index specifies the columns of the table. There is the breakfast column, the lunch column, and the dinner column. Thus, each component of the array, such as SPECIAL (WED, DINNER), is referenced by two index values and belongs to the type FOOD.

Unlike one-dimensional array initialization, which can use a single **for** loop, two-dimensional array initialization requires nested **for** loops. Each loop ranges over the values of a different index:

```
for DAY in DAYS_OPEN loop -- rows
    for MEAL in MEAL_TYPE loop -- columns
        SPECIAL (DAY, MEAL) := SPAM;
    end loop;
end loop;
```

As with one-dimensional arrays, two-dimensional arrays can be initialized to an aggregate, either when the array is declared or by using an assignment statement. The aggregate may use either positional or named notation for each of its dimensions. For a two-dimensional array, there are four consistent combinations possible for writing the aggregate. (There are other possible combinations if one inconsistently changes, for instance, between named and positional notation for each row of an array.) The four consistent combinations are as follows:

1. Positional notation for the rows and the columns
2. Named notation for the rows and positional notation for the columns

Arrays   **101**

3. Positional notation for the rows and named notation for the columns
4. Named notation for the rows and the columns

Combination 1 uses positional notation for the rows (DAYS_OPEN) and the columns (MEAL_TYPE). In the following aggregate, each row represents the specials for a particular day (WED, THURS, FRI, and SAT), and each column represents the meals (breakfast, lunch, and dinner):

```
SPECIAL :=
   ( (SPAM,    HOT_DOG,   MEAT_LOAF),
     (EGGS,    SPAM,      HOT_DOG),
     (SPAM,    SPAM,      BURGER),
     (SPAM,    BURGER,    MEAT_LOAF) );
```

With combination 1, it is difficult to see which special applies to which day and to which meal.

Combination 2 uses named notation for the rows (DAYS_OPEN) and positional notation for the columns (MEAL_TYPE). This aggregate is easier to read than the combination 1 aggregate. However, it is still not very clear which meal is for breakfast, lunch, or dinner:

```
SPECIAL :=
 ( WED   => (SPAM,    HOT_DOG,   MEAT_LOAF),
   THURS => (EGGS,    SPAM,      HOT_DOG),
   FRI   => (SPAM,    SPAM,      BURGER),
   SAT   => (SPAM,    BURGER,    MEAT_LOAF) );
```

Combination 3 uses positional notation for the rows (DAYS_OPEN) and named notation for the columns (MEAL_TYPE). To make the code more readable, the meals for a given day are listed vertically instead of horizontally. In this combination, it is difficult to see which breakfast, lunch, or dinner special applies to which day:

```
SPECIAL := ( ( BREAKFAST => SPAM,
               LUNCH     => HOT_DOG,
               DINNER    => MEAT_LOAF ),
             ( BREAKFAST => EGGS,
               LUNCH     => SPAM,
               DINNER    => HOT_DOG ),
             ( BREAKFAST => SPAM,
               LUNCH     => SPAM,
               DINNER    => BURGER ),
             ( BREAKFAST => SPAM,
               LUNCH     => BURGER,
               DINNER    => MEAT_LOAF) );
```

Combination 4 uses named notation for both the rows (DAYS_OPEN) and the columns (MEAL_TYPE). Once again, to make the code more readable, the meals for a given day are listed vertically instead of horizontally. This aggregate is easier to read than the preceding aggregates, because all values of the two indexes are clearly labeled. For instance, at a glance, we can see that hot dog is the Thursday dinner special:

```
SPECIAL :=
   ( WED   =>  ( BREAKFAST =>  SPAM,
                 LUNCH     =>  HOT_DOG,
                 DINNER    =>  MEAT_LOAF ),
     THURS =>  ( BREAKFAST =>  EGGS,
                 LUNCH     =>  SPAM,
                 DINNER    =>  HOT_DOG ),
     FRI   =>  ( BREAKFAST =>  SPAM,
                 LUNCH     =>  SPAM,
                 DINNER    =>  BURGER ),
     SAT   =>  ( BREAKFAST =>  SPAM,
                 LUNCH     =>  BURGER,
                 DINNER    =>  MEAT_LOAF) );
```

Of course, it takes time to type all this information and to indent all the aggregate items carefully. In the long run, however, this extra effort will be rewarded. Your code will be easier to understand, maintain, and modify.

The preceding examples of aggregates do not violate the rule that array aggregates cannot mix positional and named notation. This rule applies only to portions of an aggregate that are in the same parenthetical grouping in a multidimensional aggregate. For instance, look at the aggregate shown in combination 2. WED, with its associated meals, is in the same parenthetical grouping as THURS, with its associated meals, and so on. Therefore, if the WED row is referenced using named notation, the THURS, FRI, and SAT rows must also be referenced using named notation. However, the three meals for WED might use named notation, while the three meals for THURS use positional notation, and so on.

Using named notation effectively documents which value is being assigned to which array component. However, named notation is only effective if descriptive names have been assigned to the index values. Arrays that use integer indexes, which are not typically descriptive, should usually employ positional notation for their aggregates. Consider the following two-dimensional array:

type MATRIX_TYPE **is array** (1..2, 1..3) **of** INTEGER;
MATRIX: MATRIX_TYPE;

We can initialize MATRIX just using positional notation (combination 1), as follows:

Arrays

```
MATRIX := (  ( 1, 2, 3 ),
             ( 4, 5, 6 ) );
```

This aggregate is easy to read. The following aggregates (combination 2, followed by combination 3) use positional and named notation:

```
MATRIX := (  1 => ( 1, 2, 3),       --rows are named
             2 => ( 4, 5, 6) );
MATRIX := (  (1 => 1,  2 => 2,  3 => 3 ),    -- columns are named
             (1 => 4,  2 => 5,  3 => 6 ) );
```

The worst-looking aggregate (combination 4) uses named notation for the rows and the columns:

```
MATRIX := (  1 => ( 1 => 1, 2 => 2, 3 => 3),
             2 => ( 1 => 4, 2 => 5, 3 => 6) );
```

In the MATRIX examples, combination 1 is the easiest to read, and combination 4 is the hardest to read. In the previous two-dimensional SPECIAL array, the reverse is true. The difference, again, has to do with whether or not the index values of the array have descriptive names. In the SPECIAL array, index values such as WED and LUNCH are meaningful names. In the MATRIX array, the index values 1, 2, and 3 have no meaning except as indicators of position, and position is best conveyed using positional notation.

ANONYMOUS ARRAY TYPES

Anonymous arrays are arrays that do not belong to any named type. Each anonymous array is considered to be a one-of-a-kind array whose type is anonymous (nameless). To better understand anonymous arrays, let us first look once more at an array that belongs to a named type. For contrast, we will then make this array an anonymous type.

```
subtype ITEMS_IN_STOCK is INTEGER range 0..1_000;
type ITEM is (COMPUTERS, CRTS, PRINTERS, DISK_DRIVES);
type INVENTORY is array (ITEM) of ITEMS_IN_STOCK;
MARCH_INVENTORY, APRIL_INVENTORY: INVENTORY;
```

Note that APRIL_INVENTORY and MARCH_INVENTORY are two arrays that belong to the array type named INVENTORY. Since these arrays belong to the same type, they are assignment compatible and may be tested for equality, inequality, and other relationships that will be discussed later:

```
MARCH_INVENTORY :=(COMPUTERS => 27, CRTS => 9,
                   PRINTERS => 5, DISK_DRIVES => 10);
APRIL_INVENTORY := MARCH_INVENTORY;
   -- OK, since both arrays are of the same type
```

The effect of this array assignment is to assign each component value of MARCH_INVENTORY to the corresponding component of APRIL_INVENTORY. This one assignment statement, in other words, does the work of the following four assignment statements:

```
APRIL_INVENTORY (COMPUTERS) := MARCH_INVENTORY
    (COMPUTERS);
APRIL_INVENTORY (CRTS) := MARCH_INVENTORY (CRTS);
APRIL_INVENTORY (PRINTERS) := MARCH_INVENTORY (PRINTERS);
APRIL_INVENTORY (DISK_DRIVES) := MARCH_INVENTORY
    (DISK_DRIVES);
```

Whereas more than one array may belong to the same named type, every anonymous array belongs to its own unique anonymous type. This is true even when the anonymous arrays are defined in the same declaration:

```
MARCH_INVENTORY, APRIL_INVENTORY: array (ITEM) of
     ITEMS_IN_STOCK;
   -- anonymous arrays
```

MARCH_INVENTORY and APRIL_INVENTORY are not explicitly declared to belong to any array type; thus, they belong to different anonymous types. Due to type incompatibility, these arrays cannot be assigned or compared to one another. Thus, the following assignment is illegal:

```
APRIL_INVENTORY := MARCH_INVENTORY;
    -- illegal; type mismatch
```

Type conversion cannot be used to circumvent this type incompatibility, since these arrays do not have a type name that can be used as a type conversion operator. (Type conversion will be discussed in this chapter in "Operations on Arrays.")

Anonymous arrays, therefore, should be used only when one does not need more than one array of the same type and when one's sense of data abstraction does not require an abstract array type. Discussions of other restrictions that apply to anonymous arrays will be deferred to the relevant chapters in this book.

DYNAMIC ARRAYS

Dynamic arrays are arrays whose size is not determined until runtime. Suppose that the upper bound of an index of an array named DYNAMIC is interactively set at runtime by the user of the program. If the user, for example, enters 1000, then DYNAMIC will have an index range from 1 to 1000. A first attempt at writing this code might result in the following:

```
procedure DYNAMIC_ARRAY is
    LIMIT: POSITIVE;
    GET (LIMIT);      -- compilation error; executable code cannot be
                      -- placed in declarative part
    DYNAMIC: array (1..LIMIT) of FLOAT;
begin
    . . .
end DYNAMIC_ARRAY;
```

The problem with this code, as indicated, is that it is illegal to place an executable statement, GET (LIMIT), in the declarative part of a procedure. Yet, this statement must be executed before the value of LIMIT is used to set the array bounds of DYNAMIC. (The declarative part includes all the code between the keywords **is** and **begin**.)

A second attempt at writing this code might result in the following:

```
procedure DYNAMIC_ARRAY is
    LIMIT: POSITIVE;
begin
    GET (LIMIT);
    DYNAMIC: array (1..LIMIT) of FLOAT;-- compilation error;
                                       -- declarations cannot be
                                       -- placed in statement part
    . . .
end DYNAMIC_ARRAY;
```

This code is also illegal, because a declaration cannot be placed in the statement part of a procedure. (The statement part includes all the code between the keywords **begin** and **end**.) A third and successful attempt at writing this code follows:

```
procedure DYNAMIC_ARRAY is
    LIMIT: POSITIVE;
begin
    GET (LIMIT);
    declare
        DYNAMIC: array (1..LIMIT) of FLOAT;
```

begin
    -- executable statements go here
end;
end DYNAMIC_ARRAY;

The problem of placing a declaration within the statement part of the code is solved by using a block statement. A block statement is an executable statement that begins with the keyword **declare**, followed by declarations; then the keyword **begin**, followed by executable statements; then the keyword **end**. The block statement is useful in situations like the previous example because the block statement contains a declarative part and yet can be placed wherever executable statements are allowed. Thus, declarations can be placed in the statement part of a procedure if the declarations are embedded in the declarative part of a block statement. More information on block statements will be given in Chapter 7.

UNCONSTRAINED ARRAY TYPES

Ada excels at data abstraction, and the unconstrained array type is a paragon of data abstraction. Unconstrained array types allow Ada programmers to declare arrays that differ only in size (the number of index values in a given dimension) to be the same type. An unconstrained array type, then, does not include information about the size of the array; that is, the array indexes are not constrained to a particular range of values. Determination of the array size is deferred until an array is declared to belong to this unconstrained array type.

The following is an example of an unconstrained array type:

type ARRAY_TYPE **is array** (INTEGER **range** <>) **of** INTEGER;

Instead of supplying a discrete range after the keyword **range**, we use the symbol, <>, called a box, to indicate that no constraint is imposed on the range of integer index values. When arrays are declared to belong to type ARRAY_TYPE, array index bounds must be supplied. These index bounds, or index constraints, take the form of a discrete range, which is appended to ARRAY_TYPE:

    ROW_OF_3: ARRAY_TYPE (1..3);
    ROW_OF_4: ARRAY_TYPE (1..4);
    ROW_OF_5: ARRAY_TYPE (0..4);
    ROW_OF_6: ARRAY_TYPE (-3..2);

ROW_OF_3 has a length (size) of 3, ROW_OF_4 has a length of 4, ROW_OF_5 has a length of 5, and ROW_OF_6 has a length of 6. Even though these arrays have different lengths (and in some cases, different lower index bounds), they all belong to the same type, ARRAY_TYPE.

Instead of explicitly constraining each array as it is declared, a subtype can be used to set a constraint. In the next example, the subtype ROW_OF_4 constrains the index to values from 1 to 4. Arrays A, B, and C are then declared to be of this subtype:

type ARRAY_TYPE **is array** (INTEGER **range** <>) **of** INTEGER;
subtype ROW_OF_4 **is** ARRAY_TYPE (1..4);
A, B, C: ROW_OF_4;

Unconstrained arrays may be one-dimensional, as in the preceding examples, or multidimensional, as in the following example:

type MATRIX_TYPE **is array** (INTEGER **range** <>, INTEGER **range** <>)
    of INTEGER;
FOUR_BY_FOUR: MATRIX_TYPE (1..4, 1..4);
THREE_BY_THREE: MATRIX_TYPE (1..3, 1..3);
subtype TWO_BY_THREE **is** MATRIX_TYPE (1..2, 1..3);
A, B, C: TWO_BY_THREE;

This example is like the preceding example, except that two array indexes must be constrained.

STRINGS

Strings are discussed in this chapter on arrays because a string is an unconstrained one-dimensional array of characters. In the Ada package STANDARD, strings are defined as follows:

type STRING **is array** (POSITIVE **range** <>) **of** CHARACTER;
    -- defined in the package STANDARD

Because a string is an unconstrained array type, constraints must be supplied when an object is declared to be a string. (Or, as mentioned previously, subtypes can be used to set a constraint.) For example, in the declaration that follows, MY_CAT is defined as a string variable constrained to a length of 13:

MY_CAT: STRING (1..13);

An array aggregate containing 13 characters can then be assigned to MY_CAT:

MY_CAT := ('M', 'e', 'o', 'w', ' ',',','T', 's', 'e', '-', 't', 'u', 'n', 'g');

This notation is unnatural and awkward. In most computer languages, the entire string is placed in quotes. Ada allows the same convention:

   MY_CAT := "Meow Tse-tung";

A double quote that is part of the string is indicated with two double quotes:

   PUT ("Physicists say that ""strings are super!""");

This statement outputs: Physicists say that "strings are super!"

Let us now declare a few more strings:

   MY_BOA: STRING (1.. 15) := "Julius Squeezer";
   MY_COBRA: STRING (1.. 11) := "Herman Hiss";
   MY_CANARY: STRING (1..4) := "Pete";
   MY_SECOND_CANARY: STRING (1..6) := "Repete";

Note that the string variables are given a size constraint that exactly matches the size of the string aggregates (also called string literals) that are being assigned to them. For instance, MY_BOA, which is a string variable of length 15, is assigned the value "Julius Squeezer", which is 15 characters long. Strings, as well as other kinds of arrays, can only be assigned to one another if they have the same size. Consider this declaration:

   PET_NAME: STRING (1..5);

Because PET_NAME is a string variable of length 5, the following assignments are illegal:

   PET_NAME := "Pete";   -- illegal; "Pete" contains less than 5 characters
   PET_NAME := "Repete"; -- illegal; "Repete" contains more than 5
                         -- characters

Thus, Ada does not have predefined variable length strings. If variable length strings are needed, then a utility to support variable length strings should be written.

Although the size of a string variable is set by a constraint, the size of a string constant may be inferred from the size of the aggregate being assigned to it:

   NASTIEST_PET: **constant** STRING := "Parmenides";

In this declaration, the string constant NASTIEST_PET gets the upper value of its constraint, 1..10, from the length of the aggregate being assigned to it, "Parmenides".

When working with strings, it is sometimes useful to select a substring, or in Ada's terminology, a string slice. String slices are taken by specifying the desired index range. For example, consider the declaration

    MY_COBRA: STRING (1 .. 11) := "Herman Hiss";

The following slice can be made:

    MY_HUSBAND: STRING (1.. 6) := MY_COBRA (1..6);
        -- assigns the value "Herman"

In this declaration, MY_COBRA (1..6) is a string slice, consisting of the first 6 characters ("Herman") of the 11-character string MY_COBRA. This slice is then assigned to the string variable MY_HUSBAND.

In the next declaration, the string slice MY_COBRA (8..11) yields the 4-character string "Hiss", which is assigned to the string variable MY_FAVORITE_SOUND:

    MY_FAVORITE_SOUND: STRING (1..4) := MY_COBRA (8..11);
        -- assigns the value "Hiss"

A slice can be dynamically set; that is, the upper or lower bound of a slice can be set at runtime. If the upper bound is less than the lower bound, then the slice is null. The result is a null string, indicated by two double quotes with nothing between them: "". A null string is legal; no compiler error will be generated.

Strings are the most common type of array to slice. However, in Ada, any type of one-dimensional array can be sliced. Other examples of array slicing are given in this chapter in "Operations on Arrays."

In addition to array slicing, concatenation is another common string operation. Concatenating strings means to join them. In Ada, the catcatenation operator is the ampersand symbol, &. Consider the following declarations:

    MY_CANARY: STRING (1..4) := "Pete";
    MY_SECOND_CANARY: STRING (1..6) := "Repete";

The following concatenation yields the value "Pete and Repete", which is then assigned to the string MY_BIRDS:

    MY_BIRDS: STRING (1..15) := MY_CANARY & " and " &
                                MY_SECOND_CANARY;
        -- assigns "Pete and Repete"

Any type of one-dimensional discrete array (an array whose components are of a discrete type) may be concatenated, not just strings. An example of an integer array concatenation appears in "Operations on Arrays."

When a string slice is assigned a value, the rest of the string is not automatically padded with blanks. This is shown in the following code:

```
declare
    MY_BOA: STRING (1.. 15) := "Julius Squeezer";
    MY_COBRA: STRING (1.. 11) := "Herman Hiss";
begin
    MY_BOA (1..6) := MY_COBRA (1..6);
        -- MY_BOA = "Herman Squeezer", not "Herman     "
end;
```

Although MY_BOA (1..6) is assigned the value "Herman", the remaining slice, MY_BOA (7..15), still contains " Squeezer". The entire string, MY_BOA (1..15), therefore has the value "Herman Squeezer". If only the value "Herman" is desired, then the remainder of the string must be padded with blanks:

```
MY_BOA := MY_COBRA (1..6) & "         ";
```

Failing to pad a string with blanks is one common programming pitfall. Another common pitfall is confusing strings of length 1 with a character. Strings and characters are distinct types. Consider the following declaration:

```
MY_NEWT: STRING (1..16) := "Sir Isaac Newton";
```

Given this declaration, the string slice MY_NEWT (1..1) is not the same as MY_NEWT (1). The string slice MY_NEWT (1..1) yields the string "S", whereas MY_NEWT (1) yields the value of the first component of MY_NEWT, which is the character 'S'. Thus, MY_NEWT (1..1) and MY_NEWT (1) may not be assigned or compared to one another:

```
if  MY_NEWT (1..1) /= MY_NEWT (1) then   -- will not compile; mixed types
    MY_NEWT (1..1) := MY_NEWT (1);       -- same problem
end if;
```

Even though strings and characters are different types, the concatenation operator can operate on either of them. Thus, "Ad" & 'a' yields "Ada".

Another common pitfall is to break a single string across multiple lines. In Ada, this is illegal:

```
PUT ( "EGOIST, n. A person of low taste, more interested in himself than in
        me. (Ambrose Bierce)" ); -- will not compile; cannot break up a string
```

Therefore, string concatenations are particularly handy when a string cannot fit on one line:

PUT ("EGOIST, n. A person of low taste, more interested in himself " &
       "than in me. (Ambrose Bierce)"); -- legal

Now that we have discussed string slicing and concatenation, let us consider a program that uses both operations:

```
with TEXT_IO; use TEXT_IO;
procedure STRING_SEARCH is
    SEARCH_STRING: STRING (1..45) :=
        "Self-actualization through programming in Ada";
    TARGET: STRING (1..2) := "ro"; -- forbid null strings
    subtype LOOP_BOUNDS is NATURAL
        range 1 .. (SEARCH_STRING'LENGTH - TARGET'LENGTH + 1);
    UPPER: constant NATURAL := TARGET'LENGTH - 1;
    TIMES_FOUND: NATURAL := 0;
begin
    for LOWER in LOOP_BOUNDS loop
        if SEARCH_STRING (LOWER..(LOWER + UPPER)) = TARGET then
            TIMES_FOUND := TIMES_FOUND + 1;
        end if;
    end loop;
    PUT_LINE ("The target word, """ & TARGET & """, was found"
              & NATURAL'IMAGE (TIMES_FOUND) & " times.");
end STRING_SEARCH;
```

This procedure searches a string, "Self-actualization through programming in Ada", for a target string, "ro", and counts the number of times that the target string is found. When this program is run, the following is output:

The target word, "ro", was found 2 times.

During each iteration through the **for** loop, a successive dynamic substring—SEARCH_STRING(1..2), SEARCH_STRING(2..3), SEARCH_STRING(3..4), . . . , SEARCH_STRING(44..45)—is compared with the target string "ro". Whenever a match is found, TIMES_FOUND is incremented by 1. Note how the expression NATURAL'IMAGE (TIMES_FOUND) is concatenated with the strings. By using this IMAGE attribute to convert a natural number to its string representation, we are able to output our answer using only one PUT_LINE statement instead of multiple PUT statements. By using the IMAGE attribute, we also avoid having to generically instantiate the INTEGER_IO package in order to output the integer value TIMES_FOUND.

In addition to the concatenation operator, there are other useful operators, called relational operators: =, /=, <, <=, >, >=. These relational operators can be used to compare strings of the same length or of different lengths. The following Boolean expressions are all true:

"Julius Squeezer" > "Herman Hiss"
"Pete" < "Repete"
"?" > "+"

The last expression is true because of the order in which the characters "?" and "+" are listed in the ASCII character set contained in the package STANDARD. As we will show in "Operations on Arrays," these relational operators can apply to any one-dimensional discrete array, not just strings.

In addition to the predefined string type contained in the package STANDARD, there may be user-defined string types. For instance, one can define the set of Morse code characters as an array of characters consisting only of dots, dashes, and spaces:

```
procedure USER_DEFINED_STRING is

    type DOTS_DASHES_AND_SPACES is ('.', '-', ' ');
    type MORSE_CODE is array (POSITIVE range <>) of
          DOTS_DASHES_AND_SPACES;
    ADA: MORSE_CODE (1..10);

    A: constant MORSE_CODE := ".- ";
    B: constant MORSE_CODE := "-... ";
    C: constant MORSE_CODE := "-.-. ";
    D: constant MORSE_CODE := "-.. ";
begin
    ADA := A & D & A; -- assigns ".- -.. .- "
end USER_DEFINED_STRING;
```

Note that string literals of the user-defined string MORSE_CODE may be placed within a pair of double quotes, just like literals of the predefined type STRING.

As shown in the following code, caution must be exercised when declaring a user-defined string constant:

```
declare
    type DOTS_DASHES_AND_SPACES is ('.', '-', ' ');
    SYMBOL: DOTS_DASHES_AND_SPACES;
    type MORSE_CODE is array (INTEGER range <>) of
                DOTS_DASHES_AND_SPACES;
    A: constant MORSE_CODE := ".- ";    -- LOOK OUT!
begin
    SYMBOL := A (1);                    -- constraint error
    SYMBOL := A (INTEGER'FIRST);        -- OK
end;
```

The important difference between this code and the original example is that, in this code, the unconstrained array type MORSE_CODE has an integer index instead of a positive index. This difference seems innocuous, but the consequence of using an integer index may surprise you. If you try to access the first component of the constant array A by writing A (1), the compiler will raise a constraint error. The problem is that, since no explicit constraint is imposed on the index of A, the compiler makes INTEGER'FIRST the first index value. On a standard 16-bit computer, INTEGER'FIRST is not 1 but -32,768! This is not a problem in our original example, where we declare the index to be POSITIVE, because POSITIVE'FIRST is 1.

We can avoid this problem by initializing A using named notation:

   A: **constant** MORSE_CODE := (1 => '.', 2 => '-', 3 => ' ');

This use of named notation forces the index range of A to be 1..3 instead of -32768..-32766. Alternatively, we can supply an index constraint:

   A: **constant** MORSE_CODE (1..3) := ".- ";

BOOLEAN VECTORS

A vector is just a fancy name for a one-dimensional array. Boolean vectors are one-dimensional arrays with Boolean components such as the following:

   type BOOLEAN_VECTOR **is array** (POSITIVE **range** <>) **of** BOOLEAN;

Boolean vectors are not of a predefined type; they are user defined.

Boolean vectors are mentioned in a separate section because they are the only type of array that can be operated on by the logical operators **and**, **or**, **xor**, and **not**. In particular, these logical operators operate on two one-dimensional Boolean vectors of the same type and length:

```
declare
    type BOOLEAN_VECTOR is array (POSITIVE range <> ) of BOOLEAN;
    T: constant BOOLEAN := TRUE;
    F: constant BOOLEAN := FALSE;
    A: BOOLEAN_VECTOR (1..4) := (T, F, T, F);
    B: BOOLEAN_VECTOR (1..4) := (T, F, F, T);
    C: BOOLEAN_VECTOR (1..4);
begin
    C := not A;        -- yields (F, T, F, T)
    C := A and B;      -- yields (T, F, F, F)
    C := A or B;       -- yields (T, F, T, T)
    C := A xor B;      -- yields (F, F, T, T)
end;
```

After the unconstrained array BOOLEAN_VECTOR is declared, the constants T and F are initialized to the Boolean literals TRUE and FALSE, respectively. Throughout the rest of the code, T and F can then be used. As can be inferred from this code, the logical operators apply to each of the corresponding Boolean components of the two arrays, and the result is an aggregate, not a single Boolean value. For instance, consider the Boolean expression A **and** B, which appears in the preceding code. If the value of A is (T, F, T, F) and the value of B is (T, F, F, T), then A **and** B yield (T, F, F, F):

	(T, F, T, F)	-- value of A
and	(T, F, F, T)	-- value of B
	(T, F, F, F)	-- value of A **and** B

ARRAY OF ARRAYS

In Ada, it is possible to have an array of arrays. It is even possible to have an array of arrays of arrays, and so on, although these data structures soon get too complex to easily comprehend. The following is an example of an array of arrays:

```
declare
    INT_VALUE: INTEGER;
    type TWO_BY_THREE is array (1..2, 1..3) of INTEGER;
    type ARRAY_OF_2_BY_3 is array (1..3) of TWO_BY_THREE;
    ARRAY_OF_ARRAY: ARRAY_OF_2_BY_3 := ( (    (1,   2,   3),
                                              (4,   5,   6) ),
                                         (    (7,   8,   9),
                                              (10, 11, 12) ),
                                         (    (13, 14, 15),
                                              (16, 17, 18) ) );
begin
    INT_VALUE := ARRAY_OF_ARRAY (3) (1, 2); -- assigns 14
        -- first row, second column of third 2 by 3 array
    ...
end;
```

ARRAY_OF_ARRAY, as we can see from the aggregate being assigned to it, consists of 3 components. Each component is a 2 by 3 array of type TWO_BY_THREE.

The last statement of the preceding code contains some unusual syntax. The expression ARRAY_OF_ARRAY (3) (1, 2) selects a component of a component. That is, the expression selects the integer value in the first row, second column, of the third 2 by 3 array. This is more easily shown by introducing an intermediate variable. The following two statements are logically equivalent to the last line of code in the preceding example:

INTERMEDIATE_VARIABLE := ARRAY_OF_ARRAY (3);
INT_VALUE := INTERMEDIATE_VARIABLE (1, 2);

INTERMEDIATE_VARIABLE, which is assumed to belong to type TWO_BY_THREE, is first set to the third 2 by 3 array:

((13, 14, 15),
  (16, 17, 18))

Then, the variable INT_VALUE is set to the first row, second column, of this array aggegate. The value in this position is 14.

In Ada, an array of arrays is not the same thing as a multidimensional array. Thus, the following statement is not allowed:

INT_VALUE := ARRAY_OF_ARRAY (1, 2, 3); -- not allowed

ARRAY ATTRIBUTES

Array attributes are characteristics of arrays. Arrays have four frequently used attributes: FIRST, LAST, RANGE, and LENGTH. These attributes apply to arrays and to constrained array types. Furthermore, these attributes give characteristics of the array index, not characteristics of the array components.

Consider the following one-dimensional array, CONDUCTOR, which stores information on how well various materials carry electric current:

```
type MATERIAL is (WOOD, GLASS, WATER, SALT_WATER, PLASTIC,
    SUPERCONDUCTOR, RUBBER, METAL);
type RATING is (PERFECT, EXCELLENT, GOOD, FAIR, POOR,
    WORTHLESS);
CONDUCTOR: array (MATERIAL) of RATING :=
    ( WOOD             => POOR,
      GLASS            => WORTHLESS,
      WATER            => FAIR,
      SALT_WATER       => GOOD,
      PLASTIC          => WORTHLESS,
      SUPERCONDUCTOR   => PERFECT,
      RUBBER           => WORTHLESS,
      METAL            => EXCELLENT );
```

In Chapter 3, we saw how the attributes FIRST and LAST apply to scalar types. These attributes can also apply to arrays. The attributes FIRST and LAST give the first and last index values of an array. CONDUCTOR'FIRST, therefore, gives WOOD, and CONDUCTOR'LAST gives METAL. Note that WOOD and METAL are the first and last index values of the array, not the first and last component values of the array, which in this case are POOR and EXCELLENT.

The attribute LENGTH gives the length (size) of the array. Because the CONDUCTOR array has an index that can assume any of 8 possible values, CONDUCTOR'LENGTH is 8.

The attribute RANGE gives the discrete range of the array index. CONDUCTOR'RANGE thus gives the range WOOD..METAL. (Note that CONDUCTOR'RANGE is the same as CONDUCTOR'FIRST..CONDUCTOR'LAST.) This means that CONDUCTOR'RANGE can be used wherever the range WOOD..METAL can be used, for instance, in **for** loops, or as constraints in declarations. The following two **for** loops are thus logically equivalent:

```
for SUBSTANCE in WOOD..METAL loop
    CONDUCTOR (SUBSTANCE) := POOR;
end loop;

for SUBSTANCE in CONDUCTOR'RANGE loop -- WOOD..METAL
    CONDUCTOR (SUBSTANCE) := POOR;
end loop;
```

Be careful not to append the RANGE attribute to an enumeration type, such as MATERIAL. The range attribute only applies to arrays and array types. This restriction is no problem since the type name MATERIAL can be used to represent the discrete range WOOD..METAL (which in this example is the same as CONDUCTOR'RANGE). Also be careful not to confuse the attribute RANGE with the keyword **range**.

The array attributes FIRST, LAST, LENGTH, and RANGE also apply to multidimensional arrays. In such arrays, the attributes are followed by a number in parentheses, sometimes called a parameter. This parameter specifies the array dimension to which the attribute refers. The parameter does not refer to a particular index value but to an index range defining a dimension.

Consider an anonymous 2 by 6 (2 rows, 6 columns) integer array named MATRIX:

```
MATRIX: array (1..2, 0..5) of INTEGER := (  (12, 24, 15, 33, 11, 43),
                                            (72, 91, 54, 26, 56, 81) );
```

The MATRIX array contains two index ranges, 1..2 and 0..5. The range 1..2 refers to the first dimension (the rows) of MATRIX, and the range 0..5 refers to the second dimension (the columns) of MATRIX. When we apply an array attribute to MATRIX, we can specify the array dimension to which the attribute applies. We select the first or second dimension by placing 1 or 2 in parentheses, following the array attribute. MATRIX'FIRST(1) yields the value of 1, because it refers to the lower bound of the first dimension of

MATRIX, that is, the first index value in the range 1..2. MATRIX'LAST(2) yields the value of 5, because it refers to the upper bound of the second dimension of MATRIX, that is, the last index value in the range 0..5. MATRIX'RANGE(1) yields the discrete range 1..2 of the first dimension of MATRIX. MATRIX'LENGTH(2) yields the value of 6, because it refers to the length of the second dimension, that is, the number of values in the second index range, 0..5.

The following is a list of array attributes as they apply to MATRIX:

MATRIX'FIRST (1)   -- yields 1
MATRIX'FIRST (2)   -- yields 0
MATRIX'LAST (1)   -- yields 2
MATRIX'LAST (2)   -- yields 5
MATRIX'LENGTH (1)   -- yields 2
MATRIX'LENGTH (2)   -- yields 6
MATRIX'RANGE (1)   -- yields 1..2
MATRIX'RANGE (2)   -- yields 0..5

When writing attributes, the attribute parameter may be omitted. When the attribute parameter is omitted for multidimensional arrays, the first dimension is assumed. In other words, MATRIX'FIRST is the same as MATRIX'FIRST (1), MATRIX'RANGE is the same as MATRIX'RANGE (1), and so on. It is considered good programming practice, however, not to omit the attribute parameter when using multidimensional arrays, except, perhaps, when it makes no difference. For example, the length of the diagonal of a 5 by 5 array can just as meaningfully be determined with LENGTH (1) as with LENGTH (2). Hence, the parameter for LENGTH may be omitted. One-dimensional arrays, of course, do not need an attribute parameter, because there is only one dimension that can be selected.

The RANGE attribute is frequently used when looping through the indexes of a multidimensional array. In the two-dimensional array MATRIX, we can explicitly use the discrete ranges 1..2 and 0..5:

```
for ROW in 1..2 loop                    -- row index
    for COLUMN in 0..5 loop             -- column index
        MATRIX (ROW, COLUMN) := 0;
    end loop;
end loop;
```

However, it is better to use MATRIX'RANGE(1) instead of 1..2 and MATRIX'RANGE(2) instead of 0..5:

```
for ROW in MATRIX'RANGE(1) loop         -- row index
    for COLUMN in MATRIX'RANGE(2) loop  -- column index
        MATRIX (ROW, COLUMN) := 0;
    end loop;
end loop;
```

Array attributes generalize code and help localize changes that may be needed in the future. For instance, suppose that MATRIX is redefined so that the row index has a range 1..3 and the column index has a range 1..5. If the attributes MATRIX'RANGE(1) and MATRIX'RANGE(2) are consistently used throughout the code, then the modified ranges are automatically handled. MATRIX'RANGE(1) will now be 1..3, and MATRIX'RANGE (2) will now be 1..5.

In the preceding example, array attributes improve the code but are not absolutely required. However, there are certain cases where array attributes are required. In the following example, the nested procedure ADD_COMPONENTS must use array attributes:

```
with TEXT_IO; use TEXT_IO;
procedure MAIN is
    package INT_IO is new INTEGER_IO (INTEGER);
    use INT_IO;
    type VECTOR is array (INTEGER range <>) of INTEGER;
    VECTOR_OF_3: VECTOR (1..3) := (3, 1, 6);
    VECTOR_OF_4: VECTOR (2..5) := (9, 2, 5, 7);

    procedure ADD_COMPONENTS (V: VECTOR) is
        SUM : INTEGER := 0;
    begin
        -- an array attribute is needed since the actual size of array V
        -- can vary from call to call
        for J in V'RANGE loop
            SUM := SUM + V (J);
        end loop;
        PUT (SUM);
    end ADD_COMPONENTS;

begin -- MAIN
    ADD_COMPONENTS (VECTOR_OF_3); -- prints 10
    ADD_COMPONENTS (VECTOR_OF_4); -- prints 23
end MAIN;
```

In this program, the procedure ADD_COMPONENTS is placed within the declarative part of the procedure MAIN. The procedure MAIN uses ADD_COMPONENTS to add all the components of a vector.

The first line of the declaration of ADD_COMPONENTS merits careful scrutiny:

procedure ADD_COMPONENTS (V: VECTOR) **is** . . .

This line introduces some subtle concepts that will be further explained in the next chapter. The parameter, V, is a "dummy" parameter that is passed an actual value when ADD_COMPONENTS is invoked (activated). Since V belongs to an unconstrained array type, VECTOR, V is passed arrays of different sizes. The procedure ADD_COMPONENTS takes these different-sized arrays and adds their components. To accomplish this, the attribute V'RANGE (which is the same as V'FIRST .. V'LAST) is used. This attribute determines the index range of the array being passed in as an actual parameter value. For instance, when ADD_COMPONENTS is called with the parameter VECTOR_OF_3, V'RANGE has the value 1..3. When ADD_COMPONENTS is called with the parameter of VECTOR_OF_4, V'RANGE has the value 2..5.

OPERATIONS ON ARRAYS

As we have shown in preceding sections of this chapter, many different operations on arrays are possible. Some operations can apply only to a specific kind of array; other operations can apply to any array. The term "operations" is used in a liberal sense to include all the following: array attributes, logical operations, concatenation, array slicing, assignments, type conversions, and relational operations.

We have already discussed four frequently used array attributes in the section on array attributes. These array attributes can apply to any array or constrained array type. We have also discussed logical operators in the section on Boolean vectors. The logical operators apply only to one-dimensional Boolean arrays of the same length.

In addition, we have seen how concatenation and array slicing are used for strings. Although these operations are most frequently used on strings, they can be similarly applied to any one-dimensional discrete array:

```
declare
    type VECTOR is array (INTEGER <>) of INTEGER;
    V1: VECTOR (1..4) := (1, -2, 3, -5);
    V2: VECTOR (-2..1) := (-3, -4, -1, 0);
    V3: VECTOR (0..3);
begin
    V3 := V1 (1..2) & V2 (0..1); -- yields (1, -2, -1, 0)
        . . .
end;
```

In this code, V3 is assigned the concatenated values of the array slice V1 (1..2) and the array slice V2 (0..1). The slice V1 (1..2) yields the aggregate (1, -2). The slice V2 (0..1) yields the aggregate (-1, 0). (Be careful with the slice V2 (0..1). Because the index range of V2 is -2..1, the index range 0..1 covers the last two index values of V2, not the first two index values.) Therefore, V1(1..2) & V2(0..1) yields (1, -2) & (-1, 0), which yields the final result, (1, -2, -1, 0).

The next operation to be considered is the assignment. We have already seen examples where one array is assigned to another array. Two arrays of the same type may be assigned to each other if they have the same shape and size (the same number of index values in each dimension). Consider the following example:

```
declare
    type MATRIX_TYPE is array (INTEGER range <>,
        INTEGER range <>) of INTEGER;
    P : MATRIX_TYPE (0..1, 2..5):= (  (1, 3, 8, 9),
                                      (2, 5, 7, 6) );
    Q : MATRIX_TYPE (3..4, 1..4);
    R : MATRIX_TYPE (1..5, 1..3);
begin
    Q := P; -- OK
    R := Q; -- illegal; the arrays have different shapes
end;
```

In this code, array P can be legally assigned to array Q, even though the range of their corresponding indexes differs: the range of the first index of P is 0..1, and the range of the first index of Q is 3..4. The second indexes also have different corresponding ranges. Even though the ranges are different, P can be assigned to Q because P'LENGTH (1) = Q'LENGTH (1) and P'LENGTH (2) = Q'LENGTH (2).

Another array operation is type conversion. Arrays that belong to different types cannot be assigned or compared to one another. This restriction can sometimes be circumvented by performing type conversion. An array can be converted to another type of array, however, only when each array has the same shape and size, the same corresponding index types, and the same component type. In the next example, arrays A and B belong to different types but share the characteristics just mentioned. Therefore, array B may be assigned to array A if array B is first converted to the same type as array A, and vice versa. Array A belongs to type ROW_A. Array B can be converted to type ROW_A by using the type name ROW_A as a type conversion operator:

```
declare
    type ROW_A is array (INTEGER range <>) of FLOAT;
    type ROW_B is array (INTEGER range <>) of FLOAT;
    A: ROW_A (1..4) := (1.0, 2.0, 3.0, 4.0);
    B: ROW_B (1..4) := ( 5.0, 6.0, 7.0, 8.0);
begin
    A := B;              -- will not compile; mixed types
    A := ROW_A (B);      -- OK; B converted to type ROW_A
    B := ROW_B (A);      -- OK; A converted to type ROW_B
end;
```

Next, we will discuss the relational operators: =, /=, <, >, <=, and >=. We have already seen how these operators are used on strings. These operators can also be used on other types of arrays. Any two arrays, not just strings, can be tested for equality (=) and inequality (/=), as long as they belong to the same type. The other relational operators, however, impose a further restriction. These other operators (<, >, <=, >=) can be used only on one-dimensional discrete arrays. Thus, we cannot test whether multidimensional arrays are greater than or less than one another. Neither can we test whether one-dimensional real arrays are greater than or less than one another.

There is a specific method for testing whether one array is greater than or less than another array. This method is a generalization of the way that words are alphabetized. This is as expected, since words are strings, which are arrays of characters. Two arrays are compared by comparing, in turn, each of their corresponding components, from left to right, until a difference is found, or until all the components of one or both arrays have been exhausted. If a difference in a corresponding component is detected, then the array possessing the component with the smaller value is considered to be "less than" the other array, regardless of what components may follow. Thus, "DO" < "IF", and (2,5) < (9,3). Now assume that all of the components of one array have been exhausted and no difference in a corresponding component has been detected. If additional components remain for the second array, then the first array is considered to be "less than" the second array. Thus, "DO" < "DONE", and (2,5) < (2,5,2,3). Finally, two arrays are considered to be equal if they have the same number of components and all corresponding components are equal. Thus, "DONE" = "DONE", and (3,1,2) = (3,1,2).

Table 5.1 summarizes our discussion of the various array operations and the restrictions that apply. Note that Ada's strong typing mandates that binary operators operate only on arrays of the same type. Keep in mind, though, that this restriction can sometimes be circumvented by using type conversion. Also keep in mind that if two arrays are of the same type, then it follows that their component types are the same and their corresponding index types are the same. However, it does not follow that the arrays are the same size or that their corresponding index ranges are the same.

Both arrays and records are composite types, that is, types that consist of multiple components. Whereas every component of an array must belong to the same type, components of a record may belong to different types. The next chapter discusses records.

Table 5.1 Operations on Arrays

Operation	Restrictions
Array Attributes (FIRST, LAST, LENGTH, RANGE)	None
Logical Operators (**not**, **and**, **or**, **xor**)	Must be one-dimensional Boolean arrays of same length and type
Concatenation (&)	Must be one-dimensional discrete arrays of same type
Array Slicing	Must be one-dimensional arrays
Assignments (:=)	Arrays must be same size and type
Type Conversions	Arrays must be same size and have same component type and corresponding index types
Relational Operators (<, >, <=, >=)	Must be one-dimensional discrete arrays of same type
Equality Testing (=, /=)	Arrays must be same type

EXERCISES

1. Which one of the following is <u>not</u> allowed when initializing a one-dimensional integer array with integer indexes from 1 to 4?

    a. A : ARRAY_TYPE := (1, 2, 0, 0);
    b. A : ARRAY_TYPE := (1, 2, **others** => 0);
    c. A : ARRAY_TYPE := (1, 2, 3..4 => 0);
    d. A : ARRAY_TYPE := (2 => 2, 1 => 1, 4 => 0, 3 => 0);
    e. A : ARRAY_TYPE := (1 => 1, 2 => 2, 3..4 => 0);

2. Which of the following is <u>not</u> allowed when initializing the two-dimensional array SNOW?

    Declarations:

    type LOCATION **is** (LOS_ANGELES, SEATTLE, FARGO);
    subtype YEAR **is** INTEGER **range** 1987 .. 1989;
    type SNOW_ARRAY **is array** (LOCATION, YEAR) **of** BOOLEAN;
    SNOW: SNOW_ARRAY;

Arrays   **123**

a. SNOW := ((FALSE, FALSE, FALSE),
             (FALSE, TRUE, TRUE),
             (TRUE, TRUE, TRUE));

b. SNOW := (LOS_ANGELES => (1987 => FALSE,
                                1988 => FALSE,
                                1989 => FALSE),
             SEATTLE =>   (1987 => FALSE,
                                1988 => TRUE,
                                1989 => TRUE),
             FARGO =>   (1987 => TRUE,
                                1988 => TRUE,
                                1989 => TRUE));

c. SNOW := (LOS_ANGELES => (**others** => FALSE),
             SEATTLE =>   (1987 => FALSE,
                                1988 => TRUE,
                                1989 => TRUE),
             FARGO =>   (**others** => TRUE));

d. SNOW := (**others** => (**others** => TRUE));

e. SNOW := (LOS_ANGELES => (1987 => FALSE,
                                1988 => FALSE,
                                1989 => FALSE),
                              (1987 => FALSE,
                                1988 => TRUE,
                                1989 => TRUE),
                              (1987 => TRUE,
                                1988 => TRUE,
                                1989 => TRUE));

f. SNOW := ((**others** => FALSE),
                              (1987 => FALSE,
                                1988 | 1989 => TRUE),
             others =>   (**others** => TRUE));

3. Consider the following declarations:

   type BOOLEAN_VECTOR **is array** (POSITIVE **range** <>) **of**
       BOOLEAN;
   A: BOOLEAN_VECTOR (1..4) := (TRUE, TRUE, FALSE, FALSE);
   B: BOOLEAN_VECTOR (1..4) := (TRUE, FALSE, FALSE, TRUE);

Evaluate each of the following expressions:

a. A **xor** B
b. A **and** B
c. A **or** B
d **not** (A **and** B)
e. A **or** (**not** B **xor** A)

4. STRING is predefined as which of the following?

   a. **type** STRING **is array** (1..100) **of** CHARACTER;
   b. **type** STRING **is array** (NATURAL **range** <>) **of** CHARACTER;
   c. **type** STRING **is array** (INTEGER **range** <>) **of** CHARACTER;
   d. **type** STRING **is array** (POSITIVE **range** <>) **of** CHARACTER;

5. Consider the following declarations:

   type DAYS_OF_WEEK **is** (MON, TUES, WED,THURS, FRI, SAT, SUN);
   type DAYS_OPEN **is array** (DAYS_OF_WEEK) **of** BOOLEAN;
   OPEN : DAYS_OPEN;

   Which attempt to represent the discrete range MON to SUN is illegal?

   a. MON .. SUN
   b. DAYS_OF_WEEK **range** MON .. SUN
   c. OPEN'RANGE
   d. OPEN'FIRST..OPEN'LAST
   e. DAYS_OF_WEEK'FIRST .. DAYS_OF_WEEK'LAST
   f. DAYS_OF_WEEK
   g. DAYS_OF_WEEK'RANGE
   h. DAYS_OPEN'RANGE

6. Evaluate each of the following expressions. If the expression results in an error, then give the reason for the error.

   Assumed Declarations:

   type SOLAR_SYSTEM **is** (MERCURY, VENUS, EARTH, MARS, JUPITER, SATURN, URANUS, NEPTUNE, PLUTO);
   type PLANETS **is array** (SOLAR_SYSTEM) **of** BOOLEAN;
   RINGED_PLANETS: **constant** PLANETS := (FALSE, FALSE, FALSE, FALSE, TRUE, TRUE, TRUE, TRUE, FALSE);
   type MATRIX_TYPE **is array** (0..1, 2..5) **of** INTEGER;
   MATRIX: MATRIX_TYPE := ((1, 2, 3, 4),
                                               (5, 6, 7, 8));

   a. SOLAR_SYSTEM'POS (MERCURY)
   b. SOLAR_SYSTEM'SUCC (PLUTO)
   c. SOLAR_SYSTEM'VAL(1)
   d. SOLAR_SYSTEM'FIRST
   e. RINGED_PLANETS'RANGE

f. RINGED_PLANETS'FIRST
g. RINGED_PLANETS'SUCC (JUPITER)
h. RINGED_PLANETS'LENGTH
i. PLANETS'FIRST
j. PLANETS'RANGE
k. MATRIX'LAST (2)
l. MATRIX'LENGTH (1)
m. MATRIX'RANGE (2)
n. MATRIX'FIRST
o. MATRIX_TYPE'RANGE (1)
p. (PLUTO < URANUS) **xor** (MATRIX (1, 2) < MATRIX (0, 2))

7. State whether each of the following code segments is correct. If it is incorrect, explain what is wrong.

a. **declare**
```
    C, D : array (1..3) of FLOAT;
begin
    C := (1.1, 2.2, 3.3);
    D := C;
end;
```

b. SUPER : STRING (1..20) := "Symmetry";

c. **declare**
```
    type MATRIX is array (INTEGER range <>, INTEGER range <>)
        of FLOAT;
    A : MATRIX (1..2, 0..1);
    B : MATRIX (5..6, 1..2) := ( (1.0, 2.0),
                                 (4.0, 5.0) );
begin
    A := B;
end;
```

d. **declare**
```
    type LIST is array (INTEGER range <>) of INTEGER;
    type ROW is array (INTEGER range <>) of INTEGER;
    L: LIST (1..5) := (7, 2, 0, 1, -2);
    R: ROW (-2..2);
begin
    R := ROW (L);
end;
```

8. What will the following code fragment output?

```
declare
    LANGUAGE: STRING(1..3) := "ADA";
    SENSOR: STRING(1..5) := "ROVER";
begin
    SENSOR (2..4) := LANGUAGE;
    PUT_LINE (SENSOR);
end;
```

9. What is the value of V3?

```
declare
   type VECTOR is array (INTEGER range <>) of INTEGER;
   V1: VECTOR (0..4) := (1, 2, 3, 4, 5);
   V2: VECTOR (1..5) := (6, 7, 8, 9, 10);
   V3: VECTOR (2..6);
begin
   V3 := V1 (0..1) & V2 (2..3) & V2 (1..1);
   . . .
end;
```

10. Consider the following declarations:

```
type INT is array (INTEGER range <>) of INTEGER;
A: INT (1..2) := (3, 2);
B: INT (0..1) := (5, 0);
C: INT (1..4) := (3, 2, 1, 1);
D: INT (1..2) := (5, 0);
```

Which one of the following Boolean expressions is false?

a. A < B
b. C < B
c. B <= D
d. C < A

11. Which eight of the following lines contain errors?

```
declare
   type MATH_OP is ('+', '-', '*', '/');
   type P is array (1..3) of MATH_OP;
   P1, P2: P := ('*', '+', '-');
   type Q is array (0..2) of MATH_OP;
   Q1, Q2: Q;
   type R is array (POSITIVE range <>) of MATH_OP;
   R1: R;
   R2: R(1..3) := ('-', '-', '-');
   R3: constant R := "++--**//";
begin
   Q1 := '-';
   Q2 := "****";
   Q1 (3) := '/';
   Q1 (1) := '&';
   Q1 := R3;
   Q1 := R3 (1..3);
   Q1 := Q (R3 (1..3));
   R3 (1) := '+';
   if R2 < R3 then
      PUT ("R2 is less than R3");
```

```
        end if;
        if R2(1..1) = R2(1) then
            PUT ("This is amazing!");
        end if;
    end;
```

12. Write a program that reads 10 real numbers, finds the smallest of these numbers, subtracts this smallest number from each of the other 9 numbers, and prints the results.

13. Consider the following types:

    type STRANGE_CLAIMS **is** (UFOS, UNICORNS, GHOSTS, ESP, ASTROLOGY, SANTA_CLAUS, CHANNELING, PSYCHIC_SURGERY, BIGFOOT, LOCH_NESS_MONSTER);

    type LIKELIHOOD **is** (CERTAIN, VERY_LIKELY, LIKELY, FIFTY_FIFTY, UNLIKELY, VERY_UNLIKELY, IMPOSSIBLE, NO_OPINION);

    Declare an array called BELIEVE_IN and store what you believe is the likelihood of each of these strange claims. For a unicorn hunter, for instance, BELIEVE_IN (UNICORNS) might have the value of CERTAIN.

14. Rewrite each of these anonymous arrays as named arrays:

    a. MINIMAL_ENERGY: **array** (ANIMAL) **of** KILOCALORIES;
    b. PIXEL_ON: **array** (X_COORD, Y_COORD) **of** BOOLEAN;

15. Show five different ways that each component of the following anonymous array can be initialized to TRUE:

    A: **array** (1..4) **of** BOOLEAN;

16. Rewrite the example of an array of arrays presented in this chapter as a three-dimensional array.

Chapter 6

RECORDS

Ada has two kinds of composite objects that consist of multiple components: arrays and records. The previous chapter discussed arrays; this chapter will discuss records.

Arrays and records have certain basic features in common. An entire array or record is referenced by a single identifier. An individual component may also be specified. In addition, both arrays and records can be assigned an aggregate, which is a complete set of values for the composite object. An aggregate can be written using positional or named notation.

The essential difference between arrays and records is that every component of an array must be of the same type, whereas the components of a record may be of different types. An array, for example, cannot have both integer and character components. A record, however, may have an integer component, a character component, a Boolean component, and so on.

This chapter is divided into two main sections: record types without discriminants and record types with discriminants. Objects (records) of a record type without discriminants must all have the same kind of components and number of components. (By "same kind of components," we are referring to the corresponding components of different records, not different components within the same record.) Records of a record type with discriminants may differ from each other in the kind of components, number of components, or size of components.

129

RECORD TYPES WITHOUT DISCRIMINANTS

The most basic and frequently used kind of records are those declared without discriminants. Record types without discriminants are declared as follows:

    type *record name* **is**
        record
            record components
        end record;

The keyword **type** is followed by the record name and the keywords **is record**. The declaration ends with the keywords **end record**. The record components are declared between **record** and **end record**. These record component declarations appear exactly like variable declarations. Each component has a unique indentifier and can assume values of the specified type. Consider, for example, the following record type declaration, which defines POSITION in terms of an X coordinate and a Y coordinate:

    type POSITION **is**
        record
            X_COORD: INTEGER;
            Y_COORD: INTEGER;
        end record;

The identifiers X_COORD and Y_COORD, which appear to the left of a colon, name the record components. Both record components are declared to be of type INTEGER.

Once type POSITION is defined, records can be declared to belong to this type. In the following declaration, an entire record is represented by a single identifier, POINT:

    POINT: POSITION;

The individual components of POINT, X_COORD and Y_COORD, may be selected using dot notation. The first component of POINT is selected by writing POINT.X_COORD. The second component of POINT is selected by writing POINT.Y_COORD. Once selected, operations can be performed on these components as if they were regular integer variables. For instance, the components may be assigned values:

    POINT.X_COORD := 1;
    POINT.Y_COORD := 2;

As an alternative to assigning values separately to each component of a record, an entire record can be assigned an aggregate:

POINT := (1, 2);   -- positional notation

Record aggregates (also known as record literals) resemble array aggregates. The previous aggregate is written using positional notation. Since the value 1 appears first, this value is assigned to the first record component, X_COORD. The second value is assigned to the second record component, Y_COORD.

Just as with array aggregates, named notation may also be used:

POINT := (X_COORD => 1, Y_COORD => 2);   -- named notation

The name of the record component appears to the left of the arrow, =>. The value being assigned to this component is placed to the right of the arrow. When using named notation, the order in which items are listed is irrelevant. The preceding aggregate may therefore be written as follows:

POINT:= (Y_COORD => 2, X_COORD => 1);   -- named notation

Since coordinate values are frequently written as ordered pairs of numbers, positional notation works well in this case. Usually, however, named notation is preferred over positional notation because it helps document what is represented by each component value of the record.

Record aggregates may not only be used in assignment statements. Like array aggregates, record aggregates may also appear in declarations:

POINT: POSITION := (1, 2);

Also, like array aggregates, record aggregates, under certain conditions, may use the vertical bar or the keyword **others**. In our example, since both components of POSITION belong to the same type, the vertical bar may be used to assign the same value to both components:

POINT := (X_COORD | Y_COORD => 2);
    -- if component is X_COORD or Y_COORD, assign it 2

The same result may also be accomplished with the keyword **others**:

POINT:= (**others** => 2);   -- assigns 2 to both components

As with array aggregates, **others** must always appear as the last item in a record aggregate.

So far, we have mentioned the similarities between array aggregates and record aggregates. Let us now consider a few differences. One difference is that, unlike array aggregates, record aggregates may mix named and positional notation. The only restriction is that all the items listed in positional notation precede the items listed in named notation. The following mixed notation is legal:

```
POINT := (1, Y_COORD => 2);        -- mixed notation
```

The next assignment, however, is illegal because named notation is used before positional notation:

```
POINT := (X_COORD => 1, 2);        -- illegal; positional notation must be
                                   -- used before named notation
```

Finally, unlike array aggregates, record aggregates may not use a discrete range:

```
POINT := (X_COORD .. Y_COORD => 2); -- illegal; cannot use ranges
```

Now that we have discussed similarities and differences between array and record aggregates, let us discuss a feature of record types that no other data type in Ada possesses: record types can be assigned an initial default value. Consider the following code:

```
type POSITION is
    record
        X_COORD: INTEGER range 0 .. 1023 := 0;  -- initialized to 0
        Y_COORD: INTEGER range 0 .. 1023 := 0;  -- initialized to 0
    end record;
```

When a record of type POSITION is declared, both its components assume the default value of 0 unless this default is overridden:

```
POINT_1: POSITION;
    -- both record components have default values of 0

POINT_2: POSITION := (1, 1);
    -- default component values overridden
```

Note that we also included a range constraint in the component declarations: **range** 0..1023. If values of X_COORD or Y_COORD wander outside this range, a constraint error is raised.

Whenever two or more record components have the same type definitions, they may be combined in the same declaration. The previous version of POSITION may thus be written as follows:

```
type POSITION is
    record
        X_COORD, Y_COORD: INTEGER range 0 .. 1023 := 0;
    end record;
```

Let us now consider the predefined operations for records. Fewer such operations exist for records than for arrays. For instance, whereas one may test whether one array is greater than or less than another array, such relational operations are not defined for records. The only predefined operations that may be performed on records are assignments, and tests for equality and inequality. Illegal and legal record operations are shown in the following code:

```
-- assumes POSITION is visible
declare
    POINT_1: POSITION := (3, 1);
    POINT_2: POSITION := POINT_1;
begin
    if POINT_1 /= POINT_2 then
        PUT_LINE ("Not equal, but will make equal");
        POINT_2 := POINT_1;
    elsif POINT_1 > POINT_2 then  -- illegal; > is undefined for records
        PUT_LINE ("POINT_1 is greater than POINT_2");
    end if;
end;
```

In this code, the following assignment statement replaces the value of POINT_2 with a new record value:

```
POINT_2 := POINT_1;
```

Such an assignment is logically equivalent to the following two statements:

```
POINT_2.X_COORD := POINT_1.X_COORD;
POINT_2.Y_COORD := POINT_1.Y_COORD;
```

In addition to declaring record variables, such as POINT_1 and POINT_2, a programmer may also declare record constants:

```
HOME: constant POSITION := (0, 0);
```

As with all constants, HOME can be read from but not written to (given a value):

```
HOME.X_COORD := 1;  -- error; HOME is a constant
```

Whereas both components of POSITION belong to the same type, components of a given record can belong to different types. This is illustrated by the following record, which stores information about galaxies:

```
type GALAXY_CLASSIFICATION is (SPIRAL, ELLIPTICAL, BARRED,
    IRREGULAR);

type GALAXY is
    record
```

```
        GALAXY_NAME: STRING (1..10) := (others => ' ');
        DISTANCE: FLOAT range 0.0 .. 1_000.0; -- millions of light years
        CLASSIFICATION: GALAXY_CLASSIFICATION;
    end record;

    NEIGHBOR: GALAXY := (  GALAXY_NAME    => "Andromeda ",
                           DISTANCE       => 2.2,
                           CLASSIFICATION => SPIRAL );
```

The three components—GALAXY_NAME, DISTANCE, and CLASSIFICATION—belong to three different types: STRING, FLOAT, and GALAXY_CLASSIFICATION. Consider the first type, STRING. Recall that a string is a one-dimensional unconstrained array of characters. To select the first character of the string assigned to the GALAXY_NAME component of NEIGHBOR, we can write

```
    NEIGHBOR.GALAXY_NAME(1) -- selects 'A' from "Andromeda "
```

Not only can an array, such as NEIGHBOR.GALAXY_NAME, be a component of a record; a record can also be a component of a record. Such a nested record is shown in the following declarations:

```
type LANGUAGE_TYPE is (PASCAL, ADA, FORTRAN, COBOL, C);
type SOFTWARE_ENGINEERING_PRINCIPLES is
    record
        STRONG_TYPING: BOOLEAN;
        INFORMATION_HIDING: BOOLEAN;
        CONCURRENT_PROCESSING: BOOLEAN;
        EXCEPTION_HANDLING: BOOLEAN;
    end record;

type COMPUTER_LANGUAGE is
    record
        LANGUAGE: LANGUAGE_TYPE;
        FEATURES: SOFTWARE_ENGINEERING_PRINCIPLES;  -- nested
                                                    -- record
        ANSI_STANDARD: INTEGER range 1955 .. 2010; -- date of adoption
    end record;
OFFICIAL_DOD_LANGUAGE: COMPUTER_LANGUAGE;
```

Note that FEATURES is a record that is a component of another record, COMPUTER_LANGUAGE. To reference a component of the nested record, FEATURES, one must use dot notation twice:

```
if OFFICIAL_DOD_LANGUAGE.FEATURES.STRONG_TYPING then
    -- references a component of a component
    PUT (OFFICIAL_DOD_LANGUAGE.LANGUAGE);
    PUT (" is a strongly typed language");
end if;
```

Nested records may be assigned aggregates in a similar manner as records that are not nested. The aggregate for the nested record is placed within the aggregate for the record that is not nested (the outer record):

```
-- positional notation
OFFICIAL_DOD_LANGUAGE: COMPUTER_LANGUAGE :=
    ( ADA, (TRUE, TRUE, TRUE, TRUE), 1983 );
```

As shown, the nested aggregate is placed in parentheses. Positional notation is used throughout this nested aggregate. Named notation can also be used, as follows:

```
-- named notation
OFFICIAL_DOD_LANGUAGE: COMPUTER_LANGUAGE :=
    ( LANGUAGE      =>   ADA,
      FEATURES      =>   ( STRONG_TYPING            => TRUE,
                           INFORMATION_HIDING       => TRUE,
                           CONCURRENT_PROCESSING    => TRUE,
                           EXCEPTION_HANDLING       => TRUE ),
      ANSI_STANDARD =>   1983 );
```

The notation used in an aggregate is independent of the notation used in any of its nested aggregates. In the following example, a record aggregate uses named notation, and its nested aggregate uses positional notation:

```
OFFICIAL_DOD_LANGUAGE: COMPUTER_LANGUAGE :=
    ( LANGUAGE      =>   ADA,
      FEATURES      =>   (TRUE, TRUE, TRUE, TRUE),
      ANSI_STANDARD =>   1983 );
```

In the previous chapter on arrays, we mentioned arrays of records. Now that we understand records, we can show how such a data structure is declared:

```
type ARRAY_OF_LANGUAGES is array (1 .. 10) of
    COMPUTER_LANGUAGE;
    -- assumes COMPUTER_LANGUAGE is visible
LANGUAGE_LIST: ARRAY_OF_LANGUAGES;
```

To reference, for instance, the LANGUAGE component of the first record in the array LANGUAGE_LIST, we write

```
LANGUAGE_LIST(1).LANGUAGE
```

To reference the INFORMATION_HIDING component of the FEATURES component of the third record in the array, we write

```
LANGUAGE_LIST(3).FEATURES.INFORMATION_HIDING
```

In the examples presented so far, records of a given type have exactly the same kind of components and number of components. The next section will show how record types with discriminants can be used to declare records that differ from one another in the kind of components, number of components, or size of components.

RECORD TYPES WITH DISCRIMINANTS

Record types with discriminants can be used to define records to be of the same type even though the kind, number, and size of the components may differ between records. The notion of "sameness" is thus raised to a higher level of abstraction. Objects can conceptually be of the same type even if their internal structure differs. The criterion for deciding which objects belong to the same type can therefore be based on conceptual considerations without concern for the object's physical structure.

Record types with discriminants are used frequently to declare variant records. Variant records are those that differ from one another in the kind or number of components. In addition, record types with discriminants can be used to declare records whose component size varies. These two uses of discriminated record types will be discussed in the following subsections. Less common uses for discriminated record types will be covered in a third subsection.

Variant Records

The following problem illustrates the need for variant records. Suppose that a record type is needed to store information about a collection of music recordings. These recordings are on three different kinds of media: phonograph records, cassettes, and compact disks. We could tackle this problem by using three different record types without discriminants: one type to store information about phonograph recordings, one to store information about cassette recordings, and a third to store information about compact disk recordings:

```
type MUSIC_TYPE is (CLASSICAL, JAZZ, NEW_AGE, BLUEGRASS, FOLK,
                    POP);
subtype YEAR is INTEGER range 1920 .. 2020;
type SPEED_TYPE is (LP, FORTY_FIVE);
type PHONOGRAPH_RECORDING is -- phonograph record information
    record
        MUSIC: MUSIC_TYPE;
        YEAR_RECORDED: YEAR;
```

```
      SPEED: SPEED_TYPE;
      SCRATCHED: BOOLEAN;
   end record;

type LENGTH_TYPE is (SIXTY_MINUTE, NINETY_MINUTE);
type TAPE_TYPE is (METAL, CHROMIUM_OXIDE, NORMAL);
type CASSETTE_RECORDINGS is -- cassette information
   record
      MUSIC: MUSIC_TYPE;
      YEAR_RECORDED: YEAR;
      LENGTH: LENGTH_TYPE;
      TAPE: TAPE_TYPE;
      NOISE_REDUCTION: BOOLEAN;
   end record;

type COMPACT_DISK_RECORDING is -- compact disk information
   record
      MUSIC: MUSIC_TYPE;
      YEAR_RECORDED: YEAR;
   end record;
```

The three record type declarations have two components in common: MUSIC and YEAR_RECORDED. The other components are different for each record type, because different information needs to be stored depending on the recording medium. Information about being scratched, for instance, applies only to phonograph records, and information about being made of chromium oxide applies only to cassette tapes. Because different information is needed for each record type, the internal structure of each record type differs.

Even though the internal structure of the three record types differs, it still makes conceptual sense to categorize the three types as a single type. This single type can be used to store any information about music recordings. To create a single record type to hold information about recordings made on phonograph records, cassette tapes, and compact disks, a discriminant should be used. (Without a discriminant, "merging" all three record types into one type would be contrived and confusing, because for each recording medium, some of the components would not apply.) A discriminant is a record "parameter" whose value determines which set of alternative components a record acquires. The following record type, RECORDING, has a discriminant, DEVICE, of type RECORDING_MEDIUM. The values of DEVICE—PHONOGRAPH_RECORD, CASSETTE, and COMPACT_DISK—select the set of record components appropriate for each of these recording media:

```
type MUSIC_TYPE is (CLASSICAL, JAZZ, NEW_AGE, BLUEGRASS, FOLK,
                    POP);
subtype YEAR is INTEGER range 1920 .. 2020;
type RECORDING_MEDIUM is ( PHONOGRAPH_RECORD, CASSETTE,
                           COMPACT_DISK);
```

```ada
type SPEED_TYPE is (LP, FORTY_FIVE);
type LENGTH_TYPE is (SIXTY_MINUTE, NINETY_MINUTE);
type TAPE_TYPE is (METAL, CHROMIUM_OXIDE, NORMAL);

type RECORDING ( DEVICE: RECORDING_MEDIUM ) is
    record
        MUSIC: MUSIC_TYPE;                  -- invariant part
        YEAR_RECORDED: YEAR;

        case DEVICE is                      -- variant part
            when PHONOGRAPH_RECORD =>       -- variant with two
                                            -- components
                SPEED: SPEED_TYPE;
                SCRATCHED: BOOLEAN;
            when CASSETTE =>                -- variant with three
                                            -- components
                LENGTH: LENGTH_TYPE;
                TAPE: TAPE_TYPE;
                NOISE_REDUCTION: BOOLEAN;
            when COMPACT_DISK =>            -- variant with no components
                null;
        end case;

    end record;
```

The record type RECORDING consists of two parts: the invariant part and the variant part. The invariant part consists of components that do not vary. These components are common to every record belonging to type RECORDING. In this example, the invariant part consists of the components MUSIC and YEAR_RECORDED.

The variant part consists of alternative sets of components that are selected according to the value of the discriminant, DEVICE. This variant part closely resembles the structure of a **case** statement. The four rules that govern the **case** statement, presented in Chapter 4, also apply here. However, unlike a **case** statement, which controls the execution of code, this structure controls the declaration of record components.

Note that the variant part follows the invariant part. This ordering is required. Thus, the components MUSIC or YEAR_RECORDED cannot be declared after the keywords **end case**.

Let us now examine the variant record type, RECORDING, in detail. RECORDING has a discriminant, DEVICE, of type RECORDING_MEDIUM:

type RECORDING (DEVICE: RECORDING_MEDIUM) **is**

As mentioned, this discriminant, which is a record component that acts like a record parameter, can assume the values PHONOGRAPH_RECORD, CASSETTE, and COMPACT_DISK. These discriminant values determine which group of components is selected from the variant part of the record type. Discriminant values are supplied when a record of type RECORDING is declared:

SONGS_FOR_101_UKULELES: RECORDING (CASSETTE);
NEW_WAVE_ACCORDION: RECORDING (PHONOGRAPH_RECORD);
THE_SHMATTE_RAG: RECORDING (COMPACT_DISK);

These discriminants may optionally be written using named notation, as follows:

-- named notation
SONGS_FOR_101_UKULELES: RECORDING (DEVICE => CASSETTE);
NEW_WAVE_ACCORDION : RECORDING (DEVICE =>
    PHONOGRAPH_RECORD);
THE_SHMATTE_RAG: RECORDING (DEVICE => COMPACT_DISK);

In named notation, the name of the discriminant is placed to the left of the arrow, and the discriminant value to the right of the arrow.

Once a record is declared with a discriminant, it is constrained. This means that the value of the discriminant may never be changed. For example, since the record, SONGS_FOR_101_UKULELES, is declared with the discriminant CASSETTE, this record may only be used to store information about cassette recordings.

The record SONGS_FOR_101_UKULELES has six components. The first component, DEVICE, is the discriminant. The next two components, MUSIC and YEAR_RECORDED, are taken from the invariant part of the record type and do not depend on the value of the discriminant DEVICE. The remaining components, however, are selected from the variant part of the record type, according to the value of DEVICE. Since the value of DEVICE is CASSETTE, the **when** clause for CASSETTE is chosen, and the three components listed in that **when** clause are selected: LENGTH, TAPE, and NOISE_REDUCTION.

The record NEW_WAVE_ACCORDION is declared with a discriminant value of PHONOGRAPH_RECORD and therefore has five components: the discrimant, DEVICE; the two invariant components, MUSIC and YEAR_RECORDED; plus two components in the variant part, SPEED and SCRATCHED. The record THE_SHMATTE_RAG is declared with a discriminant value of COMPACT_DISK. The **when** clause for COMPACT_DISK does not have any components. Therefore, THE_SHMATTE_RAG only consists of the discriminant DEVICE plus the invariant components MUSIC and YEAR_RECORDED.

A **when** clause with no components requires the "do nothing" keyword **null**, because it is illegal to have an "empty" **when** clause. Furthermore, the **when** clause for COMPACT_DISK is required even though COMPACT_DISK has no components in the variant part. The **when** clause is needed since, as with the regular **case** statement, every possible discriminant value—PHONOGRAPH_RECORD, CASSETTE, and COMPACT_DISK—must be explicitly covered. If one or more **when** clauses use the keyword **null**, they may be combined by using the keyword **others**:

   when others => **null**;

The **when others** clause thus handles all the discriminant values that do not select any components in the variant part.

Once SONGS_FOR_101_UKULELES and the other records are declared with a discriminant, their components may be selected. Once selected, operations can be performed on these components as if they were regular variables. For instance, the components may be assigned values:

```
SONGS_FOR_101_UKULELES.TAPE := METAL;
NEW_WAVE_ACCORDION.SPEED := LP;
THE_SHMATTE_RAG.MUSIC := POP;
```

If an inappropriate value is assigned to these components, a constraint error will be raised:

```
SONGS_FOR_101_UKULELES.SCRATCHED := TRUE;
   -- error; record does not have this component
NEW_WAVE_ACCORDION.TAPE := CHROMIUM_OXIDE;
   -- error; record does not have this component
```

Since the discriminant, DEVICE, is a record component, it may be selected just like any other record component:

```
if SONGS_FOR_101_UKULELES.DEVICE = PHONOGRAPH_RECORD
   then . . .
```

An error, however, will be raised if one attempts to assign a value to only the discriminant component:

```
SONGS_FOR_101_UKULELES.DEVICE := PHONOGRAPH_RECORD;
   -- constraint error; cannot change the discriminant
NEW_WAVE_ACCORDION.DEVICE := PHONOGRAPH_RECORD;
   -- cannot even reassign the same value to a discriminant
```

Discriminant values cannot be changed because, as previously mentioned, these records are constrained.

Instead of separately assigning values to each record component, an aggregate may be assigned to the entire record. As shown in the following three examples, the aggregate must be complete and must therefore contain every record component, including the value of the discriminant:

```
SONGS_FOR_101_UKULELES :=
    (   DEVICE              =>  CASSETTE,
        -- discriminant with value CASSETTE required
        MUSIC               =>  POP,
        YEAR_RECORDED       =>  1955,
        LENGTH              =>  NINETY_MINUTES,
        TAPE                =>  NORMAL,
        NOISE_REDUCTION     =>  FALSE );
NEW_WAVE_ACCORDION :=
    (   DEVICE              =>  PHONOGRAPH_RECORD,
        -- discriminant with value PHONOGRAPH_RECORD required
        MUSIC               =>  NEW_AGE,
        YEAR_RECORDED       =>  1989,
        SPEED               =>  FORTY_FIVE,
        SCRATCHED           =>  TRUE );
THE_SHMATTE_RAG :=
    (   DEVICE              =>  COMPACT_DISK,
        -- discriminant with value COMPACT_DISK required
        MUSIC               =>  JAZZ,
        YEAR_RECORDED       =>  1957 );
```

As indicated in the comments, the value of the discriminant used in the aggregate must match the discriminant that was used to constrain the record. For instance, recall that when THE_SHMATTE_RAG was declared, it was constrained to COMPACT_DISK. An attempt to alter this discriminant value, such as changing it to CASSETTE, results in a constraint error:

```
THE_SHMATTE_RAG :=
    (   DEVICE          =>  CASSETTE,   -- constraint error
                                        -- cannot change discriminant
        MUSIC           =>  JAZZ,
        YEAR_RECORDED   =>  1957 );
```

In addition to being used in assignment statements, aggregates may be used in declarations:

```
THE_SHMATTE_RAG: RECORDING (COMPACT_DISK) :=
    (COMPACT_DISK, JAZZ,1957);
```

In this declaration, positional notation is used. Note that the discriminant, COMPACT_DISK, must appear on both sides of the assignment operator. On the left side, the discriminant constrains the record. On the right side, the discriminant appears as one of the record components required to make the aggregate complete. The discriminant, of course, must appear the same on both sides of the operator.

In all of the examples seen so far, the discriminant of the record cannot change. Records can be declared, however, whose discriminants can change.

The discriminant of a record can be changed only if the record is unconstrained. A record is unconstrained only if it is declared without a discriminant constraint. A record can be declared without a discriminant constraint only if its record type is declared with a default discriminant value. Consider, for example, the following record type declaration, in which the discriminant POISONOUS is given the default value of TRUE:

```
type VENOM_TYPE is (HEMOTOXIC, NEUROTOXIC);
type SNAKE (POISONOUS: BOOLEAN := TRUE) is -- given default initial value
   record
      case POISONOUS is
         when TRUE =>
            VENOM: VENOM_TYPE;
         when FALSE =>
            CONSTRICTOR: BOOLEAN;
      end case;
   end record;
```

As a result of the default value given to POISONOUS, a record of type SNAKE can be declared with or without a discriminant constraint. The following declaration does not have a discriminant constraint:

```
GREEN_MAMBA: SNAKE;        -- unconstrained record
                           -- initially takes default discriminant value
```

Since a discriminant constraint is not provided, GREEN_MAMBA is an unconstrained record that takes the default discriminant value of TRUE. This discriminant value may later be overridden and changed as many times as desired. When overriding this discriminant value, however, one cannot just change the discriminant:

```
GREEN_MAMBA.POISONOUS := FALSE; -- illegal;
      -- to change discriminant, assign value of entire record
```

To override this discriminant value, one must change the value of an entire record. The compiler can thus guarantee that a record's discriminant value is always in agreement with the record's other components. The value of the entire record may be changed by, for instance, assigning it a record variable or a record aggregate:

```
declare
    MY_SNAKE: SNAKE := ( POISONOUS    => FALSE,   -- unconstrained
                         CONSTRICTOR  => TRUE );
    YOUR_SNAKE: SNAKE;                             -- unconstrained
begin -- in both statements, an entire record value is assigned
    YOUR_SNAKE := MY_SNAKE;
    MY_SNAKE := ( POISONOUS =>  TRUE,
                  VENOM     =>  HEMOTOXIC );
end;
```

In the first declaration, MY_SNAKE is declared and initialized to an aggregate with the discriminant value of FALSE. This value overrides the default discriminant value of TRUE. Note that even though a discriminant value is provided to the right of the assignment operator, no discriminant constraint is provided to the left of the operator. The record is thus unconstrained.

The second declaration defines the record YOUR_SNAKE. Since no discriminant is provided, the default value of TRUE is assumed. The next line assigns the record, MY_SNAKE, to YOUR_SNAKE. This assignment is legal since an entire record value is being assigned. As a result of this assignment, the discriminant value of YOUR_SNAKE, which had the default value TRUE, is assigned the value FALSE. The last statement assigns a record aggregate to MY_SNAKE, which changes the discriminant value of MY_SNAKE to TRUE.

Records belonging to the type SNAKE may thus be declared as unconstrained records. Records belonging to this type, however, may optionally be declared as constrained records. To declare a constrained record, provide a discriminant constraint, just as if the record belonged to a record type without a default discriminant value. When the discriminant constraint is provided, the default value of TRUE is overridden. The following record, BOOMSLANG, is declared with a discriminant value of TRUE:

```
BOOMSLANG: SNAKE (POISONOUS => TRUE); -- constrained record
```

Even though the discriminant constraint, TRUE, is the same as the default value, the effect is to constrain the record. Thus, BOOMSLANG must spend the rest of its life with this discriminant value of TRUE. (Of course, BOOMSLANG could have been initially constrained with the discriminant value of FALSE.)

Discriminated records can also be constrained by using subtypes:

```
declare
    subtype POISONOUS_SNAKE is SNAKE ( POISONOUS => TRUE );
    -- all records of this subtype are constrained
    GREEN_MAMBA: POISONOUS_SNAKE := (TRUE, NEUROTOXIC);
begin
    GREEN_MAMBA := ( FALSE, FALSE );   -- constraint error;
                                       -- cannot change discriminant
end;
```

As shown, GREEN_MAMBA is constrained since it is declared to be a record of a constrained record subtype. Note that the use of subtypes does not allow us to omit the discriminant value from the record aggregate.

As mentioned, whenever an attempt is made to change the discriminant of a constrained record, a constraint error is raised. To avoid raising such an error, if you want to change the discriminant of a record but are uncertain whether the record is constrained, use the CONSTRAINED attribute:

```
if not GREEN_MAMBA'CONSTRAINED then
    GREEN_MAMBA := ( FALSE, FALSE );   -- only changes discriminant if
                                        -- GREEN_MAMBA is
                                        -- unconstrained
end if;
```

The expression GREEN_MAMBA'CONSTRAINED is TRUE when GREEN_MAMBA is constrained; otherwise, this expression is FALSE.

The following code illustrates the rules governing constrained and unconstrained records:

```
-- assume type SNAKE is visible
declare
    A: SNAKE;                                -- unconstrained
    B: SNAKE := (TRUE, HEMOTOXIC);           -- unconstrained
    C: SNAKE (TRUE);                         -- constrained
    D: SNAKE (FALSE) := (FALSE, FALSE);      -- constrained
begin
    A := B;                  -- OK
    C := B;                  -- OK; discriminant not changed
    C := D;                  -- constraint error; can't change discriminant
    A := D;                  -- OK
    D := B;                  -- constraint error; can't change discriminant
    B := D;                  -- OK
    B := (FALSE, TRUE);      -- OK
    D := (FALSE, TRUE);      -- OK
    C := (FALSE, FALSE);     -- constraint error; can't change discriminant
end;
```

Records are constrained or unconstrained according to the conditions shown in Figure 6.1.

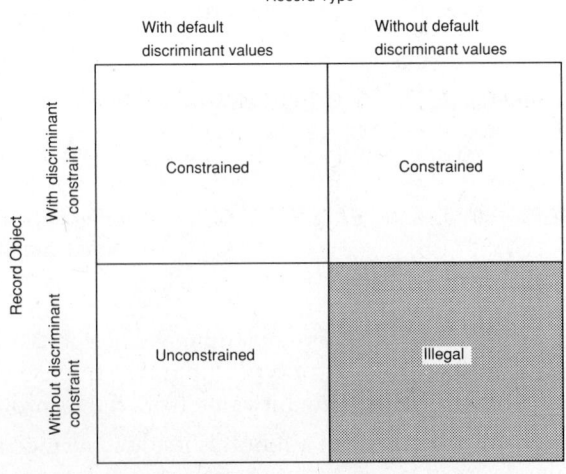

Figure 6.1 Conditions under which record objects are constrained or unconstrained

Whether a variant record is constrained or unconstrained, certain restrictions apply. One restriction was already mentioned: the variant part of a record must follow the invariant part. Another restriction is that variant records may only include a single variant part. In other words, the record type declaration may contain only a single **case** construct. The following code, which contains two **case** constructs, is therefore illegal:

```
type PROGRAMMER_TYPE is (SYSTEM, APPLICATION);
type PROJECT_LANGUAGE is (ADA, PASCAL);

type PROJECT (   PROGRAMMER: PROGRAMMER_TYPE;
                 LANGUAGE: PROJECT_LANGUAGE ) is
   record
      case PROGRAMMER is
         when SYSTEM =>
            COMPILER_EXPERIENCE: BOOLEAN;
         when APPLICATION =>
            GRAPHICS_EXPERIENCE: BOOLEAN;
      end case;

      case LANGUAGE is -- illegal; cannot have another case construct
         when ADA =>
            YEAR_OF_ADA_EXPERIENCE: BOOLEAN;
         when PASCAL =>
            MONTH_OF_PASCAL_EXPERIENCE: BOOLEAN;
      end case;

   end record;
```

One **case** construct, however, can be nested in another case construct:

```
type FURNITURE_TYPE is (COFFEE_TABLE, DINING_TABLE);
type MATERIAL_TYPE is (WOOD, GLASS);
type WOOD_TYPE is (MAHOGANY, MAPLE, CEDAR, WALNUT, TEAK,
                   PADUKA);
type HARDNESS_SCALE is (SOFT, MEDIUM, HARD);
type COLOR_TYPE is (GREEN, GRAY, COLORLESS);
type SALE_ITEMS ( FURNITURE: FURNITURE_TYPE;
                  MATERIAL: MATERIAL_TYPE  ) is
   record
      case FURNITURE is
         when COFFEE_TABLE =>
            case MATERIAL is -- nested case construct
               when WOOD =>
                  KIND: WOOD_TYPE;
                  HARDNESS: HARDNESS_SCALE;
               when GLASS =>
                  CLEAR: BOOLEAN;
                  BEVELED: BOOLEAN;
                  COLOR: COLOR_TYPE;
            end case;
```

```
      when DINING_TABLE =>
        THICKNESS: FLOAT range 0.1 .. 3.0;
  end case;
end record;
```

Since the record type SALE_ITEMS has two discriminants—FURNITURE and MATERIAL—each with two possible values, four combinations of these values exist. These combinations are illustrated by the following declarations:

```
TABLE_1: SALE_ITEMS := ( FURNITURE => COFFEE_TABLE,
                         MATERIAL  => WOOD,
                         KIND      => TEAK,
                         HARDNESS  => MEDIUM );
TABLE_2: SALE_ITEMS := ( FURNITURE => COFFEE_TABLE,
                         MATERIAL  => GLASS,
                         CLEAR     => FALSE,
                         BEVELED   => TRUE,
                         COLOR     => GRAY );
TABLE_3: SALE_ITEMS := ( FURNITURE => DINING_TABLE,
                         MATERIAL  => WOOD,
                         THICKNESS => 2.0 );
TABLE_4: SALE_ITEMS := ( FURNITURE => DINING_TABLE,
                         MATERIAL  => GLASS,
                         THICKNESS => 0.5 );
```

There is another restriction that applies to all records but is most likely to cause problems with variant records: every component of a record type must have a unique identifier. This restriction applies even if the record components belong to different variants:

```
type COUNTRY is (USA, FRANCE);
type AMERICAN_MONEY is (DOLLAR, CENTS);
type FRENCH_MONEY is (FRANC, CENTIMES);
type MONEY_TYPE (NATION: COUNTRY) is
  record
    case NATION is
      when USA =>
        MONEY: AMERICAN_MONEY;
      when FRANCE =>
        MONEY: FRENCH_MONEY; -- illegal; record component
                             -- MONEY appears twice
    end case;
  end record;
```

The problem with this record type is that the record component MONEY appears twice. (However, the component MONEY could be used in two different record types.)

Records with Different Sized Components

We have seen how discriminants can be used to declare variant records, that is, records with different kinds and numbers of components. There is another common use for discriminants: to set the size of a record component. This can be done if the component belongs to an unconstrained array type. In such cases, a discriminant may be used to set the size of the array. Consider, for instance, the following record type:

type INSTRUCTOR (NAME_LENGTH: POSITIVE := 10) **is**
   record
      NAME: STRING (1 .. NAME_LENGTH);
   end record;

This record type has a discriminant, NAME_LENGTH, which is used to set the size of the array of characters, NAME. (Recall that a string is defined as a one-dimensional unconstrained array of characters.) The following code declares two records to belong to record type INSTRUCTOR:

declare
   MY_ADA_INSTRUCTOR, MY_PASCAL_INSTRUCTOR: INSTRUCTOR;
begin
   MY_ADA_INSTRUCTOR.NAME := "Augusta   ";
     -- takes default length of 10
   MY_PASCAL_INSTRUCTOR := (NAME_LENGTH =>   6,
                                    NAME   =>   "Blaise");
end;

Since the record MY_ADA_INSTRUCTOR is declared without a discriminant value, the default value of 10 applies and NAME is assigned the string "Augusta   ". (This string must be padded with 3 blanks so that its total length is 10.) The record MY_PASCAL_INSTRUCTOR overrides this default value by assigning 6 to NAME_LENGTH, thereby setting the length of NAME to fit the length of "Blaise". (Thus, no padding is required.)

   Beware of a common pitfall that programmers encounter when an unconstrained record uses a discriminant to set an array size. In this situation, some compilers will consume a great deal of computer memory. The reason is that, for ease of implementation, these compilers will reserve enough memory to hold the largest possible record value. Consider, for instance, the preceding declaration of MY_ADA_INSTRUCTOR. Since this record is unconstrained, its discriminant, NAME_LENGTH, may assume various values throughout its life. The largest possible value follows:

   MY_ADA_INSTRUCTOR := (NAME_LENGTH => POSITIVE'LAST,
                                 NAME   =>(**others** => '!'));

On a standard 16-bit computer, POSITIVE'LAST might be 32,767. An Ada compiler might thus reserve storage space needed to hold a record with an array of this length. To avoid such a possible waste of memory, use subtypes to limit the range of values that a discriminant may assume:

```
subtype NAME_RANGE is INTEGER range 1 .. 20;
type INSTRUCTOR (NAME_LENGTH: NAME_RANGE := 10) is
    record
        NAME: STRING (1 .. NAME_LENGTH);
    end record;
```

Since the discriminant has a maximum value of 20, the Ada compiler should reserve no more storage space than is needed to hold a record with an array of length 20.

In the previous record type, a single discriminant sets the index bounds of a one-dimensional array component. In the next record type, two discriminants are used to set the index bounds of a two-dimensional array:

```
subtype SIZE is INTEGER range 1 .. 20;
type MATRIX_TYPE is array (SIZE range <>, SIZE range <>) of INTEGER;

type TABLE_TYPE (ROWS, COLUMNS: SIZE) is
    record
        MATRIX: MATRIX_TYPE (1 .. ROWS, 1.. COLUMNS);
    end record;

M1: TABLE_TYPE (ROWS => 2, COLUMNS => 4);   -- named notation
M2: TABLE_TYPE (3, 7);                       -- positional notation
```

TABLE_TYPE has two discriminants. The first discriminant, ROWS, is used to set the number of rows for MATRIX. The second discriminant, COLUMNS, is used to set the number of columns for MATRIX. M1.MATRIX is declared with 2 rows and 4 columns, and M2.MATRIX is declared with 3 rows and 7 columns. In this example, the record component MATRIX is declared to belong to the type MATRIX_TYPE. Usually, one has the option of declaring an array object, such as MATRIX, as an anonymous array type. This cannot be done for arrays in component declarations of a record (whether or not the record is a discriminated record):

```
subtype SIZE is INTEGER range 1 .. 20;
type TABLE (ROWS, COLUMNS: SIZE) is
    record
        MATRIX: array (1..ROWS, 1..COLUMNS) of INTEGER;
            -- illegal; record component cannot be declared
            -- as an anonymous array
    end record;
```

Let us consider yet another restriction: discriminants may only appear by themselves; they may not be part of a larger expression:

```
subtype SIZE is INTEGER range 1 .. 20;
type MATRIX_TYPE is array (SIZE range <>, SIZE range <>) of INTEGER;
type TABLE_TYPE (ROWS, COLUMNS: SIZE) is
    record
        MATRIX: MATRIX_TYPE (0 .. ROWS - 1, 0 .. COLUMNS - 1);
            -- illegal; discriminant cannot be part of expression
    end record;
```

The problem with this example is that the discriminants ROWS and COLUMNS do not appear by themselves. They are used as part of the larger expressions, ROWS - 1 and COLUMNS - 1.

Two Other Uses of Discriminated Records

As we have seen, discriminants can be used to establish the variant part of a record or to establish the bound of array index of a record component. A discriminant may also be used to initialize a record component:

```
type TEST_SCORE ( SCORE: NATURAL ) is
    record
        TOP_SCORE: NATURAL := SCORE;
    end record;
ADA_CLASS: TEST_SCORE (97);
```

ADA_CLASS is declared with a discriminant of 97. This discriminant value is used to initialize the record component, TOP_SCORE. To reference this top score, select the TOP_SCORE component of the ADA_CLASS record:

```
ADA_CLASS.TOP_SCORE -- has the value 97
```

Finally, a discriminant can be used to constrain a record component that is itself a discriminated record:

```
type INNER (A: BOOLEAN) is
    record
        case A is
            when TRUE =>
                INT: INTEGER;
            when FALSE =>
                null;
        end case;
    end record;
type OUTER (B: BOOLEAN) is
    record
        case B is
            when TRUE =>
                C: INNER (B); -- discriminated record component
```

```
            when others =>
                null;
            end case;
       end record;
```

Note that the component, C, of the record type OUTER, is itself a discriminated record. Also note that the discriminant of OUTER, B, is used to constrain the component, C.

Nested discriminated records, such as those of type OUTER, are initialized like nested records without discriminants. Just remember to include the value for the discriminants in addition to the value for the other components:

```
DEMO: OUTER (TRUE) := ( B => TRUE,
                        C => (A => TRUE, INT => 3) );
```

Since the discriminant value of B is also used as the discriminant value of A, the values of B and A must be the same.

In summary, discriminants may be used four ways: to select the variant part of a record; to set the index bound of an array in a record component declaration; to initialize a variable in a component declaration; and finally, to constrain a record in a component declaration. These are the only ways that discriminants can be used. Avoid the common pitfall of attempting to use a discriminant as, for instance, a range constraint in a variable declaration:

```
type ( PERFECT_SCORE: POSITIVE ) is
    record
        SCORE: INTEGER range 0 .. PERFECT_SCORE;
            -- illegal; cannot use a discriminant
            -- as a range constraint for a variable declaration
    end record;
```

This concludes our discussion of records. The next chapter will discuss blocks, procedures, and functions.

EXERCISES

1. Explain the differences between records and arrays.

2. Define a record type that may be used to represent fractions.

3. Initialize the components of the record type defined in exercise 2 so that the default value of the numerator is 0 and the default value of the denominator is 1.

4. Define a record type whose components represent the year, month, and day.

5. Which three of the following assignments are illegal?
   declare
     type COMPLEX **is**
       record
         REAL, IMAGINARY: FLOAT;
       end record;
     C: COMPLEX;
   begin
     C.REAL := 1.0; C.IMAGINARY := 3.2;
     C := (2.4, 9.9);
     C := (**others** => 0.0);
     C := (REAL .. IMAGINARY => 0.0);
     C := (REAL | IMAGINARY => 0.0);
     C := (5.2, IMAGINARY => 1.8);
     C := (3.2, REAL => 3.1);
     C := (IMAGINARY => 2.2, REAL => 1.1);
     C := (REAL => 3.2, 5.1);
   end;

6. What will each of the following PUT statements output?
   with TEXT_IO; **use** TEXT_IO;
   procedure OUTPUT **is**
     type PHILOSOPHER **is**
       record
         NAME: STRING (1..12) := "Heraclitus ";
       end record;
     PRE_SOCRATIC: PHILOSOPHER;
     MODERN: PHILOSOPHER := (NAME => "Wittgenstein");
   begin
     PUT (PRE_SOCRATIC.NAME (1));
     NEW_LINE;
     PUT (PRE_SOCRATIC.NAME (1..3) &
         PRE_SOCRATIC.NAME (12) &
         MODERN.NAME (1..3));
     NEW_LINE;
   end OUTPUT;

7. Consider the following declarations:
   type R1 **is**
     record
       D: INTEGER **range** 1 .. 10;
       E: CHARACTER **range** 'A' .. 'Z';
     end record;

```
type R2 is
  record
    A: BOOLEAN;
    B: FLOAT;
    C: R1;
  end record;
R: R2;
```

Given these declarations, which one of the following record aggregates is illegal? Why?

a. R := (TRUE, 2.4, (5, 'C'));

b. R := (A => TRUE,
         B => 2.4,
         C => (D => 5, E => 'C'));

c. R := (TRUE, 2.4, C => (5, 'C'));

d. R := (A => TRUE,
         B => 2.4,
         C => (5, 'C'));

e. R := (TRUE, 2.4, (D => 5, E => 'C'));

f. R := (TRUE, 2.4, C => (5, E => 'C'));

g. R := (A => TRUE, B => 2.4, (D => 5, E => 'C'));

8. Consider the following declarations:

```
type GENDER is (MALE, FEMALE, NEITHER);
type ADULT (SEX: GENDER) is
  record
    AGE: INTEGER range 0..120;
    case SEX is
      when MALE =>
        MALE_CHAUVINIST: BOOLEAN;
        BEARDED: BOOLEAN;
      when FEMALE =>
        USE_PERFUME: BOOLEAN;
      when NEITHER =>
        null;
    end case;
  end record;

COSMOLOGIST: ADULT (FEMALE);
COSMETOLOGIST: ADULT (MALE);
COSMOGONIST: ADULT (NEITHER);
```

Assign each of the three records—COSMOLOGIST, COSMETOLOGIST, and COSMOGONIST—a legal set of aggregate values.

9. Modify the variant record type, ADULT, of exercise 8, so that unconstrained records may be declared. Declare several different unconstrained records and assign them aggregate values that change their default discriminant values.

10. Find the errors in this code:

    declare
      type REC (VAL: BOOLEAN) **is**
        record
          case VAL **is**
            when TRUE =>
              X: INTEGER;
            when FALSE =>
              Y: CHARACTER;
          end case;
        end record;
      A: REC;
      B: REC (TRUE);
      C: REC (FALSE);
      D: REC := (TRUE, 7);
      E: REC (TRUE) := (TRUE, 9);
      F: REC (TRUE) := (FALSE, 'X');
    begin
      B := (TRUE, 12);
      C := (TRUE, 25);
      E := (FALSE, 'S');
      B := (TRUE, 'B');
      C := (FALSE, 6);
    end;

11. Consider the following record type:

    type REC (VAL: BOOLEAN := TRUE) **is**
      record
        case VAL **is**
          when TRUE =>
            X: INTEGER;
          when FALSE =>
            Y: CHARACTER;
        end case;
      end record;

    Given the preceding declaration, which of the following records, A to G, are constrained?

      A: REC;
      B: REC (TRUE);
      C: REC (FALSE);
      D: REC := (TRUE, 7);

```
E: REC := (FALSE, 'A');
F: REC (TRUE) := (TRUE, 9);
G: REC (FALSE) := (FALSE, 'C');
```

12. Which of the following assignment statements raise a constraint error?

    ```
    declare
       type ALTERNATIVE is (RENT, BUY);
       type OPTION (CHOICE: ALTERNATIVE := RENT ) is
          record
             case CHOICE is
                when RENT =>
                   MONTHLY_RATE: POSITIVE;
                when BUY =>
                   FIXED_RATE: BOOLEAN;
             end case;
          end record;

       RISKY: OPTION;
       POPULAR: OPTION := (BUY, TRUE);
       WORST: OPTION (RENT);
       BEST: OPTION (BUY) := (BUY, FALSE);
    begin
       RISKY := POPULAR;
       RISKY := BEST;
       WORST := (BUY, FALSE);
       WORST := (RENT, 1200);
       WORST := POPULAR;
       WORST := BEST;
       BEST := POPULAR;
       POPULAR := BEST;
       POPULAR := (BUY, TRUE);
       POPULAR := (RENT, 750);
       BEST := (BUY, TRUE);
       BEST := (RENT, 375);
    end;
    ```

13. Explain what is wrong with each of the following record types. (Every example contains an error.)

    a. ```
       type REC (VAL1, VAL2: BOOLEAN) is
          record
             case VAL1 is
                when TRUE =>
                   W: INTEGER;
                when FALSE =>
                   X: CHARACTER;
             end case;
             case VAL2 is
                when TRUE =>
       ```
       ```

```
            Y: INTEGER;
         when FALSE =>
            Z: CHARACTER;
      end case;
   end record;
```

b. **subtype** SIZE **is** INTEGER **range** 1..100;
   type REC (LIMIT: SIZE) **is**
      record
         ROW: **array** (1..LIMIT) **of** BOOLEAN;
      end record;

c. **subtype** SIZE **is** INTEGER **range** 1..100;
   type ROW_TYPE **is array** (SIZE **range** <>) **of** BOOLEAN;
   type REC (LIMIT: SIZE) **is**
      record
         ROW: ROW_TYPE (1 .. LIMIT + 1);
      end record;

d. **type** REC (LIMIT: POSITIVE) **is**
      record
         INT: INTEGER **range** 1 .. LIMIT;
      end record;

e. **type** REC (VAL: BOOLEAN) **is**
      record
         case VAL **is**
            when TRUE =>
               X: INTEGER;
            when FALSE =>
               X: CHARACTER;
         end case;
      end record;

f. **type** SELECTION **is** (ALPHA, BETA, GAMMA);
   type REC (VAL: SELECTION) **is**
      record
         case VAL **is**
            when ALPHA =>
               X: INTEGER;
            when GAMMA =>
               Y: CHARACTER;
         end case;
      end record;

Chapter 7

BLOCKS, PROCEDURES, AND FUNCTIONS

Blocks, procedures, and functions are units of code that contain a declarative part, an executable statement part, and optional exception handlers. (Exception handlers will be discussed in Chapter 11.) The declarative part contains declarations of types, subtypes, variables, constants, procedures, functions, and packages. These declarations bring the objects into existence, allocate the computer memory needed to store them, and sometimes initialize them to a particular value. These objects are local objects: they exist only as long as the block, procedure, or function in which they reside is active. When the unit of code in which they reside is finished executing, the local objects cease to exist. The executable statement part, which we will refer to as simply the statement part, contains executable statements such as assignments and control statements. At least one statement must appear in the statement part of a block, procedure, or function. The "do-nothing" statement, **null**, satisfies this requirement.

Procedures and functions are collectively known as subprograms. There are three basic differences between subprograms and blocks. First, subprograms can be separately compiled. Block statements cannot be separately compiled but must be embedded in some larger unit that is compilable. Second, embedded subprograms can only be placed in the declarative part of a unit. Block statements can only be placed in the statement part of a unit. Third, subprograms can be invoked. Block statements cannot be invoked.

To invoke (call) a subprogram is to activate it. Subprograms can be invoked as many times as needed from wherever in the code they are needed. A subprogram is invoked by a single command. Whenever the subprogram is finished executing, control passes to the statement following the command that invoked the subprogram. Thus, the need for redundant code is reduced. On the other hand, a block must be duplicated wherever it is needed in the code.

This chapter continues the discussion of blocks, procedures, and functions. Specific features of procedures and functions will then be covered.

BLOCKS

Blocks (block statements) were introduced in Chapter 3. Recall that a block statement has the following structure:

declare
    declarations
begin
    statements
end;

A block statement begins with the keyword **declare**, followed by a declarative part containing declarations of local objects. After the declarative part is the keyword **begin**, followed by one or more executable statements. After the executable statements, the block statement terminates with the keyword **end**. If there are no declarations, then the keyword **declare** is optional. Block statements without declarations, however, do not serve any purpose unless they contain exception handlers.

The entire block statement is considered to be an executable statement, even though it contains a declarative part. Thus, a block statement can appear wherever an executable statement is allowed. A block statement can even be placed in the statement part of another block statement:

```
--assume PUT is visible
declare
    A: INTEGER := 1;
    B: INTEGER := 2;
begin
    PUT (A);      -- outputs 1
    PUT (B);      -- outputs 2
    declare       -- beginning of inner block
        C: INTEGER := 3;
        D: INTEGER := 4;
    begin
        PUT (A);  -- outputs 1
        PUT (B);  -- outputs 2
        PUT (C);  -- outputs 3
```

```
            PUT (D);      -- outputs 4
        end;              -- end of inner block

        PUT (A);          -- outputs 1
        PUT (B);          -- outputs 2
        PUT (C);          -- error; C is not available
        PUT (D);          -- error; D is not available
    end;
```

Note that the inner block can access objects A and B, which are declared in the outer block. However, the outer block cannot access objects C and D, which are declared in the inner block and only exist within this inner block. As soon as the inner block is finished executing, these objects cease to exist and are, therefore, inaccessible to the outer block.

An inner block, then, can access objects that are declared in an outer block. But what happens when an inner block declares an object with the same name as one of the objects declared in an outer block? This situation is illustrated in the following code:

```
declare
    A: INTEGER := 1;
    B: INTEGER := 2;
begin
    PUT (A);          -- outputs 1
    PUT (B);          -- outputs 2

    declare           -- beginning of inner block
        A: INTEGER := 3;
    begin
        PUT (A);      -- outputs 3
        PUT (B);      -- outputs 2
    end;              -- end of inner block

    PUT (A);          -- outputs 1
    PUT (B);          -- outputs 2
end;
```

Note that both the inner block and the outer block have declared a variable A. In such situations, within the inner block, the inner A "hides" the outer A. In other words, if the variable A is accessed within the inner block, it is the inner A that is accessed, not the outer A.

But what if, within the inner block, we want to access the A declared in the outer block? To do this, we assign an identifier to the outer block, just as we assigned an identifier to a loop statement in Chapter 4. The identifier, which can be any valid Ada name, can then be used to reference hidden variables like the outer A. For instance, we can identify the outer block as OUTER, by placing

    OUTER:

before the keyword **declare**. The identifier OUTER must also be placed at the end of the block, after the keyword **end**. (Although a block identifier or a loop identifier <u>must</u> be placed after the keyword **end**, placement of a subprogram identifier after the keyword **end** is optional.) When an identifier, such as OUTER, is given to the outer block, then the outer variable A can be accessed by the inner block through the use of dot notation: OUTER.A. The following example shows how this is accomplished:

```
OUTER:
declare
    A: INTEGER := 1;
    B: INTEGER := 2;
begin
    PUT (A);              -- outputs 1
    PUT (B);              -- outputs 2

    INNER:                -- beginning of inner block
    declare
        C: INTEGER := A;  -- A here is OUTER A
        A: INTEGER := 3;
    begin
        PUT (A);          -- outputs 3
        PUT (B);          -- outputs 2
        PUT (C);          -- outputs 1
        PUT (INNER.A);    -- outputs 3
        PUT (OUTER.A);    -- outputs 1
    end INNER;            -- end of inner block

    PUT (A);              -- outputs 1
    PUT (B);              -- outputs 2
    PUT (C);              -- error; C not available
    PUT (INNER.A);        -- error; INNER.A not available
    PUT (OUTER.A);        -- outputs 1
end OUTER;
```

Note that we gave an identifier, INNER, to the inner block. This identifier, which is not required, makes code more readable by allowing the programmer to state explicitly which variable A is being accessed. Even with the notation INNER.A, however, the outer block still cannot access the inner A. Also note that, within the inner block, C is declared before A. Since the outer A is not hidden until after C is declared, when C is initialized to A, it is initialized to the outer A. Thus, the order of declarations is significant. If these two declarations were written in reverse order, C would be initialized to the value of the inner A. This is because the outer A would be hidden by the inner A before C is declared.

According to the scope rule, the scope of an object extends from the end of its declaration to the end of the block in which it is declared. In the previous example, the scope of the outer A extends from the point in the code after it is declared to the end of the outer block. The scope of the inner

A extends from the point after it is declared to the end of the inner block. The scope of B and C are similarly defined.

According to the visibility rule, an object is visible from the end of its declaration to the end of the block in which it is declared, except when hidden by objects with the same identifier. In the previous example, the variable A declared in the outer block is thus directly visible in the outer block but not within areas of the inner block where the inner A is visible. An object is "directly visible" if it can be directly accessed simply by using its name without dot notation. The variable B declared in the outer block is directly visible to the end of the code because it is not hidden by any declarations in the inner block. These scope and visibility rules apply to nested subprograms as well as to nested block statements. (See exercise 4 of this chapter.)

Because a block is an executable statement that may contain a declarative part, a block statement enables us to place declarations within the statement part of the code. We saw an example of this use of a block statement in Chapter 5 when we discussed dynamic arrays. Another such example follows, in which the subtype PERCENT_RANGE is given an upper limit at runtime:

```
declare
    subtype PERCENT is INTEGER range 0 .. 100;
    HIGHEST_PERCENT: PERCENT;
begin
    PUT ("Enter the greatest possible percent.");
    GET (HIGHEST_PERCENT);
    declare
        subtype PERCENT_RANGE is PERCENT range
            PERCENT'FIRST.. HIGHEST_PERCENT;
        ...
    begin
        ...
    end;
end;
```

At runtime, a user enters the highest possible percentage value that needs to be considered. This value is then used to place an upper bound on the subtype PERCENT_RANGE. The inner block statement is needed here because the declaration of PERCENT_RANGE must follow the executable statement GET (HIGHEST_PERCENT). Without this inner block statement, in other words, the subtype declaration for PERCENT_RANGE would be illegal, because it would be located in the executable part of the code instead of the declarative part.

Block statements are also used to define objects that are only needed throughout a small region of code. This region of code is placed in the statement part of the block. Such use of block statements is particularly useful when the objects are, for instance, large arrays that require a lot of memory. As soon as the block is exited, this memory is available for other purposes.

PROCEDURES

Procedures were first introduced in Chapter 2 and then used in succeeding chapters. The structure of a procedure should, therefore, be familiar:

>   **procedure** *procedure name (parameter definitions)* **is**
>   *declarations*
>   **begin**
>   *statements*
>   **end** *procedure name;*

A procedure is composed of two parts: the procedure specification and the procedure body. The procedure specification begins with the keyword **procedure**, followed by the procedure name and parameter definitions, if any, which are enclosed in parentheses. The procedure body begins with the keyword **is** and terminates with the keyword **end**, followed by an optional procedure name. As discussed in the beginning of this chapter, the procedure body is also divided into two parts: the declarative part and the statement part. The declarative part contains the declarations of local objects, which are placed between the keywords **is** and **begin**. The statement part contains statements that are placed between the keywords **begin** and **end**.

Procedures are frequently written with the specification and body combined into one unit. It is possible, however, to separate the procedure specification from its body and to compile each separately:

>   **procedure** *procedure name (parameter definitions);*
>   *--specification*

>   **procedure** *procedure name (parameter definitions)* **is** *-- body*
>   *declarations*
>   **begin**
>   *statements*
>   **end** *procedure name;*

The line indicates two separate compilation units. Note that the procedure body is written exactly as if the procedure specification had not been separated from it.

Procedure specifications and bodies are not only separated for separate compilation; they are more commonly separated for the correct placement of procedures in a package. When procedures are placed in a package, the procedure specifications are often placed in the package specification. The corresponding procedure bodies must be placed in the corresponding package body. This placement will be discussed in Chapter 8 on packages.

Before showing an example of a procedure, let us see how a procedure is invoked (called), which will be contrasted with how a function is invoked (called). A procedure is invoked as a statement. For instance, consider the procedure SQUARE_ROOT, which calculates the square root of a real number. This procedure, which is not shown, can be invoked as follows:

SQUARE_ROOT (9.0,RESULT);

The first parameter, 9.0, is passed to the procedure SQUARE_ROOT, which then calculates the square root of 9.0. The procedure returns the answer, 3.0, through the second parameter, RESULT. Thus, the first parameter passes in a value to the procedure, and the second parameter returns a value from the procedure back to the caller. As we will see later in this chapter, the procedure defines how the parameters are to be used.

Whereas a procedure is invoked as a statement, a function is invoked as an expression. Thus, if the procedure SQUARE_ROOT is instead written as a function, it can be invoked as follows:

RESULT := SQUARE_ROOT (9.0);

Unlike the procedure, this function has only a single parameter. This is because the result is not returned through a parameter; rather, it is returned through the function identifier SQUARE_ROOT. The function identifier appears on the right side of the assignment operator because it is an expression that yields a result. The square root of 9.0 is calculated, and the result, 3.0, is returned through the identifier, SQUARE_ROOT. The result is then assigned to the real (FLOAT) variable, RESULT.

Let us now examine a procedure that swaps the values of two integer variables. This procedure is implemented as follows:

procedure SWAP (PRE, POST: **in out** INTEGER) **is**
    TEMP: INTEGER := PRE;
begin
    PRE := POST;
    POST := TEMP;
end SWAP;

The parameter definitions of this procedure—PRE, POST: **in out** INTEGER—define two formal parameters, PRE and POST, to be **in out** parameters of type INTEGER. A formal parameter is a name that is only used within the body of a subprogram. An actual parameter is the particular object associated with the corresponding formal parameter when the subprogram is invoked. The keywords **in out** define the parameter mode. (Parameter modes will be discussed in detail in a subsequent section.) An **in**

out formal parameter is passed an actual value when the subprogram is invoked; it then returns a result when the subprogram is finished executing. (This is different from the SQUARE_ROOT procedure, whose parameters can either be used for passing in a value or returning a result, but not both.) Thus, at runtime, the two formal parameters, PRE and POST, are passed actual values when the procedure SWAP is invoked:

```
declare
    A: INTEGER := 5;
    B: INTEGER := 3;
begin
    SWAP (A,B);      -- invocation of SWAP
    . . .
end;
```

The variables A and B are actual parameters. When SWAP is invoked, A has a value of 5 that is passed to the formal parameter PRE, and B has a value of 3 that is passed to the formal parameter POST. The swap procedure then swaps these two values and returns the results to A and B. After the procedure is invoked, therefore, A has the value of 3 and B has the value of 5. Note that the actual parameter names, A and B, do not have to be the same as the formal parameter names, PRE and POST. An actual parameter, however, must belong to the same type as its associated formal parameter.

FUNCTIONS

The structure of a function is the same as the structure of a procedure, except that the function includes the keyword **return** followed by the type of result that the function returns:

function *function name (parameter definitions)* **return** *type* **is**
    declarations
begin
    statements
end *function name;*

As with procedures, parameter definitions are optional. Functions without parameters, in other words, are acceptable and are written without parentheses.

Like a procedure, a function is composed of two parts: the function specification and the function body. The function specification begins with the keyword **function**, followed by the function name and parameter definitions, if any, which are enclosed in parentheses. Next is the keyword

return, followed by the type of the result that the function returns. The function body begins with the keyword **is** and terminates with the keyword **end**, followed by an optional function name. The function body is also composed of two parts: the declarative part and the statement part. The declarative part contains declarations of local objects, which are placed between the keywords **is** and **begin** . The statement part contains executable statements, which are placed between the keywords **begin** and **end**.

As with procedures, the function specification and function body can be written as two separate program units and compiled separately. This is done in the same manner that was described for procedures. Therefore, the information will not be repeated in this section.

Let us consider a simple function that uses the membership test to check whether a character is an uppercase letter:

function UPPERCASE (CHAR: **in** CHARACTER) **return** BOOLEAN **is**
begin
    return CHAR **in** 'A' .. 'Z';
end UPPERCASE;

This function has a formal **in** parameter called CHAR that is of type CHARACTER. An **in** parameter is passed an actual value when a function is invoked; it cannot be used to return a result. In fact, unlike procedure parameters, a function parameter must be an **in** parameter and therefore can never be used to return a result. Rather, a result can only be returned by the function identifier. Since a function can only return a result through its identifier, only a single value can be returned when a function is invoked. (This single value, however, may be an array or record aggregate with multiple component values.)

In the preceding example, the function identifier, UPPERCASE, gets set to a single Boolean value by the **return** statement:

return CHAR **in** 'A' .. 'Z';

If CHAR is in the range from 'A' to 'Z', then UPPERCASE is set to TRUE; else UPPERCASE is set to FALSE. (In languages like FORTRAN, the function identifier gets set to a return value by the assignment operator.) The **return** statement also returns control to the program unit that called the function (the calling unit). Program execution then resumes with the statement following the function call. Functions must contain at least one **return** statement. Procedures, however, do not require **return** statements, because no value is being returned through the procedure identifier, and because the procedure automatically returns control to the calling unit when the procedure is finished executing. Even though procedures do not require **return** statements, **return** statements are sometimes used in procedures when a return to the calling unit is desired before the end of the procedure is reached.

Let us now embed the preceding function, UPPERCASE, in a complete Ada program. In the following program, the function UPPERCASE is used to test whether a CHARACTER input by a user is an uppercase letter:

```
with TEXT_IO; use TEXT_IO;
procedure INPUT_CHARACTER is

    LETTER: CHARACTER;
    function UPPERCASE (CHAR: CHARACTER) return BOOLEAN is
    begin
        return CHAR in 'A' .. 'Z';
    end UPPERCASE;

begin
    PUT ("Enter a character.");
    GET (LETTER);
    if UPPERCASE (LETTER) then
        PUT_LINE ("You entered an uppercase letter.");
    else
        PUT_LINE ("You did not enter an uppercase letter.");
    end if;

end INPUT_CHARACTER;
```

This procedure begins by prompting the user for a character. If the character is an uppercase letter, the procedure will output "You entered an uppercase letter." Otherwise, the procedure will output "You did not enter an uppercase letter."

Note that, within the declarative part of the procedure INPUT_CHARACTER, the object LETTER is declared before the body of the function UPPERCASE. This order is required. Within the declarative part of any unit, subprogram bodies must come after all the declarations of types, subtypes, variables, and constants.

The procedure INPUT_CHARACTER uses the function UPPERCASE as a Boolean expression in its **if** statement. When UPPERCASE is invoked, the actual parameter LETTER is passed to the formal parameter CHAR. A membership test is then performed to check whether LETTER is an uppercase letter. If the letter is uppercase, then the function returns the value TRUE; otherwise, it returns the value FALSE.

Note that UPPERCASE is embedded in the declarative part of the procedure INPUT_CHARACTER and is then invoked from the statement part of this procedure. Languages such as Pascal also use this structure. Any number of subprograms, whether functions or procedures, can be placed in the declarative part of another subprogram and then invoked from the statement part of that subprogram.

FEATURES OF PROCEDURES AND FUNCTIONS

This section covers some of the features of procedures and functions. These features are parameter modes, positional and named notation, default parameter values, subunits, subprogram library units, overloading, returning composite values, and recursive subprograms.

Parameter Modes

Parameter modes define the behavior of subprogram parameters. There are three parameter modes: **in**, **out**, and **in out**. All three parameter modes apply to procedures, but only the **in** parameter mode applies to functions. We have already briefly discussed two of these parameter modes: **in** and **in out**. This discussion will thoroughly examine all the parameter modes from two perspectives: first, from the perspective of the subprogram that is being invoked; second, from the perspective of the code that does the invoking.

Within the subprogram being invoked, an **in** parameter has a value that can be read but not changed. Such a parameter, in other words, acts like a constant because it is in a read-only mode. Recall that the **in** parameter mode is the default mode: whenever a parameter is not explicitly defined to be **in**, **out**, or **in out**, it is assumed to be an **in** parameter.

Within the procedure being invoked, an **out** parameter is in a write-only mode. In other words, an **out** parameter has no initial value and cannot be read. Before the procedure is exited, an **out** parameter must be assigned a value; otherwise, upon returning to the calling program, its value is undefined. A program that attempts to evaluate a variable with an undefined value is erroneous. When an erroneous program executes, the Ada standards do not require that a problem be detected. In practice, most Ada compilers will not detect a variable that has an undefined value unless this "garbage value" fails a range check. (For more advanced readers: the previous remarks apply to scalar parameters and not necessarily to composite parameters. This is because, unlike scalar parameters, composite parameters need not be passed by value, but, depending on the compiler, might be passed by reference.)

Within the procedure being invoked, an **in out** parameter is in a read and write mode. In other words, an **in out** parameter has an initial value that can be altered.

The differences between these three parameter modes, from the perspective of the procedure being invoked, are shown in the following example:

```
with TEXT_IO; use TEXT_IO;
procedure DEMO (  IN_PARAM: in INTEGER;
                  OUT_PARAM: out INTEGER;
                  IN_OUT_PARAM: in out INTEGER ) is
```

begin
```
   OUT_PARAM := 0;  -- OK
   OUT_PARAM := OUT_PARAM + 1;    -- illegal; can't read an out
                                  -- parameter

   if OUT_PARAM = 0 then          -- illegal; can't read an out
      PUT ("Out_Param is zero");  -- parameter
   end if;

   IN_PARAM := 1; -- illegal; can't write to an in parameter

   IN_OUT_PARAM := IN_OUT_PARAM + IN_PARAM; -- OK

   ...
end DEMO;
```

The first statement in this procedure is legal because an **out** parameter has no initial value and must be assigned a value before the procedure is finished executing. In this case, the **out** parameter is assigned the value 0:

```
OUT_PARAM := 0;
```

If the procedure DEMO fails to assign a value to OUT_PARAM, then an erroneous program results, and the problem may or may not be detected by a particular compiler.

The second statement is illegal because an attempt is being made to read the OUT_PARAM that appears on the right side of the assignment operator:

```
OUT_PARAM := OUT_PARAM + 1;
```

An **out** parameter cannot appear on the right side of an assignment operator even if it has been previously assigned a value.

The third statement is illegal for the same reason that the second statement is illegal:

```
if OUT_PARAM = 0 then
   PUT ("Out_Param is zero");
end if;
```

Once again, we are reading an **out** parameter. The parameter OUT_PARAM is being read when its value is compared to 0. Ada, then, is very strict; **out** parameters are in a write-only mode. Practically every Ada programmer has encountered this pitfall.

The fourth executable statement in DEMO is also illegal:

```
IN_PARAM := 1;
```

An **in** parameter is in a read-only mode; it already has a value, which cannot be altered. An **in** parameter, then, can never appear on the left side of the assignment operator.

The last statement in DEMO is legal:

IN_OUT_PARAM := IN_OUT_PARAM + IN_PARAM;

An **in** parameter can appear on the right side of the assignment operator, because it can be read. An **in out** parameter can also appear on the right side of an assignment operator, because it can also be read. This **in out** parameter initially has the value that was passed to it by the calling program unit. If the calling unit mistakenly passes an uninitialized variable, then the program is erroneous. Note that the **in out** parameter may appear on the left side of the assignment operator as well as on the right side, since it can be written to, as well as read from.

The preceding example, DEMO, showed how the **in**, **out**, and **in out** parameter modes are viewed within the procedure being invoked. Now we will see how these modes are viewed from the perspective of the code that does the invoking. Consider the following procedure, SQUARE_OF_DIFFERENCE, which subtracts two integer values and then squares the result:

procedure SQUARE_OF_DIFFERENCE (X, Y : **in** INTEGER;
                                                             ANSWER : **out** NATURAL) **is**
begin
    ANSWER := (X - Y) ** 2;
end SQUARE_OF_DIFFERENCE;

The following block statement shows how this procedure can and cannot be invoked:

declare
    A: INTEGER := 2;
    B: INTEGER := 5;
    C: **constant** INTEGER := 3;
begin
    SQUARE_OF_DIFFERENCE (C, 6, A);   -- OK
    SQUARE_OF_DIFFERENCE (C+1, A, B);   -- OK
    SQUARE_OF_DIFFERENCE (3, 1, 4);   -- illegal; returning a value
                                          -- to the integer literal 4
    SQUARE_OF_DIFFERENCE (A, B, C);   -- illegal; can't change the
                                          -- value of constant C
    SQUARE_OF_DIFFERENCE (A, C, 1+2);   -- illegal; can't return a
                                          -- value to expression 1 + 2
end;

The first call to SQUARE_OF_DIFFERENCE is legal:

SQUARE_OF_DIFFERENCE (C, 6, A);

The value of the constant C is passed in to the formal parameter X, 6 is passed in to Y, and the value of ANSWER is returned through the variable A. It does not matter that A is initialized to 2. The result of the procedure call, in this case, 9, is passed to variable A and replaces the value 2.

The second call is also legal:

SQUARE_OF_DIFFERENCE (C + 1, A, B);

The expression C + 1 is passed in to X, the value of A is passed in to Y, and the result, 4, is returned through the variable B.

The third call, however, is illegal:

SQUARE_OF_DIFFERENCE (3, 1, 4);

The problem is with the third parameter, 4. The literal 4 cannot be used as an actual **out** (or **in out**) parameter since the procedure result cannot be returned to a literal. In other words, the value of a literal, such as 4, cannot be changed.

The fourth call is also illegal:

SQUARE_OF_DIFFERENCE (A, B, C);

Again the problem is with the third parameter. C cannot be used to store the result of the procedure call, because C is a constant whose value cannot be changed.

The fifth call also has a problem with the third parameter:

SQUARE_OF_DIFFERENCE (A, C, 1 + 2);

The expression 1 + 2 cannot be assigned a value returned from the procedure call.

As we have seen, from the perspective of the code that does the invoking, an actual **in** parameter can be an initialized variable, a constant, a literal, or an expression. An actual **out** parameter (as well as an **in out** parameter) can only be a variable. Our discussion of the differences between the three parameter modes is summarized in the following list:

> **in:**   Has an initial value
> Is in read-only mode
> Is the default mode
> Actual parameter can be an initialized variable, a constant, a literal, or an expression

out: Has no initial value
Is in write-only mode
Must be assigned a value
Actual parameter must be a variable

in out: Has an initial value
Is in read and write mode
Actual parameter must be a variable

Positional and Named Notation

Recall from Chapters 5 and 6 that array aggregates and record aggregates can be written using positional notation or named notation. Parameters for procedures and functions can also be written using either positional or named notation. More precisely, when a procedure or function is invoked, the association between its formal parameter and actual parameter may be indicated by position or name. Consider, for example, the following declarations:

```
type BEAN_TYPE is (COLOMBIAN, KENYAN, JAMAICAN, COSTA_RICAN);
type ROAST_TYPE is (LIGHT, MEDIUM, DARK);
procedure COFFEE (BEAN: BEAN_TYPE; ROAST: ROAST_TYPE);
```

Note that since the parameter modes of BEAN and ROAST are not explicitly given, Ada assumes that they both are **in** parameters. Given these declarations, the procedure COFFEE can be called as follows:

```
COFFEE (KENYAN, MEDIUM);                          -- positional notation
COFFEE (BEAN => KENYAN, ROAST => MEDIUM);         -- named notation
COFFEE (ROAST => MEDIUM, BEAN => KENYAN);         -- named notation
COFFEE (KENYAN, ROAST => MEDIUM);                 -- mixed notation
```

These four procedure calls are logically equivalent. The first procedure call uses positional notation. The compiler associates the actual parameter that is listed first, KENYAN, with the formal parameter that is listed first, BEAN. The compiler also associates the second actual parameter, MEDIUM, with the second formal parameter, ROAST. The second procedure call uses named notation. The arrow, =>, associates the formal procedure parameter to the left of the arrow with the actual parameter to the right of the arrow. Thus, BEAN => KENYAN associates the formal parameter BEAN with the actual parameter KENYAN. The third procedure call also uses named notation. This call shows that, with named notation, the order in which the parameter pairs are listed does not matter. The fourth procedure call shows that named and positional notation may be mixed. In this case, the first parameter uses positional notation, and the second parameter uses named notation. This order of notation, positional notation followed by named notation, must be observed whenever mixed notation is used. The following procedure call is illegal because this order is reversed:

COFFEE (BEAN => JAMAICAN, MEDIUM); -- illegal

If we call procedures and functions using named notation, there are two advantages. First, the order in which the formal parameters are listed does not need to be considered; just their names need to be known. Second, if the formal parameters are assigned meaningful names, named notation helps document what the actual parameters represent.

Default Parameter Values

A useful feature that is available only for **in** parameters is the assignment of default parameter values. If a procedure or function initializes its **in** parameters to a default value, then whenever the procedure or function is called, the default value can either be accepted or overridden with a new value. Consider the following example of a procedure that outputs the sum of the absolute values of each of its parameter values. [Recall that the absolute value of a positive number is simply that number. The absolute value of a negative number, for instance, **abs** (-2), is its corresponding positive value, 2.]

```
with TEXT_IO; use TEXT_IO;
procedure SUM_OF_ABS (A, B, C, D, E: in INTEGER := 0) is
    package INT_IO is new INTEGER_IO (INTEGER);
    use INT_IO;
begin
    PUT ( abs A + abs B + abs C + abs D + abs E );
end SUM_OF_ABS;
```

Note that all the **in** parameters: A, B, C, D, and E, are initialized to a default value of 0. This procedure can be called with different numbers of parameters:

```
SUM_OF_ABS;                          -- outputs 0
SUM_OF_ABS (-2);                     -- outputs 2
SUM_OF_ABS (-2, 3);                  -- outputs 5
SUM_OF_ABS (-2, -2, 2);              -- outputs 6
SUM_OF_ABS (1, -1, 1, -1);           -- outputs 4
SUM_OF_ABS (-2, -1, -3, 1, -2);      -- outputs 9
```

In all these procedure calls, if an actual parameter is not passed in, then the default value of 0 is used. The first call does not pass in any parameters, so the default value of 0 is used for each formal parameter: A, B, C, D, and E.

The value 0 is output because 0 is the value of the sum: **abs** 0 + **abs** 0 + **abs** 0 + **abs** 0 + **abs** 0. The second call passes the value of -2 to A, but all the other parameters are assigned the default value of 0. The value 2 is output because 2 is the value of the sum: **abs** (-2) + **abs** 0 + **abs** 0 + **abs** 0 + **abs** 0. Skipping to the last call, parameters are passed to A, B, C, D, and E. Therefore, none of the default values are used. The value 9 is output because 9 is the value of the sum: **abs** (-2) + **abs** (-1) + **abs** (-3) + **abs** 1 + **abs** (-2).

Let us consider another example that uses default parameter values:

```
type BODY_TYPE is (STATION_WAGON, VAN, SEDAN, HATCHBACK,
    COUPE, CONVERTIBLE);
type COLOR_LIST is (AQUA, MAUVE, FUCHSIA, PASSION_PINK,
    CHARTREUSE, LAVENDER, MAGENTA);

procedure PURCHASE_CAR
   ( BODY: in BODY_TYPE := CONVERTIBLE;
     COLOR: in COLOR_LIST := CHARTREUSE;
     IS_FULLY_LOADED: in BOOLEAN := TRUE );
```

Note that the **in** parameter BODY is initialized to the default value CONVERTIBLE; COLOR, to the default value CHARTREUSE; and IS_FULLY_LOADED, to the default value TRUE.

Given these declarations, the following procedure calls can be made:

```
PURCHASE_CAR; -- convertible, chartreuse, true

PURCHASE_CAR (VAN); -- van, chartreuse, true

PURCHASE_CAR (COLOR => FUCHSIA); -- convertible, fuchsia, true

PURCHASE_CAR ( IS_FULLY_LOADED   => FALSE,
               BODY              => STATION_WAGON );
   -- station wagon, chartreuse, false

PURCHASE_CAR (SEDAN, PASSION_PINK, TRUE);
   -- sedan, passion pink, true

PURCHASE_CAR (COUPE, COLOR => AQUA, IS_FULLY_LOADED =>
   TRUE);
   -- coupe, aqua, true

PURCHASE_CAR ( BODY              => VAN,
               COLOR             => AQUA,
               IS_FULLY_LOADED   => TRUE );
   -- van, aqua, true
```

These procedure calls work in the same way as those of the previous procedure, SUM_OF_ABS. For example, the first procedure call does not pass in any parameters, so all the default values are used: BODY is CONVERTIBLE, COLOR is CHARTREUSE, and IS_FULLY_LOADED is TRUE. The second call passes in the parameter VAN, so only the default values CHARTREUSE and TRUE are used. All of the other calls work similarly.

If we wish to override the default values of parameters that are listed sequentially from the beginning of the list, then positional notation can be used. Thus, positional notation can be used in the following cases: when the default for BODY is overridden but not the defaults for COLOR or IS_FULLY_LOADED; when the defaults for both BODY and COLOR are overridden but not the default for IS_FULLY_LOADED; and when the defaults for all three parameters are overridden. In all other cases where one or more defaults are overridden, named notation must be used. If, for example, we want to accept the default for COLOR but want to override the defaults for BODY and IS_FULLY_LOADED, then the following procedure call can be used:

PURCHASE_CAR (BODY => HATCHBACK, IS_FULLY_LOADED => FALSE);

There is no way to accomplish this by using positional notation. That is, we cannot use positional notation and skip the second parameter by leaving it blank:

PURCHASE_CAR (HATCHBACK, ,FALSE); -- illegal

Now let us consider two other incorrect uses of positional and named notation:

PURCHASE_CAR (PASSION_PINK); -- illegal

PURCHASE_CAR (BODY => SEDAN, TRUE); -- illegal

In the first procedure call, because positional notation is used, PASSION_PINK is incorrectly associated with the formal parameter BODY. In the second call, named notation is used before positional notation, which is illegal.

Subunits

The Ada programs we have seen thus far have been structured similarly to this example:

procedure MAIN **is**

-- constants, types, and variables for MAIN
Y: INTEGER;

procedure P1 **is**
-- constants, types, and variables for P1

```
   begin
      -- executable statements for P1
   end P1;

   function F1 return INTEGER is
      -- constants, types, and variables for F1
   begin
      -- executable statements for F1
   end F1;
begin -- beginning of MAIN
   P1;
   Y := F1;
end MAIN;
```

The structure of procedure MAIN is adequate if procedure P1 and function F1 are relatively short subprograms and if enough information is known to write the bodies of P1 and F1 at the time MAIN is written. But what if P1 and F1 are large subprograms? If we embed both of these subprograms in the declarative part of procedure MAIN, the result is a huge program unit that requires substantial time to compile and is difficult to maintain and read. Or what if the implementation details of P1 and F1 are not sufficiently established to write the bodies of P1 and F1 at the time MAIN is written? We would not be able to finish writing MAIN.

To avoid these problems, we should defer writing the bodies of P1 and F1. However, we should still be able to write all of MAIN and compile it, so that the compiler can check for completeness and inconsistencies. Fortunately, Ada has a mechanism by which the bodies of P1 and F1 can be removed from MAIN and implemented later, while still allowing MAIN to be written and compiled. This mechanism is called the subunit. Subunits are subprogram (or package) bodies that are separated from the declarative part of the program unit in which they are embedded and made into a separate compilation unit. A "stub" is placed in the declarative part of the program unit to indicate where the subunit belongs. Thus, instead of placing subprogram bodies in MAIN, we can use a stub that consists of the subprogram specification followed by the keywords **is separate**. The bodies of P1 and F1 can then each eventually be written as separately compiled units. This is shown in the following code (where the lines indicate separate compilation units):

```
procedure MAIN is

   -- constants, types, and variables for MAIN
   Y: INTEGER;

   procedure P1 is separate;    -- stub for P1

   function F1 return INTEGER is separate; -- stub for F1
```

```
begin -- beginning of MAIN
    P1;
    Y := F1;
end MAIN;
```

```
separate (MAIN)
procedure P1 is
    -- constants, types, and variables for P1
begin
    -- executable statements for P1
end P1;
```

```
separate (MAIN)
function F1 return INTEGER is
    -- constants, types, and variables for F1
begin
    -- executable statements for F1
end F1;
```

To help the compiler associate P1 and F1 with the parent unit MAIN, a separate clause appears at the beginning of P1 and F1. This clause consists of the keyword **separate**, followed by the name of the parent unit, MAIN, enclosed in parentheses. No semicolon follows the parentheses.

Employing subunits does not change the behavior of the program. In the example, making P1 and F1 subunits instead of embedding them in MAIN does not affect the scope or visibility of any items in the program. P1 and F1 are still only local to MAIN. Also, a subunit can only have a single parent; a subunit cannot be shared by different parent units, each with a body stub for the subunit.

A subunit may contain a stub for another subunit in its declarative part. For instance, the preceding subunit, P1, can contain a stub for another subunit, as follows:

```
separate (MAIN)
procedure P1 is
    Y: INTEGER;
    function F2 return INTEGER is separate; -- stub for F2
begin
    Y := F2;
end P1;
```

```
separate (MAIN.P1)
function F2 return INTEGER is
    -- constants, types, and variables for F2
begin
    -- executable statements for F2
end F2;
```

Note the **separate** clause that appears at the beginning of function F2: **separate** (MAIN.P1). This clause tells the compiler that F2 has the parent P1, which in turn has the parent MAIN. The compiler must be given this complete family relationship.

Subprogram Library Units

So far we have only considered structures where subprograms, or their stubs, are placed in the declarative part of another program unit. There is another kind of structure, where the entire subprogram is compiled separately, becoming a library unit that can be accessed by other library units. The preceding nested subprogram F1, for instance, can be made into a library unit by being separately compiled. F1 can then be accessed by any other library unit that mentions F1 in its **with** clause. The subprogram P1 can also be made into a library unit. This process is shown in the following example. Procedure MAIN, which is the last compilation unit listed, accesses P1 and F1 by simply mentioning P1 and F1 in its **with** clause:

```
procedure P1 is
    -- constants, types, and variables for P1
begin
    -- executable statements for P1
end P1;
```

```
function F1 return INTEGER is
    -- constants, types, and variables for F1
begin
    -- executable statements for F1
end F1;
```

```
with P1, F1; -- makes P1 and F1 available to MAIN
            -- use clause cannot be employed
procedure MAIN is

    -- constants, types, and variables for MAIN
    Y: INTEGER;

begin -- beginning of MAIN
    P1;
    Y := F1;
end MAIN;
```

By making P1 and F1 library units, they can be accessed not only by procedure MAIN but by any other library unit that mentions them in a **with** clause. If P1 and F1 were embedded units, however, they could only be accessed within the program unit in which they were embedded; they could not be accessed by any other library unit.

Unlike many previous examples, MAIN has a **with** clause but no **use** clause. It is illegal to mention a subprogram in a **use** clause. The **use** clause applies only to packages in order to make the internal resources of the package directly visible to the users. Subprograms, unlike packages, do not offer internal resources to users. Users of a subprogram can only invoke the subprogram and access values returned by the procedure parameters or by the function identifier. The declarations of local objects contained in the declarative part of a subprogram can only be used by the subprogram and cease to exist when the subprogram is finished executing. These declarations can never be accessed by an external unit.

Overloading

As mentioned in previous chapters, overloading is when the same name is given more than one meaning. The same name can be used for several different subprograms as long as the subprogram parameters differ in number or type and as long as the subprograms are not library units (separately compiled). Consider, for instance, the following function, MINIMUM, which returns the smaller of two integer values:

```
function MINIMUM (X, Y: INTEGER) return INTEGER is
begin
    if X < Y then
        return X;
    else
        return Y;
    end if;
end MINIMUM;
```

Consider also a function that is needed to return the smaller of two real numbers. Because the processing in these two functions is the same, it makes sense to give this function the same name, MINIMUM, as the previous function:

```
function MINIMUM (X, Y: FLOAT) return FLOAT is
begin
    if X < Y then
        return X;
    else
        return Y;
    end if;
end MINIMUM;
```

The two preceding versions of MINIMUM cannot both be made into library units because library units cannot be overloaded. Every library unit must have a unique identifier. These two functions, however, may be embedded in the same program unit:

```
with TEXT_IO; use TEXT_IO;
procedure OVERLOAD is

    package INT_IO is new INTEGER_IO (INTEGER);
    package REAL_IO is new FLOAT_IO (FLOAT);
    use INT_IO, REAL_IO;

    function MINIMUM (X, Y: INTEGER) return INTEGER is
    begin
       if X < Y then
          return X;
       else
          return Y;
       end if;
    end MINIMUM;

    function MINIMUM (X, Y: FLOAT) return FLOAT is
    begin
       if X < Y then
          return X;
       else
          return Y;
       end if;
    end MINIMUM;

begin -- OVERLOAD
    PUT (MINIMUM (5, 2) );        -- outputs 2
    PUT (MINIMUM (3.6, 8.5) );    -- outputs 3.6

end OVERLOAD;
```

Ada determines which of the two overloaded MINIMUM functions is being invoked by examining their parameters. If MINIMUM is invoked with integer parameters, then the version of MINIMUM that compares integers is used. If MINIMUM is invoked with real parameters, then the version of MINIMUM that compares real numbers is used.

On rare occasions, overloaded subprograms cannot be distinguished, and the compiler cannot resolve the ambiguity. Consider, for example the following declarations:

```
type TRIANGLE is (OBTUSE, RIGHT, ACUTE);
type PERSON is (OBTUSE, NORMAL, ACUTE);

function SHARPER_THAN_MOST (T: TRIANGLE) return BOOLEAN;
function SHARPER_THAN_MOST (P: PERSON) return BOOLEAN;

PREFERABLE: BOOLEAN;
```

Given these declarations, consider the following function calls:

```
PREFERABLE := SHARPER_THAN_MOST (RIGHT);      -- OK
PREFERABLE := SHARPER_THAN_MOST (NORMAL);     -- OK
```

```
PREFERABLE := SHARPER_THAN_MOST (ACUTE);      -- ambiguous
PREFERABLE := SHARPER_THAN_MOST (OBTUSE);     -- ambiguous
```

There is no problem with the first and second function calls. In both calls, the SHARPER_THAN_MOST function that is needed can be determined by examining the type of parameter. The third and fourth calls, however, are ambiguous, and the compiler has no way of resolving the ambiguity. In the third call, the compiler has no way of determining whether ACUTE refers to an ACUTE person or an ACUTE triangle. In the fourth call, the compiler has no way of determining whether OBTUSE refers to an OBTUSE person or an OBTUSE triangle. Fortunately, such ambiguity can be resolved by qualifying ACUTE and OBTUSE, that is, by explicitly stating their type:

```
PREFERABLE := SHARPER_THAN_MOST ( TRIANGLE'(ACUTE) );   -- OK
PREFERABLE := SHARPER_THAN_MOST ( PERSON'(OBTUSE) );    -- OK
```

Recall from Chapter 4 that a qualifier consists of the type or subtype name followed by a tick mark, ', followed by the literal enclosed in parentheses. TRIANGLE'(ACUTE), for instance, selects the enumeration literal ACUTE that is of type TRIANGLE. Since two different formal parameters, T and P, are used by the functions SHARPER_THAN_MOST, the preceding ambiguities can also be resolved by specifying the formal parameter name with named notation:

```
PREFERABLE := SHARPER_THAN_MOST (T => ACUTE);   -- OK
```

In addition to overloading regular functions and procedures, we can overload a special kind of function, called an operator. Overloading operators, such as +, -, >, =, is not a new idea. Even the primordial language FORTRAN has, for instance, an overloaded addition operator. In FORTRAN, the addition operator that is used when one writes 2 + 3 is not the same as the addition operator that is used when one writes 2.4 + 3.1. FORTRAN, in other words, uses different addition operators, represented by the same plus symbol, for adding integers and for adding real numbers. Even though overloading operators is not a new idea, what is new is that in Ada, programmers can define overloaded operators.

Let us consider an example of a user-defined overloaded operator. In the following procedure, the user defines an addition operator—which can already be used to add integers and real numbers—to add two matrices:

```
procedure OVERLOAD_OPERATOR is

   type MATRIX_TYPE is array (1..2, 1..3) of INTEGER;
   X, Y, Z : MATRIX_TYPE;

   --user-defined addition operator for adding two matrices
   function "+" (A, B: MATRIX_TYPE) return MATRIX_TYPE is
      C: MATRIX_TYPE;
```

```
begin
    for J in MATRIX_TYPE'RANGE (1) loop
        for K in MATRIX_TYPE'RANGE (2) loop
            C (J, K) := A (J, K) + B (J, K);
        end loop;
    end loop;
    return C;
end "+";

begin -- OVERLOAD_OPERATOR
    X := ( (1, 2, 3),
           (4, 5, 6) );
    Y := ( (7, 5, 4),
           (1, 0, 2) );
    Z := X + Y; -- yields ( ( 8, 7, 7),
                --          ( 5, 5, 8) );
end OVERLOAD_OPERATOR;
```

The overloaded addition operator is a special kind of function. In the function specification, the function identifier is in quotes: "+". The identifier is then followed by the parameter definitions, just as if this were a regular function.

Overloading the addition operator makes sense when matrix addition is needed, because two matrices can then be added using the same familiar notation that is used in mathematics:

Z := X + Y;

We could also add two matrices by defining a function called ADD_MATRICES instead of overloading the addition operator. However, we would have to use the less natural notation:

Z := ADD_MATRICES (X, Y);

The difference between the two preceding notations is not simply a difference between the function identifiers "+" and ADD_MATRICES but a difference between two kinds of notation: infix notation and regular function notation. Infix notation, like X + Y, has one operand (object that is being operated on), X, to the left of the addition operator and the other operand, Y, to the right of it.

Using infix notation to invoke the addition operator is optional. We can invoke the addition operator using the regular notation for invoking functions:

Z := "+" (X, Y);

Blocks, Procedures, and Functions   181

In regular function notation, the identifier, "+", appears first, followed by a list of parameters in parentheses. Note that the addition operator appears in quotes. As we can see, this regular notation is not as readable as the familiar infix notation.

In the preceding example, the addition operator was overloaded. In Ada, arithmetic, logical, or relational operators can be overloaded: **, *, /, +, -, **mod**, **rem**, **abs**, **not**, **and**, **or**, **xor**, <, <=, >, >=, and &. Note that this list excludes the assignment operator, :=, the inequality operator, /=, and the short circuit logical operators, **or else** and **and then**. The operator, =, can only be overloaded in special cases that will be explained in Chapter 8. There are three restrictions that apply to overloaded operators. First, the number of parameters for a user-defined overloaded operator must be the same as for the corresponding predefined operator. For example, the relational operator, >, is defined in the package STANDARD as a binary operator—one that operates on two objects. Thus, > can only be overloaded with a user-defined operator that has two parameters.

Two operators exist, + and -, that programmers can overload with operators that have either one or two parameters. A glance at the package STANDARD, listed in Appendix C, shows why this is the case. In the package STANDARD, the operator + is overloaded four times, as follows:

function "+" (LEFT, RIGHT: INTEGER) **return** INTEGER;
function "+" (LEFT, RIGHT: FLOAT) **return** FLOAT;

function "+" (RIGHT: INTEGER) **return** INTEGER;
function "+" (RIGHT: FLOAT) **return** FLOAT;

As we can see, the first two overloaded "+" operators are binary operators that operate on INTEGER and FLOAT numbers, respectively. The second two overloaded "+" operators are unary operators that operate on INTEGER and FLOAT numbers, respectively. As a binary operator, "+" is an addition operator that adds two numbers, such as 7 + 2. As a unary operator, "+" is a positive operator that is used to indicate a positive number, such as +4. The operator "-" can similarly be used as either a binary subtraction operator or a unary negative operator.

Consider the following overloaded function specifications:

function "+" (A: MATRIX_TYPE) **return** MATRIX_TYPE;   -- OK
function "+" (A, B: MATRIX_TYPE) **return** MATRIX_TYPE;   -- OK
function "+" (A, B, C: MATRIX_TYPE) **return** MATRIX_TYPE;   -- illegal

The first overloaded "+" is a unary operator because it has only one parameter, A. This specification is legal because the package STANDARD contains a unary "+" operator. The second overloaded "+" is a binary operator, because it has two parameters: A and B. This specification is also legal. The third overloaded "+", however, has three parameters. This specification is illegal because there is no corresponding "+" operator in the package STANDARD that has three parameters.

The second restriction that applies to overloaded operators is that they cannot be separately compiled and thus cannot be library units. Overloaded operators must always be embedded in another unit such as a procedure, function, or package.

The third restriction is that a procedure identifier cannot be an operator; only a function identifier can be an operator.

Returning Composite Values

The overloaded addition operator shown in the previous section returns an array aggregate (literal). In addition to overloaded operators, regular functions and procedures can also return composite values that are array or record aggregates. The following procedure declares a function that returns an array aggregate:

```
procedure RETURN_COMPOSITE is

    type VECTOR is array (INTEGER range <>) of INTEGER;
    ROW_OF_4, V4: VECTOR (1..4);
    ROW_OF_6, V6: VECTOR (1..6);
    INT: INTEGER;

    --returns a composite result
    function ARRAY_OF_ABS (V: VECTOR) return VECTOR is
        RESULT: VECTOR (V'RANGE);
    begin
        for J in V'RANGE loop
            RESULT (J) := abs V(J);
        end loop;
        return RESULT;
    end ARRAY_OF_ABS;

begin -- RETURN_COMPOSITE

    V4 := (-31, -12, 39, -9);
    V6 := (26, -83, -1, 0, 73, -122);

    ROW_OF_4 := ARRAY_OF_ABS (V4);      -- (31, 12, 39, 9)
    ROW_OF_6 := ARRAY_OF_ABS (V6);      -- (26, 83, 1, 0, 73, 122)
    INT := ARRAY_OF_ABS (V4) (1);       -- 31
    ...
end RETURN_COMPOSITE;
```

The function ARRAY_OF_ABS returns an array aggregate that consists of the absolute values of the components of the array being passed to the function. In this example, ARRAY_OF_ABS (V4) returns the array aggregate (31, 12, 39, 9), and ARRAY_OF_ABS (V6) returns the array aggregate (26, 83, 1, 0, 73, 122).

Note that the formal parameter of the function ARRAY_OF_ABS is an unconstrained array. By using a formal parameter that is an unconstrained array, the function can accept arrays of the type VECTOR that are of any length. Of course, when the function is invoked, the array being used as an actual parameter must be constrained (its length must be set). The formal parameter, V, then acquires the index range of the actual array parameter. For example, when ARRAY_OF_ABS is invoked with the parameter V6, because V6'RANGE is 1..6, V'RANGE is also 1..6.

Also note the expression ARRAY_OF_ABS (V4) (1). This expression immediately selects the first component of the array aggregate returned by the function ARRAY_OF_ABS. In other words, the expression returns the first component of the aggregate (31, 12, 39, 9), which is 31.

Recursive Subprograms

A recursive subprogram is a subprogram that calls itself. Ada supports both recursive procedures and recursive functions. In order to better understand this concept, let us consider a recursive definition, that is, a definition that defines a word in terms of itself. A recursive definition does not have to be "viciously" circular any more than a recursive subprogram has to keep calling itself forever. A condition may be reached that ends the cycle.

Consider the following recursive definition of descendant. A descendant is either the child of a person or the descendant of a child of that person. Even though descendant is defined in terms of itself, never-ending circularity in the definition is avoided. Consider, for example, a situation where Louis gives birth to Louis_II, who gives birth to Louis_III, who gives birth to Louis_IV. Is Louis_IV a descendant of Louis? Our definition applies as follows. Louis_IV is the descendant of Louis if Louis_IV is either the child of Louis or the descendant of a child of Louis. Since Louis_IV is not the child of Louis, we must consider whether Louis_IV is a descendant of a child of Louis. The child of Louis is Louis_II. So our question now becomes whether Louis_IV is the descendant of Louis_II. Again applying our definition, Louis_IV is a descendant of Louis_II if Louis_IV is either the child of Louis_II or the descendant of a child of Louis_II. Since Louis_IV is not the child of Louis_II, we must consider whether Louis_IV is a descendant of a child of Louis_II. The child of Louis_II is Louis_III. So our question now becomes whether Louis_IV is a descendant of Louis_III. Using our definition a third time, Louis_IV is a descendant of Louis_III if Louis_IV is either the child of Louis_III or the descendant of a child of Louis_III. We have finally reached the end! Louis_IV is a descendant of Louis_III because Louis_IV is the child of Louis_III. Thus, the answer to our original question, if you still remember it, is yes; Louis_IV is a descendant of Louis.

Similar recursive definitions are used in mathematics. For instance, a factorial function is often recursively defined as follows:

N! is equal to 1 if N = 1
N! is equal to N * (N-1)! if N > 1

For those who have forgotten about factorial numbers, consider this example: 9! is equal to 9 * 8 * 7 * 6 * 5 * 4 * 3 * 2 * 1, which equals 362,880. In general, for any positive integer N, N! is equal to N * (N-1) * (N-2) * (N-3) and so on, until the last term becomes 1.

The behavior of the preceding recursive definition can be illustrated as follows:

```
9! = 9 * 8!
   = 9 * 8 * 7!
   = 9 * 8 * 7 * 6!
   = 9 * 8 * 7 * 6 * 5!
   = 9 * 8 * 7 * 6 * 5 * 4!
   = 9 * 8 * 7 * 6 * 5 * 4 * 3!
   = 9 * 8 * 7 * 6 * 5 * 4 * 3 * 2!
   = 9 * 8 * 7 * 6 * 5 * 4 * 3 * 2 * 1!
   = 9 * 8 * 7 * 6 * 5 * 4 * 3 * 2 * 1
```

Each line represents a "cycle" through the recursive definition. We begin with N being set to 9. While N > 1, we keep following the second condition of our recursive definition, replacing N! with N * (N-1)!. Thus 9! gets replaced with 9 * (9-1)! which is 9 * 8!. In the second line, 8! gets replaced with 8 * (8-1)! which is 8 * 7! and so on, until we finally reach 1!. When N becomes 1, we follow the first condition of our recursive definition and replace 1! with 1. Our processing now ends since a factorial number is no longer defined in terms of other factorial numbers.

To illustrate recursive subprograms, we will first write a factorial function that is iterative (uses a loop). Next, we will implement the same function as a recursive function.

```
with TEXT_IO; use TEXT_IO;
procedure ITERATIVE is
    package POSITIVE_IO is new INTEGER_IO (POSITIVE);
    use POSITIVE_IO;
    function FACTORIAL (N: POSITIVE) return POSITIVE is
        FACT: POSITIVE := 1;
    begin
        for J in reverse 1 .. N loop
            FACT := FACT * J;
        end loop;
        return FACT;
    end FACTORIAL;
```

```
begin -- ITERATIVE
    PUT (FACTORIAL (3));    -- outputs 6
end ITERATIVE;
```

Now let us see how this same function looks when it is written recursively:

```
with TEXT_IO; use TEXT_IO;
procedure RECURSIVE is
    package POSITIVE_IO is new INTEGER_IO (POSITIVE);
    use POSITIVE_IO;
    function FACTORIAL (N: POSITIVE) return POSITIVE is
    begin
        if N = 1 then
            return 1;
        else
            return N * FACTORIAL (N-1);
        end if;
    end FACTORIAL;

begin -- RECURSIVE
    PUT (FACTORIAL (3));    -- outputs 6
end RECURSIVE;
```

The main difference between the iterative and recursive versions of the function FACTORIAL is that the iterative function uses a loop, whereas the recursive function "cycles" by repeatedly calling itself. Note that the recursive version closely follows the mathematical algorithm.

Here is how the recursive FACTORIAL function works. The procedure RECURSIVE invokes FACTORIAL with a parameter value of 3. FACTORIAL (3) needs to return the result 3 * FACTORIAL (2). However, this result cannot be returned until FACTORIAL (2) is evaluated. FACTORIAL (2) needs to return the result 2 * FACTORIAL (1). Again, this result cannot be returned until FACTORIAL (1) is evaluated. FACTORIAL (1) finally resolves to 1. So far, this function has been "winding itself up," calling itself again and again. Now that FACTORIAL (1) is ready to return the result 1, we can start to "unwind." The result 1 is returned to FACTORIAL (1); then the result 2 * FACTORIAL (1), or 2, is returned to FACTORIAL (2); then the final result 3 * FACTORIAL (2), or 6, is returned to our original invocation, FACTORIAL (3). This winding and unwinding is shown in Figure 7.1. The winding is represented by the arrows pointing downward. The unwinding is represented by the arrows pointing up and to the left.

As mentioned in the beginning of this chapter, blocks, procedures, and functions are units of code that contain a declarative part, a statement part, and optional exception handlers. There are other such units of code, like packages. Packages are discussed in the next chapter.

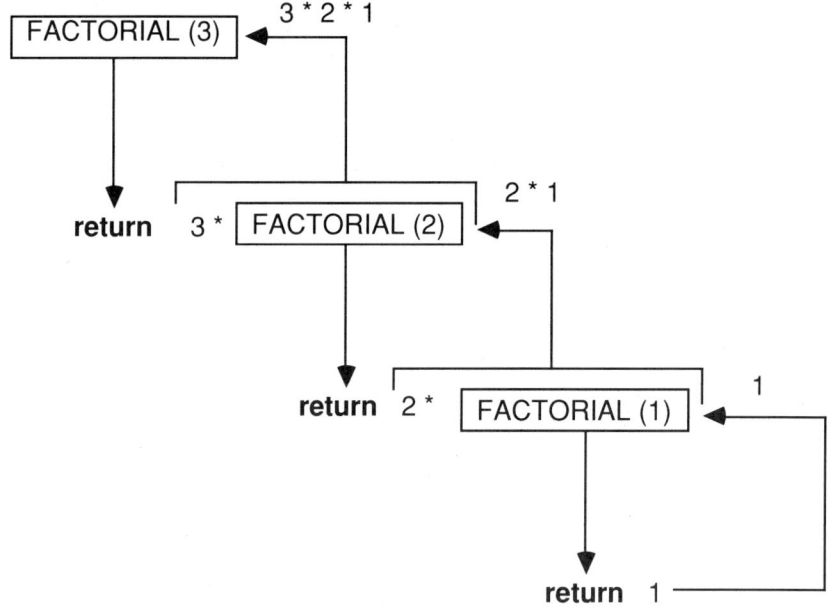

Figure 7.1 Recursive factorial function

EXERCISES

1. Consider the "twin paradox" that is a consequence of Einstein's Theory of Special Relativity. Suppose that in the distant future, we have spaceships that can travel great distances near the speed of light. Also suppose that Mary decides to travel in such a spaceship and leave her twin, Marvin, back home. According to the Theory of Special Relativity, if Mary gets into the spaceship and takes a long trip near the speed of light while Marvin stays on Earth, then a strange situation will result. When Mary returns to Earth, she will be younger than her twin Marvin.

   Write a complete Ada program that prompts a user to enter the percent of the speed of light that Mary will travel, P, and the number of Earth years, T, that she will be traveling. Have the program then calculate and output the number of years, A, that Mary will age during the trip. Make sure that the "cosmic speed" limit of light is not exceeded. (The cosmic speed limit states that nothing can accelerate to the speed of light.)

Use this formula:

$$A = T \times \sqrt{1 - \left[\frac{P}{100}\right]^2}$$

where   A = number of years that the traveler will age
P = percent of the speed of light that the traveler will be traveling
T = number of earth years that the trip takes

Note: Assume that the square root function SQRT is available and that its operand and result is type FLOAT.

2. Write a function that returns the square root of a real number, X. As a first approximation, use X/2. Keep applying the following formula until the difference between two consecutive approximations is less than 0.001.

   NEXT_APPROXIMATION =
   0.5 (LAST_APPROXIMATION + X / LAST_APPROXIMATION)

   Incorporate this square root function in exercise 1.

3. Consider the following code:

```
OUTER:
declare
   X : INTEGER := 9;
   Y : INTEGER := 2;
begin -- OUTER
   INNER:
   declare
      X : INTEGER := Y;
      Y : INTEGER := 5;
   begin -- INNER
      PUT (X);
      PUT (Y);
      PUT (OUTER.X);
      PUT (OUTER.Y);
   end INNER;
   PUT (X);
   PUT (Y);
end OUTER;
```

Write the six values that the code will output, in the order in which the values will be output: ____ ____ ____ ____ ____ ____

4. Consider the following program:

```
with TEXT_IO; use TEXT_IO;
procedure OUTER is
   package INT_IO is new INTEGER_IO (INTEGER);
   use INT_IO;
   A, B, C, D: INTEGER := 1;

   procedure MIDDLE is
      B, C: INTEGER := 2;

      procedure INNER is
         C, D: INTEGER := 3;
      begin
         PUT (A);
         PUT (B);
         PUT (C);
         PUT (D);
         PUT (OUTER.C);
         PUT (MIDDLE.C);
         PUT (MIDDLE.B);
      end INNER;

   begin -- MIDDLE
      INNER;
      PUT (A);
      PUT (B);
      PUT (C);
      PUT (D);
      PUT (OUTER.B);
   end MIDDLE;

begin -- OUTER
   MIDDLE;
   PUT (A);
   PUT (B);
   PUT (C);
   PUT (D);
end OUTER;
```

What will this program output? Test your answer by running the program.

5. Assume that you are given the following declarations:

```
type BEAN_TYPE is (COLOMBIAN, KENYAN, JAMAICAN,
                   COSTA_RICAN);
type ROAST_TYPE is (LIGHT, MEDIUM, DARK);
procedure COFFEE ( BEAN: BEAN_TYPE := COLOMBIAN;
                   ROAST: ROAST_TYPE := DARK );
```

What values do each of the following procedure invocations assign to the parameters BEAN and ROAST?

a. COFFEE (ROAST => LIGHT);
   BEAN is set to _____
   ROAST is set to_____

b. COFFEE;
   BEAN is set to _____
   ROAST is set to_____

c. COFFEE (COSTA_RICAN, ROAST => MEDIUM);
   BEAN is set to _____
   ROAST is set to_____

d. COFFEE (ROAST => MEDIUM, BEAN => JAMAICAN);
   BEAN is set to _____
   ROAST is set to_____

6. Consider this procedure specification:

   procedure CHECK (FIRST: **in** INTEGER;
                       SECOND: **in out** INTEGER;
                       RESULT: **out** BOOLEAN);

   Consider these declarations:

   X : INTEGER := 1;
   Y : **constant** INTEGER := 3;
   B : BOOLEAN;

   Which six of the following calls to CHECK are illegal and why?

   a. CHECK;
   b. CHECK (9, X, B);
   c. CHECK (Y, X, B);
   d. CHECK (X, Y, B);
   e. CHECK (X, 2, B);
   f. CHECK (2, X, TRUE);
   g. CHECK (9, X, RESULT => TRUE);
   h. CHECK (FIRST := 7, SECOND := X, RESULT := B);
   i. CHECK (FIRST => 7, RESULT => B, SECOND => X);

7. Which of the following statements are illegal and why?

   procedure DEMO (IN_PARAM : **in** INTEGER;
                       OUT_PARAM : **out** INTEGER;
                       IN_OUT_PARAM : **in out** INTEGER) **is**

```
begin
   OUT_PARAM := 4;
   IN_PARAM := 4;
   if OUT_PARAM /= IN_PARAM then
      OUT_PARAM := OUT_PARAM - IN_PARAM;
   elsif IN_PARAM = IN_OUT_PARAM then
      IN_PARAM := IN_PARAM + 1;
   else
      IN_OUT_PARAM := IN_OUT_PARAM - IN_PARAM;
   end if;
end DEMO;
```

8. When the following recursive Ada procedure is invoked with RECURSION (4), what values will be output? _____

   ```
   with TEXT_IO; use TEXT_IO;
   procedure RECURSION (P: POSITIVE) is
      package POSITIVE_IO is new INTEGER_IO (POSITIVE);
      use POSITIVE_IO;
   begin
      if P = 1 then
         return;
      else
         PUT (P);
         RECURSION (P - 1);
      end if;
      PUT (P);
   end RECURSION;
   ```

9. a. Write an overloaded function "+" that adds two complex numbers. Define your complex number as a record:

   ```
   type COMPLEX_NUMBER is
      record
         REAL : FLOAT;
         IMAGINARY : FLOAT;
      end record;
   ```

   b. Embed the overloaded addition operator in the declarative part of a procedure. Have this procedure calculate and output the sum of complex numbers A and B, where A := (7.9, 6.5) and B := (-5.2, 1.9).

10. Which three of the following four specifications are illegal, and why are they illegal?

    a. **function** SQUARE_ROOT (VALUE: **in** FLOAT;
                     IMAGINARY: **out** BOOLEAN) **return** FLOAT;

b. -- assume types MONTHS_OF_YEAR and DAYS_IN_MONTH
   -- are visible
   procedure MONTH_LENGTH (MONTH: **in**
           MONTHS_OF_YEAR := JANUARY;
           DAYS: **out** DAYS_IN_MONTH := 31);

c. **function** GET_RESPONSE **return** BOOLEAN;

d. -- assume type COMPLEX is visible
   procedure ">" (LEFT, RIGHT: **in** COMPLEX;
           RESULT: **out** BOOLEAN);

11. Explain the problem with the following code. Will the compiler necessarily detect this problem?

    procedure DISCRIMINANT (A, B, C: **in** INTEGER;
                    DISCRIM: **out** INTEGER;
                    REAL_SOLUTION: **out** BOOLEAN) **is**
        ANSWER: INTEGER;
    begin
        ANSWER := B ** 2 - 4 * A * C;
        if ANSWER >= 0 **then**
            DISCRIM := ANSWER;
            REAL_SOLUTION := TRUE;
        else
            REAL_SOLUTION := FALSE;
        end if;
    end DISCRIMINANT;

12. Write a function, SUM_OF_CUBE, that returns the sum of the cubes of up to five parameters. For example, SUM_OF_CUBE (2) returns 8, SUM_OF_CUBE (2, 3) returns 35, and SUM_OF_CUBE (2, 3, 4, 5, 6) returns 440. (Hint: use default parameter values.)

13. What is wrong with the following function?

    function CUBE (VALUE: **in** INTEGER) **return** INTEGER **is**
    begin
        CUBE := VALUE ** 3;
        return;
    end CUBE;

14. Write a function that converts lowercase letters to uppercase letters. Write a main program that uses this function to convert lowercase letters entered from the keyboard into uppercase letters.

15. Rewrite the square root function described in exercise 2 as a recursive function.

16. In the RETURN_COMPOSITE procedure presented in the "Returning Composite Values" section of this chapter, replace the ARRAY_OF_ABS function with an overloaded "+" defined as an unary operator. Be careful rewriting ARRAY_OF_ABS (V4) (1). This expression becomes "+" (V4) (1), not + V4 (1). Since the component selection has precedence over the "+" operator, +V4 (1) is the same as STANDARD. "+" (V4 (1)), which is + (-31) or -31.

Chapter 8

PACKAGES

Packages are used to bundle together related resources that provide users with a well-defined and complete service. These resources can consist of functions; procedures; other packages; and declarations of constants, variables, types, subtypes, and so on. We are already familiar with a few of the predefined packages, such as TEXT_IO, which provides input and output services. Programmers may also write their own packages. For instance, a trigonometry package might be written that supplies users with various trigonometric functions, or a graphics package might be created that allows users to draw different shapes. Once such general-purpose packages are written, their services are easily made available to any program.

A package consists of two parts: a specification and a body. This chapter begins with a discussion of package specifications, followed by a discussion of package bodies. Examples of packages are then provided that contain both specifications and bodies. The division of packages into a specification and body has certain implications for software design. These implications are explored. Next is a detailed examination of the **with** clause and the **use** clause, followed by a discussion of when to employ the **use** clause. Embedded packages are then presented. The chapter concludes with an exploration of two kinds of types that may only appear in package specifications: private types and limited private types.

PACKAGE SPECIFICATIONS

Packages usually consist of two parts—a specification and a body:

```
-- package specification
package package name is
    visible declarations
end package name;

-- package body
package body package name is
    hidden declarations
begin -- initialization
    statements
end package name;
```

The package specification begins with the keyword **package**, followed by the package name and the keyword **is**. Next come the declarations, which may include definitions of constants, variables, types, subtypes, and subprogram specifications. The package specification ends with the keyword **end**, followed optionally by the package name.

The package body begins with the keywords **package body**, followed by the package name and the keyword **is**. Next comes the declarative part of the body. As with package specifications, the declarative part of a package body may include definitions of constants, variables, types, subtypes, and subprogram specifications. Unlike package specifications, the declarative part of a package body may also contain subprogram bodies. Subprogram bodies must be placed after the definitions of the constants, variables, types, and subtypes. (This rule applies whenever subprogram bodies appear in the declarative part of a program unit.) Following the declarative part of the package body is the keyword **begin**, the executable statement part (in a package, usually referred to as the initialization part), and the keyword **end**, optionally followed by the package name.

Although a package usually consists of a specification and a body, the following user-defined package consists of only a specification:

```
package STYLES is              -- package consisting of a specification
    type HOUSE_STYLES is (QUEEN_ANNE, GOTHIC, CRAFTSMAN,
        PRAIRIE_STYLE, ENGLISH_TUDOR, MEDITERRANEAN,
        FRENCH_NORMAN, SPANISH_COLONIAL, ART_DECO,
        HIGH_TECH, STREAMLINE_MODERNE);
end STYLES;
```

Package STYLES contains a declaration of an enumeration type. Since this package is complete and does not require any underlying implementation, no package body is needed.

Once package STYLES is written, it may either be compiled independently or as part of a larger program unit, in which it is embedded. Packages that are separately compiled become library units, which can be referenced by other program units. Embedded packages, however, have more limited use, because they are only available to the unit in which they are embedded. (This is not true, however, for packages embedded within a package specification.) Until we get to the section in this chapter on embedded packages, we will assume that all packages presented are library units. This is the usual case, since the benefits of packages may be fully exploited when they are library units.

After package STYLES is compiled as a library unit, its resources become available to other program units. Other program units can reference these resources by using a **with** clause and optionally a **use** clause:

```
with TEXT_IO, STYLES; use TEXT_IO, STYLES;
procedure TASTE is
    -- HOUSE_STYLES and HIGH_TECH imported from package STYLES
    package HOUSE_IO is new ENUMERATION_IO (HOUSE_STYLES);
    use HOUSE_IO;
    HOUSE: HOUSE_STYLES;
begin
    GET (HOUSE);
    if HOUSE = HIGH_TECH then
        PUT_LINE ("This person likes supermodern");
    end if;
end TASTE;
```

The **with** clause, optionally followed by the **use** clause, is known as the context specification. The context specification defines the environment of a program unit. The environment consists of all the library units available to the program unit.

The **with** clause consists of the keyword **with**, followed by a list of program units. When the **with** clause is encountered, the Ada library is searched for the listed program units. In our example, the program units consist of the packages TEXT_IO and STYLES. When these packages are found in the Ada library, their resources are made available to procedure TASTE. Whereas the **with** clause makes these resources available, the **use** clause makes these resources directly visible. By directly visible, we mean that a resource, such as the enumeration type HOUSE_STYLES, can be referenced simply by using its name, HOUSE_STYLES. If we omit the **use** clause, resources such as HOUSE_STYLES can only be referenced using dot notation: STYLES.HOUSE_STYLES. This dot notation tells the compiler that HOUSE_STYLES is found in the package STYLES. If the **use** clause is omitted, resources of the TEXT_IO package, such as PUT_LINE, must be similarly referenced: TEXT_IO.PUT_LINE. (As we will discuss later in this chapter, if the **use** clause is omitted, other items in package STYLES would also need to be referenced using dot notation.)

PACKAGE BODIES

There are two critical distinctions between a package specification and a package body. One critical distinction is that the specification is the public (visible) part of a package and the body is the private (hidden) part. In other words, users may reference items contained in the package specification but not those contained in the package body. Items in the specification may also be referenced by the corresponding package body.

The other critical distinction is that the package specification contains the interface to the package resources, whereas the package body contains the underlying implementation of these resources. The specification contains everything that the user needs to know: the resources the package has to offer and how to use these resources. The body contains the underlying implementation that does not concern the user. To use the resources of a package, one does not have to know how these resources are implemented.

The distinction between a package specification and a package body is analogous to the distinction between a hardware interface and the inner workings of the hardware. From the user's perspective, a piece of hardware is a "black box" whose inner workings do not need to be considered. The user must only know how to plug into the black box (interface with it). Analogously, a package body is a black box whose inner workings do not need to be considered. The user only needs to know how to interface with the body through the corresponding specification. Users of a package do not need to know how the package body works any more than users of a microwave oven need to know how microwaves are generated.

The black box analogy can be pursued further. Just as the insides of a piece of hardware can be fixed, enhanced, or replaced without the interface to the hardware changing, so too can a package body be debugged, enhanced, or replaced without the interface (package specification) to the package body changing. Thus, a package body can be modified or replaced with minimal impact on the rest of the program. Such changes need not concern users, except that certain aspects of performance may be affected, such as execution speed of a program.

EXAMPLES OF PACKAGES WITH SPECIFICATIONS AND BODIES

The following package contains resources to calculate the areas of circles, rectangles, and triangles. Since code is required to perform the calculations, a package body must be provided that implements these calculations:

```
package AREA_CALCULATIONS is -- package specification
    subtype DISTANCE is FLOAT range 0.0 .. 100.0;
    function CIRCLE_AREA (RADIUS: DISTANCE) return FLOAT;
    function RECTANGLE_AREA (LENGTH, WIDTH: DISTANCE) return
        FLOAT;
    function TRIANGLE_AREA (BASE, HEIGHT: DISTANCE) return FLOAT;
end AREA_CALCULATIONS;

package body AREA_CALCULATIONS is -- package body

    function CIRCLE_AREA (RADIUS: DISTANCE) return FLOAT is
        PI: constant FLOAT := 3.1415927;
    begin
        return PI * RADIUS * RADIUS;
    end CIRCLE_AREA;

    function RECTANGLE_AREA (LENGTH, WIDTH: DISTANCE) return
        FLOAT is
    begin
        return LENGTH * WIDTH;
    end RECTANGLE_AREA;

    function TRIANGLE_AREA (BASE, HEIGHT: DISTANCE) return
        FLOAT is
    begin
        return 0.5 * BASE * HEIGHT;
    end TRIANGLE_AREA;

end AREA_CALCULATIONS;
```

The package specification of AREA_CALCULATIONS contains the declaration of the subtype DISTANCE and the specifications of the functions used to calculate the areas of circles, rectangles, and triangles. Since these functions are provided to external users, they must be placed in the public part of the package, the package specification. Only the function specifications—not the function bodies—can be placed in the package specification. This is because function specifications contain interface information (information required to call the function), and interface information belongs in the package specification. This interface information includes the name of the function, followed by parameter definitions (in parentheses) and the type of value returned by the function. This is the only information needed by the user of this package, except for comments describing the services that the package offers. The user does not need to know how the functions are implemented. The implementations of these functions are therefore contained in the function bodies, which are hidden in the package body. Keep in mind that these function bodies may be invoked from outside the package only because their corresponding function specifications are contained in the package specification.

Once the preceding package, AREA_CALCULATIONS, is independently compiled, it may be referenced by any program unit that mentions this package in its **with** clause:

```ada
with TEXT_IO, AREA_CALCULATIONS;
use TEXT_IO, AREA_CALCULATIONS;
procedure OUTPUT_AREAS is

    type SHAPE is (CIRCLE, RECTANGLE, TRIANGLE);
    OBJECT: SHAPE;
    package REAL_IO is new FLOAT_IO (FLOAT);
    package SHAPE_IO is new ENUMERATION_IO (SHAPE);
    use REAL_IO, SHAPE_IO;
    RADIUS, LENGTH, WIDTH, BASE, HEIGHT: DISTANCE;

begin -- OUTPUT_AREAS

    PUT ("Do you want to find the area of a circle, rectangle, or triangle?");
    GET (OBJECT);

    case OBJECT is

        when CIRCLE =>
            PUT_LINE ("Enter the radius of the circle as a real number: ");
            GET (RADIUS);
            PUT ("The area of the circle is ");
            PUT ( CIRCLE_AREA (RADIUS), 5, 3, 0 );
            NEW_LINE;

        when RECTANGLE =>
            PUT_LINE ("Enter the length of the rectangle as a real number: ");
            GET (LENGTH);
            PUT_LINE ("Enter the width of the rectangle as a real number: ");
            GET (WIDTH);
            PUT ("The area of the rectangle is ");
            PUT ( RECTANGLE_AREA (LENGTH, WIDTH), 5, 3, 0 );
            NEW_LINE;

        when TRIANGLE =>
            PUT_LINE ("Enter the base of the triangle as a real number: ");
            GET (BASE);
            PUT_LINE ("Enter the height of the triangle as a real number: ");
            GET (HEIGHT);
            PUT ("The area of the triangle is ");
            PUT ( TRIANGLE_AREA (BASE, HEIGHT), 5, 3, 0 );
            NEW_LINE;

    end case;

end OUTPUT_AREAS;
```

When procedure OUTPUT_AREAS executes, the user is prompted for the type of object—CIRCLE, RECTANGLE, OR TRIANGLE—whose area is to be calculated. The user response is assigned to the variable OBJECT, which is declared to be of type SHAPE. A **case** statement then selects a group of statements to execute, based on the value of OBJECT. If, for instance, OBJECT has the value of CIRCLE, then the user is prompted for the radius of the circle. The area is calculated by making a call to the CIRCLE_AREA function, and the result is output with an appropriate message.

A sample run of this program may appear as follows:

```
Do you want to find the area of a circle, rectangle, or triangle?
> circle
Enter the radius of the circle as a real number:
> 2.0
The area of the circle is    12.566
```

The user responses follow the prompt, >. Note that the answer is rounded off to the nearest thousandth. This output format is specified by the PUT statements that output the areas of the various objects. For example, the area of a circle is output by the following statement:

PUT (CIRCLE_AREA (RADIUS), 5, 3, 0);

The second parameter, 5, provides space for 5 digits to the left of the decimal point. The third parameter, 3, specifies that 3 digits are to follow the decimal point. The 0 specifies that no digits are to be used for an exponent; that is, an exponent is not to be used. Without such a format specification, the output would appear in scientific notation, such as 1.256637E+01. Formatted output will be discussed in detail in Chapter 14.

Each time one of the functions in package AREA_CALCULATIONS is called, the calculated area is returned to the caller. No information is retained in the package between each of the calls. Quite often, however, a package body hides data structures that retain their values between subprogram calls. These data structures are protected. They can only be manipulated through the subprograms provided in the package specification.

The following example illustrates such a package, where the hidden data structure is an array used to stack integer values. Before showing the code, let us briefly describe a stack.

A stack is a "last in, first out" (LIFO) data structure. Items are "pushed" on (placed in) the stack and "popped" off (taken from) the stack just as individual plates in a cafeteria are placed in a stack or removed from a stack. The plate that is removed from the top of the stack is the one that was most recently added to the stack.

The following stack package maintains an integer stack whose values can be pushed and popped using subprograms provided by the package:

```
package STACK is -- specification
    subtype STACK_ITEM is INTEGER range -10_000 .. 10_000;
    procedure PUSH (ITEM: STACK_ITEM);
    function POP return STACK_ITEM;
end STACK;
```

```
package body STACK is    -- body
   -- declarative part
   STACK_SIZE: constant INTEGER := 1_000;
   STACK_ARRAY: array (1 .. STACK_SIZE) of STACK_ITEM;
   TOP: INTEGER range 0 .. STACK_SIZE;

   procedure PUSH (ITEM: STACK_ITEM) is
   begin
      TOP := TOP + 1;
      STACK_ARRAY (TOP) := ITEM;
   end PUSH;

   function POP return STACK_ITEM is
   begin
      TOP := TOP - 1;
      return STACK_ARRAY (TOP + 1);
   end POP;

begin -- initialization part
   TOP := 0;
end STACK;
```

The package specification contains the declaration of the subtype STACK_ITEM, and the specifications of the procedure PUSH and the function POP. PUSH pushes an object belonging to STACK_ITEM onto the stack, and POP pops an object belonging to STACK_ITEM from the stack and returns the value of the object.

Now let us consider the package body, which contains the hidden implementation details. The declarative part of the package body contains the declarations of the constant STACK_SIZE, the anonymous array STACK_ARRAY, and the integer variable TOP.

STACK_SIZE is set to 1000, which places an upper limit on the number of integers that can be stacked. STACK_ARRAY is used to hold all the integer values in the stack. These integer values belong to the subtype STACK_ITEM. The subtype STACK_ITEM, declared in the package specification, is thus directly visible to the corresponding package body. Note that although the stack is implemented as an array, this fact is hidden from the users of the package. Whether the stack is implemented as an array or as some other data structure should be of no concern to the user, because this does not affect how the package is used.

Next, the integer variable TOP is declared. TOP is the index value of the last item placed in STACK_ARRAY. TOP must therefore be updated whenever integers are added to or removed from the array. Following the declaration of TOP are the bodies of the subprograms PUSH and POP. Since subprogram bodies contain implementation details rather than interface information, they must be placed in the package body rather than in the package specification. The procedure PUSH increments TOP and assigns the item to be pushed on the stack to the array component

STACK_ARRAY(TOP). The function POP decrements the value of TOP and returns the last value in the stack before TOP was decremented.

After the function, POP, comes the executable statement part of the STACK package body, which initializes TOP to 0. The statement part of a package body is unlike the statement part of subprograms. The statement part of subprograms, which must contain at least one statement, is critical because it implements the actions that the subprogram is designed to accomplish. The statement part of a package body, however, plays a minor role and is often omitted (along with the keyword **begin**). When such a part does exist, it typically just contains a few statements that initialize some of the variables, such as TOP, previously declared in the package. For this reason, the statement part of a package body is often known as the initialization part. The statement part of packages plays such a minor role because, unlike subprograms, a package is not invoked or passed parameters. (Although, as in our STACK package, a package may contain subprograms that can be invoked and passed parameters.) Hence, unlike the statement part of a subprogram, which is executed whenever the subprogram is invoked, the statement part of a package is executed only when the package is elaborated (brought into existence). If the package is a library unit, this elaboration occurs only once, before the main program begins to execute. TOP is thus initialized only once. Thereafter, every time a call is made to PUSH or POP, TOP is updated but never again initialized to 0.

Instead of initializing TOP in the statement part of the package body, we could have initialized TOP in the declarative part of the body:

TOP: INTEGER **range** 0 .. STACK_SIZE := 0;

The effect is the same as before: TOP is only initialized once, when the package is first brought into existence.

Now that we have examined the STACK package, let us consider the following program that uses its services:

```
with STACK, TEXT_IO; use STACK, TEXT_IO;
procedure USE_STACK is
    package STACK_ITEM_IO is new INTEGER_IO (STACK_ITEM);
    use STACK_ITEM_IO;
    X, Y: STACK_ITEM;
begin -- USE_STACK
    PUSH (5);
    X := 3;
    PUSH (X);
    PUT ( POP );   -- outputs 3
    Y := POP;
    PUT ( Y );     -- outputs 5
end USE_STACK;
```

USE_STACK references all three items listed in the specification of STACK: STACK_ITEM, PUSH, and POP. STACK_ITEM is used to instantiate INTEGER_IO and to declare variables X and Y. PUSH is used to push the integer values 5 and 3 onto the stack, and then POP is used to pop these two values from the stack. Since a stack is a last in, first out data structure, the values are popped from the stack in the opposite order from which they were pushed onto the stack.

When a program unit such as USE_STACK references a package, this does not preclude other program units from referencing the package. A main program may have several different program units that mention STACK in their **with** clauses. Regardless of how many program units reference the STACK package, only one stack is created. Thus, each call to PUSH or POP manipulates the same integer stack, regardless of which program unit makes the call. Furthermore, this integer stack exists throughout the lifetime of the main program. The values in the array STACK_ARRAY and the value of TOP are retained between calls to the subprograms PUSH and POP. In general, whenever variables, such as STACK_ARRAY and TOP, need to be maintained throughout a program's life, place them in the declarative part of the package body. If the variables need to be made public, place them in the package specification.

As mentioned, unlike the items declared in the specification of STACK, items declared in the body of STACK are "hidden" from the users of this package. Therefore, a program unit that mentions STACK in its **with** clause cannot reference the items STACK_SIZE, STACK_ARRAY, or TOP:

```
with STACK, TEXT_IO; use STACK, TEXT_IO;
procedure INACCESSIBLE_ITEMS is
begin
    STACK_ARRAY(1) := 7;    -- error; STACK_ARRAY not available
    TOP := 20;              -- error; TOP not available
    TOP := STACK_SIZE;      -- error; STACK_SIZE not available
end INACCESSIBLE_ITEMS;
```

By hiding implementation details from the user, the integrity of the package is protected. Users may only manipulate the stack by using the subprograms provided in the specification: PUSH and POP. Users cannot circumvent these subprograms and directly manipulate the underlying structure of the stack. For example, as shown in the preceding code, the users of STACK cannot directly insert values into STACK_ARRAY or reset the value of TOP. This is fortunate; otherwise, the users could corrupt the stack.

When developing a package, carefully consider what items should be placed in the package specification and what items should be placed in the package body. The goal is to place as many items as possible in a package body. Only the items that must be visible to users of the package should appear in a package specification. If extraneous items are placed in the package specification, users of the package can base their code on irrelevant implementation details, possibly corrupting the data structures defined in the package. For example, if the declarations of STACK_SIZE, STACK_ARRAY, and TOP were relocated to the specification of STACK, the result would be a poorly structured package. The package would still work, because every item declared in a package specification is available to the corresponding package body. However, all of the illegal operations illustrated in the previous procedure, INACCESSIBLE_ITEMS, would unfortunately be legal.

Another reason for placing as few items as possible in a package specification is to minimize the amount of recompilation time that is required when code is changed. As we will discuss in Chapter 10, changes made to a package body usually do not require other program units to be recompiled, just relinked. Changes made to a package specification, however, require that every program unit that mentions this package in its **with** clause be recompiled.

To realize the saving in recompilation time that occurs when only the package body changes, package specifications must be compiled separately from their bodies. If both are compiled as a single unit, then any changes that are made require that every program unit referencing this package also be recompiled.

DESIGNING IN ADA

A package specification and package body may each be separately compiled as long as the specification is submitted to the compiler before its associated body. Separate compilation of a package specification and a package body is particularly useful when designing a program from the top down.

In top-down design, a program, through successive refinement, is broken down into manageable, well-defined pieces called modules. Each module should be self-contained and easy to understand, and the interfaces between modules should be simple and well defined. In Ada, modules are naturally represented as packages. In top-down design, all that is initially needed is the interface information provided by package specifications. The specifications can be written and compiled without the associated bodies. In other words, program units that reference a package can be compiled, provided that the package specification has been compiled. The compiler checks the program design by testing the specifications for completeness and consistency. Completeness is checked by verifying that all the units mentioned in **with** clauses actually exist and contain the required resources. Consistency is checked by verifying that procedures and functions are called with the correct number and type of parameters. The coding of implementation details contained in the package bodies is deferred until the design has been tested by the compiler. The package bodies do not need to be fully implemented until the program is ready to be executed.

Thus, when developing Ada code using top-down design, define the package specifications before the package bodies. Since the package specifications reflect the design of the program, much effort should be taken when developing the specifications. Regardless of how well the package bodies are implemented, without well-thought-out package specifications, a poorly designed program might result.

Ada also supports bottom-up design and object-oriented design. In bottom-up design, low-level modules are pieced together by **with** clauses to form larger modules, which are, in turn, pieced together to form yet larger modules, and so on, until an entire program eventually emerges. Bottom-up design is particularly useful when many of the modules already exist for other applications. Instead of rewriting these modules, they may be easily reused, thanks to the package construct and the **with** clause. When writing library packages, therefore, keep them as general as possible so that they can be reused in future applications.

In object-oriented design, objects are defined, together with the operations that can be performed on the objects. For example, our STACK package creates an object that is a stack, together with push and pop operations that can be performed on the stack. In well-designed, object-oriented code, the objects often mirror physical objects in the real world that they are meant to simulate, and the operations often mirror physical operations that are performed on these physical objects.

THE WITH CLAUSE AND USE CLAUSE

Throughout this book, we have been employing the **with** clause and the **use** clause. This section explores these two clauses in detail. Recall that the **with** clause makes the resources of a package available, whereas the **use** clause makes these resources directly visible so that dot notation may be avoided. The **use** clause, therefore, does not determine which items are available to a program unit; it merely allows those items that are available to be referenced more concisely.

The **with** clause may mention any library unit, not just packages. A **with** clause can, for example, mention functions and procedures, as long as these functions and procedures are independently compiled to form library units. The **use** clause, however, may only mention a package. This is because the **use** clause makes the internal resources of a library unit directly visible, and the only kind of library unit that provides internal resources is a package. A subprogram does not offer internal resources to an external unit. When a subprogram is mentioned in a **with** clause, all that it provides to the external unit is the subprogram name and parameters. The **with** clause alone renders these items directly visible, so the **use** clause would have no function. Items declared within the subprogram can only be used locally and are never available to outside units. On the other hand, when a package is mentioned in a **with** clause, only the package name is directly visible. The resources in the package specification are only directly visible if the **use** clause is employed.

Unlike the **use** clause, which may optionally be placed in the declarative part of a program unit, the **with** clause must be placed before the specification of the program unit. It cannot be embedded inside another program unit:

procedure OUTER **is**
   . . .
   with P; -- illegal; **with** clause cannot be embedded
   procedure INNER **is**
   . . .

When a **with** clause precedes a package specification, the clause automatically applies to the corresponding package body. The same **with** clause can also appear with the package body, but this has no additional effect. However, when a **with** clause appears with a package body but not the associated package specification, it only applies to the body:

with A;   -- may use more than 1 **with** clause
with B;
package P **is**
   -- can access resources of A and B
end P;

with B;
with C;
package body P **is**
   -- can access resources of A, B, and C
end P;

A **use** clause may be placed after its associated **with** clause before the program unit specification, or in the declarative part of a unit. When the **use** clause appears after the **with** clause, it applies throughout the program unit, rendering the resources of the package mentioned in the **use** clause directly visible. Dot notation, however, may still be employed to make the code more understandable. When a **use** clause appears in the declarative part of a unit, it takes effect from the point in the code after it is declared, throughout the scope of the unit. Consider the following code (where the line indicates separate compilation units):

208 Rendezvous with ADA: A Programmer's Introduction

```ada
package STYLES is            -- package consisting of a specification
   type HOUSE_STYLES is (QUEEN_ANNE, GOTHIC, CRAFTSMAN,
      PRAIRIE_STYLE, ENGLISH_TUDOR, MEDITERRANEAN, ------------
      FRENCH_NORMAN, SPANISH_COLONIAL, ART_DECO,
      HIGH_TECH,  STREAMLINE_MODERNE);
end STYLES;
```

```ada
with STYLES;
procedure DEMO_USE_CLAUSE is
   YOUR_HOUSE: STYLES.HOUSE_STYLES :=
      STYLES.FRENCH_NORMAN;
   -- needs dot notation for type HOUSE_STYLES and
   -- enumeration literal FRENCH_NORMAN

   use STYLES;
   -- takes effect from here to the rest of procedure

   MY_HOUSE: HOUSE_STYLES := ART_DECO;
   -- does not need dot notation

begin

   MY_HOUSE := STREAMLINE_MODERNE;
   -- does not need dot notation

end DEMO_USE_CLAUSE;
```

Before the **use** clause is employed in the procedure DEMO_USE_CLAUSE, dot notation is needed, not only for the enumeration type HOUSE_STYLES but also for the values of HOUSE_STYLES, such as FRENCH_NORMAN. Once the **use** clause is employed, dot notation is no longer required from the point after it is declared to the end of the procedure.

The **use** clause does not always guarantee that dot notation can be avoided. Sometimes dot notation is required to resolve ambiguity. Consider, for example, the following two packages that each have an identifier named C:

```ada
package P1 is
   A, B, C: INTEGER;
end P1;
```

```ada
package P2 is
   C, D: INTEGER;
end P2;
```

Suppose that a procedure mentions these two packages in a **with** clause and a **use** clause:

```ada
with P1, P2; use P1, P2;
procedure Q is
```

```
begin
    A := 1;         -- OK
    B := 2;         -- OK
    C := 3;         -- error; C is ambiguous
    P1.C := 3;      -- OK
    P2.C := 3;      -- OK
    D := 4;         -- OK
end Q;
```

As shown, the identifier C, written without dot notation, is ambiguous; it may refer to the C in package P1 or P2. The identifier C must therefore be written using dot notation, even though the **use** clause is employed.

In the previous example, identifiers having the same name appear in two different packages. Let us now consider what happens when identifiers with the same name appear in a package and in the program unit referencing the package:

```
package P is
    A: INTEGER;
end P;
```

```
with P; use P;
procedure Q is
    A: INTEGER;   -- hides A from package P
begin
    A := 2;       -- refers to the local A
    Q.A := 2;     -- explicitly selects the local A
    P.A := 3;     -- selects the A imported from package P
end Q;
```

Even though the **use** clause is employed, the integer variable A defined in package P is not directly visible. This variable A is not directly visible because it is hidden by the local declaration of the variable A in procedure Q. Local identifiers thus hide identifiers with the same name that are imported from packages. To reference the A in package P, one must write P.A.

Before ending this section, let us consider one more property of the **with** clause. In typical Ada programs, the **with** clause is often used to tie together many program units. A question that naturally emerges is whether **with** clauses allow program units to reference resources indirectly. In other words, if unit P3 **with**s P2, which **with**s P1, does P3 have access to the resources of P1? The answer is no. This is illustrated in the following code:

```
package P1 is
    subtype T1_TYPE is INTEGER range 1 .. 100;
end P1;
```

```
with P1; use P1;
package P2 is
    subtype T2_TYPE is T1_TYPE range 1 .. 10;
end P2;
```

```
with P2; use P2;
package P3 is
    A: T1_TYPE;   -- error; resources of P1 not available
    B: T2_TYPE;   -- OK
end P3;
```

Since P3 mentions P2 in its **with** clause, P3 can reference subtype T2_TYPE of P2. P2 can, in turn, reference subtype T1_TYPE of P1. This "chain" of references, however, does not enable P3 to reference the subtype T1_TYPE.

WHEN TO EMPLOY THE USE CLAUSE

The issue of when the **use** clause should be employed is controversial. Some Ada experts and software engineers believe that the **use** clause should never be employed. Without the **use** clause, code is better documented and therefore easier to understand. Code is better documented because every imported item must be referenced with dot notation. For example, at a glance, one can tell from COORDINATE.X1 that X1 is a coordinate value defined in package COORDINATE. Without dot notation, a reader of the code encountering X1 might have trouble figuring out what X1 represents or in what package it is defined.

Let us now consider the advantages of employing the **use** clause. By employing the **use** clause, items can be referenced without dot notation. Such "unexpanded" names are concise and therefore easy to read. For instance, the function call SQUARE_ROOT (7.5) is easier to read than MATH_LIBRARY.SQUARE_ROOT (7.5).

Perhaps the biggest advantage of employing the **use** clause occurs when overloaded operators are imported. Consider, for instance, the following package, which contains overloaded operators for adding, subtracting, multiplying, and dividing complex numbers:

```
package COMPLEX_NUMBER is
    type COMPLEX is
        record
            REAL: FLOAT;
            IMAGINARY: FLOAT;
        end record;

        -- overloaded functions
```

```
      function "+" (A, B: COMPLEX) return COMPLEX;
      function "-" (A, B: COMPLEX) return COMPLEX;
      function "*" (A, B: COMPLEX) return COMPLEX;
      function "/" (A, B: COMPLEX) return COMPLEX;
   end COMPLEX_NUMBER;

   package body COMPLEX_NUMBER is

      function "+" (A, B: COMPLEX) return COMPLEX is
      begin
         return (A.REAL + B.REAL, A.IMAGINARY + B.IMAGINARY);
      end "+";

      function "-" (A, B: COMPLEX) return COMPLEX is
      begin
         return (A.REAL - B.REAL, A.IMAGINARY - B.IMAGINARY);
      end "-";

      function "*" (A, B: COMPLEX) return COMPLEX is
      begin
         return ( A.REAL * B.REAL - A.IMAGINARY * B.IMAGINARY,
             A.REAL * B.IMAGINARY + A.IMAGINARY * B.REAL );
      end "*";

      function "/" (A, B: COMPLEX) return COMPLEX is
         DENOM: FLOAT;
      begin
         DENOM := B.REAL ** 2 + B.IMAGINARY ** 2;
         return   (  (A.REAL * B.REAL + A.IMAGINARY * B.IMAGINARY) /
             DENOM,
                 (A.IMAGINARY * B.REAL - A.REAL * B.IMAGINARY) /
             DENOM );
      end "/";

   end COMPLEX_NUMBER;
```

If you are not mathematically inclined, just think of a complex number as a record consisting of two components of type FLOAT. You do not have to understand the package body to follow the discussion in this section.

Without the **use** clause, an external program unit must reference the overloaded operators "+", "-", "*", and "/", by employing dot notation: COMPLEX_NUMBER."+", COMPLEX_NUMBER."-", COMPLEX_NUMBER."*", and COMPLEX_NUMBER."/". This notation is unnatural and very difficult to read. To make matters worse, when dot notation is employed, the infix notation, where operands are placed on opposite sides of the operator, cannot be employed:

```
Z := X COMPLEX_NUMBER."+" Y; -- illegal syntax
```

Instead, the standard function notation must be used:

```
Z := COMPLEX_NUMBER."+" (X, Y);
```

This defeats the reason for using overloaded operators, which is to provide natural mathematical notation, such as

```
Z := X + Y;
```

The following procedure demonstrates the advantages of employing the **use** clause when overloaded operators are imported:

```
with COMPLEX_NUMBER;
procedure DEMONSTRATE_USE_CLAUSE is
    X, Y, Z: COMPLEX_NUMBER.COMPLEX := (2.0, 3.0);
begin
    -- without the use clause, one must employ dot notation
    -- and standard function notation
    Z := COMPLEX_NUMBER."+" (X, Y);

    declare
        use COMPLEX_NUMBER;   -- only applies to following items within
                              -- this block statement
    begin
        -- with the use clause, one can omit dot notation
        -- and employ infix notation
        Z := X + Y;
    end;

end DEMONSTRATE_USE_CLAUSE;
```

When the **use** clause is placed in the declarative part of a block statement, it applies only from the point in the code where it is declared to the end of the block. Thus, the overloaded operator, "+", imported from the package COMPLEX_NUMBER, may be referenced without dot notation only within the block statement. Throughout the rest of the code, dot notation is required.

The problem of referencing operators with dot notation not only arises when importing overloaded operators. The problem arises whenever pre-defined operators are used to manipulate items imported from external packages. For example, let us reconsider procedure TASTE, presented in the beginning of this chapter, which references the package STYLES. The following version of TASTE omits the **use** clause:

```
with TEXT_IO, STYLES; -- no use clause
procedure TASTE is
    HOUSE : STYLES.HOUSE_STYLES := STYLES.HIGH_TECH;
    -- must use dot notation for enumeration type and literals
```

```
    begin
       if  STYLES."=" (HOUSE, STYLES.HIGH_TECH) then
          -- must use dot notation for equality operator
          TEXT_IO.PUT ("This person likes supermodern");
       end if;
    end TASTE;
```

When the **use** clause is omitted, not only do identifiers of imported constants, variables, types, program units, and enumeration literals need to be written with dot notation; operators must also be written with dot notation. For instance, the equality operator, "=", must be written as STYLES."=". This is because operators that operate on a given type are imported from the same package as the type. It so happens that package STYLES does not contain an overloaded equality operator. STYLES just has available the predefined equality operator. Since procedure TASTE does not employ the **use** clause, it does not know which version of the equality operator the package STYLES has available. Therefore, if you were to write HOUSE = STYLES.HIGH_TECH, an error would be raised because the equality operator is undefined for values, such as HIGH_TECH, which are defined in package STYLES.

In procedure TASTE, the price to pay for not employing the **use** clause is high. Writing each enumeration literal with dot notation is cumbersome. More disturbing, however, is the loss of the natural notation for equality. As previously mentioned, once an operator such as "=" is written with dot notation as STYLES."=", infix notation can no longer be used. The required standard function notation is very awkward and difficult to read.

Before giving up and employing the **use** clause, let us consider another way of writing TASTE without a **use** clause:

```
    with TEXT_IO, STYLES;
    procedure TASTE is
       function "=" (LEFT, RIGHT: STYLES.HOUSE_STYLES) return
          BOOLEAN renames STYLES."=";
       HOUSE : STYLES.HOUSE_STYLES := STYLES.HIGH_TECH;
    begin
       if  HOUSE = STYLES.HIGH_TECH then  -- OK; uses the renamed "="
          TEXT_IO.PUT ("This person likes supermodern");
       end if;
    end TASTE;
```

In order to use the the natural notation for equality, this version of TASTE renames STYLES."=" to "=". Renaming does not bring new entities into existence or replace one name with another. Renaming merely provides an alternative name. In our example, as a result of renaming, the equality operator can be referenced either with the name "=" or with dot notation as STYLES."=". Renaming the equality operator is perhaps better than using dot notation, but renaming operators is still awkward and confusing.

Moreover, if the code also employed operators such as "<" and ">", each of these operators would also need to be renamed. Therefore, the best solution to our problem may be to give up trying to avoid the **use** clause. By employing the **use** clause, our problems go away, and we end up with a version of TASTE like the one in the beginning of this chapter.

Before proceeding to our next topic, a few more points need to be made about renaming. To avoid dot notation, renaming can be applied to more than just operators. One can also rename items such as variables, constants, packages, and procedures. For example, the procedure TEXT_IO.PUT can be renamed to PUT:

procedure PUT (ITEM: **in** CHARACTER) **renames** TEXT_IO.PUT;

By renaming an item to avoid dot notation, these names are made more concise, as if the **use** clause were employed. However, unlike the **use** clause, which applies to all the resources of a package, the renaming feature only applies to the individually specified items. Also, an item can be renamed to any valid Ada identifier. For example, a BASIC aficionado may rename TEXT_IO.PUT to PRINT:

procedure PRINT (ITEM: **in** CHARACTER) **renames** TEXT_IO.PUT;

Considering the pros and cons of the **use** clause, it is suggested that this clause be employed but that it be employed judiciously. The **use** clause should be considered to permit infix notation of operators. The **use** clause should also be considered when items imported from a package are self-explanatory. For example, there is little danger of misunderstanding if the identifier SQUARE_ROOT is used rather than MATH_PACKAGE.SQUARE_ROOT. The identifier SQUARE_ROOT adequately explains what the function does. Furthermore, if one wishes to know where this function comes from, it should be obvious from the package name MATH_PACKAGE, listed in the **with** clause. The **use** clause should also be considered when the imported items are well-known resources from one of the predefined packages, such as TEXT_IO. For example, there is little danger of confusion using the procedure call PUT("Hello") instead of TEXT_IO.PUT("Hello"). Anyone seeing this procedure call would automatically assume the PUT statement from the TEXT_IO package was being used.

EMBEDDED PACKAGES

So far we have only considered packages that are library units (independent program units). As previously mentioned, such packages are elaborated before the main program executes. The package then exists throughout the lifetime of the program, and its resources are available to any program unit that mentions the package in a **with** clause.

In contrast to packages that are library units, packages may be embedded (contained) within other units, such as block statements and subprograms. A package that is embedded in the declarative part of a block statement or subprogram comes into existence when it is elaborated with the rest of the declarations. It ceases to exist when the enclosing program unit ceases to exist. Embedded packages are thus re-created each time the enclosing unit is elaborated. In the beginning of each new re-creation, the statements in the initialization part of the package are executed, and declarations in the package are elaborated. No information in the package is retained from one re-creation to the next.

The following example shows a package that is embedded in the declarative part of a block statement:

```
-- contents of package Q are not available here
declare
    package Q is
        type ANSWER is (YES, NO, MAYBE);
        -- ANSWER is directly visible within Q
        RESPONSE: ANSWER := MAYBE;
    end Q;
    -- here ANSWER and its values require dot notation
    MY_RESPONSE: Q.ANSWER := Q.NO;
    use Q; -- makes Q's resources directly visible up to end of block
    YOUR_RESPONSE: ANSWER := YES;
begin
    MY_RESPONSE := YOUR_RESPONSE;
end;
-- contents of package Q are not available here
```

Package Q is brought into existence when the declarations in the block are elaborated. The package ceases to exist, along with the other declared items, as soon as the block is exited. If this block statement is reentered, the package is re-created, and the statements in the package's initialization part (not shown) are again executed. In this case, any variables declared within the package have no "memory" of the values they held during their previous life. Furthermore, the resources of the package are not available from outside the block. From inside the block, the resources are available from the point in the code where the package is declared to the end of the block. In other words, the scope of the items declared within the package specification extends beyond the package, to the end of the block in which the package is declared. As shown in the example, however, unless the **use** clause is employed, the items declared within the package specification are not directly visible outside the package.

Besides being embedded in a block statement, a package can be embedded in the declarative part of a subprogram. Such a package is re-created each time the subprogram is invoked. The package ceases to exist, along with the other items declared in the subprogram, as soon as the subprogram is finished executing:

```
procedure P is
    package Q is
        A: INTEGER := 1;
    end Q;
    B: INTEGER := Q.A; -- dot notation required
    use Q;
    C: INTEGER := A; -- dot notation not required
begin
    A := B + C;
end P;
```

Each time procedure P is invoked, package Q is re-created, and statements in the initialization part of the package body (not shown) are executed.

In addition to being embedded in block statements and subprograms, packages can be nested within other packages. The lifetime of the inner package extends throughout the lifetime of the outer package. Packages can be nested within other packages in two ways. The inner package, including the specification and body, may be placed in the body of the outer package:

```
package OUTER is
    subtype OUTER_SPEC is INTEGER;
    A: OUTER_SPEC;
end OUTER;

package body OUTER is
    subtype OUTER_BODY is INTEGER;
    B: OUTER_BODY;

    package INNER is
        C: OUTER_SPEC;
        D: OUTER_BODY;
        subtype INNER_SPEC is INTEGER;
        E: INNER_SPEC;
    end INNER;

    package body INNER is
        F: OUTER_SPEC;
        G: OUTER_BODY;
        H: INNER_SPEC;
    end INNER;

end OUTER;
```

Note that the inner package specification can reference the subtypes declared in the outer package specification and the outer package body. Furthermore, the inner package body can reference these same subtypes plus the subtype declared in the inner package specification. This inner package is only available to the body of the outer package. (Note that the package body of INNER only contains declarations of variables—there are no subprogram bodies. Such package bodies rarely serve any purpose but are presented here to illustrate scope and visibility rules.)

Alternatively, the specification of the inner package may be placed in the specification of the outer package, and the body of the inner package inside the body of the outer package:

```
package OUTER is
    subtype OUTER_SPEC is INTEGER;
    A: OUTER_SPEC;

    package INNER is
       B: OUTER_SPEC;
       subtype INNER_SPEC is INTEGER;
    end INNER;

end OUTER;

package body OUTER is
    subtype OUTER_BODY is INTEGER;
    C: OUTER_BODY;

    package body INNER is
        D: OUTER_SPEC;
        E: INNER_SPEC;
        F: OUTER_BODY;
    end INNER;

end OUTER;
```

Note that the inner package specification can reference the subtype declared in the outer package specification, and the inner package body can reference the same subtype, plus subtypes declared in the inner package specification and the outer package body. A program unit that mentions OUTER in its **with** clause can reference all the resources in the specification of OUTER, including the resources of the specification of INNER. Suppose that procedure P mentions OUTER in a **with** clause but not a **use** clause:

```
with OUTER;
procedure P is
begin
    OUTER.A := 1;
    OUTER.INNER.B := 2;
end P;
```

To reference a variable such as B, the dot notation must include the full name: OUTER.INNER.B. If the clause **use** OUTER is employed, this variable can be referenced as INNER.B. If the clause **use** OUTER.INNER is employed, then this variable can be referenced without dot notation: B.

As previously mentioned, to avoid dot notation, renaming can be used. The previous procedure P, for instance, can be written as follows:

```
with OUTER;
procedure P is
    A: INTEGER renames OUTER.A;
    B: INTEGER renames OUTER.INNER.B;
begin
    A := 1;
    B := 2;
end P;
```

The integer variable A becomes an alternative name for OUTER.A, and the integer variable B becomes an alternative for OUTER.INNER.B.

PRIVATE TYPES

As we have seen, by placing a subprogram specification in a package specification and the associated subprogram body in the package body, the subprogram is visible, but its underlying implementation is hidden. In Ada, one can define private types, which are handled similarly. A private type is visible, but its underlying implementation is hidden.

Before showing how private types are declared, let us begin by demonstrating the need for private types. Reconsider, for example, the COMPLEX_NUMBER package specification:

```
package COMPLEX_NUMBER is
    type COMPLEX is
        record
            REAL: FLOAT;
            IMAGINARY: FLOAT;
        end record;
    function "+" (A, B: COMPLEX) return COMPLEX;
    function "-" (A, B: COMPLEX) return COMPLEX;
    function "*" (A, B: COMPLEX) return COMPLEX;
    function "/" (A, B: COMPLEX) return COMPLEX;
end COMPLEX_NUMBER;
```

The following procedure uses the type COMPLEX declared in this package to define three complex numbers—X, Y, and Z:

```
with COMPLEX_NUMBER; use COMPLEX_NUMBER;
procedure WEIRD_MATH is
    X, Y, Z: COMPLEX;
    SPEED_LIMIT: FLOAT := 55.0;
begin
    X := (3.2, 4.3);
    Y := (1.2, 2.8);
    Z := X + Y;
    X.REAL := Y.IMAGINARY + SPEED_LIMIT; -- the weird part
end WEIRD_MATH;
```

This procedure initializes X and Y to record aggregates and then assigns the sum of X and Y to the complex variable Z. So far, this code uses the complex numbers X, Y, and Z, as one would expect. The next statement, however, violates our concept of a complex number:

```
X.REAL := Y.IMAGINARY + SPEED_LIMIT; -- the weird part
```

Conceptually it makes no sense to assign the sum of the imaginary component of Y and the value of SPEED_LIMIT to the real component of X. In most computer languages, programmers can only trust that users of their code do not abuse such data structures in this way. As we shall see, in Ada, programmers can prohibit such abuse of data structures by defining them as private types. Because the underlying components of a private type are hidden, users cannot abuse them.

So far, we have only encountered packages that are neatly divided into a public part, which is the package specification, and the private part, which is the package body. The package specification, however, may itself contain a private part. This private part is where the implementations of private types are defined:

```
-- package specification with a private part
package package name is
    public declarations
private
    private declarations
end package name;
```

The private part of a package specification begins with the keyword **private** and extends to the end of the specification.

The following version of the COMPLEX_NUMBER package specification makes type COMPLEX a private type:

```
package COMPLEX_NUMBER is

    type COMPLEX is private; -- private type
        -- the only operations on private types are the ones defined in
        -- this package specification, plus the operations =, /=, and :=
```

```
        function "+" (A, B: COMPLEX) return COMPLEX;
        function "-" (A, B: COMPLEX) return COMPLEX;
        function "*" (A, B: COMPLEX) return COMPLEX;
        function "/" (A, B: COMPLEX) return COMPLEX;
        function MAKE_COMPLEX (RE, IM: FLOAT) return COMPLEX;
    private                     -- private part
        -- this information is not available to users of the package

        type COMPLEX is    -- this internal representation is not available
            record         -- to users of this package
                REAL: FLOAT;
                IMAGINARY: FLOAT;
            end record;

    end COMPLEX_NUMBER;
```

Type COMPLEX is declared to be private with the keywords **is private**:

```
    type COMPLEX is private;
```

Private types are only available for packages. Private type declarations appear in the public part of the package specification. The implementations of these private types are defined in the private part of the package specification. Within this private part, private types such as COMPLEX must be fully specified, just as an ordinary type. In our example, COMPLEX is specified to be a record with two components of type FLOAT.

From a user's perspective, items placed in the private part of a package specification are "hidden" just as if these items were placed in the package body. By "hidden" we mean inaccessible, not out of sight. Users of the package can view the record COMPLEX, but, since this record is inaccessible, cannot base their code on what is viewed. Ideally, the record type COMPLEX should be placed out of sight in the package body. The only reason that the record COMPLEX is placed in the private part of the package specification, rather than in the package body, is because the compiler needs to reference COMPLEX. The compiler must know what kind of object is being declared as private and how much memory needs to be allocated for such an object. This information cannot be obtained from the corresponding package body, because, as previously mentioned, package specifications can be compiled separately, without the package bodies.

When the implementation of COMPLEX is placed in the private part of the package specification, users of the package are encouraged to think of complex numbers in the abstract mathematical sense and to ignore the fact that the numbers are implemented using a record. From the user's perspective, it makes no difference whether the complex numbers are implemented as records, arrays, or some other data structure.

Let us now revisit the procedure WEIRD_MATH and see how it is affected by the new version of COMPLEX_NUMBER, where COMPLEX is a private type:

```
with COMPLEX_NUMBER; use COMPLEX_NUMBER;
procedure WEIRD_MATH is
    A, B, C: COMPLEX;
    SPEED_LIMIT: FLOAT := 55.0;
begin
    A := (3.2, 4.3);                              -- illegal
    A := MAKE_COMPLEX (3.2, 4.3);
    B := MAKE_COMPLEX (1.2, 2.8);
    C := A + B;
    A.REAL := B.IMAGINARY + SPEED_LIMIT;  -- now illegal
end WEIRD_MATH;
```

Users of this new version of COMPLEX_NUMBER can now reference complex variables and constants as a whole but cannot reference their real and imaginary components. This means that a complex number cannot be initialized to a record aggregate (record literal):

```
A := (3.2, 4.3); -- illegal;
```

This assignment is illegal because it is based on the knowledge that COMPLEX_NUMBER is implemented as a record with two real components. This information cannot be used. To initialize a complex number to a record aggregate, the function MAKE_COMPLEX was added to the new version of the COMPLEX_NUMBER package. The body of MAKE_COMPLEX, which must be placed in the body of COMPLEX_NUMBER, appears as follows:

```
function MAKE_COMPLEX (RE, IM: FLOAT) return COMPLEX is
begin
    return (RE, IM);
end MAKE_COMPLEX;
```

This function simply returns, as a complex number, the real and imaginary components that were passed in as parameters. MAKE_COMPLEX thus provides the only way for users of the package to assign component values to a record. In general, when private types are employed, the package designer must be careful that all the needed operations on the private types are explicitly provided by subprograms defined in the public part of the package specification. (In package COMPLEX_NUMBER, we should probably also include an overloaded PUT statement for outputting complex numbers.)

In procedure WEIRD_MATH, once A and B are initialized using the MAKE_COMPLEX function, C is assigned the sum of A and B. This assignment is legal since we are operating on complex numbers as a whole.

The next statement, the objectionable assignment, is now illegal, as desired:

```
A.REAL := B.IMAGINARY + SPEED_LIMIT; -- illegal
```

This assignment is illegal because, as mentioned, the components of COMPLEX_NUMBER cannot be accessed.

By declaring a type to be private, we not only make the underlying implementation of the type inaccessible; we also restrict the predefined operations that can be performed on objects of this type. Only three predefined operations can be performed on objects of a private type: assignments and tests for equality and inequality. (A few attributes can also apply to private types.) Any additional operations must be explicitly provided in the package specification where the private type is declared. In our example, the additional operations—"+", "-", "*", and "/"—are explicitly provided in the package specification of COMPLEX_NUMBER.

Even though only three predefined operations can be performed on objects of a private type, in our example, this is not a restriction. The private type COMPLEX is implemented as a record, and records are already restricted to these three predefined operations. If a private type, though, is implemented as an integer type, then users of the package are restricted. They cannot employ the operations usually allowed for integers, such as addition, subtraction, multiplication, and division.

As we have seen, the private part of the package specification of COMPLEX_NUMBER only contains the full declaration of the private type COMPLEX. Other items, however, may be placed in this private part. For example, we may declare each component of the record COMPLEX to belong to a floating point subtype instead of to type FLOAT:

```
    ...
private
    subtype COMPONENT_TYPE is FLOAT range 0.0 .. 1_000.0;
        -- not a full declaration of a private type
    type COMPLEX is
        record
            REAL: COMPONENT_TYPE;
            IMAGINARY: COMPONENT_TYPE;
        end record;

end COMPLEX_NUMBER;
```

Subtype COMPONENT_TYPE is declared in the private part of the package specification. This is appropriate since it is merely provided to implement type COMPLEX and is of no concern to users. Private types, however, cannot be subtypes. Thus, the private type COMPLEX cannot be declared as a subtype.

Another point to consider is that, except for subprogram bodies, every item in the declarative part of a package body can be relocated to the private part of its corresponding package specification. This is not advised, however, because changes to a package are best made in the package body rather than in the package specification. As previously mentioned, changes to the package body usually do not require any other unit of code to be recompiled. Changes to a package specification require that every program unit that mentions the specification in its **with** clause also be recompiled.

Once a type is declared to be private, constants of this private type can be declared in the public part of the package specification, so they will be available to users. Declaring such constants, however, creates a dilemma. Thus far in this book, we have seen that all constants must be initialized when they are declared. Constants that belong to a private type, however, cannot be assigned an initial value because the implementation of the private type has not yet been declared. For example, suppose that we wish to declare the constant I, which represents the imaginary unit of a complex number. The imaginary unit of a complex number is represented by the record aggregate, (0.0, 1.0), where the real component is 0.0 and the imaginary component is 1.0. (Those with a mathematical background will recall that such an imaginary unit represents the square root of -1.) We cannot initialize I to the record aggregate (0.0, 1.0) in the declaration of I, because the implementation of objects of type COMPLEX has not yet been defined:

```
package COMPLEX_NUMBER is
    type COMPLEX is private;
    I: constant COMPLEX := (0.0, 1.0); -- illegal; the implementation of
                                       -- COMPLEX has not yet been defined
    ...
```

The solution to our dilemma is to use deferred constants. When a deferred constant is declared, the specification of its value is deferred until after the private type to which it belongs is fully declared:

```
package COMPLEX_NUMBER is

    type COMPLEX is private;
    I: constant COMPLEX; -- deferred constant

    function "+" (A, B: COMPLEX) return COMPLEX;
    function "-" (A, B: COMPLEX) return COMPLEX;
    function "*" (A, B: COMPLEX) return COMPLEX;
    function "/" (A, B: COMPLEX) return COMPLEX;
    function MAKE_COMPLEX (RE, IM: FLOAT) return COMPLEX;

private

    type COMPLEX is
        record
            REAL: FLOAT;
            IMAGINARY: FLOAT;
        end record;

    I: constant COMPLEX := (REAL => 0.0, IMAGINARY => 1.0);
        -- full declaration of constant

end COMPLEX_NUMBER;
```

The full declaration of the constant I, including its value, is placed in the private part of the package specification, following the full declaration of COMPLEX.

In summary, private types permit designers of a package to impose their data abstractions upon users of the package. This is accomplished in two ways. First, a private type is visible, while its underlying implementation is hidden. Users of the package can then reference a private type but cannot fiddle around with irrelevant implementation details. Second, a private type restricts the kind of operations that can be performed on its objects. Thus, only operations that make sense for a particular abstract type are allowed. (Within the package itself, however, such restrictions do not apply. The underlying representation of the private type is visible, and any operations normally available can be used.)

LIMITED PRIVATE TYPES

As previously mentioned, from outside a package, the only predefined operations that automatically apply to private types are assignments and tests for equality and inequality. The designer of the package may even forbid these operations by declaring a limited private type. With a limited private type, the only operations allowed are those provided in the package along with the type. (A few predefined attributes can apply to objects of a private type or of a limited private type. For instance, the attribute ADDRESS yields the address where an object is stored.) The programmer thus takes complete control over how objects of a limited private type are used.

Limited private types are declared just like private types, except that the keywords **is limited private** are used. The private part of the package specification is still denoted by the keyword **private**:

```
package COMPLEX_NUMBER is

    -- visible part
    type COMPLEX is limited private; -- limited private type
        -- the only operations on limited private types are the ones defined
        -- in this package specification

    function "+" (A, B: COMPLEX) return COMPLEX;
    function "-" (A, B: COMPLEX) return COMPLEX;
    function "*" (A, B: COMPLEX) return COMPLEX;
    function "/" (A, B: COMPLEX) return COMPLEX;
    function MAKE_COMPLEX (RE, IM: FLOAT) return COMPLEX;

    function "=" (A, B: COMPLEX) return BOOLEAN;
        -- takes the place of missing predefined equality test, "="
        -- as a result, "/=" is automatically overloaded
```

procedure COPY (FROM: **in** COMPLEX; TO: **out** COMPLEX);
-- takes the place of missing assignment operator, ":="

private   -- private part
-- this information is not available to users of the package

type COMPLEX **is**
  record
    REAL: FLOAT;
    IMAGINARY: FLOAT;
  end record;

end COMPLEX_NUMBER;

Outside of the package, objects belonging to a limited private type may not even be assigned to one another or tested for equality or inequality. (These restrictions, however, do not apply within the package in which the limited private type is declared.) To compensate for these missing operations, the overloaded equality operator "=" and the procedure COPY have been added to the package. Although the equality operator cannot be overloaded for normal types, it may be overloaded for limited private types. With the overloaded operator "=", users of the package can test whether objects of the limited private type COMPLEX are equal. The inequality operator "/=" cannot be explicitly declared but is implicitly provided when "=" is declared. In other words, "/=" is automatically provided since it takes its meaning from "=". Unlike the equality operator, the assignment operator, ":=", can never be overloaded. The procedure COPY, which has the effect of an assignment operator, is thus provided. For example, assuming that A and B are complex variables, the following procedure call assigns the value of A to the variable B:

COPY (FROM => A, TO => B);

The restriction against employing the assignment operator for objects of a limited private type extends to other situations where values are copied. For instance, users of a package may not declare an object of a limited private type with an assigned initial value. This means that outside of the package, constants belonging to a limited private type cannot be declared. (Once again, these restrictions only apply to external users of the package, not within the package containing the limited private type.)

In our example, declaring COMPLEX to be a limited private type is not particularly useful. Limited private types are most useful when assignments and tests for equality or inequality either do not make sense for the type in question or would be incorrect, based on the implementation of the type.

The next example is a useful version of the STACK package that defines a stack as a limited private type:

```ada
package STACK is

    type STACK_TYPE (STACK_SIZE: NATURAL) is limited private;
        -- limited private means that the only operations on stacks are the
        -- ones defined in this package specification

    function IS_EMPTY (S: in STACK_TYPE) return BOOLEAN;
    function IS_FULL (S: in STACK_TYPE) return BOOLEAN;

    procedure PUSH (S: in out STACK_TYPE; ITEM: in INTEGER);
    procedure POP (S: in out STACK_TYPE; ITEM: out INTEGER);

    function "=" (LEFT, RIGHT: in STACK_TYPE) return BOOLEAN;
    procedure COPY (FROM: in STACK_TYPE; TO: out STACK_TYPE);
    procedure CLEAR (S: in out STACK_TYPE);

private
    -- this information cannot be used by the users of the package

    type INTEGER_ARRAY is array (NATURAL range <>) of INTEGER;

    type STACK_TYPE (STACK_SIZE: NATURAL) is
        record
            STK: INTEGER_ARRAY (1 .. STACK_SIZE) := (others => 0);
            TOP: NATURAL := 0;
        end record;
end STACK;


with TEXT_IO; use TEXT_IO;
package body STACK is
    function IS_EMPTY (S: STACK_TYPE) return BOOLEAN is
    begin
        return S.TOP = 0;
    end IS_EMPTY;

    function IS_FULL (S: STACK_TYPE) return BOOLEAN is
    begin
        return S.TOP = S.STACK_SIZE;
    end IS_FULL;

    procedure PUSH (S: in out STACK_TYPE; ITEM: in INTEGER) is
    begin
        if IS_FULL (S) then
            PUT_LINE ("ERROR: Stack Overflow");
        else
            S.TOP := S.TOP + 1;
            S.STK (S.TOP) := ITEM;
        end if;
    end PUSH;

    procedure POP (S: in out STACK_TYPE; ITEM: out INTEGER) is
    begin
        if IS_EMPTY (S) then
            PUT_LINE ("ERROR: Stack Underflow");
```

```ada
        else
            ITEM := S.STK (S.TOP);
            S.TOP := S.TOP - 1;
        end if;
    end POP;

    function "=" (LEFT, RIGHT: STACK_TYPE) return BOOLEAN is
    begin
        -- only compares valid part of stacks
        return LEFT.TOP = RIGHT.TOP and then
            (LEFT.STK (1 .. LEFT.TOP) = RIGHT.STK (1 .. RIGHT.TOP) );
    end "=";

    procedure COPY (FROM: in STACK_TYPE; TO: out STACK_TYPE) is
    begin
        -- checks whether there is room in the destination stack for a copy
        if FROM.TOP > TO.STACK_SIZE then
            PUT_LINE ("ERROR: Stack Overflow");
        else
            -- copies stack items
            TO.TOP := FROM.TOP;
            TO.STK (1 .. TO.TOP) := FROM.STK (1 .. FROM.TOP);
        end if;
    end COPY;

    procedure CLEAR (S: in out STACK_TYPE) is
    begin
        -- only resets TOP; does not fill array with zeros
        S.TOP := 0;
    end CLEAR;

end STACK;
```

This package is more sophisticated that the previous stack package. We have added resources such as IS_EMPTY, which informs us whether a stack is empty; IS_FULL, which informs us whether a stack is full; the equality operator "=", which compares two stacks; the procedure COPY, which replaces the assignment operator; and the procedure CLEAR, which resets the stack to the beginning. Furthermore, PUSH and POP (POP is now a procedure) contain two parameters instead of one. The added parameter specifies the particular integer stack to manipulate. Thus, multiple integer stacks can be maintained. In addition, the stack is now implemented as a variant record type, STACK_TYPE, instead of as an array. The record discriminant, STACK_SIZE, sets the size of the stack. Therefore, users of this package may declare different sized integer stacks as follows:

```ada
    MY_STACK: STACK_TYPE (50);      -- creates an integer stack of size 50
    YOUR_STACK: STACK_TYPE (33);    -- creates an integer stack of size 33
```

To push or pop an item, include the name of the desired stack:

```
PUSH (MY_STACK, 10);     -- pushes the value 10 on MY_STACK
PUSH (YOUR_STACK, 5);    -- pushes the value 5 on YOUR_STACK
POP (MY_STACK, ITEM);    -- pops the value 10 from MY_STACK and returns
                         -- this value in the integer variable ITEM
```

Finally, note that PUSH and POP invoke the functions IS_FULL and IS_EMPTY, respectively, before attempting to push or pop an item. For example, if the stack is empty and POP is called, then POP determines that the stack is empty and outputs an error message. In Chapter 11, we will see that a better way to handle such overflow or underflow conditions is by raising user-defined exceptions. Since the specifications of IS_FULL and IS_EMPTY are placed in the package specification, these functions are also available to users of the package.

Library packages should be made as general as possible so that they can be used by many different programs. Generics are one of the most powerful methods for making packages, and other program units, as general as possible. Generics are the subject of the next chapter.

EXERCISES

1. Describe the difference between the **with** clause and the **use** clause. Describe the advantages and disadvantages of employing the **use** clause.

2. How do packages differ from subprograms? How do package specifications differ from package bodies?

3. Write a package that contains an enumeration type PERSONAL_COMPUTERS, which consists of brands of various personal computers. Include a constant of type PERSONAL_COMPUTER called BEST_COMPUTER.

4. Find all the errors in the following packages, ignoring the fact that the package bodies would rarely serve any purpose. (Lines indicate separate compilation units.)

    ```
    package P1 is
       subtype P1_SPEC is INTEGER range 1 .. 10;
       A: P1_SPEC;
    end P1;
    ```

    ```
    package body P1 is
       B: P1_SPEC;
    ```

```
      subtype P1_BODY is CHARACTER range 'A' .. 'Z';
      C: P1_BODY;
   end P1;

   with P1; use P1;
   package P2 is
      D: P1_SPEC;
      E: P1_BODY;
      subtype P2_SPEC is INTEGER range 1 .. 10;
      F: P2_SPEC;
   end P2;

   package body P2 is
      G: P1_SPEC;
      H: P1_BODY;
      I: P2_SPEC;
      subtype P2_BODY is CHARACTER range 'A' .. 'Z';
      J: P2_BODY;
   end P2;
```

5. Find all the errors in the declarative part of procedure Q, ignoring the fact that the package bodies would rarely serve any purpose:

```
   procedure Q is
      package P1 is
         subtype P1_SPEC is INTEGER range 1 .. 10;
         A: P1_SPEC;
      end P1;

      B: P1.P1_SPEC;
      use P1;
      C: P1_SPEC;
      subtype OUTSIDE is FLOAT range 0.0 .. 5.0;

      package P2 is
         D: P1_SPEC;
         E: OUTSIDE;
         subtype P2_SPEC is INTEGER range 1 .. 10;
         F: P2_SPEC;
      end P2;

      package body P1 is
         G: P1_SPEC;
         H: P2_SPEC;
         I: OUTSIDE;
         subtype P1_BODY is CHARACTER range 'A' .. 'Z';
         J: P1_BODY;
      end P1;
```

```
        package body P2 is
            K: P1_SPEC;
            L: P1_BODY;
            M: P2_SPEC;
        end P2;
    begin -- Q
        null;
    end Q;
```

6. Which variables, A to M, are available to the executable statement part of procedure Q in exercise 5?

7. Find all the errors in the following code:

```
    package P1 is
        subtype P1_SPEC is INTEGER range 1 .. 10;
    end P1;
```

```
    with P1; use P1;
    package P2 is
        A: P1_SPEC;
        subtype P2_SPEC is CHARACTER range 'A' .. 'Z';
    end P2;
```

```
    with P2; use P2;
    package P3 is
        B: P1_SPEC;
        C: P2_SPEC;
        subtype P3_SPEC is INTEGER range 0 .. 10;
    end P3;
```

```
    with P1; use P1;
    package body P3 is
        D: P1_SPEC;
        E: P2_SPEC;
        F: P3_SPEC;
    end P3;
```

8. What will each of the following PUT statements in procedure Q output? (Note: one of these PUT statements contains an error.)

```
    package P1 is
        A, B, C, D: CHARACTER := 'X';
    end P1;
```

```
        package P2 is
            C, D, E: CHARACTER := 'Y';
        end P2;
```

```
    with TEXT_IO, P1, P2; use TEXT_IO, P1, P2;
    procedure Q is
       B, C: CHARACTER := 'Z';
    begin
       -- one of these is illegal
       PUT (A); NEW_LINE;
       PUT (B); NEW_LINE;
       PUT (C); NEW_LINE;
       PUT (D); NEW_LINE;
       PUT (E); NEW_LINE;
    end Q;
```

9. Fix the errors in the following code without employing the use clause:

```
package D_SCALE is
   type D_MAJOR is (D, E, F_SHARP, G, A, B, C_SHARP);
end D_SCALE;
```

```
with TEXT_IO;
with D_SCALE;
procedure NOTE_WORTHY is
   package SCALE_IO is new ENUMERATION_IO (D_MAJOR);
   NOTE: D_MAJOR := D;
begin
   GET (NOTE);
   if NOTE = D_MAJOR'FIRST then
      PUT_LINE ("First note of scale");
   end if;
end NOTE_WORTHY;
```

10. Write a package (specification and body) that enables users to multiply and divide fractions. Represent these fractions as a record with two integer components:

```
type FRACTION is
   record
      NUMERATOR: INTEGER;
      DENOMINATOR: INTEGER;
   end record;
```

Thus, the fraction 3/5 can be represented as the record aggregate (3, 5), and the fraction 14/5 as (14, 5).

11. In case you have not done so, enhance the package you wrote for exercise 10 so that each operator returns a fraction in reduced form. For example, if the answer is (6, 15), then reduce it to (2, 5). To help reduce the fractions, you may wish to use the following recursive function:

```
function GCD (A, B: INTEGER) return INTEGER is
begin
  if B = 0 then
    return A;
  else
    return GCD (B, A mod B);
  end if;
end GCD;
```

For example, to reduce (6, 15), simply divide both 6 and 15 by GCD(6,15). Should the function GCD appear in the package specification or the package body?

12. Modify the package you wrote for exercise 11 so that type FRACTION is a private type. Add an additional subprogram to the package to allow users to assign a value (literal) to objects of type FRACTION.

13. Modify the package you wrote for exercise 12 so that the type FRACTION is a limited private type. Add new subprograms to the package to allow users to perform assignment operations and to test fractions to determine whether they are equal.

14. Enhance the package of exercises 11, 12, or 13 to enable users to also add and subtract fractions.

15. Consider the following package that contains a private type:

```
package COUNTER is
  type ELEMENT is private;
  function SET_ELEMENT return ELEMENT;
  function INCREMENT (ITEM: ELEMENT) return ELEMENT;
private
  type ELEMENT is new INTEGER;
    -- this is a "derived" type (covered in Chapter 13)
    -- type ELEMENT is a copy of type INTEGER
end COUNTER;

package body COUNTER is
  function SET_ELEMENT return ELEMENT is
  begin
    return 1;
  end SET_ELEMENT;

  function INCREMENT (ITEM: ELEMENT) return ELEMENT is
  begin
    return ITEM + 1;
  end INCREMENT;
end COUNTER;
```

Which of the following statements illegally attempt to reference items from the package COUNTER that are hidden?

```
with TEXT_IO, COUNTER; use TEXT_IO, COUNTER;
procedure DEMO is
   X, Y, Z: ELEMENT;
begin
   Z := SET_ELEMENT;
   Y := INCREMENT (Z);
   X := Z;
   if X = Y then
      PUT_LINE ("Equal");
   end if;
   if X = 2 then
      PUT_LINE ("Equals 2");
   end if;
   X := 4;
   Y := SET_ELEMENT + 1;
end DEMO;
```

16. Which statements in exercise 15 would be illegal if ELEMENT were a limited private type?

17. In one of the COMPLEX_NUMBER packages presented in this chapter, implement type COMPLEX as an array type instead of as a record type.

Chapter 9

GENERICS

Generics are a very important feature of Ada. Few other computer languages have anything resembling generics. Therefore, the concepts in this chapter should be new to most programmers, even those who already know languages such as Pascal.

Generics, or generic units, act as a template from which actual nongeneric units can be created. What makes generic units useful is that they can greatly reduce the amount of redundant code. This is similar to the way a form letter program eliminates the need to write redundant letters. Users of a form letter program create a form letter by substituting certain information, such as a person's name and address, with special symbols. When letters are printed, these special symbols are replaced with actual names and addresses, which are stored in a separate file. The letter is thus written only once, and many copies, differing only in certain information, are created.

Similarly, Ada programmers create a generic unit, substituting such information as the type (INTEGER, FLOAT, etc.) to which an object belongs with a "dummy" name, or formal parameter. When the generic unit is used as a template to create a nongeneric unit, this dummy name is replaced with the name of the actual type. This process of creating a nongeneric unit from a generic unit is known as generic instantiation. Using generic instantiation, a generic unit is thus written only once, and many actual units can be instantiated that perform the same processing but on objects of different types.

Note that generic units cannot be used in the same manner as actual units. Generic functions and procedures cannot be invoked; only the actual functions and procedures created by instantiating these generic units can be invoked. Similarly, the resources of a generic package cannot be accessed; only the resources of its instantiated "copies" may be accessed.

There are three kinds of generic units: generic functions, generic procedures, and generic packages. In this chapter, we will discuss these three kinds of generic units. As we show examples of generic units, we will also introduce three different kinds of generic parameters: type parameters, object parameters, and subprogram parameters. Subprogram parameters are sufficiently involved to merit a separate section at the end of this chapter.

GENERIC FUNCTIONS

To illustrate how generic functions can be used to eliminate redundant code, we will consider three different nongeneric functions. Each of these functions does the same processing but on objects of different data types. We will then see how a generic function enables us to eliminate the redundant code by writing the implementation of these functions only once instead of three times.

The first function compares two integers and returns the value of the larger integer:

```
function LARGER_INTEGER (X, Y: INTEGER) return INTEGER is
begin
    if X > Y then
        return X;
    else
        return Y;
    end if;
end LARGER_INTEGER;
```

Note that this function only returns the larger of two _integer_ values. If we need a function that returns the "larger" of two _character_ values, then a new function must be written. This is our second function, MAX_CHARACTER:

```
function MAX_CHARACTER (X, Y: CHARACTER)
    return CHARACTER is
begin
    if X > Y then
        return X;
```

```
        else
            return Y;
        end if;
    end MAX_CHARACTER;
```

For a third example, consider a function that, given two planets, returns the planet that is farthest from the sun. (Ignore the fact that during certain times, Pluto is closer to the sun than Neptune.)

```
    type SOLAR_SYSTEM is ( MERCURY, VENUS, EARTH, MARS, JUPITER,
                           SATURN , URANUS, NEPTUNE, PLUTO);
    function OUTER_PLANET (X, Y: SOLAR_SYSTEM) return
        SOLAR_SYSTEM is
    begin
        if X > Y then
            return X;
        else
            return Y;
        end if;
    end OUTER_PLANET;
```

Note that the reason this function "knows," for instance, that NEPTUNE > VENUS, is not because Ada compilers come with a built-in knowledge of basic astronomy but because of the order of the enumeration literals MERCURY to PLUTO.

The three functions—LARGER_INTEGER, MAX_CHARACTER, and OUTER_PLANET—basically do the same thing: they return the larger of two values. The only difference between the functions is that they operate on different types of data: integers, characters, and planets. Writing different functions to handle each data type, as we have done, results in redundant code. Redundant code is not a significant problem if the functions are as short as these three examples. However, if the functions require many lines of code, then redundant code is a problem. First, redundant code is error prone because errors can be easily introduced when duplicating many lines of source code. Second, redundant code is difficult to maintain because, if one function containing this code needs to be modified, every other function containing the same code will probably have to be modified. Third, and least important, redundant code wastes computer storage space because more space is needed to store all the duplicate source code (Ada code) and the resulting object code (binary machine code).

Some computer languages partially avoid redundant code by allowing data types to be passed in at runtime as parameters to regular subprograms. In strongly typed languages like Ada, however, types cannot be passed in at runtime because the type of every data object must be determined at compilation time.

Although data types cannot be passed to subprograms during runtime, they can be "passed" to generic units during compilation time when these units are instantiated. The result of this generic instantiation is the creation of an actual subprogram that can reference the type that was passed in. There is, therefore, no uncertainty at compilation time about the type to which any object belongs.

Let us now return to the problem of redundant code illustrated by the three preceding functions: LARGER_INTEGER, MAX_CHARACTER, and OUTER_PLANET. Instead of having three copies of essentially the same function, a single generic function can be written. From this single generic function, the three functions can be instantiated.

A generic function has two parts, a generic specification and a body:

```
-- generic specification
generic
    generic formal parameters
function function name (parameter definitions) return type;

-- body
function function name (parameter definitions) return type is
    declarations
begin
    statements
end function name;
```

The first part of the generic unit is the generic specification. The generic specification is the visible part that acts as an interface to those who instantiate the generic function. The generic specification begins with the keyword **generic**. Between the keywords **generic** and **function** is the list of formal generic parameters. Formal generic parameters act like placeholders, or replaceable dummy names. When a generic unit is instantiated, these formal generic parameters are replaced by actual parameters. Following the formal generic parameters is the standard function specification. The second part of the generic unit is the body, which is indistinguishable from the bodies of regular nongeneric functions. Note that the function specification must appear in both the generic specification and in the generic body.

The generic function from which LARGER_INTEGER, MAX_CHARACTER, and OUTER_PLANET can be instantiated appears as follows:

```
generic                                  -- generic specification
    type ITEM is (<>);
function MAXIMUM (X, Y: ITEM) return ITEM;

function MAXIMUM (X, Y: ITEM) return ITEM is    -- body
begin
    if X > Y then
        return X;
```

```
        else
            return Y;
        end if;
end MAXIMUM;
```

A generic function can have an unlimited number of formal generic parameters; the generic function MAXIMUM has only one, ITEM:

   type ITEM **is** (<>);

The keyword **type** tells us that ITEM is a formal generic type. The actual type that will replace ITEM is determined when this generic function is instantiated. The notation (<>) indicates that the actual type that will replace ITEM must be a discrete type. (As we will see, other notation is used for integer types, etc.) Following the formal generic parameter is a standard function specification for MAXIMUM.

The second part of the generic unit is the body. The body of MAXIMUM contains the implementation of the function and is the same as the bodies of functions LARGER_INTEGER, MAX_CHARACTER, and OUTER_PLANET. Note, however, that X and Y are of type ITEM, which is eventually replaced with an actual type. The body, then, can operate on objects whose types are determined at the time the generic unit is instantiated.

Given this generic function MAXIMUM, the functions LARGER_INTEGER, MAX_CHARACTER, and OUTER_PLANET can all be created by instantiating MAXIMUM as follows:

   function LARGER_INTEGER **is new** MAXIMUM (ITEM => INTEGER);
   function MAX_CHARACTER **is new** MAXIMUM (ITEM => CHARACTER);
   function OUTER_PLANET **is new** MAXIMUM (ITEM => SOLAR_SYSTEM);

As we can see, a generic instantiation of a function begins with the keyword **function**, followed by the user-supplied function name, followed by the keywords **is new**. Next comes the name of the generic function that is to be instantiated. Note that generic functions can only be instantiated to create functions, never to create procedures or packages. (A parallel remark is true for generic procedures and packages.) Following the name of the generic function, MAXIMUM, and placed within parentheses, are the actual generic parameters: INTEGER, CHARACTER, and SOLAR_SYSTEM. At the time of instantiation, these actual generic parameters are matched, either through positional or named notation, with the formal generic parameter ITEM. The three preceding instantiations use named notation, denoted by the arrow, =>. In the first instantiation, for example, the actual generic parameter, INTEGER, is matched, using named notation, with the formal generic parameter ITEM. The actual type, INTEGER, therefore, replaces the "dummy" type ITEM. Within the generic function MAXIMUM, variables X and Y, which were declared to belong to type ITEM, are now integer variables. Therefore, in the body of MAXIMUM, when a test is made whether X > Y, the values of two integer variables, X and Y, are being compared.

Be careful not to confuse the formal parameters of MAXIMUM, which are X and Y, with its generic formal parameter, ITEM. As we have seen, the generic formal parameter ITEM is passed a value when MAXIMUM is generically instantiated. The formal parameters X and Y, however, are passed actual values at runtime when the three functions created by instantiating MAXIMUM are invoked.

As shown in the following code, once the functions LARGER_INTEGER, MAX_CHARACTER, and OUTER_PLANET are created through generic instantiations, they can be used as if they were created "normally":

```
declare
    INT: INTEGER;
    CHAR: CHARACTER;
    PLANET: SOLAR_SYSTEM;
begin
    INT := LARGER_INTEGER (X => 5, Y => 1);        -- returns 5
    CHAR := MAX_CHARACTER (X => 'A', Y => 'Z');    -- returns 'Z'
    PLANET := OUTER_PLANET (X => JUPITER, Y => EARTH);
        -- returns JUPITER
    . . .
end;
```

Our problem of code redundancy is now solved. The source code that implements three functions is now contained in only one place, in the body of the generic function MAXIMUM. The object code, however, is handled differently by different compilers. Ada does not specify how object code is to be handled. Some compilers create the object code for MAXIMUM only once, no matter how many times this generic function is instantiated. Each function created by instantiating the same generic function thus shares the same object code. This results in a smaller load module but in code that takes longer to execute. Other compilers copy the object code for MAXIMUM every time this generic function is instantiated. The result is more object code but faster execution speed. The preferable approach depends on which is more important, computer memory or execution speed. An ideal compiler allows either option.

The user "tells" the Ada compiler whether space or time is more important by placing a pragma called OPTIMIZE in the declarative part of a program unit. (A pragma is a compiler directive. See Appendix B for a complete list of pragmas.) OPTIMIZE has two possible parameter values, SPACE and TIME. The following statement tells the compiler that whenever there is a trade-off between space and time, space should be the overriding concern:

pragma OPTIMIZE (SPACE);

Alternatively, the following statement tells the compiler that time should be the overriding concern:

pragma OPTIMIZE (TIME);

GENERIC PROCEDURES

Generic procedures are handled like generic functions. To demonstrate the need for generic procedures, let us again begin by considering several nongeneric procedures that perform the same tasks but on different data types. The following nongeneric procedure, PRINT_SOLAR_SYSTEM, prints all the planets of the solar system:

```
with TEXT_IO; use TEXT_IO;
procedure PRINT_SOLAR_SYSTEM is
    type SOLAR_SYSTEM is (MERCURY, VENUS, EARTH, MARS,
                JUPITER, SATURN, URANUS, NEPTUNE, PLUTO);
    package SOLAR_SYSTEM_IO is new
            ENUMERATION_IO (SOLAR_SYSTEM);
    use SOLAR_SYSTEM_IO;
begin
    for PLANET in SOLAR_SYSTEM loop
        PUT (PLANET);
        NEW_LINE;
    end loop;
end PRINT_SOLAR_SYSTEM;
```

Similarly, the next procedure, PRINT_MUSIC_TYPES, prints all the different kinds of music listed in the enumeration type MUSIC_TYPES:

```
with TEXT_IO; use TEXT_IO;
procedure PRINT_MUSIC_TYPES is
    type MUSIC_TYPES is (JAZZ, FOLK, BLUES, BLUEGRASS, KLEZMER,
                POP);
    package MUSIC_TYPE_IO is new ENUMERATION_IO (MUSIC_TYPES);
    use MUSIC_TYPE_IO;
begin
    for MUSIC in MUSIC_TYPES loop
        PUT (MUSIC);
        NEW_LINE;
    end loop;
end PRINT_MUSIC_TYPES;
```

These two procedures, PRINT_SOLAR_SYSTEM and PRINT_MUSIC_TYPES, do the same thing: they output the items of an enumeration type. The only difference between the procedures is that they output different enumeration types: planets and kinds of music. Writing different functions to handle each data type results in redundant code. This redundant code can be eliminated by writing a single generic procedure. Instead of showing this generic procedure out of context, we will show how it fits into a complete Ada program. In this program, the generic procedure PRINT_ENUMERATION_TYPE is embedded into the procedure MAIN. The result is a complete Ada program consisting of a single compilation unit:

```ada
with TEXT_IO; use TEXT_IO;
procedure MAIN is

    type SOLAR_SYSTEM is (MERCURY, VENUS, EARTH, MARS,
                          JUPITER, SATURN, URANUS, NEPTUNE,
                          PLUTO);
    type MUSIC_TYPES is (JAZZ, FOLK, BLUES, BLUEGRASS, KLEZMER,
                         POP);

    generic                                     -- generic specification
        type ENUM_TYPE is (<>);
    procedure PRINT_ENUMERATION_TYPE;

    procedure PRINT_ENUMERATION_TYPE is   -- body
        package ENUM_TYPE_IO is new ENUMERATION_IO (ENUM_TYPE);
        use ENUM_TYPE_IO;
    begin
        for ITEM in ENUM_TYPE loop
            PUT (ITEM);
            NEW_LINE;
        end loop;
    end PRINT_ENUMERATION_TYPE;

    procedure PRINT_SOLAR_SYSTEM is new      -- generic instantiation
        PRINT_ENUMERATION_TYPE (ENUM_TYPE => SOLAR_SYSTEM);

    procedure PRINT_MUSIC_TYPES is new       -- generic instantiation
        PRINT_ENUMERATION_TYPE (ENUM_TYPE => MUSIC_TYPES);

begin -- MAIN

    PRINT_SOLAR_SYSTEM; -- prints planets of solar system
    PRINT_MUSIC_TYPES; -- prints kinds of music
end MAIN;
```

The first two declarations in **procedure** MAIN define the enumeration types SOLAR_SYSTEM and TYPES_OF_MUSIC. These two declarations are followed by the specification and body of PRINT_ENUMERATION_TYPE. PRINT_ENUMERATION_TYPE is then generically instantiated, using the actual generic parameters SOLAR_SYSTEM and MUSIC_TYPES. When PRINT_ENUMERATION_TYPE is instantiated, the procedures

PRINT_SOLAR_SYSTEM and PRINT_MUSIC_TYPES are created and available to the body of procedure MAIN. When MAIN invokes PRINT_SOLAR_SYSTEM, all the planets of the solar system from MERCURY to PLUTO are output. When MAIN invokes PRINT_MUSIC_TYPES, all the types of music from JAZZ to POP are output.

Note once again that we have created two procedures—PRINT_SOLAR_SYSTEM and PRINT_MUSIC_TYPES—but coded the implementation of these procedures just once, in the body of PRINT_ENUMERATION_TYPE. We could create an indefinite number of these same procedures, each one outputting a different enumeration type, by simply instantiating PRINT_ENUMERATION_TYPE with different actual generic parameters.

Let us consider one more example of a generic procedure. This time, instead of first reviewing various versions of nongeneric procedures, we will immediately show the generic procedure. This generic procedure swaps the values of two objects:

```
generic                           --generic specification
    type ITEM is private;
procedure SWAP_THEM (LEFT, RIGHT : in out ITEM);

procedure SWAP_THEM (LEFT, RIGHT : in out ITEM) is        --body
    TEMP: ITEM := LEFT;
begin
    LEFT := RIGHT;
    RIGHT := TEMP;
end SWAP_THEM;
```

In the preceding generic specification, note the new form of the formal generic parameter, ITEM:

type ITEM **is private**;

Our previous examples used the symbol (<>) instead of the keyword **private**. The difference between (<>) and **private** has to do with the types that can be used to instantiate the generic unit.

The symbol (<>) means that the generic unit can be instantiated only with discrete types. Because of this restriction (enforced by the Ada compiler), the body of the generic unit may only contain operators that operate on discrete types. These are the relational operators =, /=, >, >=, <, and <=; the assignment operator := ; and attributes such as PRED, SUCC, FIRST, and LAST.

The keyword **private** means that the generic procedure SWAP_THEM can be instantiated with any type (except a limited private type): scalar types (INTEGER, FLOAT, BOOLEAN, etc.) and even composite types (records and arrays). But there is a price to pay. Because any type is allowed, the body of the generic unit can only contain operators that are allowed on

244 Rendezvous with ADA: A Programmer's Introduction

all data types. Only equality testing (=, /=) and assignments (:=) meet this stringent requirement. For the body of the generic procedure SWAP_THEM, however, the limited choice of operators is no problem because only the assignment operator is used.

The following code shows how the generic procedure SWAP_THEM can be instantiated with integer types, character types, enumeration types, record types, and array types:

```
declare
    procedure SWAP is new SWAP_THEM (ITEM => INTEGER);
    procedure SWAP is new SWAP_THEM (ITEM => CHARACTER);
    type AI is (NEURAL_NETWORKS, EXPERT_SYSTEMS);
    procedure SWAP is new SWAP_THEM (ITEM => AI);
    type COMPLEX is
        record
            RE, IM : FLOAT;
        end record;
    procedure SWAP is new SWAP_THEM (ITEM => COMPLEX);
    type VECTOR is array (1..5) of FLOAT;
    procedure SWAP is new SWAP_THEM (ITEM => VECTOR);
    INT_1: INTEGER := 5;
    INT_2: INTEGER := 7;
    CHAR_1: CHARACTER := 'A';
    CHAR_2: CHARACTER := 'D';
    AI_1 : AI := NEURAL_NETWORKS;
    AI_2 : AI := EXPERT_SYSTEMS;
    COMP_1: COMPLEX := (3.5, 2.1);
    COMP_2: COMPLEX := (4.4, 1.0);
    VECT_1: VECTOR := (1.0, 2.0, 3.0, 4.0, 5.0);
    VECT_2: VECTOR := (6.0, 7.0, 8.0, 9.0, 10.0);
begin
    SWAP (LEFT => AI_1, RIGHT => AI_2);
    SWAP (LEFT => INT_1, RIGHT => INT_2);
    SWAP (LEFT => CHAR_1, RIGHT => CHAR_2);
    SWAP (LEFT => COMP_1, RIGHT => COMP_2);
    SWAP (LEFT => VECT_1, RIGHT => VECT_2);
    . . .
end;
```

In this code, five overloaded instances of SWAP are created by instantiating the generic procedure SWAP_THEM. To determine which SWAP procedure is being used, the compiler checks the actual parameters of SWAP. For instance, if the actual parameters are integer variables, then the version of the SWAP procedure that swaps integer values is used.

In the first executable statement of the preceding code, the values of AI_1 and AI_2 are swapped. Before the swap is made, AI_1 has the value NEURAL_NETWORKS, and AI_2 has the value EXPERT_SYSTEMS. After the swap, their values are exchanged: AI_1 has the value EXPERT_SYSTEMS, and AI_2 has the value NEURAL_NETWORKS. The other SWAP procedures operate in the same manner.

In addition to the keyword **private** and the symbol (<>), there are other type specifications that can be used in formal generic parameters. Table 9-1 lists these formal generic type parameters, together with the operations and data types allowed.

Table 9.1 Generic Type Parameters

Type Parameters	Operations Allowed	Data Types Allowed
type ANY_TYPE **is private**;	=, /=, :=	Discrete, FLOAT, array, record, private
type DISCRETE_TYPE **is** (<>);	=, /=, :=, >, >=, <, <=, PRED, SUCC, FIRST, LAST	Discrete
type INTEGER_TYPE **is range** <>;	Integer operations	INTEGER
type FLOAT_TYPE **is digits** <>;	Real operations	FLOAT
type FIXED_TYPE **is delta** <>;	Fixed operations	Fixed

Once again, note that as we allow a greater variety of types to be used as generic type parameters, fewer operations can be used in the body of the generic unit. This is because the more types that are allowed, the fewer operations remain that can be performed on all these types. For example, generic units that allow themselves to be instantiated with any discrete type can use the operators greater than (>) and less than (<). If the generic unit, however, also allows itself to be instantiated with records, then these operators can no longer be used. It may not make sense to ask whether one record is greater than or less than another record, and Ada does not define such comparisons. As we will see later, however, such comparisons may be defined by the programmer.

GENERIC PACKAGES

The greatest opportunity for reducing redundant code is with utilities, and generic packages usually provide the best means for realizing this opportunity. (Do not confuse generic packages with the white boxes with bar codes found on many supermarket shelves.) The reason utilities provide such an opportunity for reducing redundant code is that they tend to be substantial programs that can potentially serve the needs of many different program developers. The reason that generic packages provide the best means for realizing this opportunity is that they can make utilities even more general and flexible. Thus, practically anyone can use the generic packages to instantiate their own customized packages.

Utilities include code that handles I/O and variable length strings, sorts data, creates and manipulates stacks and queues, and so on. One way that these utilities can be made very general is to make them into generic library packages. For instance, we may want to create a library package that is a stack package. This package should not just create a stack that allows, for instance, 100 integers to be stacked. Rather, this package should allow users to create stacks of different sizes and different kinds of objects. These objects should include integers, real numbers, characters, and objects of some user-defined enumeration type. We should even allow users to stack composite objects—arrays and records. If we write a generic stack package, users can then instantiate this package to create stacks of whatever kinds of objects and number of objects are desired.

Recall from Chapter 8 that a stack is a "last in, first out" (LIFO) data structure. The first example of a stack that was presented in that chapter can be rewritten as a generic package, as follows:

```
generic
    STACK_SIZE : POSITIVE;
    type ITEM is private;
package STACK is
    procedure PUSH (A : ITEM);
    function POP return ITEM;
end STACK;

package body STACK is
    STACK_ARRAY : array (1..STACK_SIZE) of ITEM;
    TOP : INTEGER range 0 .. STACK_SIZE;

    procedure PUSH (A: ITEM) is
    begin
       TOP := TOP + 1;
       STACK_ARRAY (TOP) := A;
    end PUSH;

    function POP return ITEM is
    begin
       TOP := TOP - 1;
       return STACK_ARRAY ( TOP + 1);
    end POP;
```

```
begin -- STACK
    TOP := 0;
end STACK;
```

For details on how this package works, read the discussion of stacks in Chapter 8. (As seen in Chapter 8, we could also add checks for overflow and underflow and add a subprogram to clear the stack.)

Note that the preceding generic stack package has two formal generic parameters:

```
STACK_SIZE : POSITIVE;
type ITEM is private;
```

The first formal generic parameter is an object, STACK_SIZE. Thus far in this chapter, we have only seen generic types used as formal generic parameters. This is the first time that we have seen an object used as a formal generic parameter. When the generic package, STACK, is instantiated, an actual object parameter must be provided that sets an upper limit to the size of the stack. The second formal generic parameter, ITEM, is used to establish the type of object that can be stacked.

The following code shows different ways that this package, STACK, can be instantiated and how objects can be pushed and popped from the various stacks created as a result of instantiating STACK:

```
declare
    type SMOKE_TYPES is (CIGARETTE, PIPE, CIGAR);
    type SMOKE is array (SMOKE_TYPES) of BOOLEAN;
    package STACK_REAL is new STACK (20, FLOAT);
    package STACK_100 is new STACK (100, INTEGER);
    package STACK_10 is new STACK (10, INTEGER);
    package SMOKE_STACK is new STACK (20, SMOKE);
    use STACK_REAL, STACK_100, STACK_10, SMOKE_STACK;
    X, Y : FLOAT := 1.2;
    A, B : INTEGER := 5;
    P : SMOKE := (CIGARETTE => TRUE, PIPE => FALSE, CIGAR =>
        FALSE);
begin
    . . .
    PUSH (X);
    . . .
    Y := POP;
    . . .
    STACK_10.PUSH (A); -- must qualify to avoid ambiguity
    . . .
    B := STACK_100.POP; -- must qualify to avoid ambiguity
    . . .
    PUSH (P);
    . . .
end;
```

In this code, the generic package STACK is instantiated four times. The first instantiation creates a stack capable of stacking up to 20 real (FLOAT) numbers:

package STACK_REAL **is new** STACK (20, FLOAT);

The second instantiation creates a stack capable of stacking up to 100 integers:

package STACK_100 **is new** STACK (100, INTEGER);

The third instantiation creates a stack capable of stacking up to 10 integers:

package STACK_10 **is new** STACK (10, INTEGER);

Finally, the fourth instantiation creates a stack capable of stacking up to 20 arrays of type SMOKE:

package SMOKE_STACK **is new** STACK (20, SMOKE);

After the four preceding stack packages are created, their PUSH and POP subprograms are used. Because each of these four stack packages contains its own PUSH and POP subprograms, PUSH and POP are each overloaded four times. The compiler can usually figure out which PUSH or POP subprogram is being used by examining the parameter type of the subprogram. Let us assume that the statement is PUSH (X) and that X is a real number. Because STACK_REAL is the only package that contains a PUSH procedure that pushes real numbers on a stack, the compiler knows that the PUSH procedure from the STACK_REAL package is being used. Now let us assume that the statement is PUSH (A) and that A is an integer. This statement is ambiguous. The compiler has no way of determining whether we wish to use the PUSH procedure from the package STACK_100 or from the package STACK_10. This is because both stack packages, STACK_100 and STACK_10, contain a PUSH procedure that will push integers onto a stack. As shown in the preceding code, this ambiguity is resolved by telling the compiler, using the dot notation STACK_10.PUSH(A) or STACK_100.PUSH(A), from which package to get the PUSH procedure. Similarly, dot notation must be used with the POP function to avoid ambiguity.

In the generic package STACK, the formal object parameter STACK_SIZE could have been assigned a default value:

STACK_SIZE : POSITIVE := 100;

In this case, if the STACK package is instantiated without an actual object parameter, then the default of 100 is used:

package DEFAULT_SIZE **is new** STACK (ITEM => INTEGER);

(For the advanced reader: a formal object parameter, unlike other kinds of generic formal parameters, can have the parameter modes **in** and **in out** but not **out**. As with subprograms, the **in** mode is assumed unless otherwise specified. A default value can only be assigned to a formal object that is an **in** parameter.)

Generic stack packages are a good example of a utility needed by many programs. Another example of a generic utility package is the input/output (I/O) packages that we have been instantiating throughout this book. Now that we understand generics, let us examine these packages more closely.

These generic I/O packages are contained within the nongeneric TEXT_IO package that is included with every Ada compiler. The TEXT_IO package is used for inputting and outputting strings and characters. The generic packages are used for inputting and outputting objects other than strings or characters. The four generic packages included in TEXT_IO are INTEGER_IO, FLOAT_IO, FIXED_IO, and ENUMERATION_IO. Each of these generic packages has a single formal generic type parameter. This parameter is used to specify the particular integer, floating point, fixed point, or enumeration type that is to be input or output. These four generic packages are instantiated as follows:

For integer I/O:
    package INT_IO **is new** TEXT_IO.INTEGER_IO (INTEGER);

For float I/O:
    package REAL_IO **is new** TEXT_IO.FLOAT_IO (FLOAT);

For fixed number I/O:
    type FIXED **is delta** 0.01 **range** 0.00 .. 10.00; -- to be discussed in
                                                              -- Chapter 13
    package FIXED_POINT_IO **is new** TEXT_IO.FIXED_IO (FIXED);

For enumeration I/O:
    type COINS **is** (PENNY, NICKLE, DIME, QUARTER, HALF_DOLLAR);
    package ENUM_IO **is new** TEXT_IO.ENUMERATION_IO (COINS);

If we examine the TEXT_IO package, which is included in Appendix E, we can see that the generic package specification for the ENUMERATION_IO package begins as follows:

generic
    type ENUM **is** (<>);
package ENUMERATION_IO **is** . . .

Recall that the notation (<>) indicates that any enumeration type can be used as an actual generic type parameter.

Similarly, the INTEGER_IO package specification appears in the TEXT_IO package as follows:

```
generic
    type NUM is range <>;
package INTEGER_IO is . . .
```

The notation **range** <> indicates that any INTEGER type can be used as an actual generic type parameter. Consider the following code:

```
declare -- assume TEXT_IO is visible
    subtype ONE_TO_5 is INTEGER range 1..5;
    package ONE_TO_5_IO is new INTEGER_IO (ONE_TO_5);
    package POSITIVE_IO is new INTEGER_IO (POSITIVE);
    package NATURAL_IO is new INTEGER_IO (NATURAL);
    package SHORT_INT_IO is new INTEGER_IO (SHORT_INTEGER);
    package LONG_INT_IO is new INTEGER_IO (LONG_INTEGER);
begin
    null;
end;
```

The package INTEGER_IO is first instantiated with an integer subtype ONE_TO_5. Recall from Chapter 3 that there are two predefined integer subtypes that are defined in the package STANDARD: POSITIVE and NATURAL. Some versions of the package STANDARD also include the integer types SHORT_INTEGER and LONG_INTEGER. The preceding example shows that the INTEGER_IO package can be instantiated with any of these integer types or subtypes. (The other two packages are instantiated similarly.)

GENERIC SUBPROGRAM PARAMETERS

Thus far in this chapter, we have discussed two kinds of generic parameters: type parameters and object parameters. We will now discuss a third kind of generic parameter: a subprogram parameter. Subprogram parameters are functions or procedures that are passed in when the generic unit is instantiated. To understand better the need for generic subprogram parameters, let us compare the private types discussed in this chapter (those used as generic parameters in generic specifications) with the private types encountered in Chapter 8 during our discussion of packages.

Recall from Chapter 8 that private types can be used in packages to hide the underlying structure or implementation of a type contained in the package specification. In both package specifications and generic specifications, operations on private types are restricted to assignments and to tests for equality and inequality. There is, however, this difference in perspective: users of a package containing a private type cannot assume anything about the private type. Therefore, the users can only perform assignments and tests for equality and inequality on objects of this private type. Developers of the package, however, know the actual makeup of the private type and can exploit this knowledge to perform additional operations on objects of this type. This situation is reversed when private types are used in generic specifications. Users who instantiate a generic unit know everything about the type they are passing in to match the private type. Developers of the generic unit, however, cannot know what actual type the user will be passing in to match the private type.

Thus, the following dilemma is created. If the users of a generic unit do not have any restrictions imposed and can instantiate the generic unit with any data type, then the developers are very restricted. They are limited to using only operations that apply to all data types. Conversely, if the developers wish to use operations that cannot apply to every data type, then the users of the generic unit are restricted. They can only instantiate this generic unit with certain data types. Ada solves this dilemma by using generic subprogram parameters.

First, to illustrate the dilemma, let us return to the generic function MAXIMUM that we discussed at the beginning of this chapter. The specification of this function is as follows:

generic
    type ITEM **is** (<>);
function MAXIMUM (X, Y: ITEM) **return** ITEM;

This generic specification uses the symbol (<>) to indicate that this generic unit can be instantiated only with discrete types. But what if we want to have this function work on real numbers, and even on arrays and records? We could try replacing the symbol (<>) with the keyword **private**, which results in the following version of the generic function MAXIMUM:

generic
    type ITEM **is private**;
function MAXIMUM (X, Y: ITEM) **return** ITEM;

function MAXIMUM (X, Y: ITEM) **return** ITEM **is**
begin
    if X > Y **then**   -- illegal operation on private types
        return X;
    else
        return Y;
    end if;
end MAXIMUM;

Because our generic formal parameter, ITEM, is a private type, we can instantiate this function with real numbers, arrays, records, or any other type. However, there is a problem. The only operations allowed on private types are assignments and tests for equality and inequality, yet the body of this generic function uses the greater than operator, >. This is illegal, and the compiler will raise an error.

Fortunately, there is a solution to our dilemma. We can let our generic formal parameter, ITEM, remain a private type and can also allow the operator, >, to appear in the generic body. To do this, however, we must place a special burden on those who instantiate this generic function. Whoever instantiates this package must define what is meant by the operator, >. Thus, users of this generic function MAXIMUM may instantiate MAXIMUM with a record type, but they must also define what is meant when one record is "greater than" another record. As the following code illustrates, such a definition is supplied to the generic unit through the formal generic subprogram parameter:

```
generic
    type ITEM is private;
    with function ">" (LEFT, RIGHT: ITEM) return BOOLEAN;
function MAXIMUM (X, Y: ITEM) return ITEM;

function MAXIMUM (X, Y: ITEM) return ITEM is
begin
    if X > Y then
        return X;
    else
        return Y;
    end if;
end MAXIMUM;
```

The formal generic subprogram parameter, ">", is preceded by the keywords **with function.** The keyword **with** is unrelated to the **with** used in context specifications. This keyword is used solely to remove ambiguity, so that the compiler knows that the function ">" is a generic subprogram parameter and not the name of the generic function itself. If the keyword **with** is not included, the code appears as follows:

```
generic
    type ITEM is private;
function ">" (LEFT, RIGHT: ITEM) return BOOLEAN;
```

The compiler then interprets the name of this generic function to be ">", not MAXIMUM.

In our example, when the generic function MAXIMUM is instantiated, the formal subprogram parameter, ">", which serves as a placeholder, is replaced with an actual function. This is illustrated in the following example, in which the generic function MAXIMUM is instantiated to create actual functions that compare whether one record is "greater than" another record:

```ada
with MAXIMUM;
procedure COMPARE_PEOPLE is
   type PERSONALITY_TYPE is (LOATHSOME, TOLERABLE, LOVABLE);
   type ADULT is
      record
         HEIGHT: INTEGER range 36..86; -- inches
         PERSONALITY: PERSONALITY_TYPE;
         AGE: INTEGER range 0..130; -- years
      end record;
   MELBA: ADULT := ( HEIGHT      => 67,
                     PERSONALITY => TOLERABLE,
                     AGE         => 28 );
   ZELDA: ADULT := ( HEIGHT      => 60,
                     PERSONALITY => LOATHSOME,
                     AGE         => 55 );
   GILDA: ADULT := ( HEIGHT      => 77,
                     PERSONALITY => LOVABLE,
                     AGE         => 87 );
   TALLER_PERSON, OLDER_PERSON, NICER_PERSON: ADULT;

   function OLDER_THAN (X, Y: ADULT) return BOOLEAN is
   begin
      return X.AGE > Y.AGE;
   end OLDER_THAN;

   function TALLER_THAN (X, Y: ADULT) return BOOLEAN is
   begin
      return X.HEIGHT > Y.HEIGHT;
   end TALLER_THAN;

   function NICER_THAN (X, Y: ADULT) return BOOLEAN is
   begin
      return X.PERSONALITY > Y.PERSONALITY;
   end NICER_THAN;

   function TALLER is new MAXIMUM ( ITEM => ADULT,
                                    ">"  => TALLER_THAN);

   function OLDER is new MAXIMUM ( ITEM => ADULT,
                                   ">"  => OLDER_THAN);

   function NICER is new MAXIMUM ( ITEM => ADULT,
                                   ">"  => NICER_THAN);

begin -- COMPARE_PEOPLE

   TALLER_PERSON := TALLER (MELBA, GILDA);           -- returns GILDA
   OLDER_PERSON  := OLDER (MELBA, ZELDA);            -- returns ZELDA
   NICER_PERSON  := NICER (MELBA, ZELDA);            -- returns MELBA
   NICER_PERSON  := NICER (NICER_PERSON, GILDA);     -- returns GILDA
   ...
end COMPARE_PEOPLE;
```

The procedure COMPARE_PEOPLE compares people on the basis of their age, height, and personality. This procedure determines whether one person is older, taller, or nicer than another person.

The first line of this code makes the generic unit MAXIMUM available through the context specification **with** MAXIMUM. This is possible because generic units such as MAXIMUM can be made into library units by being separately compiled. The generic function MAXIMUM is used by the procedure COMPARE_PEOPLE to create, through generic instantiation, three new functions: TALLER, OLDER, and NICER.

COMPARE_PEOPLE works as follows. Several people—MELBA, ZELDA, and GILDA—are defined as records, of type ADULT, that have three components: HEIGHT, PERSONALITY, and AGE. These three components are then used by three functions: OLDER_THAN, TALLER_THAN, NICER_THAN. These functions define what it means to say that one adult is taller, nicer, or older than another adult. For instance, the function TALLER_THAN can determine whether MELBA is taller than ZELDA by checking whether the record components MELBA.HEIGHT > ZELDA.HEIGHT. Similarly, function OLDER_THAN can determine whether MELBA is older than ZELDA by checking whether MELBA.AGE > ZELDA.AGE. The function NICER_THAN can determine whether MELBA is nicer than ZELDA by checking whether MELBA.PERSONALITY > ZELDA.PERSONALITY. This last comparison yields the desired result because values of the enumeration type PERSONALITY_TYPE are specifically listed in order of increasing niceness: LOATHSOME, TOLERABLE, and LOVABLE.

The functions TALLER_THAN, OLDER_THAN, and NICER_THAN are used as actual subprogram parameters when the generic function MAXIMUM is instantiated. The function TALLER, for example, is created by generically instantiating MAXIMUM with the type ADULT and the function TALLER_THAN. The function TALLER resembles the template, MAXIMUM, from which it was created, except for these differences: X and Y that were declared in MAXIMUM to be of type ITEM are now of type ADULT. In addition, the function ">" that appears in the body of MAXIMUM is replaced by the function TALLER_THAN. The function TALLER, therefore, behaves as if its body were written as follows, where TALLER_THAN (X, Y) is true or false depending on whether or not X.HEIGHT > Y.HEIGHT:

```
function TALLER (X, Y: ADULT) return ADULT is
begin
    if TALLER_THAN (X, Y) then
        return X;
    else
        return Y;
    end if;
end TALLER;
```

Within COMPARE_PEOPLE, the actual generic subprogram parameters used to instantiate MAXIMUM are OLDER_THAN, TALLER_THAN, and NICER_THAN. But what if we just want to use the predefined function ">", contained in the package STANDARD, as the actual subprogram parameter for comparing integers? This can be accomplished by instantiating the generic function MAXIMUM as follows:

function LARGER_INT **is new** MAXIMUM (ITEM => INTEGER, ">" => ">");

This instantiation creates a function called LARGER_INT that can be used to return the larger of two integers. In the peculiar notation ">" => ">", the ">" to the left of the arrow represents the formal generic subprogram parameter. The ">" to the right of the arrow represents the actual generic subprogram parameter. We can qualify the actual subprogram parameter, ">", as follows: STANDARD.">". This qualification clarifies the code by explicitly stating that the ">" function, which is being passed to the generic function MAXIMUM, is the standard ">" function contained in the STANDARD package and not a user-defined overloaded function.

Let us consider another example that uses subprogram parameters. Such parameters are sometimes used in mathematical programs. The following program creates the functions AVERAGE_SQUARE and AVERAGE_CUBE by instantiating the generic function AVERAGE with the function parameters SQUARE and CUBE:

```
with TEXT_IO; use TEXT_IO;
procedure AVERAGE_TERM is
    package REAL_IO is new FLOAT_IO (FLOAT);
    use REAL_IO;

    function SQUARE (X: INTEGER) return INTEGER is
    begin
        return X ** 2;
    end SQUARE;

    function CUBE (X: INTEGER) return INTEGER is
    begin
        return X ** 3;
    end CUBE;

    generic
        with function VALUES (PARAM: INTEGER) return INTEGER;
        function AVERAGE (BEGINNING, ENDING: INTEGER) return FLOAT;

    function AVERAGE (BEGINNING, ENDING: INTEGER) return FLOAT is
        SUM_OF_TERMS: FLOAT := 0.0;
    begin
        for INDEX in BEGINNING .. ENDING loop
            SUM_OF_TERMS := SUM_OF_TERMS +
                FLOAT ( VALUES (INDEX) );
```

```
        end loop;
        return SUM_OF_TERMS / FLOAT (ENDING - BEGINNING + 1);
    end AVERAGE;

    function AVERAGE_SQUARE is new AVERAGE (VALUES =>
        SQUARE);

    function AVERAGE_CUBE is new AVERAGE (VALUES => CUBE);
begin
        PUT ( AVERAGE_SQUARE (BEGINNING => 1, ENDING => 4));
        NEW_LINE;
        PUT ( AVERAGE_CUBE (BEGINNING => 10, ENDING => 15));
        NEW_LINE;
end AVERAGE_TERM;
```

In this program, the function call

AVERAGE_SQUARE (BEGINNING => 1, ENDING => 4)

returns the average value of N^2 for values of N from 1 to 4:

$(1^2 + 2^2 + 3^2 + 4^2) / 4$

The function call

AVERAGE_CUBE (BEGINNING => 10, ENDING => 15)

returns the average value of N^3 for values of N from 10 to 15:

$(10^3 + 11^3 + 12^3 + 13^3 + 14^3 + 15^3) / 6$

Functions such as AVERAGE_CUBE, therefore, return the average value of their terms (10^3, 11^3, 12^3, etc.) by adding all these terms and dividing by the number of these terms. Of course, the generic function AVERAGE can be instantiated with function parameters much more complex than the functions SQUARE and CUBE.

Before ending our discussion of subprogram parameters, let us see how these parameters can be given a default name. In the preceding generic function AVERAGE, for instance, the clause

with function VALUES (PARAM: INTEGER) **return** INTEGER;

could be replaced with

with function VALUES (PARAM: INTEGER) **return** INTEGER **is** SQUARE;

This second version uses the function name SQUARE as a default name for the actual subprogram parameter. To use SQUARE as a default name,

SQUARE must be visible at the point where AVERAGE is declared. This requirement is satisfied in the program AVERAGE_TERM. Given this second version, AVERAGE can be instantiated without a generic parameter:

function AVERAGE_SQUARE **is new** AVERAGE;

In this case, since the formal subprogram parameter is omitted, the default SQUARE is used.

Another method for assigning a default subprogram parameter is as follows:

with function ">" (LEFT, RIGHT: ITEM) **return** BOOLEAN **is** <>;

This strange-looking notation is used to make the name of the default subprogram parameter the same as the name of the formal subprogram parameter. In this case, therefore, the default subprogram name is ">". This default function, ">", could be the one that is defined in the STANDARD package. Alternatively, it could be a user-defined overloaded function that is visible at the point of instantiation. If we use this default in MAXIMUM, the preceding LARGER_INT function can be created with the following instantiation of MAXIMUM:

function LARGER_INT **is new** MAXIMUM (ITEM => INTEGER);

For a final example of how generics can be used, consider a method for sorting items, sometimes called an insertion sort. An insertion sort, probably the simplest of all the sorting algorithms, works in the same way that you sort your hand during a game of cards. You start with one item (which is considered already sorted). Then you get a second item and insert it where it belongs. Then you get a third item and insert it where it belongs. You keep getting and inserting items until every item is inserted. While the insertion sort is not the most efficient sort, it performs well for very small lists of less than 100 items and is easy to implement.

Before showing the generic insertion sort procedure, let us consider a nongeneric version that sorts integer arrays of type VECTOR:

type VECTOR **is array** (1 .. 10) **of** INTEGER;

Arrays of type VECTOR have a length of 10 and index values that range from 1 to 10. The nongeneric sort procedure appears as follows:

```
-- nongeneric version of an insertion sort for integer arrays of length 10
procedure INSERTION_SORT (V: in out VECTOR) is
    J: INTEGER;
    TEMP: INTEGER;
```

```ada
begin
    -- loop invariant: V (1 .. K - 1) is already sorted
    for K in 2 .. 10 loop
        J := K;
        TEMP := V(J);

        while J > 1 and then V (J - 1) > TEMP loop
            V (J) := V (J - 1);
            J := J - 1;
        end loop;

        V (J) := TEMP;
    end loop;
end INSERTION_SORT;
```

Now let us consider the generic version of the insertion sort:

```ada
-- generic version of an insertion sort
generic
    type ITEM is private;
    type INDEX is (<>);
    type VECTOR is array (INDEX range <>) of ITEM;
    with function ">" (LEFT, RIGHT: ITEM) return BOOLEAN;
procedure INSERTION_SORT (V: in out VECTOR);

procedure INSERTION_SORT (V: in out VECTOR) is
    J: INDEX;
    TEMP: ITEM;
begin
    -- loop invariant: V ( FIRST .. PRED(K) ) is already sorted
    for K in INDEX'SUCC(V'FIRST) .. V'LAST loop
        J := K;
        TEMP := V(J);

        while J > V'FIRST and then V ( INDEX'PRED( J ) ) > TEMP loop
            V (J) := V ( INDEX'PRED( J ) );
            J := INDEX'PRED( J );
        end loop;

        V (J) := TEMP;
    end loop;
end INSERTION_SORT;
```

To make the insertion sort generic, attributes are extensively used. For example, INDEX'SUCC(V'FIRST) is used instead of the second index value 2 (in the nongeneric version) for the lower bounds of the **for** loop. In addition, V'LAST is used instead of the last index value, 10. These attributes enable this generic sort procedure to be used for arrays with index ranges other than from 1 to 10. For instance, if an array has index values from 5 to 15, then INDEX'SUCC(V'FIRST) yields the second index value, 6, and V'LAST yields the last index value, 15. But this generic version will even work for noninteger index values. For example, if the values of INDEX belong to the enumeration type DAY that contains the values MONDAY to SUNDAY, then this generic procedure still works! INDEX'SUCC(V'FIRST) yields the second index value, TUESDAY, and V'LAST yields the last index value, SUNDAY.

The only restriction that applies to this generic procedure is that it does not work for indexes that are enumeration types with only one value such as the following:

type ONE **is** (LONELY);

In other words, this generic program assumes that INDEX'SUCC(V'FIRST), which yields the second index value, is always legal. Since it is rather ridiculous to sort arrays that can never have more than one item, this is not an unreasonable restriction.

The generic sort procedure has a long list of generic formal parameters. The first parameter, ITEM, is used to specify the kind of items that are to be sorted. The second parameter, INDEX, is used to specify the index range. The third parameter, VECTOR, is an unconstrained array of type ITEM with an index of type INDEX. When instantiating this generic procedure, the actual array type parameter, matched with VECTOR, must also be unconstrained; its component type must be the type that was matched with ITEM; and its index type must be the type that was matched with INDEX. The fourth parameter, ">", allows one to define what it means for an item of type ITEM to be greater than another item. This generic procedure can therefore be used to sort items such as records for which the relational operators are not predefined. Although the formal generic parameter, ">", implies that the array items are sorted in ascending order, one may instantiate INSERTION_SORT so that the sort is performed in descending order. To accomplish this, match the formal generic parameter, ">", with the actual parameter, "<":

">" => "<"

The following procedure instantiates the generic INSERTION_SORT and uses its instance, SORT, to sort an array of planets.

```
with TEXT_IO, INSERTION_SORT; use TEXT_IO;
procedure SORT_LIST is
    type SOLAR_SYSTEM is (MERCURY, VENUS, EARTH, MARS,
        JUPITER, SATURN, URANUS, NEPTUNE, PLUTO);
    subtype INDEX_TYPE is INTEGER range 0 .. 100;
    type PLANETS is array (INDEX_TYPE range <>) of SOLAR_SYSTEM;
    procedure SORT is new INSERTION_SORT
                        ( ITEM      => SOLAR_SYSTEM,
                          INDEX     => INDEX_TYPE,
                          VECTOR    => PLANETS,
                          ">"       => ">" );
```

```
   SORT_ME: PLANETS (5 .. 13) := ( JUPITER, MARS, PLUTO, EARTH,
      MERCURY, VENUS, SATURN, NEPTUNE, URANUS);

   package SOLAR_SYSTEM_IO is new ENUMERATION_IO
      (SOLAR_SYSTEM);
   use SOLAR_SYSTEM_IO;
begin
   for HEAVENLY_BODY in SORT_ME'RANGE loop
      PUT (SORT_ME (HEAVENLY_BODY));   -- outputs planets in unsorted
                                       -- order
      PUT (" ");
   end loop;
   NEW_LINE;

   SORT (SORT_ME); -- returns array sorted by planet's position from sun

   for HEAVENLY_BODY in SORT_ME'RANGE loop
      PUT (SORT_ME (HEAVENLY_BODY)); -- output planets in sorted order
      PUT (" ");
   end loop;
   NEW_LINE;
end SORT_LIST;
```

The planets are first output in their unsorted order. The SORT procedure is then used to sort the planets, and they are output in their correct order.

Generic units, as well as subprograms and packages, can be separately compiled. The next chapter discusses such compilation units in detail.

EXERCISES

1. When should generic units be used?

2. Consider the following specification:

   ```
   generic
      type ITEM_LIST is (<>);
      type ITEMS_IN_STOCK is range <>;
      type ITEM_ID is private;
   procedure STOCK;
   ```

   Which of the following instantiations are illegal, and why?

   a. **type** BLUEGRASS_INSTRUMENTS **is** (GUITAR, BASS, FIDDLE, BANJO, MANDOLIN);
      subtype CATEGORY_TYPE **is** INTEGER **range** 0 .. 20;
      procedure NUMBER_OF_BLUEGRASS_INSTRUMENTS **is new** STOCK

```
             ( ITEM_LIST          => BLUEGRASS_INSTRUMENTS,
               ITEMS_IN_STOCK    => NATURAL,
               ITEM_ID           => CATEGORY_TYPE );
```

b. **type** HARMONICAS **is** (DIATONIC, CHROMATIC, CHORD, BASS);
   type ID **is**
      record
         MAKE: STRING (1..15);
         MODEL: INTEGER **range** 1..999;
      end record;
   procedure HARMONICAS_IN_STOCK **is new** STOCK
             (ITEM_LIST   => HARMONICAS,
               ITEMS_IN_STOCK   => INTEGER,
               ITEM_ID   => ID);

c. **type** MANDOLIN_TYPES **is** (MANDOLIN, MANDOLA,
         MANDOCELLO, MANDOBASS);
   procedure MANDOLINS_AVAILABLE **is new** STOCK
             (ITEM_LIST   => MANDOLINS,
               ITEMS_IN_STOCK   => FLOAT,
               ITEM_ID   => POSITIVE);

3. Write a generic procedure called FIRST_AND_LAST that returns the first and last value of an enumeration type. Instantiate this procedure using several user-defined enumeration types of your choice. For example, you can create the procedure END_MONTHS by instantiating this generic unit with the enumeration type consisting of the months of the year. The procedure call

   END_MONTHS (FIRST, LAST);

   would then return JANUARY for the parameter FIRST and DECEMBER for LAST.

4. Consider the following generic package specification

   generic
      UPPER_BOUNDS: POSITIVE := 80; -- default of 80
   package CHARACTERS_PER_LINE **is**
      LINE: **array** (1 .. UPPER_BOUNDS) **of** CHARACTER;
   end CHARACTERS_PER_LINE;

   Write a program that instantiates this generic package with a generic parameter value of 40. Have the program then use the array, LINE, to output a 40-character message.

5. Consider the following generic procedure:

   generic
      with function F (A: INTEGER) **return** INTEGER;
   procedure OUTPUT_TERM (B: INTEGER);

```
procedure OUTPUT_TERM (B: INTEGER) is
begin
   PUT_LINE ("Parameter: " & INTEGER'IMAGE (B) );
   PUT_LINE ("Function value: " & INTEGER'IMAGE (F (B) ) );
end OUTPUT_TERM;
```

Write a program that instantiates this generic procedure with a function that returns the cube of a number. Using this instantiated procedure, have the program output the parameter 3 and its cube, 9.

6. Rewrite the generic stack package presented in this chapter as a generic queue package.

Chapter 10

COMPILATION UNITS

Compilation units are units of code that are separately compiled. There are several advantages to breaking code up into separate compilation units. First, when a change is made to a compilation unit, possibly only that unit will need to be recompiled. If the code is not broken up into several compilation units, then any change, no matter how minor, requires recompilation of the entire program. Second, code can be more easily farmed out to programmers working on the same project. Programmers can work on their own compilation units without fear of undoing the work of others. Third, the code is easier to read and maintain because the modular structure of the program is easier to discern.

Not every unit of code can be separately compiled. Block statements, for instance, cannot be separately compiled; they must always be embedded in a larger unit of code. However, subprograms (procedures and functions), packages, and generics can be separately compiled.

In this chapter, we will first discuss the differences between two kinds of compilation units: primary units, also known as library units, and secondary units. (Throughout the book, we have used the term "library unit" instead of "primary unit." In this chapter, however, since we are continually contrasting primary units with secondary units, the alternative name seems more appropriate.) Next, we will discuss compilation dependencies, followed by an explanation of how these dependencies affect the order in which units must be compiled. We will then explore how units that are modified and compiled again (recompiled) might require the recompilation of other units. The impact of these compilation issues on compiling and developing entire Ada programs will finally be discussed.

PRIMARY UNITS AND SECONDARY UNITS

Recall that compilation units—subprograms, packages, and generics—are each divided into two parts: a specification and a body. The body is further broken down into a declarative part and a statement part; however, this level of division is irrelevant to this chapter.

A primary unit usually consists of just a program specification. A specification defines how the user interfaces with the program unit. A secondary unit consists of a program body. A program body contains the implementation of the program unit.

The following examples show how compilation units are divided into primary and secondary units. A special kind of secondary unit, called a subunit, is also shown.

Procedures

Primary Unit:
```
-- specification
procedure GREETINGS;
```

Secondary Unit:
```
-- body (with specification)
procedure GREETINGS is
begin
    PUT ("Hello");
end GREETINGS;
```

or

Primary Unit:
```
-- body (with specification)
procedure GREETINGS is
begin
    PUT ("Hello");
end GREETINGS;
```

Secondary Unit: None

Functions

Primary Unit:
```
--specification
function CUBE (A: INTEGER) return INTEGER;
```

Secondary Unit:
```
--body (with specification)
function CUBE (A: INTEGER) return INTEGER is
begin
    return A ** 3;
end CUBE;
```

or

Primary Unit:
```
-- body (with specification)
function CUBE (A: INTEGER) return INTEGER is
begin
    return A ** 3;
end CUBE;
```

Secondary Unit: None

Packages

Primary Unit:
```
-- specification
package COMPUTER_LANGUAGES is
   type LANGUAGE is (FORTRAN, PASCAL, ADA);
   function BETTER_LANGUAGE (A, B: LANGUAGE)
      return LANGUAGE;
end COMPUTER_LANGUAGES;
```

Secondary Unit:
```
-- body
package body COMPUTER_LANGUAGES is
   function BETTER_LANGUAGE (A, B: LANGUAGE)
      return LANGUAGE is
   begin
      if  A > B then
         return A;
      else
         return B;
      end if;
   end BETTER_LANGUAGE;
end COMPUTER_LANGUAGES;
```

Generics

Primary Unit:
```
-- specification
generic
   type ITEM is (<>);
function MAXIMUM (X, Y: ITEM) return ITEM;
```

Secondary Unit:
```
-- body
function MAXIMUM (X, Y: ITEM) return ITEM is
begin
   if  X > Y then
      return X;
   else
      return Y;
   end if;
end MAXIMUM;
```

Subunits

Primary Unit: None

Secondary Unit:
```
-- body (with specification)
separate (MAIN)
procedure SUBUNIT is
begin
   PUT ("I am a subunit and my parent is MAIN");
end SUBUNIT;
```

Note that procedures and functions may be submitted for compilation in two different ways. Consider, for instance, the previous example of procedure GREETINGS:

```
procedure GREETINGS is
begin
    PUT ("Hello");
end GREETINGS;
```

The body of this procedure actually contains its own specification: **procedure GREETINGS**. Thus, the procedure body may form either a primary or a secondary unit. The compiler determines whether the procedure body is a primary or a secondary unit, as follows. If the specification is submitted to the compiler before the body, the body becomes a secondary unit when it is submitted to the compiler. This is rarely done. More commonly, the procedure body is made into a primary unit. This is done by submitting only the body to the compiler. The body then becomes a primary unit, and there is no associated secondary unit.

Functions may also be submitted for compilation in the two ways just described for procedures. In general, then, subprogram bodies may either form primary or secondary units, depending on whether the subprogram specification is compiled first.

As shown, packages are broken down into primary and secondary units in a straightforward manner. When a package specification is compiled, it becomes a primary unit. When the corresponding package body is later compiled, it becomes a secondary unit. Recall that there may or may not be a corresponding package body. A package that does not contain executable code can be written simply as a package specification; no corresponding package body is required. Such a package, therefore, just consists of a primary unit.

As with packages, generics are also broken down into primary and secondary units in a straightforward manner. When a generic specification is compiled, it becomes a primary unit. When the corresponding generic body (which is indistinguishable from a nongeneric body) is later compiled, it becomes a secondary unit. Many implementations require that the primary and secondary units of a generic unit be submitted in the same compilation, that is, as a single file.

Subunits are bodies that are separated from the declarative part of the program unit in which they are embedded and made into a separate compilation unit. Subunits are unique because they are the only secondary units that do not have a corresponding primary unit. Subunits do not have corresponding primary units because the only possible candidate for being a primary unit—the specification of the subunit—is not even a compilation unit. The specification of the subunit (and body stub of the subunit) must be contained in the subunit's parent unit.

Subunits that are subprogram bodies were shown in Chapter 7. Subunits, however, may also be package bodies:

```
procedure MAIN is
    package P is
        . . .
    end P;
    package body P is separate; -- body stub
begin
    . . .
end MAIN;
```

```
-- subunit P
separate (MAIN)
package body P is
    . . .
end P;
```

In this case, the body of P is removed from the declarative part of MAIN and replaced by a body stub:

package body P is separate;

Subunit P is separately compiled and forms a secondary unit without a corresponding primary unit. Note that, as with subunits that are subprogram bodies, subunits that are package bodies must begin with the **separate** clause. The **separate** clause gives the name of the subunit's parent unit, which contains the subunit's body stub and corresponding specification.

In summary, primary units usually consist of package specifications, generic specifications, and subprogram bodies (which include their specifications). Secondary units usually consist of package bodies, generic bodies, or subunits.

COMPILATION DEPENDENCIES

Now that we have explained the differences between primary and secondary units, let us see how compilation dependencies between these units are created. Compilation dependencies—whereby the compilation of one unit depends on the prior compilation of another unit—are created in three different ways.

First, compilation dependencies are created through the use of subunits. A subunit is dependent on its parent. The parent of a subunit may be either a primary or secondary unit, but the subunit is always a secondary unit.

Second, compilation dependencies are created whenever a unit is written that consists of both a primary and secondary unit. In such cases, the secondary unit (the body) depends on its associated primary unit (its specification).

Third, compilation dependencies are created through the use of the **with** clause. A unit is dependent on other units that are mentioned in its **with** clause. This dependency created by using the **with** clause, however, is formed on a primary unit, not on a secondary unit. Thus, if a **with** clause of a procedure mentions a package, then the procedure only depends on the package's primary unit (its specification), not on the package's secondary unit (its body). Note that the **with** clause may be used by a primary or secondary unit. For example, if the specification of a package mentions a procedure in a **with** clause, then the specification of the package depends on the procedure. The corresponding body of the package indirectly depends on this procedure. That is, the package body depends on the package specification, which, in turn, depends on the procedure. Conversely, if the body of a package mentions a procedure in a **with** clause, then the body of the package depends on the procedure; the corresponding specification of the package does not depend on the procedure.

In general, then, primary units may depend on other primary units but not on secondary units. Secondary units may depend on primary units or on other secondary units.

COMPILATION ORDER

Whenever there are compilation dependencies, a certain compilation order must be followed: dependent units must be compiled after the units on which they depend are compiled. Consider the three compilation dependencies just discussed. As a result of these dependencies: a subunit must be compiled after its parent unit is compiled; a unit that has a **with** clause must be compiled after the primary units mentioned in this clause are compiled; and secondary units must be compiled after their associated primary units are compiled.

To illustrate compilation order, consider the following Ada program, MAIN, which consists of six separate compilation units. (A line is used to indicate separate compilation units.)

```
with P1;                    -- P1 specification (spec) must be compiled
procedure MAIN is           -- before MAIN
begin
    . . .
end MAIN;
```

```
-- package P1 spec
with P2;                        -- P2 must be compiled before P1 spec
package P1 is                   -- P1 spec must be compiled before P1 body
   . . .
end P1;
```

```
-- package P1 body
package body P1 is
   . . .
end P1;
```

```
procedure P2 is                 -- P2 must be compiled before P3
   procedure P3 is separate;
begin
   . . .
end P2;
```

```
-- subunit P3
separate (P2)
procedure P3 is                 -- P3 must be compiled before P4
   procedure P4 is separate;
begin
   . . .
end P3;
```

```
-- subunit P4
separate (P2.P3)
procedure P4 is
begin
   . . .
end P4;
```

In this program, because package P1 appears in the **with** clause of procedure MAIN, MAIN is dependent on the primary unit of P1 (P1's specification) and must be compiled after the specification for P1 is compiled. The package P1 specification, in turn, mentions procedure P2 in a **with** clause and is thus dependent on P2. P2, therefore, must be compiled before the specification of P1. Note that the package P1 specification also has an associated body. Specifications must always be submitted for compilation before their associated bodies. Now let us examine procedure P2. Note that P2 contains a procedure body stub for P3. This means that the subunit, P3, depends on its parent unit, P2. P2, therefore, must be compiled before P3. Finally, note that P3, in turn, contains a procedure body stub, in this case, for P4. Procedure P3 must therefore be compiled before P4. The following list summarizes the pairs of compilation orderings that we have discussed:

$P1_{spec}$ **before** MAIN
P2 **before** $P1_{spec}$
$P1_{spec}$ **before** $P1_{body}$
P2 **before** P3
P3 **before** P4

RECOMPILING DEPENDENT UNITS

Compilation order determines which units need to be recompiled after a unit is modified. When a unit is modified, only units that depend on this modified unit must be recompiled. As a first example, let us assume that, in the preceding program, MAIN, the specification for package P1 is modified and recompiled. Two other compilation units must then also be recompiled: MAIN and the package P1 body. The reason for this, as shown in the preceding list of paired compilation orderings, is that both procedure MAIN and the package P1 body depend on the package P1 specification.

As a second example, let us suppose that procedure P3 is modified and then recompiled. Because the subunit P4 depends on P3, P4 must also be recompiled. No other units depend on P3, so no other units need to be recompiled.

As a third example, let us suppose that the package P1 body is modified and recompiled. In this case, because no other unit depends on the package P1 body, no other unit needs to be recompiled. This is assuming, however, that no changes are made to the parameters of any subprogram body located in the package P1 body. If changes are made to these parameters, then the P1 body will not compile unless parallel changes have first been made to the subprogram specification located in the package P1 specification. This is necessary so that users of the P1 package can correctly invoke this subprogram. For instance, reconsider the following example, given in the beginning of this chapter:

Primary Unit:
```
-- specification
package COMPUTER_LANGUAGES is
   type LANGUAGE is (FORTRAN, PASCAL, ADA);
   function BETTER_LANGUAGE (A, B: LANGUAGE)
      return LANGUAGE;
end COMPUTER_LANGUAGES;
```

Secondary Unit:
```
package body COMPUTER_LANGUAGES is -- body
   function BETTER_LANGUAGE (A, B: LANGUAGE)
      return LANGUAGE is
```

```
               begin
                  if  A > B then
                     return A;
                  else
                     return B;
                  end if;
               end BETTER_LANGUAGE;
            end COMPUTER_LANGUAGES;
```

In this example, assume that we add a third parameter, C, to the function body located in the package body of COMPUTER_LANGUAGES:

function BETTER_LANGUAGE (A, B, C: LANGUAGE) **return** LANGUAGE
   is . . .

We must then add a C to the parameters of the BETTER_LANGUAGE function specification, located in the package specification of COMPUTER_LANGUAGES.

In general, though, changes made to a package body or any other secondary unit do not require that other units be recompiled. Thus, it is important to keep secondary units separate from their associated primary units. If a primary unit and a secondary unit are both contained in the same file and no provision is made for their separation, then when this file is submitted to the compiler, the primary and secondary units are recompiled together, even if changes are only made to the secondary unit. This results in the unnecessary recompilation of other units that depend on the primary unit.

As we have seen, whenever a unit is recompiled, all the units that depend on it must also be recompiled. The Ada compiler system (Ada compiler, linker, and Ada library system) assists in such situations by ensuring that the recompilation of a unit does not make other units obsolete. In other words, the compiler system keeps track of all the compilation dependencies and does not allow a compilation unit to be successfully recompiled unless all of its dependent units are also recompiled. The failed compilation unit is not added to the Ada library and cannot render any other library unit obsolete. The integrity of the Ada library is thus protected. It is fortunate that the Ada compiler system keeps track of all the compilation dependencies, because this task would be difficult without computer assistance. But how does the Ada compiler system enforce a compilation order that is consistent with all the dependencies that exist between a program's compilation units? The Ada Language Reference Manual does not specifically answer this question. A user-friendly compiler system might automatically recompile, in proper order, all the units that need to be recompiled. A less friendly compiler system might instruct a user to manually recompile each unit that needs to be recompiled, perhaps one unit at a time.

COMPILING AN ENTIRE ADA PROGRAM

Now that we have considered paired compilation orderings and recompiling dependent units, let us consider the compilation of the entire Ada program MAIN. This program is shown in the section on compilation order. (The compilation of an entire Ada program consisting of many units is not normally performed, except, for example, when an Ada program is ported to another computer with a different Ada compiler. Usually, units of code are compiled as they are written or modified.) When compiling MAIN, the compiler system must satisfy all of the paired compilation orderings listed previously. But these paired compilation orderings can be satisfied by different complete compilation orderings of the entire program, such as the following:

P2 **before** P3 **before** P4 **before** P1$_{spec}$ **before** P1$_{body}$ **before** MAIN

or

P2 **before** P1$_{spec}$ **before** MAIN **before** P1$_{body}$ **before** P3 **before** P4

or

P2 **before** P3 **before** P1$_{spec}$ **before** MAIN **before** P4 **before** P1$_{body}$

Any of these complete orderings is correct. One can select any of these complete orderings or any other complete ordering that satisfies all the required paired compilation orderings.

DEVELOPING ADA PROGRAMS

Let us now consider how the development of Ada programs is affected by the fact that primary units do not depend on secondary units. When a program is developed, the compiler can test the design before the implementation details are written. To have the compiler test the design, only the primary units need to be compiled, because they contain all of the information on how units interface with one another. The secondary units, which contain the underlying program implementation, do not need to be written and compiled until the program is ready to run.

During compilation, the compiler system tests the program design by making consistency and completeness checks.

Consistency checks include checks that subprograms are being called with the correct number and type of parameters. Included are checks for circular dependencies. Circular dependencies occur when two primary units mention each other in **with** clauses. This is illegal since each unit requires that the other be compiled first.

```
--illegal circularity
with P2;
package P1 is -- depends on P2
    -- public part
end P1;
```

```
with P1;
package P2 is -- depends on P1
    -- public part
end P2;
```

In this example, the specifications of P1 and P2 depend on each other. One way to avoid this circularity is to relocate the **with** clauses to the package bodies:

```
-- legal
package P1 is
    -- public part
end P1;
```

```
package P2 is
    -- public part
end P2;
```

```
with P2;
package body P1 is
    -- private part
end P1;
```

```
with P1;
package body P2 is
    -- private part
end P2;
```

The body of P1 now depends on the specification of P2, and the body of P2 depends on the specification of P1. This does not result in a circularity problem. A consequence of the solution, however, is that the resources of P1 are only available to the body of P2, and the resources of P2 are only available to the body of P1. If the package specifications require each other's resources, then this solution will not work. In such cases, the packages must be restructured or combined so that circularity between their specifications is avoided.

During compilation, the compiler system also checks for completeness. Completeness checks include checks that a primary unit that is mentioned in a **with** clause actually exists. Included are checks that a package that is mentioned in the **with** clause of a unit contains all of the resources that the unit assumes it contains.

The bodies of compilation units—procedures, functions, and packages—as well as blocks and tasks, contain a declarative part and a statement part. There is an additional part that we have not yet discussed: exception handlers. The next chapter will explore these exception handlers.

EXERCISES

1. Answer true or false.
    a. Block statements can be separately compiled.   T F
    b. Primary units are also known as library units.   T F
    c. The body of a subprogram may form either a primary or a   T F
       secondary unit.
    d. Every secondary unit must have a corresponding primary   T F
       unit.
    e. The compiler can test the design of a program before the   T F
       implementation details are written.
    f. A subunit is dependent on its parent.   T F
    g. A primary unit usually consists of a body.   T F
    h. Ada protects the integrity of its library.   T F
    i. A unit is dependent on other units that are mentioned in   T F
       its **with** clause.
    j. A subunit must be compiled before its parent unit is   T F
       compiled.
    k. For a compiler to test the design of a program, only the   T F
       primary units need to be compiled.
    l. The Ada standards require that the specification of a   T F
       generic unit be separately compilable.
    m. A package body may be compiled before its corresponding T F
       specification.
    n. Compilation units have two parts: a specification and a   T F
       body. The body contains a declarative part and a statement
       part.
    o. Every primary unit must have a corresponding secondary T F
       unit.
    p. In general, changes made to secondary units do not require T F
       that other units be recompiled.

q. Typically only one compilation ordering is possible for a   T F
program consisting of many compilation units.

2. Explain how a subprogram body may form either a primary or a secondary unit.

3. Explain three ways that compilation dependencies are created.

4. Given the following compilation units, write pairs of compilation orderings.

   with P1, P2;
   procedure MAIN **is**
   begin
   . . .
   end MAIN;

   ---

   with P3;
   procedure P1 **is**
   begin
   . . .
   end P1;

   ---

   package P3 **is**
   . . .
   end P3;

   ---

   package P2 **is**
      procedure P4;
   end P2;

   ---

   package body P2 **is**
      procedure P4 **is separate**;
   end P2;

   ---

   separate (P2)
   procedure P4 **is**
   begin
   . . .
   end P4;

5. List two different complete compilation orderings that satisfy all of the paired compilation orderings in exercise 4.

Chapter 11

EXCEPTIONS

There are two common kinds of errors that programmers encounter: compilation errors and runtime errors. Compilation errors are errors that are encountered when code is being compiled. Runtime errors are errors that are encountered while code is running. This chapter is concerned with runtime errors.

In Ada, runtime errors are called exceptions, because they are exceptions to the normal, expected processing. During runtime, for example, an array index may go out of bounds or the value of a variable may go out of range.

Exception handlers are Ada constructs that handle exceptions. Exception handlers determine the kind of exception that was raised and then take appropriate action. By using exception handlers, an otherwise fatal error that causes a program to abort can be intercepted. Remedial action can then be taken to allow, if possible, the program to continue running.

This chapter will discuss predefined exceptions and user-defined exceptions. Information will be included on how to handle both kinds of exceptions with exception handlers. The propagation (passing) of exceptions will then be explored. The chapter will conclude with a discussion of suppressing exceptions.

PREDEFINED EXCEPTIONS

There are five exceptions defined in the package STANDARD that is supplied with every Ada compiler. Each of these predefined exceptions is identified with a name:

CONSTRAINT_ERROR
NUMERIC_ERROR
STORAGE_ERROR
TASKING_ERROR
PROGRAM_ERROR

These predefined exceptions are automatically raised (announced) when certain runtime errors are encountered. The CONSTRAINT_ERROR is raised whenever a value goes out of bounds. For instance, an attempt may be made to assign a value that is out of bounds to an array index or a variable. You have undoubtedly received messages mentioning constraint errors whenever such errors caused your programs to abort. The NUMERIC_ERROR is raised when illegal or unmanageable mathematical operations are performed, such as dividing by 0. The STORAGE_ERROR is raised when the computer runs out of available memory. The TASKING_ERROR is raised, for instance, when a call is made to a task that is no longer active. (Tasks will be covered in Chapter 15.) The PROGRAM_ERROR is raised for exceptions that do not fall into the categories of constraint, numeric, storage, or tasking errors. For instance, the PROGRAM_ERROR is raised when the end of a function is reached without a **return** statement having been encountered. For a more complete description of these predefined exceptions, consult the Ada Language Reference Manual.

Without the use of exception handlers, whenever one of these exceptions is raised, the program aborts, usually with a message from the Ada runtime environment, stating which of these five exceptions is raised. (The Ada runtime environment is the runtime system provided with the Ada compiler.) Consider the following block statement:

```
-- assume the GET for integers is visible
declare
    INPUT: INTEGER range 1..10;
begin
    PUT_LINE ("Enter an integer from 1 to 10");
    GET (INPUT);
    NEW_LINE;
    PUT_LINE ("Good for you!");
end;
```

This block statement instructs the user to enter an integer within the range from 1 to 10. The value entered is given to the variable INPUT, which is constrained to values in the range from 1 to 10. If the user enters a value such as 11, then a CONSTRAINT_ERROR is raised, because the variable INPUT is assigned a value that is out of range. If the Ada program that includes this block statement does not contain exception handlers, then the program aborts, and control returns to the Ada environment. Instead of allowing the program to automatically abort, the programmer can take control by placing in this block statement an exception handler that deals with constraint errors. After the exception is handled, the program can then continue to execute.

Exception handlers are placed at the end of a block statement, or at the end of the body of a subprogram, package, generic unit, or task. In each of these cases, the keyword **exception** is used to indicate that an exception handler follows. The exception handler, then, resides between the keywords **exception** and **end**. Exception handlers are placed in a block statement, as follows:

declare
    declarations
begin
    statements
exception
    exception handler
end;

Consider the following block statement, which contains an exception handler:

declare
    INPUT: INTEGER **range** 1..10;
begin
    PUT_LINE ("Enter an integer from 1 to 10");
    GET (INPUT);
    NEW_LINE;
    PUT_LINE ("Good for you!");
exception
    when CONSTRAINT_ERROR => PUT_LINE ("I said from 1 to 10!");
end;

When this segment of code executes, if a user enters a legal value, from 1 to 10, then the code outputs the message "Good for you!" The exception handler is then bypassed, and control passes to the line of code (not shown) following this block statement. Here is a sample run of this block (with the user response indicated by the prompt, >):

    Enter an integer from 1 to 10
    >7
    Good for you!

Now let us examine what happens when the user enters an illegal value, outside the range of 1 to 10:

```
Enter an integer from 1 to 10
>11
I said from 1 to 10!
```

When the user enters the value 11, a CONSTRAINT_ERROR is raised. As soon as the error is raised, the remaining statements in the statement part of the block, NEW_LINE and PUT_LINE ("Good for you!"), are bypassed, and the exception handler is executed.

Within the exception handler, which is similar to a **case** statement, the keyword **when** is followed by the name of an exception, an arrow, and the statements to be executed whenever the exception is raised. (Also, the exception handler, like the **case** statement, may use the vertical bar and the **when others** clause.)

The exception handler, wherever it appears, has the following structure:

```
exception
    when exception choice => statements
    when exception choice => statements
        . . .
    when exception choice => statements
end;
```

After an exception handler is done executing, control passes beyond the unit that contains the exception handler. For block statements, "beyond the unit" means to the statement following the block statement.

In the previous example, the user is only given one opportunity to enter a valid integer, because after the exception is raised, control passes to the statement following the block statement. This is user unfriendly. Let us attempt to modify the code so that the user is given unlimited chances to enter a valid integer:

```
declare
    INPUT: INTEGER range 1..10;
begin
    << TRY_AGAIN >>
    PUT_LINE ("Enter an integer from 1 to 10");
    GET (INPUT);
    NEW_LINE;
    PUT_LINE ("Good for you!");
exception
    when CONSTRAINT_ERROR =>   PUT_LINE ("I said from 1 to 10!");
                               goto TRY_AGAIN; -- will not compile
end;
```

This code seems to be just what is needed. When a constraint error is raised, an error message is output and a **goto** statement passes control back to the statement that prompts the user for input. However, this code will not work. As already stated, when the exception handler is done executing, control always passes beyond the unit that raised the exception. The Ada standards explicitly forbid the **goto** statement to return control to the unit that raises the exception.

The solution to the problem is to place the entire block statement that contains the exception handler in a loop. If an exception is raised, the exception handler executes, the block statement is exited, and we loop back to the beginning of the block statement, where the user is once again prompted for input. This is demonstrated in the following Ada program:

```
with TEXT_IO; use TEXT_IO;
procedure TRY_AGAIN is
    package INT_IO is new INTEGER_IO (INTEGER);
    use INT_IO;
begin
    loop -- keep looping until valid input is entered
        declare
            INPUT: INTEGER range 1..10;
        begin
            PUT_LINE ("Enter an integer from 1 to 10");
            GET (INPUT);
            NEW_LINE;
            PUT_LINE ("Good for you!");
            exit; -- valid input received, so exit loop
        exception
            when CONSTRAINT_ERROR =>
                    PUT_LINE ("I said from 1 to 10!");
        end;
    end loop;
end TRY_AGAIN;
```

USER-DEFINED EXCEPTIONS

In addition to the five predefined exceptions, programmers can define their own customized exceptions. The following program contains two such user-defined exceptions:

```
with TEXT_IO; use TEXT_IO;
procedure USER_DEFINED_EXCEPTION is
```

```
        AGE: FLOAT range 0.0..120.0;
        TOO_YOUNG, TOO_OLD: exception; -- user-defined exceptions
        package REAL_IO is new FLOAT_IO (FLOAT);
        use REAL_IO;
   begin -- USER_DEFINED_EXCEPTION
        PUT_LINE ("Enter your age in years");
        GET (AGE);
        if AGE < 18.0 then
            raise TOO_YOUNG;
        elsif AGE > 80.0 then
            raise TOO_OLD;
        end if;
        PUT_LINE ("You qualify for skydiving");

   exception -- exception handler
        when CONSTRAINT_ERROR =>
            PUT_LINE ("You are not being serious");
        when TOO_YOUNG =>
            PUT_LINE ("Sorry, you must be at least 18 to do skydiving");
        when TOO_OLD =>
            PUT_LINE ("Sorry, you cannot do skydiving if you are over 80");

   end USER_DEFINED_EXCEPTION;
```

Before discussing how this program works, note that the exception handler belongs to a procedure, not to a block statement. As with block statements, exception handlers in procedures (as well as in functions) are placed between the keywords **exception** and **end**:

```
procedure procedure name (parameter definitions) is
    declarations
begin
    statements
exception
    exception handler
end procedure name;
```

In the preceding procedure, USER_DEFINED_EXCEPTION, two user-defined exceptions are declared: TOO_YOUNG and TOO_OLD. These user-defined exceptions appear in the declarative part of the program unit as identifiers that are declared as exceptions:

   TOO_YOUNG, TOO_OLD: **exception**;

The syntax, then, resembles the syntax used to declare variables. Do not, however, be mislead into thinking that exceptions can be treated like variables. Unlike variables, exception identifiers are not objects; they cannot be used in assignment statements, in expressions, or as subprogram parameters.

Unlike the five predefined exceptions, which are automatically raised, user-defined exceptions are not automatically raised because the compiler has no idea when to raise them. The programmer must decide when to raise these exceptions. In the program USER_DEFINED_EXCEPTION, the exception TOO_YOUNG is raised when someone enters a valid age (between 0.0 and 120.0) that is less than 18.0 years old, and the exception TOO_OLD is raised when someone enters a valid age that is over 80.0 years old. These user-defined exceptions are explicitly raised in the statement part of the program unit by the statement consisting of the keyword **raise**, followed by the name of the exception. (A predefined exception can also be explicitly raised, for example, **raise** CONSTRAINT_ERROR. However, this is rarely recommended since it may be hard to determine whether the exception was raised automatically by the compiler or explicitly by the programmer.)

The exception handler in USER_DEFINED_EXCEPTION handles the exceptions TOO_YOUNG and TOO_OLD by outputting appropriate messages. When the user-defined exception TOO_YOUNG is raised, the program outputs "Sorry, you must be at least 18 to do skydiving." When TOO_OLD is raised, the program outputs "Sorry, you cannot do skydiving if you are over 80." In addition to the two user-defined exceptions, the exception handler handles a predefined exception, the constraint error. This constraint error is automatically raised whenever a user enters an age that lies outside of the range 0.0 to 120.0. In this case, the program outputs the message, "You are not being serious." (Exceptions should only be raised in abnormal or emergency situations; it is debatable whether such situations exist in this program.)

PROPAGATION OF EXCEPTIONS

In the last few examples, the program unit that raises an exception contains an exception handler that handles that exception. Once the exception is handled and the unit is exited, processing proceeds normally. But what if the unit that raises an exception does not contain an exception handler? In such situations, the exception is not forgotten. Rather, the exception propagates (passes) one level beyond the unit. The meaning of "one level beyond the unit" varies, depending on whether the exception propagates from a main program, a block statement, or a subprogram. (Packages will be discussed later in this section.) As we have seen, when an exception propagates from a main program, it propagates to the Ada runtime environment, and the program aborts. When an exception propagates from a block, it propagates to the unit enclosing the block. When an exception propagates from a subprogram, it propagates to the unit that last invoked the subprogram. In each of these cases, the exception propagates to one level beyond the unit. If the unit at this new level contains the appropriate exception handler, the exception is handled. If not, the exception is automatically propagated to yet a higher level. If an exception is raised that has no exception handler at any level, then the exception continues being propagated until it reaches the main program, which propagates it to the Ada environment.

The propagation path of an exception is determined at runtime. For example, a subprogram can propagate exceptions to any unit that invokes it. At runtime, it is determined which units invoke the subprogram and which exceptions, if any, the subprogram raises. (The exceptions themselves, however, are not created at runtime but exist throughout the execution of the program.)

The following example unconditionally raises an exception to show how exceptions raised in a procedure are propagated to the unit that last called the procedure:

```
with TEXT_IO; use TEXT_IO;
procedure HANDLE_EXCEPTION is
    WE_ARE_IN_DEEP_KIMCHEE: exception;

    procedure RAISE_AN_EXCEPTION is
    begin
        raise WE_ARE_IN_DEEP_KIMCHEE;
    end RAISE_AN_EXCEPTION;

begin
    RAISE_AN_EXCEPTION;
    PUT ("This sentence will never be output");
exception
    when WE_ARE_IN_DEEP_KIMCHEE =>
        PUT_LINE ("We are in deep kimchee!");
end HANDLE_EXCEPTION;
```

In this example, the procedure HANDLE_EXCEPTION calls the procedure RAISE_AN_EXCEPTION, which raises the user-defined exception WE_ARE_IN_DEEP_KIMCHEE. Since RAISE_AN_EXCEPTION does not have an exception handler, control passes back to HANDLE_EXCEPTION, and its exception handler is immediately executed. Thus, when this program runs, the message "We are in deep kimchee!" is output.

As we have seen, exceptions are propagated when the unit that raises the exception does not have an exception handler. There are two other situations where exceptions are propagated. First, an exception is propagated when the unit that raises an exception has an exception handler, but this exception handler does not handle the particular exception that is raised. This is possible because, although exception handlers resemble **case** statements, they differ in this respect: in **case** statements, every possible value of the **case** expression must be covered in a **when** clause; in exception handlers, it is not necessary for every possible exception that can be raised to be covered in a **when** clause. (Similarly to the **case** statement, however, the same exception cannot be covered by more than one **when** clause.)

In the preceding example, the exception handler contains a handler for the exception WE_ARE_IN_DEEP_KIMCHEE. Consider what happens, however, if the exception handler of this example appears as follows:

```
exception
    when CONSTRAINT_ERROR =>
        PUT_LINE ("Constraint error raised");
end HANDLE_EXCEPTION;
```

In this case, even though an exception handler exists, it does not handle the particular exception that is raised. Therefore, the exception is automatically propagated just as if there were no exception handler.

Second, an exception is propagated when the exception handler itself raises an exception. Thus far, we have only seen exceptions being explicitly raised outside the exception handler. However, programmers may raise an exception *within* an exception handler when the exception handler cannot fully handle the exception. Let us explain this process in greater detail.

In general, an exception handler should attempt to recover from each possible exception so that damage to the data structures, disk files, and so on, is minimized and program execution can continue. However, such a full recovery is not always possible for a single exception handler. In such cases, an exception handler may require the assistance of other exception handlers in higher-level units. To get this assistance, an exception handler may re-raise the exception (raise the same exception again) or raise a new exception. The raised exception then propagates to a higher unit that may have its own exception handler. This other exception handler has the same option of raising the exception. Thus, multiple levels of exception handlers may be required to fully handle an exception.

To raise an exception within an exception handler, the keyword **raise** is used, optionally followed by an exception identifier:

```
exception
    when STORAGE_ERROR =>
        PUT_LINE ("Out of memory");
        raise OVERFLOW;
            -- propagates this exception
end;
```

After the message "Out of memory" is output, the user-defined OVERFLOW exception is raised. This raised exception propagates to a higher unit that may be better equipped to deal with this emergency.

If the keyword **raise** used within an exception handler is not followed by an exception identifier, then the same exception is raised that caused the exception handler to be executed:

```
    exception
        when STORAGE_ERROR =>
            PUT_LINE ("Out of memory");
            raise; -- propagates STORAGE_ERROR
    end;
```

In this case, STORAGE_ERROR is reraised.

As previously mentioned, when an exception handler exists that does not handle the particular exception that is raised, the exception is automatically propagated just as if there were no exception handler. To avoid such automatic propagation, exception handlers must be written to handle every possible exception, including exceptions that are anonymous. An exception is anonymous if its identifier is not visible to the exception handler. An identifier is not visible to the exception handler when the exception handler lies beyond the scope of the unit in which the exception is declared. However, even though an identifier is not visible beyond the scope of the unit in which it is declared, the exception itself can be propagated beyond the unit.

The only way to write an exception handler to handle such anonymous exceptions is to use the **when others** clause. Before showing how this clause is used, we will give an example of an anonymous exception. The following modified version of the HANDLE_EXCEPTION program is an example in which, because of Ada's scoping rules, an exception handler contained in an outer unit cannot access an exception identifier that is declared in an inner unit:

```
with TEXT_IO; use TEXT_IO;
procedure HANDLE_EXCEPTION is

        procedure RAISE_AN_EXCEPTION is
            WE_ARE_IN_DEEP_KIMCHEE: exception;
        begin
            raise WE_ARE_IN_DEEP_KIMCHEE;
        end RAISE_AN_EXCEPTION;

begin
        RAISE_AN_EXCEPTION;
        PUT ("This sentence will never be output");
exception
        when WE_ARE_IN_DEEP_KIMCHEE =>
            PUT_LINE ("We are in deep kimchee!");
            -- will not compile because this exception is not visible here
end HANDLE_EXCEPTION;
```

In this program, the exception identifier, WE_ARE_IN_DEEP_KIMCHEE, is declared in the inner procedure, RAISE_AN_EXCEPTION, but is unavailable to the outer procedure, HANDLE_EXCEPTION. The exception WE_ARE_IN_DEEP_KIMCHEE still propagates to the outer procedure, but its identifier is not visible to the outer procedure. Thus, the exception becomes anonymous. (Anonymous exceptions lose their anonymity if they are eventually propagated to a unit where their identifier is once again visible.) Because this exception is anonymous, it cannot be explicitly mentioned in an exception handler. As previously stated, the only way for an exception handler to handle such anonymous exceptions is through a **when others** clause. This clause works similarly to the **when others** clause in the **case** statement. The clause is executed whenever an exception is raised that is not explicitly covered by the other **when** clauses. The following exception handler contains a **when others** clause that is executed whenever an exception is raised that is not a storage error, a numeric error, or a constraint error:

```
exception
    when STORAGE_ERROR =>
        PUT_LINE ("Out of memory");
    when CONSTRAINT_ERROR | NUMERIC_ERROR =>
        PUT_LINE ("Illegal entry");
    when others =>
        PUT_LINE ("Some other exception was raised");
        raise; -- propagate the exception
end HANDLE_EXCEPTION;
```

The **when others** clause must appear on its own; in other words, it cannot be combined with other exception identifiers through use of a vertical bar. In addition, when the **when others** clause is used, it must appear as the last **when** clause in the exception handler.

Note that CONSTRAINT_ERROR and NUMERIC_ERROR are combined in a single **when** clause. In practice, it is very difficult to distinguish between the conditions that raise the CONSTRAINT_ERROR and those that raise the NUMERIC_ERROR. In fact, which error will be raised in a given situation may vary from one compiler to the next. It is therefore recommended that both these exception identifiers be combined with the vertical bar.

As shown in the previous exception handler, using **raise** without an identifier is the only way that anonymous exceptions can be reraised. If the **when others** clause is entered, the message "Some other exception was raised" is output and the exception, whatever it is, is raised again. (Note that **raise** without an exception identifier can only appear inside an exception handler.)

We have seen how exceptions raised in blocks and subprograms are propagated. Now let us consider how exceptions that are raised in packages are propagated. In a package, an exception handler is placed in the package body, as follows:

```
package body package name is
    hidden declarations
begin -- initialization
    statements
```

exception
   exception handler
end *package name*;

The exception handler in a package can only handle errors in the statement part (initialization part) of the package body. For an example, consider the following stack package:

```
package STACK is
    procedure PUSH (A : INTEGER);
    function POP return INTEGER;
    STACK_OVERFLOW: exception;
    STACK_UNDERFLOW: exception;
end STACK;
```

```
package body STACK is
    STACK_SIZE: constant := 1_000;
    STACK_ARRAY : array (1 .. STACK_SIZE) of INTEGER;
    TOP: INTEGER range 0 .. STACK_SIZE;

    procedure PUSH (A: INTEGER) is
    begin
       if TOP = STACK_SIZE then
          raise STACK_OVERFLOW;
       end if;
       TOP := TOP + 1;
       STACK_ARRAY (TOP) := A;
    end PUSH;

    function POP return INTEGER is
    begin
       if TOP = 0 then
          raise STACK_UNDERFLOW;
       end if;
       TOP := TOP - 1;
       return STACK_ARRAY ( TOP + 1);
    end POP;
begin -- STACK initialization
    TOP := 0;
end STACK;
```

This package is identical to the first example of a package presented in Chapter 8, except that exception handling features have been added. This package contains two user-defined exceptions: STACK_OVERFLOW and STACK_UNDERFLOW. These two exceptions, raised within the subprograms PUSH and POP, are defined in the package specification. STACK_OVERFLOW is raised whenever an attempt is made to push an item onto a stack that is full. STACK_UNDERFLOW is raised whenever an attempt is made to pop an item from a stack that is empty.

Suppose that the following exception handler is placed in the body of this STACK package:

```
   ...
begin -- STACK initialization
    TOP := 0;
exception -- only executed when TOP is assigned an illegal value
    when CONSTRAINT_ERROR =>
        PUT_LINE ("Stack package initialization error");
end STACK;
```

Although an exception handler is contained in the package body, the user-defined exceptions raised by the subprograms PUSH and POP are not handled by this exception handler. Whenever these user-defined exceptions are raised, they propagate to the unit that last invoked these subprograms. The exception handler of the package is only executed when an exception is raised in the statement part of the package body. In the preceding example, there is only one statement in this part of the package:

TOP := 0;

Thus, unless TOP is assigned an illegal value, the exception handler is never executed.

Let us deliberately assign the illegal value of -1 to TOP. The CONSTRAINT_ERROR will be raised, and the exception handler will be executed:

```
   ...
begin -- STACK initialization
    TOP := -1; -- this will trigger the following exception
exception
    when CONSTRAINT_ERROR =>
        PUT_LINE ("Stack package initialization error");
end STACK;
```

The CONSTRAINT_ERROR is raised and the message "Stack package initialization error" is output when the package is elaborated (created). STACK is elaborated once, before the execution of the main program.

If a library package (which is a primary unit) such as STACK raises an exception that is not handled by its exception handler, or if it does not have an exception handler, then the main program aborts.

Let us now return to package STACK. The following program illustrates how this stack package can be used:

```
with TEXT_IO, STACK; use TEXT_IO, STACK;
procedure STACK_DEMO is
```

```ada
    package INT_IO is new INTEGER_IO (INTEGER);
    use INT_IO;
    INT: INTEGER;

begin -- STACK_DEMO

    -- place 2 integers in the stack
    PUSH (8);
    PUSH (4);

    INT := POP;
    PUT ( INT );       -- outputs 4

    INT := POP;
    PUT ( INT );       -- outputs 8

    INT := POP;        -- raises STACK_UNDERFLOW exception
    PUT ( INT );

exception
    when STACK_OVERFLOW => PUT_LINE ("Stack is full");
    when STACK_UNDERFLOW => PUT_LINE ("Stack is empty");
    when others => PUT_LINE ("An unknown error occurred");

end STACK_DEMO;
```

In this program, two integers are pushed onto the stack and then popped from the stack. When an attempt is made to pop a third integer from the stack, the STACK_UNDERFLOW exception is raised by the procedure POP. The exception handler contained in STACK_DEMO is then executed, and the message "Stack is empty" is output to the screen.

So far we have only considered exceptions that are raised as statements are being executed. Exceptions may also be raised as declarations are being elaborated. (This includes exceptions that are raised when a package located in a declarative part of a program unit is elaborated.) The following example raises an exception as the variable N is being elaborated:

```ada
with TEXT_IO; use TEXT_IO;
procedure OUTER is

    procedure INNER is
        N: POSITIVE := 0; -- constraint error during elaboration
    begin
        null;
    exception
        when CONSTRAINT_ERROR =>
            PUT_LINE ("Constraint error handled in procedure INNER");
    end INNER;

begin -- OUTER
    INNER; -- raise a constraint error produced during elaboration
```

```
    exception
        when CONSTRAINT_ERROR =>
            PUT_LINE ("Constraint error handled in procedure OUTER");
    end OUTER;
```

When this program executes, only this single message is output: "Constraint error handled in procedure OUTER". Even though the constraint error is raised in procedure INNER, and even though INNER has an exception handler that handles constraint errors, the exception handler is never executed. This is because the constraint error is raised as the declarations in INNER are elaborated. Whenever an exception is raised during elaboration, instead of being handled by the exception handler of that unit, the error propagates to one level beyond the unit. Therefore, in our example, the exception raised in the procedure INNER is immediately propagated to the procedure that last invoked INNER, namely, OUTER. Similarly, a block statement that raises an exception during elaboration propagates this exception to the unit enclosing the block. A library package that raises an exception during elaboration causes the main program to abort.

SUPPRESSING EXCEPTIONS

One advantage of Ada is that many checks are performed at runtime to ensure that array indexes do not go out of bounds, that variables do not get assigned a value that is out of range, and so on. However, there is a price to pay: larger object code and slower execution speed. In real-time applications where there are stringent space and time constraints, runtime error checking may be too costly. A solution, although a controversial one, is to use exception suppression.

Exception suppression turns off various runtime error checking. This should only be considered when execution speed or object code size is critical, because once exceptions are turned off, previously detectable errors go undetected. This is why exception suppression is controversial. As all seasoned programmers know, any large chunk of code might have nasty errors lurking around, even if the code has been successfully executing for years. (Exception suppression, of course, should never be used to deliberately hide errors.)

Some Ada compilers allow exception suppression to be specified when the compiler is run. Exceptions may then be turned on or off each time the code is compiled, without the need to alter Ada source code. This feature, however, is outside of the language requirements of Ada. The Ada language requirements do specify a pragma (a compiler directive) called SUPPRESS, which turns off runtime error checks. This pragma, however, is an optional Ada feature and, therefore, may not be fully implemented on your compiler. If it is not implemented, the compiler will ignore the pragma and, possibly, issue a warning.

In Ada, many different kinds of runtime error checking can be suppressed. For a full list of all pragmas that turn off runtime error checking, consult the Ada Language Reference Manual. The following is a list of pragmas that turn off range checks and index range checks:

```
pragma SUPPRESS (RANGE_CHECK);
    -- suppresses range checking
pragma SUPPRESS (RANGE_CHECK, INTEGER);
    -- suppresses range checking only for objects of type INTEGER
pragma SUPPRESS (RANGE_CHECK, X);
    -- suppresses range checking only for object X
pragma SUPPRESS (INDEX_CHECK);
    -- suppresses index range checking for arrays
```

These pragmas, which are placed in the declarative part of a unit, only affect the code of the unit in which they are placed.

Let us briefly consider each of the pragmas in the preceding list. The first pragma suppresses all range checking. Thus, if a variable is assigned a value that is out of range, or if an array index is assigned a value that exceeds its bounds, then no exceptions will be raised in the unit of code that contains this pragma. The second pragma only suppresses range checks for objects that are of type INTEGER. The third pragma only suppresses range checks for the object X. The last pragma only suppresses range checks for array indexes.

An example of exception suppression follows:

```
declare
    pragma SUPPRESS (RANGE_CHECK);
    subtype ONE_OR_TWO is INTEGER range 1..2;
    M, N: ONE_OR_TWO;
    OUT_OF_BOUNDS: INTEGER := 3;
begin
    M := OUT_OF_BOUNDS;  -- no error produced
    N := OUT_OF_BOUNDS;  -- no error produced
    . . .
end;
```

In this block statement, all range checking is suppressed. Therefore, when M and N are assigned values that are out of range, no exception is raised.

The next example of exception suppression is similar to the previous example, except that range checking is only suppressed for the variable M. Therefore, when M and N are assigned values that are out of range, an exception is raised only when N is assigned the out-of-range value:

```
declare
    subtype ONE_OR_TWO is INTEGER range 1..2;
    M, N: ONE_OR_TWO;
    pragma SUPPRESS (RANGE_CHECK, M);
    OUT_OF_BOUNDS: INTEGER := 3;
begin
    M := OUT_OF_BOUNDS; -- no error produced
    N := OUT_OF_BOUNDS; -- constraint error raised
    . . .
end;
```

The ability to suppress exceptions for a particular object, such as a variable, may seem peculiar, but it does have uses. Programs often spend a significant amount of time running the same few statements over and over again. Suppressing exception checks on particular objects within this code can make a substantial difference in the overall execution speed of the program. Exception suppression may be localized to a few objects within this code by enclosing this code within a block statement. The advantage of localizing exception suppression is that careful analysis and thorough testing may first be performed to ensure that the code in question can never raise an exception.

In this chapter, we discussed exceptions and exception handlers. The next chapter will cover access types.

EXERCISES

1. Consider the following function:

```
function FLAWED is (A: INTEGER; OK: BOOLEAN) return
        INTEGER is
    ANSWER: INTEGER range 0..100;
    OOPS: exception;
begin
    if OK then
        ANSWER := 100 / A;
        return ANSWER;
    else
        raise OOPS;
    end if;
exception
    when CONSTRAINT_ERROR => return -1;
    when NUMERIC_ERROR => return 0;
    when OOPS => return 1;
    when others => return -99;
end FLAWED;
```

Given this function, what is the result of the following expressions?

    a.   FLAWED (1, TRUE)
    b.   FLAWED (-10, TRUE)
    c.   FLAWED (-10, FALSE)
    d.   FLAWED (0, TRUE)
    e.   FLAWED (0, FALSE)

2. Consider the following procedure:

```
with TEXT_IO, READ_TEMPERATURE; use TEXT_IO;
procedure MONITOR_TEMPERATURE is
   TEMPERATURE: INTEGER range -30..1_000;
   TOO_HOT, TOO_COLD: exception;
begin
   loop
      READ_TEMPERATURE (TEMPERATURE);
      if TEMPERATURE > 800 then
         raise TOO_HOT;
      elsif TEMPERATURE < (-10) then
         raise TOO_COLD;
      end if;
   end loop;
exception
   when TOO_HOT =>
      PUT_LINE ("Sound alarm");
   when TOO_COLD =>
      PUT_LINE ("Turn on heater");
   when others =>
      PUT_LINE ("Evacuate building);
end MONITOR_TEMPERATURE;
```

What, if anything, does MONITOR_TEMPERATURE output when the procedure READ_TEMPERATURE returns the following TEMPERATURE values?

    a.   500
    b.   950
    c.   0
    d.   1020
    e.   -14
    f.   -32

3. What will the following code output?

    a. -- assume package TEXT_IO is visible
```
      declare
         NEG: INTEGER := -10;
         POS: POSITIVE := 10;
```

```
     begin
        POS := NEG;
        PUT_LINE ("Will this be output?");
     exception
        when CONSTRAINT_ERROR => PUT_LINE ("Out of bounds");
     end;
```

b. ```
   with TEXT_IO; use TEXT_IO;
   procedure MAIN is
      package REAL_IO is new FLOAT_IO (FLOAT);
      use REAL_IO;
      PI: constant FLOAT := 3.14159;

      function TO_DEGREES (ANGLE: in FLOAT) return FLOAT is
         DEGREES: FLOAT range 0.0 .. 360.0;
      begin
         DEGREES := 180.0 * ANGLE / PI;
         return DEGREES;
      exception
         when CONSTRAINT_ERROR | NUMERIC_ERROR =>
            PUT_LINE ("Angle not in the range 0 to 2 PI");
            return -99.0;
      end TO_DEGREES;

   begin
      PUT (TO_DEGREES (PI / 4.0));
      NEW_LINE;
      PUT (TO_DEGREES (3.0 * PI));
      NEW_LINE;
      PUT (TO_DEGREES (PI));
      NEW_LINE;
   exception
      when others =>
         PUT_LINE ("Error occurred");
   end MAIN;
   ```

c. ```
   with TEXT_IO; use TEXT_IO;
   procedure MAIN is
      package REAL_IO is new FLOAT_IO (FLOAT);
      use REAL_IO;
      PI: constant FLOAT := 3.14159;

      function TO_DEGREES (ANGLE: in FLOAT) return FLOAT is
         DEGREES: FLOAT range 0.0 .. 360.0;
      begin
         DEGREES := 180.0 * ANGLE / PI;
         return DEGREES;
      end TO_DEGREES;

   begin
      PUT ( TO_DEGREES ( PI / 4.0 ) );
      NEW_LINE;
      PUT ( TO_DEGREES ( 3.0 * PI ) );
   ```

```
            NEW_LINE;
            PUT ( TO_DEGREES ( PI ) );
            NEW_LINE;
         exception
            when CONSTRAINT_ERROR | NUMERIC_ERROR =>
               PUT_LINE ("Angle not in the range 0 to 2 PI");
            when others =>
               PUT_LINE ("Error occurred");
         end MAIN;
```

4. What is wrong with the following code?

```
      with TEXT_IO; use TEXT_IO;
      procedure MAIN is
         procedure ERROR is
            OOPS: exception;
         begin
            raise OOPS;
         end ERROR;
      begin
         ERROR;
      exception
         when OOPS =>
            PUT_LINE ("OOPS");
      end MAIN;
```

5. What will the following procedures output?

   a.
   ```
      with TEXT_IO; use TEXT_IO;
      procedure MAIN is
      begin
         declare
            ZIKES: exception;
         begin
            raise ZIKES;
         end;
      exception
         when others => PUT_LINE ("A problem has occurred");
      end MAIN;
   ```

   b.
   ```
      with TEXT_IO; use TEXT_IO;
      procedure OUTER is
         procedure MIDDLE is
            procedure INNER is
               OOPS: exception;
            begin -- INNER
               raise OOPS;
            end INNER;
   ```

```
      begin -- MIDDLE
        PUT_LINE ("Calling INNER");
        INNER;
        PUT_LINE ("Finished calling INNER");
      end MIDDLE;
    begin -- OUTER
      PUT_LINE ("Calling MIDDLE");
      MIDDLE;
      PUT_LINE ("Finished calling MIDDLE");
    exception
      when CONSTRAINT_ERROR => PUT_LINE ("Constraint error");
      when others => PUT_LINE ("A problem has occurred");
    end OUTER;
```

c. ```
    with TEXT_IO, P; use TEXT_IO, P; -- package P follows
    procedure MAIN is
    begin
       Q; -- defined in package P
    exception
       when CONSTRAINT_ERROR =>
          PUT_LINE ("A problem has occurred);
    end MAIN;
    ```

```
package P is
   procedure Q;
end P;
```

```
with TEXT_IO; use TEXT_IO;
package body P is
   POS: POSITIVE;
   procedure Q is
   begin
      POS := -5;
   end Q;
begin -- P initialization
   POS := -10;
exception
   when CONSTRAINT_ERROR =>
      PUT_LINE ("Bad initialization");
end P;
```

6. Write a procedure that checks the amount of change received after an item is purchased. If the amount received is too little, then have the procedure raise the user-defined exception OVERPAID. If the amount received is too much, then have the procedure raise the user-defined exception UNDERPAID. Incorporate an exception handler that takes appropriate action whenever one of these exceptions is raised.
```

Chapter 12

ACCESS TYPES

Access types are used to declare values that access dynamically allocated variables. Dynamically allocated variables differ from the variables previously presented in this book, which have been declared variables. As the name implies, a declared variable is brought into existence by being declared:

>   WHOLE_NUMBER: INTEGER;

In this case, WHOLE_NUMBER is declared to be a variable of type INTEGER. Once the variable is declared, it may be referenced by its name, WHOLE_NUMBER.

In contrast to a declared variable, a dynamically allocated variable is brought into existence by what is known as an allocator. Allocators will be discussed later in this chapter. Furthermore, unlike declared variables, dynamically allocated variables are referenced, not by a name, but by an access value that acts like a "pointer" to the variable. (An access value is a value of an access type).

Access values are thus conceptually similar to pointers that are found in other programming languages. Both access values and pointers "point" to various objects. An access value is not the value of the object to which it points but usually the address of the object to which it points. (In Ada, one is not guaranteed that the access value is the same as the address of the object being accessed. Even though this is often the case, a compiler is free to implement access values in some other way.) Do not be concerned with how addresses are represented by a given computer. Instead of thinking of access values as being address values, simply think of access values as pointers that point to objects.

Despite the similarities between pointers supported by other languages and access values supported by Ada, there some significant differences. In general, pointers do not belong to a type. An access value, however, belongs to an access type. Furthermore, pointers are free to roam around in memory and point to objects belonging to different types. Access values, however, may only access one type of object. The type of object that they may access is specified by the access type to which they belong. Thus an access value that belongs to a character access type may only access character objects, never integer objects, Boolean objects, and so on.

Furthermore, Ada avoids a common pitfall that programmers often encounter when working with pointers: the dangling pointer. Dangling pointers are those that attempt to point to objects that no longer exist. In Ada, this cannot happen because an object's existence is maintained as long as it is being accessed by one or more access values. In an attempt to dissociate itself from such problems, Ada does not use the term "pointer" as part of its official lingo. We will digress from strict Ada terminology, however, and refer to access values as pointers.

There are different reasons to use access types. First, access types reduce the need for redundant data. Instead of keeping and maintaining multiple copies of the same data, one can have different pointers pointing to the same data. Second, it can be much faster to reference a large data structure by pointing to it than by copying it into a variable. Third, as shown at the end of this chapter, certain data structures, such as linked lists, are naturally implemented using pointers.

This chapter begins with a discussion of the different properties of pointers. This is followed by an explanation of how pointers can be used to create data structures known as linked lists.

POINTERS

As mentioned, although "pointers" (access values) point to objects, they cannot point to just any object. In Ada, all objects belong to a type, and pointers are no exception. Due to Ada's strong typing, a pointer may point only to objects specified by the access type to which it belongs. For instance, an integer pointer can only point to integer objects (variables). This is shown pictorially in Figure 12.1. In this figure, INTEGER_POINTER belongs to an integer access type and points to an integer variable whose value is 5. The variable containing the integer 5 is a dynamically allocated variable and therefore is not associated with a name; it can only be referenced through a pointer. If INTEGER_POINTER is reset to point to a different integer variable, then this variable containing 5 can no longer be referenced. The compiler is free to reuse the memory that was allocated to store this variable.

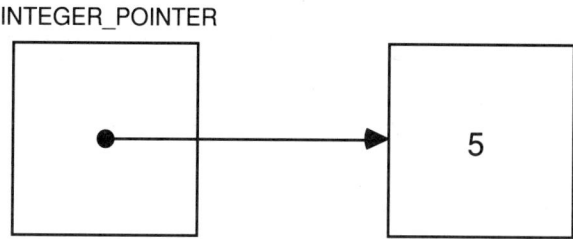

Figure 12.1 An integer pointer

We have shown a single pointer pointing to a single object. More than one pointer can point to the same object, as shown in Figure 12.2. In such cases, the two pointers are said to be equal. Two pointers can also point to different objects with the same value, as shown in Figure 12.3. In such cases, the two pointers are not equal.

The access type to which a pointer belongs is determined when the pointer is declared. The following code declares POINTER_1 and POINTER_2 to belong to the access type INTEGER_ACCESS_TYPE:

type INTEGER_ACCESS_TYPE **is access** INTEGER;
POINTER_1, POINTER_2: INTEGER_ACCESS_TYPE;

The first declaration defines type INTEGER_ACCESS_TYPE. The keyword **type** is followed by the type identifier and the keywords **is access**. After the keyword **access** is the type name, INTEGER, which specifies the type of

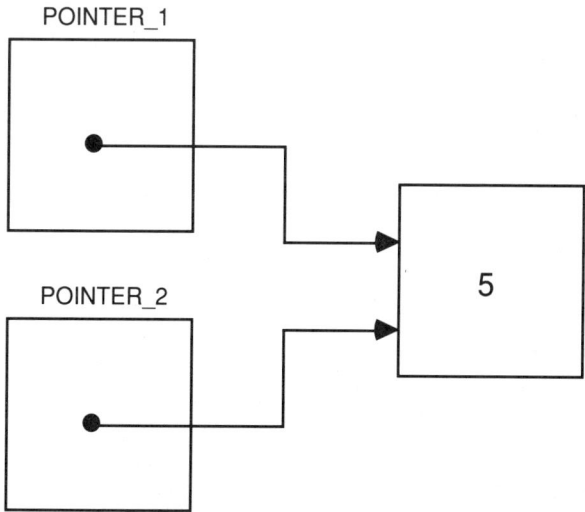

Figure 12.2 Two integer pointers that are equal

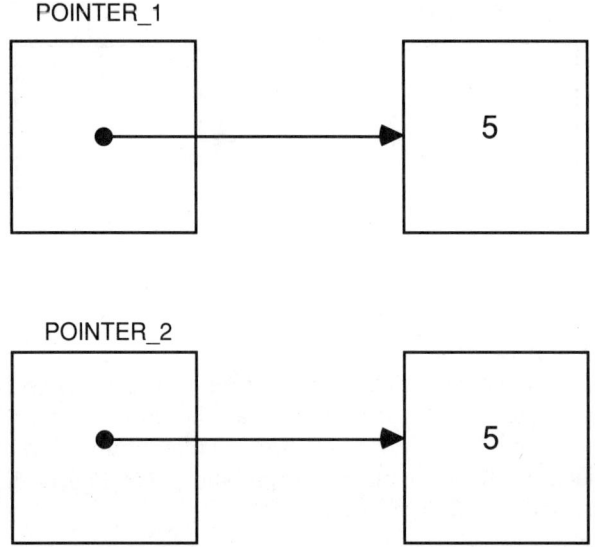

Figure 12.3 Two integer pointers that are not equal

objects that may be pointed to. The second declaration defines the variables, POINTER_1 and POINTER_2, to be of type INTEGER_ACCESS_TYPE. This means that POINTER_1 and POINTER_2 may point only to integer objects.

Optional constraints may be specified in access type declarations:

type INTEGER_ACCESS_TYPE **is access** INTEGER **range** 1..10;
POINTER_1, POINTER_2: INTEGER_ACCESS_TYPE;

In this case, POINTER_1 and POINTER_2 can only point to integer variables containing values in the range from 1 to 10. If an attempt is made to point to an integer value outside of this range, then a constraint error is raised.

In the preceding declarations, POINTER_1 and POINTER_2 are declared to be integer pointers, but they do not yet actually point to any integer variables. When a pointer is not pointing to anything, we say that it is a **null** pointer. Every pointer has an initial default value of **null**. Pointers can also be explicitly made into **null** pointers by being initialized to the keyword **null**:

POINTER_1, POINTER_2: INTEGER_ACCESS_TYPE := **null**;

Null is a legal value for all pointers.

In addition to being initialized to **null**, pointers may also be initialized to point to a variable:

```
type CHARACTER_ACCESS_TYPE is access CHARACTER;
CHARACTER_POINTER: CHARACTER_ACCESS_TYPE := new
    CHARACTER;
```

The first declaration defines the character access type CHARACTER_ACCESS_TYPE. The second declaration defines the variable, CHARACTER_POINTER, to be of type CHARACTER_ACCESS_TYPE. Note the use of the keyword **new**, which is called an allocator. An allocator dynamically creates a variable and accesses it with a pointer. In our example, the allocator creates a character variable that is pointed to by CHARACTER_POINTER. Note that no character value has been assigned to this character variable. The result of these two declarations is shown in Figure 12.4. The box pointed to is left blank to indicate a character variable whose value is undefined.

When pointers are declared, the variable to which they point can be assigned an initial value:

```
POINTER_1, POINTER_2: INTEGER_ACCESS_TYPE := new INTEGER'(5);
```

The allocator, **new**, is followed by a qualified expression that provides initial values of 5 to each of the dynamically allocated variables that are being pointed to. The type name, INTEGER, is followed by a tick mark, ', then the value 5 in parentheses. As a result of this declaration, POINTER_1 and POINTER_2 each point to a <u>different</u> integer variable containing the value of 5 (as shown in Figure 12.3).

So far we have seen the allocator **new** used when pointers are declared. The allocator **new** can also be used in assignment statements:

```
declare
    type LARGE_STAR is (BETELGEUSE, ANTARES, HERCULIS, CETI,
        PEGASI, ALDEBARAN, ARCTURUS);
    type STAR_ACCESS_TYPE is access LARGE_STAR;
    STAR_POINTER: STAR_ACCESS_TYPE;
```

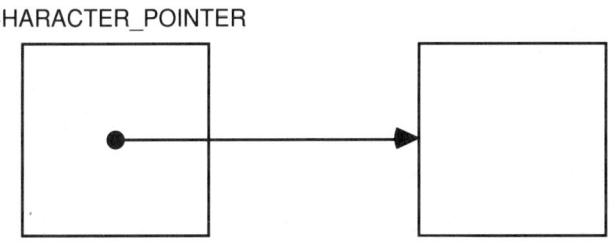

Figure 12.4 Pointer that points to character whose value is undefined

```
begin
    STAR_POINTER := new LARGE_STAR'(BETELGEUSE);
        -- assignment statement using allocator new
end;
```

As a result of the assignment statement, STAR_POINTER points to a variable containing the value BETELGEUSE.

With assignment statements, the same pointer can be made to point to different objects throughout execution of the code:

```
INTEGER_POINTER := new INTEGER'(7);
INTEGER_POINTER := new INTEGER'(9);
INTEGER_POINTER := new INTEGER'(6);
```

In each of these assignment statements, memory is dynamically allocated for different integer variables containing different values. First, the integer variable containing the value 7 is created, then the integer variable containing the value 9, then the variable containing 6. Each time a new variable is created, the previous variable becomes inaccessible because INTEGER_POINTER is no longer pointing to it. (We are assuming that the variable is not being pointed to by another pointer.) But what happens to the memory that was allocated to store an object once the object is no longer accessible? Production quality Ada compilers will automatically reclaim the memory for other uses. Such "garbage collecting," however, is not required by the Ada standards. If you are using an Ada compiler that does not provide this service, then you may wish to explicitly indicate which objects are no longer needed, so that the memory for these objects can be reclaimed. Be careful, however, when doing this. If you reclaim the memory occupied by an object that is still being pointed to, then an erroneous program results. Programmers interested in explicitly reclaiming memory should read about the predefined generic library procedure, called UNCHECKED_DEALLOCATION, in the Ada Language Reference Manual.

Now that we have seen how to assign a value to the object that the pointer points to, let us see how to access that value. This is done by using a dot followed by the keyword **all**, as shown in the following program:

```
with TEXT_IO; use TEXT_IO;
procedure DEMO is
    type CHARACTER_ACCESS_TYPE is access CHARACTER;
    CHARACTER_POINTER: CHARACTER_ACCESS_TYPE;
begin
    CHARACTER_POINTER := new CHARACTER'('Z');
    PUT (CHARACTER_POINTER.all);
        -- outputs Z (the value of the object being pointed to)
    NEW_LINE;
end DEMO;
```

As shown in Figure 12.5, CHARACTER_POINTER.**all** represents the value of the variable pointed to by CHARACTER_POINTER.

Be careful not to confuse the value of a pointer with the value of the variable that it points to. Consider the following code:

```
declare
    type BOOLEAN_ACCESS_TYPE is access BOOLEAN;
    POINTER_1: BOOLEAN_ACCESS_TYPE := new BOOLEAN'(TRUE);
    POINTER_2: BOOLEAN_ACCESS_TYPE := new BOOLEAN'(FALSE);
begin
    POINTER_1.all := POINTER_2.all;
        -- the variable pointed to by POINTER_1 is assigned the value of the
        -- variable pointed to by POINTER_2
    POINTER_1 := POINTER_2;
        -- POINTER_1 now points to the same variable as POINTER_2
end;
```

Note how the assignment statement POINTER_1.**all** := POINTER_2.**all** differs from the assignment statement POINTER_1 := POINTER_2. The first statement assigns the value of the variable pointed to by POINTER_2 to the variable pointed to by POINTER_1. The value being assigned is the Boolean value FALSE. The second statement assigns the value of POINTER_2 to POINTER_1. The result is that POINTER_1 now points to the same object as POINTER_2. The difference between these two assignment statements is shown in Figure 12.6.

Throughout this book, we have seen that objects of different types may not mix. This restriction applies to pointers as well. Even though two pointers point to the same type of object, the pointers themselves are incompatible (may not mix) if they belong to different types. In the following code, even though the pointers CHAR_PTR_1 and CHAR_PTR_2 both point to characters, they are incompatible because one belongs to type CHAR_ACCESS_1 and the other belongs to type CHAR_ACCESS_2:

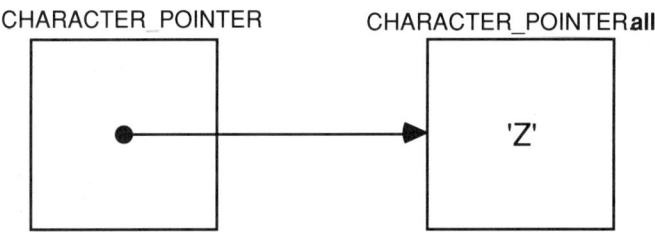

Figure 12.5 Using **.all** to reference the value of a variable pointed to

306 Rendezvous with ADA: A Programmer's Introduction

INITIAL CONDITION

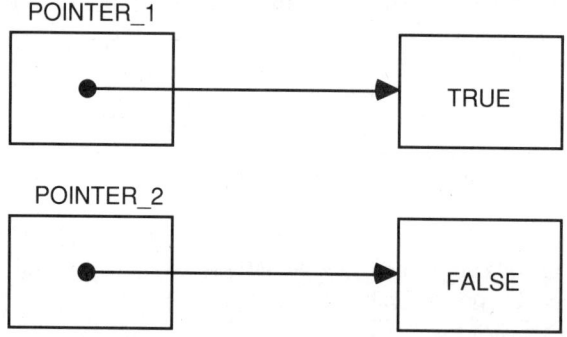

POINTER_1.**all** := POINTER_2.**all** ;

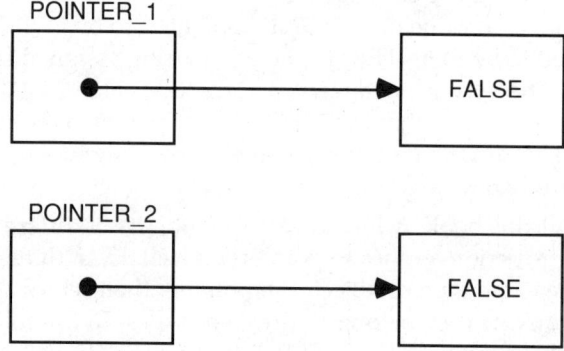

POINTER_1 := POINTER_2;

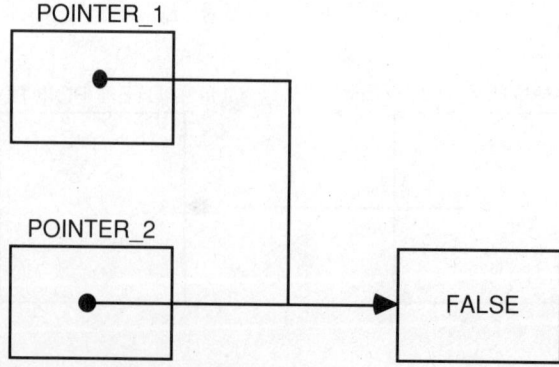

Figure 12.6 Value of pointer versus value of accessed variable

```
declare
    type CHAR_ACCESS_1 is access CHARACTER;
    type CHAR_ACCESS_2 is access CHARACTER;
    CHAR_PTR_1: CHAR_ACCESS_1 := new CHARACTER'('A');
    CHAR_PTR_2: CHAR_ACCESS_2 := new CHARACTER'('B');
begin
    CHAR_PTR_1 := CHAR_PTR_2;        -- illegal; mixed types
    CHAR_PTR_1.all := CHAR_PTR_2.all;  -- OK
end;
```

The first assignment is illegal since, as just explained, an attempt is being made to assign a pointer belonging to the type CHAR_ACCESS_2 to a pointer belonging to a different type, CHAR_ACCESS_1. The second assignment, however, is legal because the types are not mixed: a character value, CHAR_PTR_2.all, is assigned to a character variable, CHAR_PTR_1.all.

So far, all the pointers that we have declared have been variables. Pointers may also be declared as constants:

```
declare
    type INTEGER_ACCESS_TYPE is access INTEGER;
    CONSTANT_POINTER: constant INTEGER_ACCESS_TYPE := new
        INTEGER'(6);
    INTEGER_POINTER: INTEGER_ACCESS_TYPE := new INTEGER'(1);
begin
    CONSTANT_POINTER := INTEGER_POINTER;
        -- illegal; cannot change where it points
    CONSTANT_POINTER.all := INTEGER_POINTER.all; -- OK
        -- only changes value of the variable being pointed to
end;
```

The first executable statement, CONSTANT_POINTER := INTEGER_POINTER, is illegal because a constant pointer must forever point to the same object. The second executable statement, however, is legal, because only the value of the variable being pointed to is being changed. Thus, a constant pointer must only be constant with respect to what variable it points to, not with respect to the value of the variable being pointed to.

When using pointers, be careful to allocate a variable before attempting to access it:

```
declare
    type ACCESS_INT is access INTEGER;
    A, B: ACCESS_INT;
begin
    A := new INTEGER'(7);
    B.all := A.all;   -- null access violation
            -- no variable has been allocated for B
end;
```

The problem with this code is that B.**all** attempts to access the variable "pointed to" by B before this variable exists! To correct this code, first allocate a variable for B to point to:

```
declare
    type ACCESS_INT is access INTEGER;
    A, B: ACCESS_INT;
begin
    A := new INTEGER'(7);
    B := new INTEGER;     -- allocates a variable for B to point to
    B.all := A.all;
end;
```

Pointers may not only point to scalar variables, such as integer, floating point, character, and Boolean variables. Pointers may also point to composite variables: arrays and records. The following example declares a pointer, NAME, that points to an array of characters (a string):

```
with TEXT_IO; use TEXT_IO;
procedure STRING_POINTER is
    type NAME_ACCESS_TYPE is access STRING;
    NAME_POINTER: NAME_ACCESS_TYPE;
begin
    NAME_POINTER := new STRING'("Ada");
    PUT_LINE (NAME_POINTER.all);        -- outputs Ada
    PUT (NAME_POINTER (2));             -- outputs d
    NEW_LINE;
end STRING_POINTER;
```

NAME_POINTER points to a string variable with an initial value of "Ada". The value "Ada" can be referenced by using the keyword **all**:

NAME_POINTER.**all** -- selects the string Ada

In addition to selecting the value of the entire array, we can select a component of the array. To do this, we specify an index, with or without the keyword **all**:

NAME_POINTER.**all** (2) -- selects character d
NAME_POINTER (2) -- also selects d

The keyword **all** is optional because, since the pointer is not a composite object, there is no doubt that we are referring to the object being pointed to rather than the pointer itself.

Pointers are most frequently used to point to records. (The reason for this will become apparent in the next section.) In the following code, pointers STAR_PTR_A and STAR_PTR_B point to records of type STAR_RECORD:

```
with TEXT_IO; use TEXT_IO;
procedure STAR_SIZE is

   type LARGE_STAR is (BETELGEUSE, ANTARES, HERCULIS, CETI,
         PEGASI, ALDEBARAN, ARCTURUS);
   subtype LARGER_THAN_OUR_SUN is INTEGER range 10 .. 1_000;
      -- diameter of star as compared with our sun
   subtype DISTANCE_IN_PARSECS is INTEGER range 4 .. 500;
      -- 1 parsec = 3.26 light years distance

   type STAR_RECORD is
      record
         NAME: LARGE_STAR;
         SIZE: LARGER_THAN_OUR_SUN;
         DISTANCE: DISTANCE_IN_PARSECS;
      end record;

   type STAR_ACCESS_TYPE is access STAR_RECORD;

   package STAR_IO is new ENUMERATION_IO (LARGE_STAR);
   package INT_IO is new INTEGER_IO (INTEGER);
   use STAR_IO, INT_IO;
   STAR_PTR_A, STAR_PTR_B: STAR_ACCESS_TYPE;

begin
   STAR_PTR_A := new STAR_RECORD'( NAME     => BETELGEUSE,
                                   SIZE     => 700,
                                   DISTANCE => 150 );
   STAR_PTR_B := new STAR_RECORD;
   STAR_PTR_B.all := STAR_PTR_A.all;
   PUT ( STAR_PTR_B.NAME );      -- outputs component value
                                 -- BETELGEUSE
   NEW_LINE;   -- same as STAR_PTR_B.all.NAME
   PUT ( STAR_PTR_B.SIZE );      -- outputs component value 700
   NEW_LINE;                     -- same as STAR_PTR_B.all.SIZE
   PUT ( STAR_PTR_B.DISTANCE ); -- outputs component value 150
   NEW_LINE;    -- same as STAR_PTR_B.all.DISTANCE
end STAR_SIZE;
```

As shown in this code, an entire record aggregate may be accessed using the notation **.all**. Individual components of the record are selected by using a dot followed by the name of the component. Once again, when selecting a record component, the keyword **all** is optional but is generally not used.

LINKED LISTS

The examples shown so far in this chapter have limited use. Pointers, however, are very useful because they can connect objects to form data structures such as linked lists, binary trees, and directed graphs. In this section, we will show how pointers are used to create one of the simpler data structures, linked lists. A linked list is a data structure where one item points to another item, which in turn points to another item, and so on. The result is a list of items that are linked together with pointers, as shown in Figure 12.7. Each item of a linked list is typically a record. One of the components of the record is a pointer that points to the next record in the list.

Linked lists have several advantages over alternative data structures, such as arrays of records. A primary advantage of a linked list over an array of records is that computer memory is conserved because memory is allocated only as needed. For each record added to the linked list, memory needed to store the new record is dynamically allocated. Furthermore, as records are removed from the linked list, memory is dynamically deallocated, that is, given back to the computer to be used as needed. In contrast, the size of an an array of records must be established before it is used. Once the array size is established, its size cannot change as the program executes. Thus, when using an array of records, a fixed amount of storage is allocated, which is often much greater than the amount of storage needed. Or conversely, the array may overflow if too many records are added and the size of the array is exceeded.

Another advantage of a linked list is that items may be added to or removed from any location within the list simply by resetting a few pointer values. Thus, the order of items in the list can be maintained with minimal processing. For an array of records, however, if an item needs to be added at a particular location in the array, then all of the array components from that point on need to be shifted to make room for the new item. Similarly, when an item is removed from an array of records, shifting may be required to close the "hole."

Despite these advantages of linked lists over arrays of records, linked lists do have a few disadvantages. For instance, more memory is needed to store a record in a linked list than to store a record component of an array, because extra memory is required to store the pointers. More important,

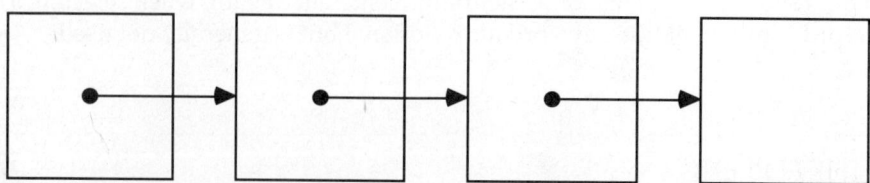

Figure 12.7 Linked list

however, is that an item in a linked list cannot be directly referenced. It can only be referenced by traversing the list from the beginning, until the item is found. In an array of records, a component can be directly referenced with an index value.

Let us now consider a linked list where each item is a record that contains information about a restaurant. Once such a list is constructed, we will write procedures to manipulate the list. One procedure will be able to search the list for a particular restaurant record. Another procedure will be able to add a restaurant record to the list; another procedure, to delete a restaurant record from the list; and another, to output the entire list.

As shown in Figure 12.8, each record of the linked list contains four components: a restaurant name; the type of food served; the average price per meal; and a pointer, NEXT, which points to the next record in this list. Since this fourth component is a pointer, it must belong to an access type that specifies the type of object it can point to. The type of object it can point to are records that belong to this linked list. The pointer is therefore a component of the very type of object that it can point to. This creates a dilemma, as shown in the following declarations:

```
type ETHNICITY is (CHINESE, JAPANESE, FRENCH, KOREAN, MEXICAN,
    ITALIAN, JEWISH, AMERICAN, GERMAN);
subtype NAME_TYPE is STRING ( 1 .. 20 );
subtype PRICE_TYPE is FLOAT range 0.0 .. 150.0;
type RESTAURANT_RECORD is
    record
        NAME: NAME_TYPE;
        FOOD: ETHNICITY;
        AVERAGE_PRICE: PRICE_TYPE;
        NEXT: access RESTAURANT_RECORD;
            -- illegal; cannot refer to RESTAURANT_RECORD until after it is
            -- fully declared
    end record;
```

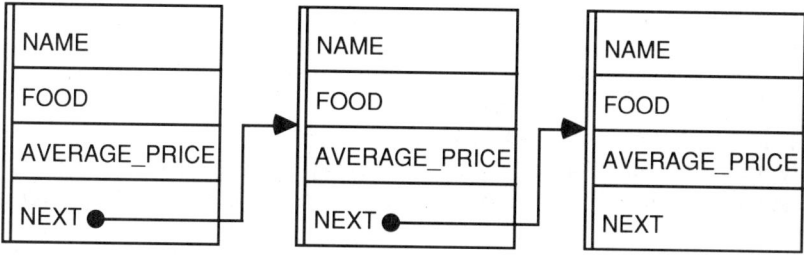

Figure 12.8 Linked list of records

The first three components of the record type RESTAURANT_RECORD are variables of the type NAME_TYPE, ETHNICITY, and PRICE_TYPE. The fourth component is a pointer, NEXT, of the RESTAURANT_RECORD access type. This pointer is a component of the same record type to which it points. Therefore, the declaration for this pointer must reference the very record type of which it is a component. This, unfortunately, is illegal. RESTAURANT_RECORD cannot be referenced by one of its own components. RESTAURANT_RECORD can only be referenced after it has been fully declared, that is, after the keywords **end record**.

Let us try a different approach to defining RESTAURANT_RECORD. Instead of defining the access type in the component declaration for NEXT, let us define the access type before the record type:

```
type ETHNICITY is (CHINESE, JAPANESE, FRENCH, KOREAN, MEXICAN,
    ITALIAN, JEWISH, AMERICAN, GERMAN);
subtype NAME_TYPE is STRING ( 1 .. 20 );
subtype PRICE_TYPE is FLOAT range 0.0 .. 150.0;

type RESTAURANT_ACCESS_TYPE is access RESTAURANT_RECORD;
    -- illegal; RESTAURANT_RECORD has not yet been defined
type RESTAURANT_RECORD is
    record
        NAME: NAME_TYPE;
        FOOD: ETHNICITY;
        AVERAGE_PRICE: PRICE_TYPE;
        NEXT: RESTAURANT_ACCESS_TYPE;
    end record;
```

Unfortunately, this approach also fails. RESTAURANT_RECORD needs to be defined before it is used in the declaration of RESTAURANT_ACCESS_TYPE.

We are thus caught in a "chicken and egg" problem. The access type and the record type reference each other. A type must be declared before it can be referenced. Therefore, the access type must be defined before the record type can reference it, and vice versa. Fortunately, there is a solution to this dilemma, which involves the use of an incomplete type declaration:

```
type ETHNICITY is (CHINESE, JAPANESE, FRENCH, KOREAN, MEXICAN,
    ITALIAN, JEWISH, AMERICAN, GERMAN);
subtype NAME_TYPE is STRING ( 1 .. 20 );
subtype PRICE_TYPE is FLOAT range 0.0 .. 150.0;
type RESTAURANT_RECORD; -- incomplete type declaration
type RESTAURANT_ACCESS_TYPE is access RESTAURANT_RECORD;
```

```
type RESTAURANT_RECORD is -- complete type declaration
   record
      NAME: NAME_TYPE;
      FOOD: ETHNICITY;
      AVERAGE_PRICE: PRICE_TYPE;
      NEXT: RESTAURANT_ACCESS_TYPE; -- pointer
   end record;
```

In this example, the incomplete type declaration consists of the single statement:

```
type RESTAURANT_RECORD; -- incomplete type declaration
```

This incomplete declaration makes the identifier, RESTAURANT_RECORD, available to subsequent declarations without defining the nature of the type. The complete declaration of RESTAURANT_RECORD must follow the incomplete declaration. Note that the access type, RESTAURANT_ACCESS_TYPE, is placed between the incomplete declaration and the complete declaration. Between these two declarations, only access types can reference the incomplete type declaration.

Now that we have defined the record type for our linked list, let us define a few records and link them together. The first record contains information about the Chinese restaurant "Wok N Roll" and is placed at the head of the list with the following declaration:

```
HEAD: RESTAURANT_ACCESS_TYPE := new
   RESTAURANT_RECORD'(  NAME           => "Wok N Roll    ",
                        FOOD           => CHINESE,
                        AVERAGE_PRICE  => 9.45,
                        NEXT           => null       );
```

Since this record does not point to any other record, we initialized the pointer, NEXT, to **null**. This is shown pictorially in Figure 12.9.

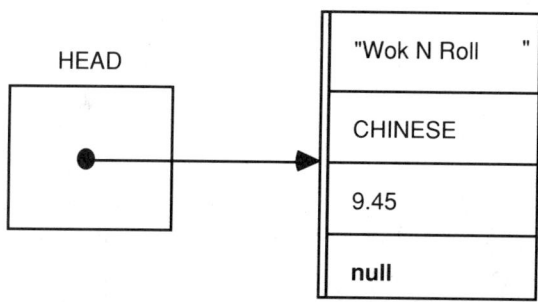

Figure 12.9 Linked list with one record

Let us now add the German restaurant "Frank N Stein" as the second record in our list:

```
HEAD.NEXT:= new
     RESTAURANT_RECORD'(  NAME           => "Frank N Stein   ",
                          FOOD           => GERMAN,
                          AVERAGE_PRICE  => 12.75,
                          NEXT           => null       );
```

After this statement is executed, the pointer of "Wok N Roll" now points to the newly allocated record, "Frank N Stein". This is shown in Figure 12.10.

Now that we understand the structure of linked lists, let us create a package that contains procedures for adding items to a linked list, deleting items from this list, searching this linked list, and outputting this linked list:

package RESTAURANT_LINKED_LIST **is**

   type ETHNICITY **is** (CHINESE, JAPANESE, FRENCH, KOREAN,
         MEXICAN, ITALIAN, JEWISH, AMERICAN, GERMAN);
   subtype NAME_TYPE **is** STRING (1 .. 20);
   subtype PRICE_TYPE **is** FLOAT **range** 0.0 .. 150.0;

   type RESTAURANT_RECORD; -- incomplete type declaration
   type RESTAURANT_POINTER **is access** RESTAURANT_RECORD;
   type RESTAURANT_RECORD **is** -- complete type declaration
      record
         NAME: NAME_TYPE;
         FOOD: ETHNICITY;
         AVERAGE_PRICE: PRICE_TYPE;
         NEXT: RESTAURANT_POINTER;
      end record;

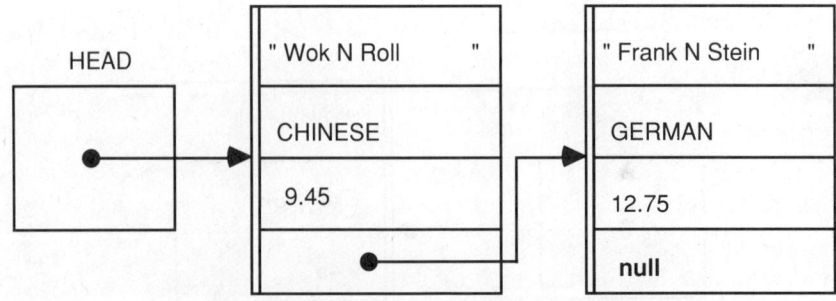

Figure 12.10   Linked list with two records

Access Types **315**

```
procedure ADD_TO_LIST (NEW_ENTRY: in RESTAURANT_RECORD);
procedure GET (NEW_RESTAURANT: out RESTAURANT_RECORD);
procedure DELETE_FROM_LIST (TARGET: in NAME_TYPE);
procedure SEARCH_LIST (TARGET: in NAME_TYPE);
procedure OUTPUT_LIST;
end RESTAURANT_LINKED_LIST;
```

```
with TEXT_IO; use TEXT_IO; -- not needed in the specification
package body RESTAURANT_LINKED_LIST is

    HEAD, TAIL: RESTAURANT_POINTER := null;

    package FOOD_IO is new ENUMERATION_IO (ETHNICITY);
    package PRICE_IO is new FLOAT_IO (PRICE_TYPE);
    use FOOD_IO, PRICE_IO;
    -- procedure to add a record to the linked list
    procedure ADD_TO_LIST (NEW_ENTRY: in
            RESTAURANT_RECORD) is
        ITEM_TO_ADD: RESTAURANT_POINTER;
    begin
        ITEM_TO_ADD := new RESTAURANT_RECORD'(NEW_ENTRY);
        TAIL.NEXT := ITEM_TO_ADD;
        TAIL := ITEM_TO_ADD;
        PUT_LINE (". . . Added");
    end ADD_TO_LIST;

    -- procedure to get information for a record
    procedure GET (NEW_RESTAURANT: out RESTAURANT_RECORD) is
    begin
        PUT_LINE ("Enter restaurant name:");
        GET (NEW_RESTAURANT.NAME);
        PUT_LINE ("What kind of food is served?");
        GET (NEW_RESTAURANT.FOOD);
        PUT_LINE ("What is the average price per meal?");
        GET (NEW_RESTAURANT.AVERAGE_PRICE);
    end GET;

    -- procedure to delete a record from the linked list
    procedure DELETE_FROM_LIST (TARGET: in NAME_TYPE) is
        PREVIOUS: RESTAURANT_POINTER := HEAD;
        CURRENT: RESTAURANT_POINTER := HEAD.NEXT;
    begin
        if CURRENT = null then -- if null list, then nothing to delete
            PUT_LINE ("Cannot delete; list is empty");
            return;
        end if;
        loop
            if CURRENT.NAME = TARGET then -- found it
                if CURRENT.NEXT = null then -- TARGET is last item in list
                    PREVIOUS.NEXT := NULL;
                    TAIL := PREVIOUS;
```

```ada
                else                          -- TARGET is within list
                    CURRENT := CURRENT.NEXT;
                    PREVIOUS.NEXT := CURRENT;
                end if;
                PUT_LINE (". . . Deleted");
                return;
            end if;
            if CURRENT.NEXT = null then -- end of list and item not found
                PUT_LINE ("Item not found);
                return;
            end if;
            PREVIOUS := CURRENT; -- advance pointers
            CURRENT := CURRENT.NEXT;
        end loop;
end DELETE_FROM_LIST;

-- procedure to search the linked list for record with specified
-- restaurant name
procedure SEARCH_LIST ( TARGET: in NAME_TYPE ) is
    RESTAURANT: RESTAURANT_POINTER := HEAD; -- search from the
                                                          -- head
begin
    PUT ("RESTAURANT");
    SET_COL (25);
    PUT ("FOOD SERVED");
    SET_COL (43);
    PUT ("AVERAGE PRICE");
    NEW_LINE;
    loop
        if RESTAURANT.NAME = TARGET then -- found it
            PUT (RESTAURANT.NAME);
            SET_COL (25);
            PUT (RESTAURANT.FOOD, 18);
            PUT (RESTAURANT.AVERAGE_PRICE, 3, 2, 0);
            NEW_LINE;
            exit;
        elsif RESTAURANT.NEXT = null then -- not found
            PUT_LINE ("Restaurant " & TARGET & " not found.");
            exit;
        else
            RESTAURANT := RESTAURANT.NEXT; -- still need to search
        end if;
    end loop;
end SEARCH_LIST;

-- procedure to output all the information in the linked list
procedure OUTPUT_LIST is
    RESTAURANT: RESTAURANT_POINTER := HEAD.NEXT;
        -- start with record after dummy header
```

```
    begin
      PUT ("RESTAURANT");
      SET_COL (25);
      PUT ("FOOD SERVED");
      SET_COL (43);
      PUT ("AVERAGE PRICE");
      NEW_LINE;
      while RESTAURANT /= null loop
        PUT (RESTAURANT.NAME);
        SET_COL (25);
        PUT (RESTAURANT.FOOD, 18);
        PUT (RESTAURANT.AVERAGE_PRICE, 3, 2, 0);
        NEW_LINE;
        RESTAURANT := RESTAURANT.NEXT; -- point to next item
      end loop;
    end OUTPUT_LIST;

begin  -- initialization part
       -- create linked list, initialize pointers, create "dummy" header entry
  HEAD := new RESTAURANT_RECORD;
  HEAD.NAME := "GOURMAND'S DATABASE ";
  TAIL := HEAD;

end RESTAURANT_LINKED_LIST;
```

This package defines a linked list of records, plus operations that may be performed on this list. The operations are provided by five procedures: ADD_TO_LIST, which adds an item to the linked list; GET, which gets information for a record; DELETE_FROM_LIST, which deletes a specified record from the list; SEARCH_LIST, which searches for a specified record; and finally, OUTPUT_LIST, which outputs the information contained in each record of the linked list.

Note that the package body contains an executable statement (initialization) part. In this part, two pointers, HEAD and TAIL, are initialized to point to a "dummy" header record:

```
HEAD := new RESTAURANT_RECORD;
HEAD.NAME := "GOURMAND'S DATABASE ";
TAIL := HEAD;
```

The effect of this code is shown pictorially in Figure 12.11. To make Figures 12.11 through 12.18 less cluttered, the record components dealing with the kind of food and the average price per meal are not shown. Furthermore, the names of restaurants are not placed in quotes, and trailing blanks are ignored.

The header record does not contain actual information about a restaurant but contains a title for the linked list: GOURMAND'S DATABASE. By having a header record, the linked list can be created and initialized

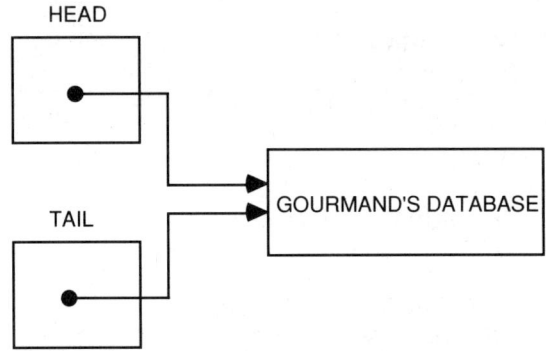

Figure 12.11 Initial condition of linked list

without requiring meaningful record information. Both pointers, HEAD and TAIL, are kept updated so that HEAD always points to the dummy header record and TAIL always points to the last record in the list. Let us now discuss each procedure contained in the package.

The ADD_TO_LIST procedure adds a record to the end of the linked list. When ADD_TO_LIST is invoked with, for example, the restaurant record for "Wok N Roll", this record value is passed to the formal parameter NEW_ENTRY. The following statement then creates a pointer ITEM_TO_ADD, which points to the new entry, "Wok N Roll":

ITEM_TO_ADD := **new** RESTAURANT_RECORD'(NEW_ENTRY);

This is shown in Figure 12.12.

Next, the pointer of the header record (TAIL.NEXT) is changed to point to the new record:

TAIL.NEXT := ITEM_TO_ADD;

This is shown in Figure 12.13.

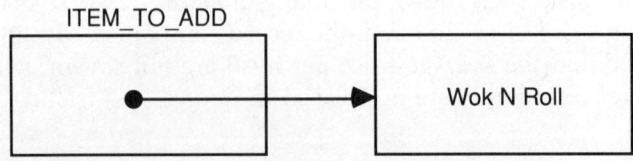

Figure 12.12 Pointer to a record to be added to linked list

Access Types **319**

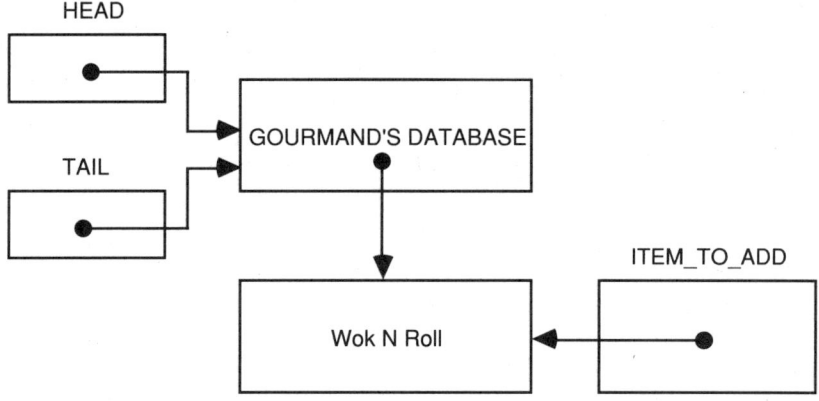

Figure 12.13 Header record updated to point to new record

Finally, TAIL is updated to point to the new record:

TAIL := ITEM_TO_ADD;

This is shown in Figure 12.14. ITEM_TO_ADD is left pointing to the last item, with no ill effects.

Suppose that ADD_TO_LIST is invoked once again, this time with the record for "Frank N Stein". A pointer to "Frank N Stein", ITEM_TO_ADD, is created, and the last record in the list, "Wok N Roll", is directed to point to this new record (Figure 12.15). TAIL is then updated to point to the new record (Figure 12.16). ITEM_TO_ADD is left pointing to the last item, with no ill effects.

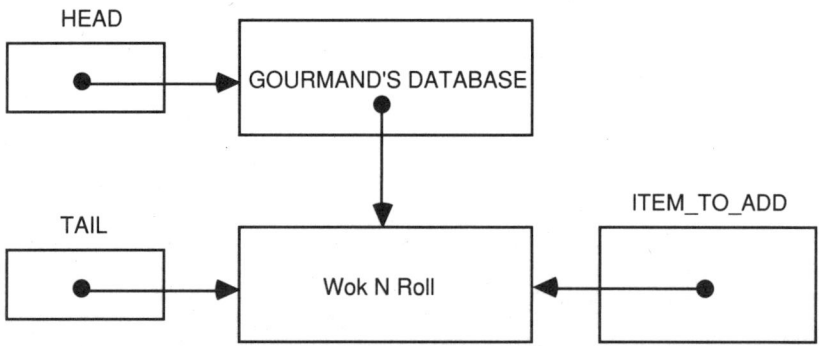

Figure 12.14 TAIL updated to point to end of list

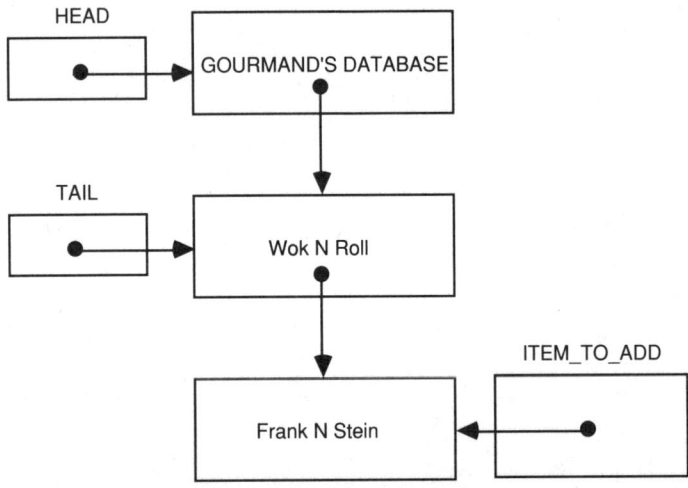

Figure 12.15 Last record in list updated to point to new record

The next procedure defined in RESTAURANT_LINKED_LIST is GET. This procedure simply prompts the user for information needed to initialize a new record. This new record may then be added to the list by the ADD_TO_LIST procedure.

The next procedure, DELETE_FROM_LIST, removes a record with the specified restaurant name from the list. Removing a record from the list is a

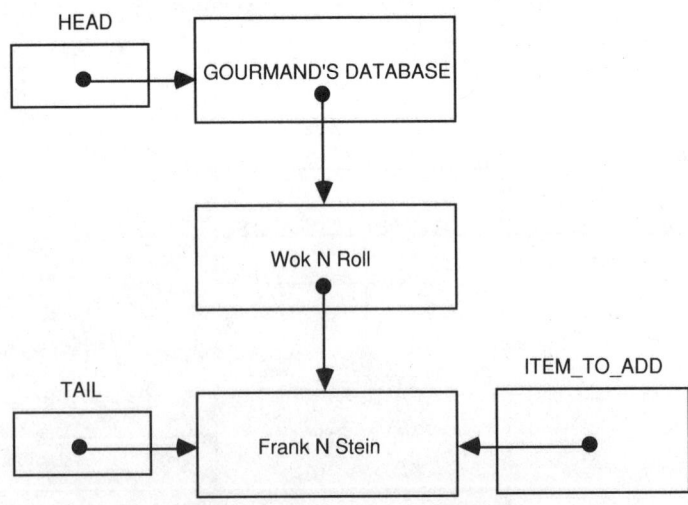

Figure 12.16 TAIL updated to point to last record

bit more complex than adding a record to the list. Two pointers, PREVIOUS and CURRENT, traverse the list together. PREVIOUS points to the record listed immediately before the record pointed to by CURRENT. Initially, PREVIOUS points to the dummy header record, and CURRENT points to the next record (or to **null** if there is no such record):

PREVIOUS: RESTAURANT_POINTER := HEAD;
CURRENT: RESTAURANT_POINTER := HEAD.NEXT;

Now assume the initial situation shown in Figure 12.17. Suppose that we wish to delete the record "Wok N Roll". To do this, DELETE_FROM_LIST is invoked with the restaurant name, "Wok N Roll". This name is passed to the formal parameter TARGET. DELETE_FROM_LIST then checks whether the list is empty (except, of course, for the header record):

if CURRENT = **null then** . . .

If the list is empty, then no records can be deleted. A message is output and the procedure terminates. If the list is not empty, then a loop is entered and a check is made to see whether CURRENT is pointing to the target record, "Wok N Roll":

if CURRENT.NAME = TARGET **then** . . .

In the situation shown in Figure 12.17, the target record has been found.

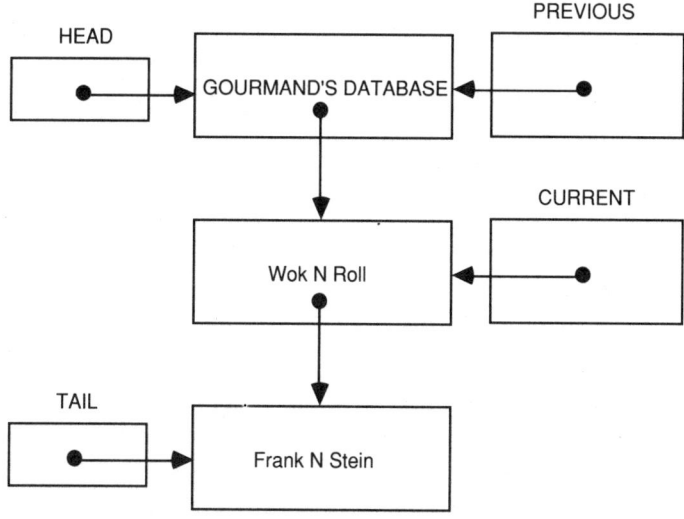

Figure 12.17 Initial condition for DELETE_FROM_LIST

At this point, different actions are taken depending on whether or not the record to be deleted is at the end of the list. If the record is not at the end of the list, then CURRENT is advanced. The record pointed to by PREVIOUS is updated to point to the same object pointed to by CURRENT:

CURRENT := CURRENT.NEXT;
PREVIOUS.NEXT := CURRENT;

This is shown in Figure 12.18. Since no records point to "Wok N Roll", this record is inaccessible. A compiler can thus use the memory taken up by "Wok N Roll" for other purposes.

If the record to be deleted were at the end of the list, then the pointer of the preceding record would be set to **null**:

PREVIOUS.NEXT := **null**;

TAIL then would be set to point to this preceding record:

TAIL := PREVIOUS;

If the end of the list had been reached and the record still had not been found, then a message would be output that the record did not exist.

The next procedure, SEARCH_LIST, searches for a record with the specified restaurant name. SEARCH_LIST keeps traversing the linked list until

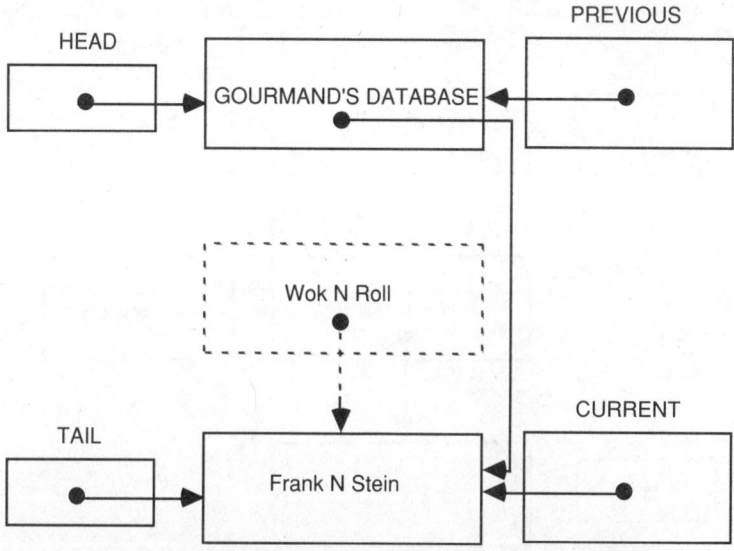

Figure 12.18 Pointers of CURRENT and header records updated

either it reaches the end without finding the record or until it finds the record. If the record is found, the information for this record is output. SEARCH_LIST traverses the list using the statement:

RESTAURANT := RESTAURANT.NEXT;

Each time this statement is executed, RESTAURANT.NEXT points to the next record in the list.

The procedure SEARCH_LIST uses several different features to format the output into columns. The procedure SET_COL places output at a specified column. The PUT procedure used for outputting the kind of food contains a second parameter, which specifies the minimum field width for the output. The PUT procedure used for outputting the average price contains a second, third, and fourth parameter used for formatting. The second parameter specifies the minimum number of spaces to the left of the number's decimal point. The third parameter specifies the number of digits to the right of the decimal point. The fourth parameter, when set to 0, specifies that scientific notation (exponents) is not to be used. These formatting features, plus many others, will be discussed in Chapter 14.

The last procedure, OUTPUT_LIST, uses the same method of traversing the list as SEARCH_LIST and outputs the information contained in all the records of the list, except the dummy header record.

Now that we have examined the contents of the RESTAURANT_LINKED_LIST package, let us consider how a program can use this package:

```
with TEXT_IO, RESTAURANT_LINKED_LIST;
use TEXT_IO, RESTAURANT_LINKED_LIST;
procedure RESTAURANTS is

    CHOICE: INTEGER range 1.. 5;
    NEW_RESTAURANT: RESTAURANT_RECORD;
    RESTAURANT_NAME: NAME_TYPE;
    package INT_IO is new INTEGER_IO (INTEGER);
    use INT_IO;

begin
    PUT_LINE ("THE GOURMAND'S DATABASE");

    loop
      NEW_LINE;
      PUT_LINE ("Enter your choice (1 to 5):");
      PUT_LINE ("   1. Enter a new restaurant.");
      PUT_LINE ("   2. Delete a restaurant entry.");
      PUT_LINE ("   3. Search for a restaurant entry.");
      PUT_LINE ("   4. List all of the entries.");
      PUT_LINE ("   5. Exit the program.");
      GET (CHOICE);
```

```ada
      case CHOICE is
         when 1 =>
            GET ( NEW_RESTAURANT ); -- uses overloaded GET procedure
            ADD_TO_LIST ( NEW_RESTAURANT );
         when 2 =>
            PUT_LINE ("Enter name of restaurant you want deleted:");
            GET (RESTAURANT_NAME);
            DELETE_FROM_LIST ( RESTAURANT_NAME );
         when 3 =>
            PUT_LINE ("Enter name of restaurant to search:");
            GET (RESTAURANT_NAME);
            SEARCH_LIST ( RESTAURANT_NAME );
         when 4 =>
            OUTPUT_LIST;
         when 5 =>
            exit;
      end case;
   end loop;

   PUT_LINE ("Have a gastronomically rewarding day!");
end RESTAURANTS;
```

This program mentions the RESTAURANT_LINKED_LIST package in its **with** clause and uses all of the procedures in this package. The procedures are invoked depending on the selections made by the user. The program keeps prompting the user with a list of choices until the user decides to exit the program. The following is a sample run of this program:

THE GOURMAND'S DATABASE

Enter your choice (1 to 5):
    1. Enter a new restaurant.
    2. Delete a restaurant entry.
    3. Search for a restaurant entry.
    4. List all of the entries.
    5. Exit the program.
> 1
Enter restaurant name:
> "Tortured Taco   "
What kind of food is served?
> MEXICAN
What is the average price per meal?
> 7.75

Enter your choice (1 to 5):
    1. Enter a new restaurant.
    2. Delete a restaurant entry.
    3. Search for a restaurant entry.
    4. List all of the entries.
    5. Exit the program.
> 1

Enter restaurant name:
> **"Quark Soup   "**
What kind of food is served?
> **AMERICAN**
What is the average price per meal?
> **15.85**

Enter your choice (1 to 5):
    1. Enter a new restaurant.
    2. Delete a restaurant entry.
    3. Search for a restaurant entry.
    4. List all of the entries.
    5. Exit the program.
> **1**
Enter restaurant name:
> **"Casa de Corned Beef "**
What kind of food is served?
> **JEWISH**
What is the average price per meal?
> **8.95**

Enter your choice (1 to 5):
    1. Enter a new restaurant.
    2. Delete a restaurant entry.
    3. Search for a restaurant entry.
    4. List all of the entries.
    5. Exit the program.
> **4**

RESTAURANT	FOOD SERVED	AVERAGE PRICE
Tortured Taco	MEXICAN	7.75
Quark Soup	AMERICAN	15.85
Casa de Corned Beef	JEWISH	8.95

Enter your choice (1 to 5):
    1. Enter a new restaurant.
    2. Delete a restaurant entry.
    3. Search for a restaurant entry.
    4. List all of the entries.
    5. Exit the program.
> **2**
Enter name of restaurant you want deleted:
> **"Quark Soup   "**
. . . Deleted

Enter your choice (1 to 5):
    1. Enter a new restaurant.
    2. Delete a restaurant entry.
    3. Search for a restaurant entry.
    4. List all of the entries.
    5. Exit the program.
> **3**

Enter name of restaurant to search:
> **"Casa de Corned Beef "**

RESTAURANT	FOOD SERVED	AVERAGE PRICE
Casa de Corned Beef	JEWISH	8.95

Enter your choice (1 to 5):
    1. Enter a new restaurant.
    2. Delete a restaurant entry.
    3. Search for a restaurant entry.
    4. List all of the entries.
    5. Exit the program.
> 5

Have a gastronomically rewarding day!

Linked lists are just one of the data structures that can be implemented using pointers. A discussion of other data structures is beyond the scope of this book.

Access types are one of Ada's more advanced types. The next chapter considers other advanced types, such as derived types and fixed point types.

EXERCISES

1. Which of the following statements contain errors? Explain the errors.

   ```
   declare
       type CHARACTER_POINTER is access CHARACTER;
       type INTEGER_POINTER is access INTEGER range 1 .. 9;
       CHAR_PTR: CHARACTER_POINTER;
       INT_PTR: INTEGER_POINTER;
   begin
       CHAR_PTR := new CHARACTER'('A');
       INT_PTR := new INTEGER'(11);
   end;
   ```

2. Pictorially show the difference between the two assignment statements in the statement part of this block:

   ```
   declare
       type INTEGER_ACCESS_TYPE is access INTEGER;
       INT_POINTER_1: INTEGER_ACCESS_TYPE := new INTEGER'(1);
       INT_POINTER_2: INTEGER_ACCESS_TYPE := new INTEGER'(2);
   begin
       INT_POINTER_1.all := INT_POINTER_2.all;
       INT_POINTER_1 := INT_POINTER_2;
   end;
   ```

3. What values do each of the following PUT statements output?

    ```
    with TEXT_IO; use TEXT_IO;
    procedure OUTPUT_ITEMS is
       type STRING_ACCESS_TYPE is access STRING;
       STRING_POINTER: STRING_ACCESS_TYPE;
    begin
       STRING_POINTER := new STRING'("Sesquipedalian");
       PUT (STRING_POINTER.all);
       NEW_LINE;
       PUT (STRING_POINTER (10) &
            STRING_POINTER (9) &
            STRING_POINTER (13) );
       NEW_LINE;
    end OUTPUT_ITEMS;
    ```

4. Which of the following statements contain errors? Explain the errors.

    ```
    declare
       type NATURAL_POINTER is access NATURAL;
       type POSITIVE_POINTER is access POSITIVE;
       NAT: NATURAL_POINTER := new NATURAL'(0);
       POS: POSITIVE_POINTER := new POSITIVE'(1);
    begin
       NAT := POS;
       POS := NAT;
       POS.all := NAT.all;
       NAT.all := POS.all;
    end;
    ```

5. What will the following program output?

    ```
    with TEXT_IO; use TEXT_IO;
    procedure DEMO is
       package INT_IO is new INTEGER_IO (INTEGER);
       use INT_IO;
       type R is
          record
             A: INTEGER;
             B: CHARACTER;
          end record;
       type R_POINTER is access R;
       POINTER: R_POINTER := new R'(2, 'C');
    begin
       PUT (POINTER.A);
       NEW_LINE;
       PUT (POINTER.B);
    end DEMO;
    ```

6. Find the error in the following code:
   ```
   declare
      type R is
         record
            A: INTEGER;
            B: CHARACTER;
         end record;
      type R_POINTER is access R;
      P1, P2: R_POINTER;
   begin
      P1 := new R'( A => 5,
                    B => 'a' );
      P2.all := P1.all;
   end;
   ```

7. Modify the program RESTAURANTS and the package RESTAURANT_LINKED_LIST presented in this chapter so that the program asks the user to enter the type of food desired and then prints all the restaurants that feature that kind of food.

8. Modify the program RESTAURANTS and the package RESTAURANT_LINKED_LIST presented in this chapter so that the program prompts the user for both the type of food desired and the maximum average price per meal. Have the program then output all the restaurants, if any, that satisfy these requirements.

9. Modify the package RESTAURANT_LINKED_LIST to add items to the front of the list (after the header record) instead of to the back of the list.

Chapter 13

MORE ABOUT TYPES

In this chapter, we will discuss some of the more advanced aspects of types. We will begin by discussing universal types, which consist of numeric literals and special kinds of constants called named numbers. We will next explore derived types, which are types derived from existing types. Fixed point types will then be covered. A fixed point type consists of real numbers in which the decimal point is at a fixed location. Finally, we will discuss implicit conversion of universal types.

UNIVERSAL TYPES

Universal types include the universal integer type and the universal real type. The universal integer type consists of integer literals and integer named numbers. The universal real type consists of real literals and real named numbers. This classification of universal types is shown in Figure 13.1. Recall from Chapter 3 that integer literals are whole numbers that do not contain a decimal point, such as 7, 0, and 32. Real literals are numbers that contain a decimal point (fractional part), such as 3.2, 0.0, and 15.2. Integer literals automatically belong to the universal integer type, and real literals automatically belong to the universal real type.

Integer named numbers and real named numbers are, as the name implies, numbers that are represented by a name. Named numbers are special kinds of constants that are declared in number declarations. Number declarations appear like regular constant declarations, except that the

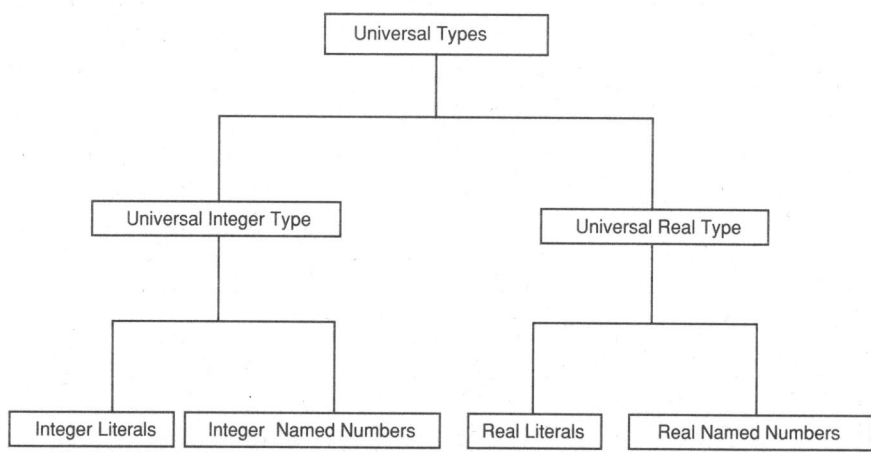

Figure 13.1 Classification of universal types

name of a type is omitted. To contrast these two forms of declarations, consider the following regular constant declaration:

    DOZEN: **constant** INTEGER := 12; -- DOZEN is a regular integer
                                                                   -- constant that belongs to
                                                                   -- type INTEGER

Now consider the following number declaration:

    DOZEN: **constant** := 12; -- DOZEN is a named number that
                                        -- belongs to type universal integer

In the number declaration, the keyword **constant** is not followed by the name of a type, such as INTEGER. Rather, the compiler determines the type by examining the value being assigned to the named number DOZEN. Because the integer literal 12 is assigned to DOZEN, the compiler determines that DOZEN belongs to a universal integer type. The programmer cannot explicitly declare an object to belong to a universal integer or universal real type, because there are no predefined type identifiers, such as UNIVERSAL_INTEGER or UNIVERSAL_REAL, that the programmer can use. Note that variables cannot belong to a universal type.

Real named numbers are declared similarly to integer named numbers:

    PI: **constant** := 3.1415927; -- PI is a named number that
                                              -- belongs to type universal real

Since PI is initialized to a real literal, it belongs to the type universal real.

Declarations having the form of a number declaration can only be used to declare named numbers. The following declaration is therefore illegal:

QUESTION: **constant** := '?'; -- error

The primary advantage of using number declarations instead of regular constant declarations is that number declarations are more portable between computers. Consider, for example, the following regular constant declaration:

SPEED_OF_LIGHT: **constant** INTEGER := 186_000;

This declaration will probably be legal on a 32-bit computer but not on a 16-bit computer. On 32-bit computers, INTEGER'LAST (the largest integer supported) is often 2,147,483,647, because this is the largest positive integer value that can be contained in a 32-bit word. The integer literal 186_000, used in the preceding declaration, is less than this maximum integer value, so no problems arise. On 16-bit computers, however, INTEGER'LAST is often 32,767, because this is the largest positive integer value that can be contained in a 16-bit word. On these 16-bit computers, the preceding regular constant declaration will raise a constraint error, because we are attempting to initialize a constant to an integer value that is larger than INTEGER'LAST.

To make the preceding regular constant declaration portable, rewrite it as a number declaration:

SPEED_OF_LIGHT: **constant** := 186_000;

This number declaration, unlike the previous declaration, is legal on 16-bit and 32-bit computers, as well as on computers with other word sizes. This number declaration is legal on all these computers because, by making SPEED_OF_LIGHT belong to a universal type, it does not have any practical size constraints; it is not limited to the range of values of the predefined type INTEGER. Rather, a named number can assume a range of values that must be at least as great as any of the predefined integer types, such as LONG_INTEGER, that are supported by a particular system. To determine the smallest and largest predefined integers on a given system, access the package SYSTEM, which contains system dependent constants, and output MIN_INT and MAX_INT. (Similarly, objects belonging to the universal real type have a range that must be at least as great as any of the real types supported by a particular system.)

There is a second advantage, although a very minor one, of using number declarations instead of regular constant declarations: code may execute faster. This is because, when named numbers are combined with other named numbers or numeric literals, the resulting expression is evaluated at compilation time, not at runtime. However, with any good optimizing compiler, there is little, if any, difference in execution speed.

Expressions consisting only of named numbers or numeric literals are called literal expressions. The following program outputs examples of literal expressions:

```ada
with TEXT_IO; use TEXT_IO;
procedure LITERAL_EXPRESSIONS is

    package INT_IO is new INTEGER_IO (INTEGER);
    package REAL_IO is new FLOAT_IO (FLOAT);
    use INT_IO, REAL_IO;

    -- the following are number declarations
    DOZEN: constant := 12;
    BAKERS_DOZEN: constant := DOZEN + 1;
    PI: constant := 3.1415927;
    CIRCUMFERENCE_OF_UNIT_CIRCLE: constant := 2.0 * PI;
    ZERO, ZILCH, ALL_GONE, NONE: constant := 0;

begin -- LITERAL_EXPRESSIONS

    -- this code outputs literal expressions that only contain named
    -- numbers and numeric literals
    PUT ( CIRCUMFERENCE_OF_UNIT_CIRCLE );
    PUT ( 7 + 2 - 1 );
    PUT ( 5 * DOZEN + BAKERS_DOZEN );
    PUT ( ALL_GONE - ZILCH );

end LITERAL_EXPRESSIONS;
```

As shown in this code, named numbers can be initialized to literal expressions, such as DOZEN + 1 or 2.0 * PI. Named numbers may not be initialized to nonliteral expressions, such as the following:

```ada
DOZEN: constant INTEGER := 12;
BAKERS_DOZEN: constant := DOZEN + 1;  -- illegal; DOZEN is not
                                      -- a named number
```

This code is illegal because it attempts to initialize the named number BAKERS_DOZEN to the nonliteral expression DOZEN + 1. The expression DOZEN + 1 is a nonliteral expression because DOZEN belongs to type INTEGER, not to type universal integer.

It should be mentioned that certain attributes yield numeric values that belong to the universal integer type or the universal real type. For instance, the attribute POS yields a universal integer that represents the position of an item in a discrete type. Note that since POS may have a dynamic parameter (one that is evaluated at runtime), when POS appears in an expression, the expression might not be evaluated at compilation time. Hence, although literal expressions are evaluated at compilation time, not every expression that yields a universal integer or a universal real result is evaluated at compilation time.

Before ending our discussion of universal types, let us consider universal types as they relate to strong typing. Ada enforces strong typing with fanatic fervor. Objects of different types cannot be assigned or compared to one another and cannot appear in the same expression. However, even Ada is forgiving on rare occasions. For instance, universal integers may mix with any integer type, and universal real numbers may mix with any real (floating point or fixed point) type. Thus an expression such as INT + 2, where INT belongs to the INTEGER type, is legal. We do not need to convert explicitly the universal integer 2 to an INTEGER type because Ada implicitly converts it for us. This issue will be discussed further after we cover derived types and fixed point types in the next two sections of this chapter.

Ada is also forgiving in that universal real numbers and universal integers may appear in the same expression. The result is always of type universal real. The rules governing the mixing of universal types follow: (1) Universal real numbers may be multiplied by universal integers and vice versa; (2) Universal real numbers may be divided by universal integers, but universal integers may not be divided by universal real numbers; and (3) No other forms of mixed type expressions are allowed, such as adding or subtracting universal real numbers and integers from one another. These rules are illustrated in the following block statement:

declare
    REAL: FLOAT;
    TWO: **constant** := 2;
    ONE_HALF: **constant** := 0.5;
begin
    REAL := 2.0 * 5;   -- yields 10.0
    REAL := 5 * 2.0;   -- yields 10.0
    REAL := 5.0 / 2;   -- yields 2.5
    REAL := 2 / 5.0;   -- will not compile
    REAL := TWO * ONE_HALF;   -- yields 1.0
    REAL := ONE_HALF * TWO;   -- yields 1.0
    REAL := ONE_HALF / TWO;   -- yields 0.25
    REAL := TWO / ONE_HALF;   -- will not compile
    REAL := 5.0 + 2;   -- will not compile
    REAL := 5.0 - 2;   -- will not compile
    REAL := TWO + ONE_HALF;   -- will not compile
    REAL := TWO - ONE_HALF;   -- will not compile
    REAL := (TWO * 1.0) - ONE_HALF; -- yields 1.5
end;

The last statement in the example merits closer scrutiny:

    REAL := (TWO * 1.0) - ONE_HALF;

Universal real numbers cannot be subtracted from universal integers. However, multiplying the universal integer TWO by 1.0 has the effect of a type conversion. In other words, TWO * 1.0 yields the universal real number 2.0, from which the universal real number ONE_HALF can then be subtracted. This is the only way to "convert" a universal integer to a universal real number; there is no explicit type, UNIVERSAL_REAL, that can be used as a type conversion operator.

DERIVED TYPES

A derived type creates a new type from an existing "parent type":

    type PERCENT **is new** INTEGER **range** 0 .. 100; -- derived type

Derived type declarations resemble subtype declarations:

    subtype PERCENT **is** INTEGER **range** 0 .. 100; -- subtype

Syntactically, these type declarations differ in only two ways. First, derived type declarations begin with the keyword **type**; subtype declarations begin with the keyword **subtype**. Second, derived type declarations, unlike subtype declarations, contain the keyword **new**.

Despite the similar appearance between subtype and derived type declarations, there are major differences. Recall from Chapter 3 that a subtype does not introduce a new type but merely places an optional constraint on the values of its base type. A derived type, however, creates a new type from an existing parent type. (Note the terminology: a subtype is based on a base type, but a derived type is derived from a parent type.) Since a subtype does not introduce a new type, objects of a subtype may mix with objects of its base type. Furthermore, objects of different subtypes created from the same base type may mix. Since a derived type introduces a new type, objects of a derived type may <u>not</u> mix with objects of its parent type. Furthermore, objects of different derived types may not mix, even when they are created from the same parent type.

Although objects of different derived types may not mix, this restriction can be circumvented by using type conversion. The name of a derived type can be used as a type conversion operator. The following block statement shows illegal type mixing and shows how type conversion can be used to circumvent the problem:

    declare
        type PERCENT **is new** INTEGER **range** 0 .. 100;
        SCORE: PERCENT := 0;
        INT: INTEGER := 22;
    begin
        INT := SCORE;   -- error; mixed types
        SCORE := INT;   -- error; mixed types
        INT := INTEGER (SCORE);   -- OK; convert to INTEGER
        SCORE := PERCENT (INT);   -- OK; convert to PERCENT
    end;

In this block statement, the derived type PERCENT has a range constraint. Range constraints, however, are optional. As the following declarations show, derived types may be declared with or without a range constraint:

```
-- without range constraints
type NEW_INTEGER is new INTEGER;
type NEW_REAL is new FLOAT;
type ITSY_BITSY_INTEGER is new SHORT_INTEGER;
type REAL_LARGE is new LONG_FLOAT;

-- with range constraints
type ONE_TO_FIVE is new INTEGER range 1 .. 5;
type ZERO_TO_FIVE is new FLOAT range 0.0 .. 5.0;
```

In the first declaration, the derived type NEW_INTEGER is defined to be a new integer type that assumes the same range of values as its parent type, INTEGER. Although NEW_INTEGER is a "copy" of INTEGER, with the same range of values as INTEGER, objects of these two types may not mix. The second declaration defines the derived type NEW_REAL to be a copy of its parent type FLOAT. The third declaration defines the derived type ITSY_BITSY_INTEGER to be a copy of its parent type SHORT_INTEGER. The integer type SHORT_INTEGER—along with LONG_INTEGER, SHORT_FLOAT, and LONG_FLOAT—is optionally supplied by some Ada compilers in the package STANDARD. Although the range of values for SHORT_INTEGER is implementation dependent, SHORT_INTEGER provides a smaller range of values than type INTEGER. This means that fewer bits are allocated for an object of type SHORT_INTEGER than are allocated for an object of type INTEGER. The fourth declaration defines the type REAL_LARGE to be a copy of the predefined type LONG_FLOAT. LONG_FLOAT, if provided, is used when large real numbers are needed. Again, the range of values supported by this type is implementation dependent; however, LONG_FLOAT provides a greater range of values than type FLOAT. The fifth declaration contains a range constraint: type ONE_TO_FIVE is defined as an integer type constrained to the values from 1 to 5. Finally, the sixth declaration defines the type ZERO_TO_FIVE to be a floating point type constrained to the values from 0.0 to 5.0.

In the preceding section, we saw how number declarations can make code more portable. Code can also be made more portable by using special forms of the derived type declarations, called integer type definitions and floating point type definitions.

To illustrate the need to make code more portable, consider the following regular derived type declaration:

```
type INVENTORY is new INTEGER range 0 .. 50_000;
```

This derived type declaration will work on a 32-bit computer where INTEGER'LAST is 2,147,483,647, but it will raise a constraint error on a 16-bit computer where INTEGER'LAST is 32,767.

We could attempt to make this declaration more portable by using the predefined integer type LONG_INTEGER:

```
type INVENTORY is new LONG_INTEGER range 0 .. 50_000;
```

The range of values for type LONG_INTEGER is implementation dependent; however, when available, type LONG_INTEGER provides a greater range of values than type INTEGER. On a 16-bit computer, LONG_INTEGER might be stored in a double word of 32 bits, in which case LONG_INTEGER'LAST is 2,147,483,647. On such a computer, the previous type declaration does not result in an error, and hence the code is more portable.

However, there is a problem with this solution. If we port our code to a 32-bit computer, then numbers of type LONG_INTEGER might be stored in a double word of 64 bits. The preceding declaration thus wastes computer memory, because the largest object of type INVENTORY, 50,000, can be stored as type INTEGER (in 32 bits) rather than as type LONG_INTEGER.

In summary, defining the parent type of INVENTORY as INTEGER has the disadvantage of not being very portable. On the other hand, defining the parent type of INVENTORY as LONG_INTEGER, while increasing portability, has the disadvantage of potentially wasting computer memory. The solution to this dilemma is to use an integer type definition:

```
-- integer type definition
type INVENTORY is range 0 .. 50_000;
     -- enhances portability by letting the compiler decide whether the
     -- parent type is SHORT_INTEGER, INTEGER, LONG_INTEGER, etc.
```

Integer type definitions differ from other derived type declarations as follows: the specification of a parent type, such as **new** INTEGER, is omitted. Because of this omission, the compiler selects the most appropriate parent type to handle the range of values on the particular computer. In other words, the programmer does not select the parent type; instead, the selection is made by the compiler. On some computers, the compiler may select INTEGER as the parent type; on other computers, the compiler may select LONG_INTEGER as the parent type. By letting the compiler select the parent type, we not only increase code portability; we also trust the compiler to select the most efficient representation of our type on a particular computer.

The more advanced reader should note that the preceding integer type definition is actually a subtype of an anonymous derived type, whose parent type is SHORT_INTEGER, INTEGER, LONG_INTEGER, or some other integer type selected by the particular compiler:

```
type anonymous is new some integer type;
subtype INVENTORY is anonymous range 0 .. 50_000;
```

In addition to integer type definitions, there are floating point type definitions, which are also special forms of the derived type. The following floating point type definition has an accuracy constraint:

```
-- floating point type definition with accuracy constraint
type TINY_REAL is digits 3;
   -- increases portability by letting compiler decide whether the
   -- parent type is FLOAT, SHORT_FLOAT, or LONG_FLOAT
```

In floating point type definitions, words such as "**new** FLOAT," which appear in other derived type declarations, are omitted. As with integer type definitions, the result of this omission is that the programmer does not select the parent type; the selection is made by the compiler. Note the accuracy constraint: **digits** 3. This accuracy constraint indicates that the values of the type TINY_REAL need only be accurate to 3 significant digits. The accuracy constraint is provided to enable the compiler to select the most appropriate parent type. An object of TINY_REAL, therefore, might not distinguish between the values 3.111 and 3.112. The following real literals each contains 3 significant digits:

   3.11, 2.22E7, 0.00452, 12.3E-3, 745000.0

Note that leading and trailing zeros, as well as exponents, do not count as significant digits.

Floating point definitions may contain range constraints in addition to accuracy constraints:

```
-- floating point type definition with accuracy and range constraint
type CHANGE is digits 4 range 0.0 .. 99.99;
```

In this example, objects of type CHANGE are represented by at least 4 significant digits and are constrained to the range from 0.0 to 99.99.

So far we have seen derived types derived from predefined types. Derived types may also be derived from user-defined types:

```
type COLOR is (WHITE, TAN, BEIGE, GREY);
type STOVE_COLOR is new COLOR range WHITE..BEIGE;
   -- derived from parent type COLOR
type REFRIGERATOR_COLOR is new COLOR;
   -- derived from parent type COLOR
```

Both STOVE_COLOR and REFRIGERATOR_COLOR are derived from the parent type COLOR, which is a user-defined type. By creating these derived types, the programmer maintains the distinction between stove color and refrigerator color; the color of a stove cannot inadvertently be compared or assigned to the color of a refrigerator.

Derived types inherit basic predefined operations from their parent type. In the preceding example, since the parent type is an enumeration type, the operations (attributes) FIRST, LAST, POS, VAL, SUCC, and PRED apply. Thus, the derived types STOVE_COLOR and REFRIGERATOR_COLOR inherit these operations from their parent type COLOR. Such expressions as the following are therefore allowed:

```
STOVE_COLOR'FIRST                        -- yields WHITE
REFRIGERATOR_COLOR'SUCC (WHITE) -- yields TAN
    -- inherits attribute operations from the parent type COLOR
```

As a second example, consider a derived type whose parent type is type INTEGER:

```
declare
    type STOVES_IN_STOCK is new INTEGER range 0 .. 200;
    NUMBER_OF_STOVES: STOVES_IN_STOCK := 25;
begin
    NUMBER_OF_STOVES := 2 * NUMBER_OF_STOVES + 1;
        -- OK; inherits arithmetic operations from the parent type, INTEGER
end;
```

In this example, the derived type STOVES_IN_STOCK inherits the arithmetic operations from its parent type, INTEGER.

Besides inheriting such basic predefined operations, a derived type inherits operations defined in the visible part of a package where its parent type is declared. Consider, for example, the following package specification:

```
package COORDINATES is
    type POINT is
        record
            X_COORDINATE: FLOAT range 0.0 .. 10_000.0;
            Y_COORDINATE: FLOAT range 0.0 .. 10_000.0;
        end record;
    function DISTANCE (POINT_A, POINT_B: in POINT) return FLOAT;
end COORDINATES;
```

This package declares a type, POINT, and a function, DISTANCE, which operates on objects of type POINT. Suppose that another program unit defines a derived type whose parent type is POINT. Since DISTANCE is defined in the same package specification as type POINT, the derived type inherits the function DISTANCE. DISTANCE may thus operate on objects belonging to this derived type, as shown in the following code:

```
with TEXT_IO, COORDINATES; use TEXT_IO, COORDINATES;
procedure AS_THE_CROW_FLIES is
    type INTERSECTION is new POINT;
        -- type POINT declared in the package specification COORDINATES
    HOLLYWOOD_AND_VINE: INTERSECTION := (2_301.3, 198.1);
    PICO_AND_SEPULVEDA: INTERSECTION := (2_294.6, 203.0);
    package REAL_IO is new FLOAT_IO (FLOAT);
    use REAL_IO;
begin
    PUT ( "The distance between the corner of Hollywood and Vine " &
          "and the corner of Pico and Sepulveda is ");
```

```
      PUT ( DISTANCE ( HOLLYWOOD_AND_VINE, PICO_AND_SEPULVEDA ) );
         -- the function DISTANCE is inherited from the package
         -- specification of COORDINATES
      NEW_LINE;
   end AS_THE_CROW_FLIES;
```

Now let us consider a situation where a derived type does not inherit all the operations of its parent type. The following package specification defines the function SQUARE_ROOT but does not define the type FLOAT, on which this function operates:

```
package MATH_LIBRARY is
    function SQUARE_ROOT (X: FLOAT) return FLOAT;
end MATH_LIBRARY;
```

The following procedure defines a derived type, NEW_FLOAT, whose parent type is FLOAT:

```
with MATH_LIBRARY; use MATH_LIBRARY;
procedure NOT_INHERITED is
    type NEW_FLOAT is new FLOAT;
    X: NEW_FLOAT: = 2.0;
    subtype POSITIVE_FLOAT is FLOAT range 1.0 .. 1.0E6;
    Y: POSITIVE_FLOAT: = 3.0;
begin
    Y := SQUARE_ROOT (Y); -- OK
    Y := SQUARE_ROOT (X); -- illegal; SQUARE_ROOT not inherited
end NOT_INHERITED;
```

NEW_FLOAT does not inherit the function SQUARE_ROOT because its parent type, FLOAT, is not defined in the same package specification as SQUARE_ROOT. (FLOAT is defined in the package STANDARD.) Note that there is no problem invoking SQUARE_ROOT with a parameter belonging to the subtype POSITIVE_FLOAT. The subtype POSITIVE_FLOAT has the same operations as its base type, FLOAT, because, unlike a derived type, a subtype does not introduce a new type. A subtype just places an optional constraint on the range of values of its base type.

FIXED POINT TYPES

Real types consist of floating point types and fixed point types. Numbers belonging to the floating point type were discussed in Chapter 3. We will now discuss numbers belonging to the fixed point type.

Unlike floating point numbers, where the decimal point can shift to different locations, in fixed point numbers, the decimal point is "fixed" at a particular location. Also, whereas floating point numbers have a margin of error that is relative to the magnitude (absolute value) of the number, fixed point numbers have a margin of error that is a fixed quantity.

A fixed point type is not a predefined type; there is no predefined type identifier such as FIX that can be used in type declarations. Rather, the programmer must define a fixed point type by specifying a fixed point constraint and a range constraint (using real literals or static real expressions):

type SALARY **is delta** 0.01 **range** 0.00 .. 1_000.00;
 -- fixed point type declaration

Fixed point type declarations begin with the keyword **type**, followed by the name of the fixed point type, the keywords **is delta**, and the fixed point constraint. The fixed point constraint is followed by the keyword **range** and a range constraint. The fixed point constraint establishes the absolute margin of error, the smallest amount by which the fixed point number is guaranteed to be able to change, and the location of the decimal point.

In the preceding declaration, the fixed point constraint sets the absolute margin of error to 0.01. This means that an object of type SALARY may be inaccurate by no more than ±0.01. For instance, a number of type SALARY with an actual value of 5.02 may be represented as 5.02 ±0.01, which is 5.01, 5.02, or 5.03. With fixed point numbers, the margin of error does not vary with the size of the number, as it does with floating point numbers. (With floating point numbers, the margin of error depends on the absolute value of the floating point number: the larger the absolute value, the greater the margin of error.)

In the preceding declaration, the fixed point constraint also establishes the smallest amount by which the fixed point number is guaranteed to be able to change. Numbers of type SALARY may increase or decrease by amounts at least as small as 0.01. Such numbers cannot necessarily be increased or decreased by, for instance, amounts as small as 0.003, because this is a finer resolution than specified by the fixed point constraint 0.01.

Finally, the fixed point constraint of SALARY establishes the location of the decimal point. Since the range constraint is from 0.0..1_000.00, objects of type SALARY can assume the following values:

   0.00, 0.01, 0.02, 0.03, ..., 999.97, 999.98, 999.99, 1000.00

Note in these values that the decimal point is fixed so that there are only two digits to the right of it.

When using fixed point numbers in expressions, the following rules apply: (1) Fixed point numbers may be added and subtracted from one another, which results in a fixed point number in both cases; (2) Fixed point numbers may be multiplied and divided by each other, but the result (which is an anonymous predefined type called universal fixed) must be explicitly converted using a type conversion operator; and (3) Fixed point numbers

More About Types   **341**

may be multiplied and divided by integer numbers (resulting in a fixed point number) but not by floating point numbers. These rules are illustrated in the following block statement:

```
declare
    type FIXED_TYPE is delta 0.001 range -100.000 .. 100.000;
    FIXED_A, FIXED_B: FIXED_TYPE := 0.002;
    INT: INTEGER := 3;
    FLT: FLOAT := 4.0;
begin
    FIXED_A := FIXED_B + INT;                        -- will not compile
        -- for addition, both operands must be fixed
    FIXED_A := FIXED_B - INT;                        -- will not compile
        -- for subtraction, both operands must be fixed
    FIXED_A := FIXED_A + FIXED_B;                    -- OK
    FIXED_A := FIXED_A - FIXED_B;                    -- OK
    FIXED_A := FIXED_B * INT;                        -- OK
    FIXED_A := INT * FIXED_B;                        -- OK
    FIXED_A := FLT * FIXED_B;                        -- will not compile
    FIXED_A := FIXED_B / INT;                        -- OK
    FIXED_A := INT / FIXED_B;                        -- OK
    FIXED_A := FLT / FIXED_B;                        -- will not compile
    FIXED_A := FIXED_A * FIXED_B;                    -- will not compile
        -- must explicitly convert
    FIXED_A := FIXED_TYPE (FIXED_A * FIXED_B);       -- OK
    FIXED_A := FIXED_A / FIXED_B;                    -- will not compile
        -- must explicitly convert
    FIXED_A := FIXED_TYPE (FIXED_A / FIXED_B);       -- OK
end;
```

In all the statements where the expression is OK, the result of the expression is a fixed point number of type FIXED_TYPE.

IMPLICIT CONVERSION OF UNIVERSAL TYPES

In the section of this chapter on universal types, we mentioned that universal integers may mix with any integer type and that universal real numbers may mix with any floating point or fixed point type. This is demonstrated in the following program:

```
with TEXT_IO; use TEXT_IO;
procedure IMPLICIT_CONVERSION is

    INT: constant INTEGER := 1;
    UNIVERSAL_INT: constant := 2;
    type NEW_INT_TYPE is new INTEGER;
```

```
         NEW_INT: constant NEW_INT_TYPE := 3;
         FLOATING: constant FLOAT := 1.0;
         UNIVERSAL_REAL: constant := 2.0;
         type NEW_FLOAT_TYPE is new FLOAT;
         NEW_FLOAT: constant NEW_FLOAT_TYPE := 3.0;
         type FIXED_TYPE is delta 0.1 range 0.0..10.0;
         FIXED: constant FIXED_TYPE := 4.0;

         package INT_IO is new INTEGER_IO (INTEGER);
         package NEW_INT_IO is new INTEGER_IO (NEW_INT_TYPE);
         package FLOATING_IO is new FLOAT_IO (FLOAT);
         package NEW_FLOAT_IO is new FLOAT_IO (NEW_FLOAT_TYPE);
         package FIX_IO is new FIXED_IO (FIXED_TYPE);
         use INT_IO, NEW_INT_IO, FLOATING_IO, NEW_FLOAT_IO, FIX_IO;

begin
         PUT (UNIVERSAL_INT + INT); NEW_LINE;
         -- UNIVERSAL_INT implicitly converted to type INTEGER

         PUT (UNIVERSAL_INT + NEW_INT); NEW_LINE;
         -- UNIVERSAL_INT implicitly converted to type NEW_INT_TYPE

         PUT (UNIVERSAL_REAL + FLOATING); NEW_LINE;
         -- UNIVERSAL_REAL implicitly converted to type FLOAT

         PUT (UNIVERSAL_REAL + NEW_FLOAT); NEW_LINE;
         -- UNIVERSAL_REAL implicitly converted to type NEW_FLOAT_TYPE

         PUT (UNIVERSAL_REAL + FIXED); NEW_LINE;
         -- UNIVERSAL_REAL implicitly converted to type FIXED_TYPE

         PUT (9 + NEW_INT); NEW_LINE;
         -- 9 implicitly converted to type NEW_INT_TYPE

         PUT (6.3 + FLOATING); NEW_LINE;
         -- 6.3 implicitly converted to type FLOAT

end IMPLICIT_CONVERSION;
```

In this code, the universal integers are implicitly converted to the required integer types: INTEGER or NEW_INT_TYPE. The universal real numbers are also implicitly converted to the required real type: FLOAT, NEW_FLOAT_TYPE, or FIXED_TYPE. Implicit conversion is handy since literals, named numbers, and universal expressions may be used without having to worry about explicit type conversion.

We have seen throughout this book that whenever input or output is performed, the TEXT_IO package needs to be referenced. As shown in this chapter and in previous chapters, whenever objects of a newly defined type are input or output, the appropriate generic input/output package within the TEXT_IO package must first be instantiated. In the next chapter, we will examine some of the other resources provided by the TEXT_IO package. In addition, we will examine other standardized input/output packages that are used for file manipulation.

EXERCISES

1. Describe the main differences between subtypes and derived types.

2. Which two of the following declarations are illegal?

    declare
       A: **constant** := 5.2;
       B: **constant** FLOAT := A;
       C: **constant** := B;
       D: **constant** := A - 4.9;
       E: INTEGER := 5;
       F: **constant** := E;
    begin
       null;
    end;

3. What is the main advantage of the declaration

    OUNCES_IN_TON: **constant** := 35_274;

    over the declaration

    OUNCES_IN_TON: **constant** INTEGER := 35_274;

4. Consider the following declarations:

    A: **constant** := 2;
    B: **constant** INTEGER := 5;
    C: INTEGER := 20;
    D: **constant** := 6;

    Which of the following are literal expressions?

    a. 7 + 9
    b. 2 + A - D
    c. A * B
    d. C - 1

5. Which of the following statements result in an error?

    declare
       type DERIVED_TYPE **is new** INTEGER;
       DERIVED: DERIVED_TYPE := 6;
       INT: INTEGER := 9;
    begin
       INT := 5;
       DERIVED := 5;
       INT := DERIVED + 5;
       DERIVED := INT + 5;
       DERIVED := DERIVED_TYPE (INT) + 5;
    end;

6. Explain the main advantage of the declaration

    type INFRARED **is range** 7E3 .. 1E6; -- Angstroms

    over the declaration

    type INFRARED **is new** INTEGER **range** 7E3 .. 1E6; -- Angstroms

7. Which of the following expressions result in an error?

    ```
    declare
        QUARTER: constant := 0.25;
        FIVE: constant : = 5;
        F: FLOAT;
    begin
        F := 5.2 - 1;
        F := 5 * 2.5;
        F := 6.0 / 3;
        F := 6 / 3.0;
        F := 1.0 + 1;
        F := 2 * QUARTER;
        F := FIVE / QUARTER;
        F := QUARTER / FIVE;
        F := (1.0 * 7) + QUARTER;
    end;
    ```

8. Consider the following package specification:

    ```
    package MATH_RESOURCES is
        type DEGREE is range 0 .. 360;
        function SINE (ANGLE: DEGREE) return FLOAT;
        function FACTORIAL (N: POSITIVE) return POSITIVE;
    end MATH_RESOURCES;
    ```

    Explain what is wrong with the following procedure that references MATH_RESOURCES:

    ```
    with MATH_RESOURCES; use MATH_RESOURCES;
    procedure MATH is
        type QUADRANT_I is new DEGREE range 0 .. 90;
        type SMALL_POSITIVE is new POSITIVE range 1 .. 7;
        ANGLE: QUADRANT_I := 45;
        P: SMALL_POSITIVE := 6;
        N: POSITIVE := 5;
        F: FLOAT;
    begin
        N := FACTORIAL (N);
        F := SINE (ANGLE);
        N := FACTORIAL (P);
    end MATH;
    ```

9. Which of the following statements result in an error?

   declare

      type INCREMENTS **is delta** 0.2 **range** -50.0 .. 50.0;
      CHANGE: INCREMENTS;
      ONE_DELTA: INCREMENTS := 0.2;
      TWO_DELTAS: INCREMENTS := 0.4;
      FIVE_DELTAS: INTEGER := 1;
      HALF_DELTA: FLOAT := 0.1;

   begin

      CHANGE := ONE_DELTA - FIVE_DELTAS;
      CHANGE := 2 * TWO_DELTAS;
      CHANGE := ONE_DELTA + TWO_DELTAS;
      CHANGE := ONE_DELTA * TWO_DELTAS;
      CHANGE := FIVE_DELTAS / ONE_DELTA;
      CHANGE := INCREMENTS (ONE_DELTA / TWO_DELTAS);
      CHANGE := FIVE_DELTAS * TWO_DELTAS;
      CHANGE := HALF_DELTA * TWO_DELTAS;
      CHANGE := ONE_DELTA + 0.4;
      CHANGE := INCREMENTS (ONE_DELTA * TWO_DELTAS);
      CHANGE := FIVE_DELTAS + TWO_DELTAS;

   end;

Chapter 14

INPUT/OUTPUT

Computers process numbers and manipulate textual information at enormous speeds and with great accuracy. For computers to be useful, however, they must be able to communicate this information with the outside world. Data must be input to the computer and output from the computer. Such input/output (I/O) operations are the topic of this chapter.

I/O operations are not intrinsic to the Ada language. In other words, there are no built-in features of Ada that handle I/O. Instead, all I/O is handled through the resources contained in packages. Every Ada compiler, for instance, must supply a predefined TEXT_IO package that contains our familiar I/O procedures PUT, NEW_LINE, and GET.

In this chapter, we will discuss the contents of three standard predefined I/O packages: TEXT_IO, SEQUENTIAL_IO, and DIRECT_IO. The specifications of these three packages are contained in Appendixes E, F, and G, respectively, of this book. TEXT_IO is a nongeneric package, although it contains four generic packages: INTEGER_IO, FLOAT_IO, FIXED_IO, and ENUMERATION_IO. SEQUENTIAL_IO and DIRECT_IO are generic packages. The generic I/O packages must be instantiated with a data type before I/O can be performed on objects of that type. After the discussion of these packages, we will explore the IO_EXCEPTIONS package, which contains the exceptions that may be raised during I/O operations. The chapter will conclude with a section on referencing unprintable characters.

TEXT_IO PACKAGE

The TEXT_IO package is used to input and output human readable text consisting of strings and characters. As we have seen in Chapter 9, the TEXT_IO package also contains generic packages that are used to input and output integers, real numbers, and objects belonging to enumeration types. The structure of the TEXT_IO package is shown in Figure 14.1. This package is the largest predefined I/O package. Many of its I/O services will be discussed for the first time in this chapter.

Throughout this book, we have performed basic I/O operations using procedures such as PUT and GET from the TEXT_IO package. By examining

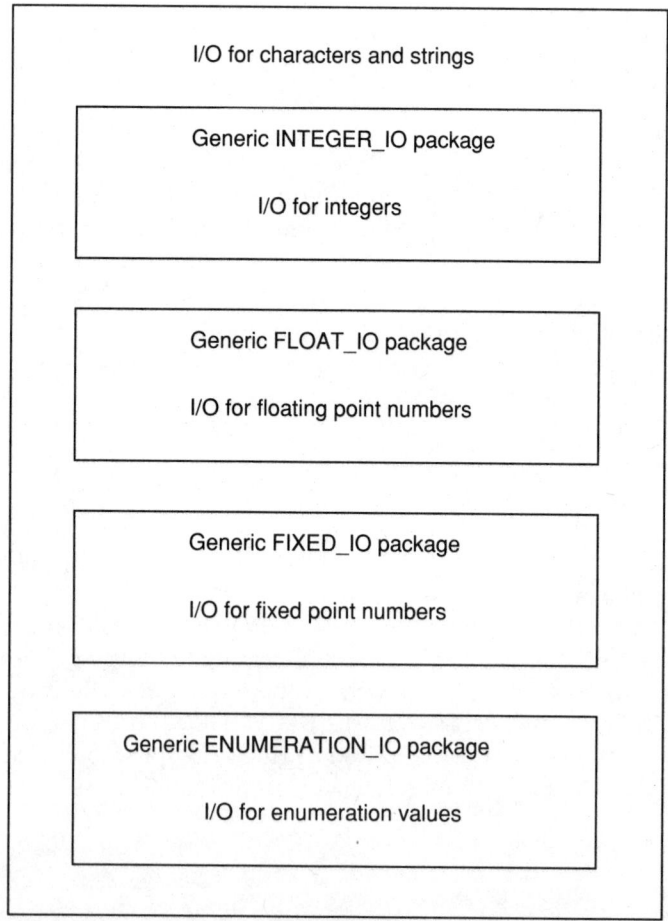

Figure 14.1 Structure of TEXT_IO package

the TEXT_IO package and its nested generic packages (see Appendix E), you will observe that PUT and GET have many overloaded versions. There are 16 different overloaded PUT procedures and 16 different overloaded GET procedures! In addition, these overloaded procedures have parameters that we have not yet discussed. Many of these parameters can be used for formatting I/O. Formatting I/O means specifying the physical layout of the data to be input or output. Formatted output is often used to produce visually pleasing reports. In such reports, numbers typically line up in vertical columns, floating point numbers have a set number of digits to the right of their decimal points, headers appear at specific lines and columns, and so on. Formatted input specifies the columns from which data are to be read by the computer. For example, for a particular input, columns 1 through 9 might contain social security numbers; columns 10 through 19, telephone numbers; and so on.

In addition to formatting I/O, many of the overloaded versions of PUT and GET have a parameter that directs input and output to and from files rather than to and from the standard I/O device. (We have been assuming that the standard I/O device consists of a keyboard for inputting information and a video screen for outputting information.) A file consists of a collection of data, typically on a magnetic disk. Large amounts of data can be stored in files over long periods of time and can be read or updated as needed.

We will begin by discussing the TEXT_IO services for formatting I/O. We will then discuss the TEXT_IO services for handling file I/O.

Formatting I/O

The TEXT_IO package provides many services for formatting I/O. We will first discuss some of the overloaded PUT and GET procedures. We will then cover PUT_LINE and GET_LINE. Finally, we will explore controlling columns, lines, and pages.

PUT Procedures

Out of the 16 overloaded PUT procedures, 6 output to the standard output device. These 6 procedures output characters, strings, integers, floating point numbers, fixed point numbers, and enumeration values. Two of these 6 PUT procedures are contained within the TEXT_IO package, outside of any nested generic packages. These 2 PUT procedures output characters and strings:

```
-- assume TEXT_IO is visible
PUT (ITEM => 'A');       -- outputs A (the character)
PUT (ITEM => "Ada");     -- outputs Ada (the string)
```

Both these procedure calls employ named notation using the formal parameter ITEM.

Now let us consider the PUT procedures contained in the generic packages. When outputting integers to the standard I/O device, the PUT procedure contained in the generic INTEGER_IO package is used. Since this PUT procedure is placed within a generic package, its instance (instantiated copy) is only available when the INTEGER_IO package is instantiated with some integer type parameter. Consider, for example, when the INTEGER_IO package is instantiated with a derived integer type, TINY_POSITIVE:

```
type TINY_POSITIVE is new POSITIVE range 1 .. 100;
-- assumes that TEXT_IO is visible
package POS_IO is new TEXT_IO.INTEGER_IO (TINY_POSITIVE);
```

This instantiation of INTEGER_IO creates an instance of the PUT procedure for objects of type TINY_POSITIVE. Each instantiation of the INTEGER_IO package creates another overloaded instance of the PUT procedure. For example, the following instantiation creates another instance of PUT:

```
package INT_IO is new TEXT_IO.INTEGER_IO (INTEGER);
```

This new instance of PUT is just like the preceding one but applies to objects of type INTEGER rather than to objects of type TINY_POSITIVE. As shown in the following code, each of these two newly created PUT procedures can only output objects of the appropriate integer type:

```
with TEXT_IO; use TEXT_IO;
procedure OUTPUT is

    type TINY_POSITIVE is new POSITIVE range 1 .. 100;
    package POS_IO is new INTEGER_IO (TINY_POSITIVE);
    package INT_IO is new INTEGER_IO (INTEGER);

    -- there are two instances of PUT: one for objects of type
    -- TINY_POSITIVE and one for objects of type INTEGER

    POS: TINY_POSITIVE := 1;
    INT: INTEGER := -2;
begin
    POS_IO.PUT (POS);       -- outputs 1
    INT_IO.PUT (INT);       -- outputs -2
    POS_IO.PUT (INT);       -- error; parameter of wrong type
end OUTPUT;
```

In this example, each PUT procedure is called with a single parameter. PUT may also be called with two additional parameters that have the formal parameter names WIDTH and BASE. These optional parameters specify the field width and number base. WIDTH establishes the minimum number of spaces (columns) allotted to the outputted integer. If the integer fits in the allotted space with room to spare, then it is placed at the right

Input/Output **351**

end of the field, and the extra space is padded with blanks. Whenever columns of integers are required to line up on the right side, the width must be sufficient to accommodate all the integers being output. For negative integers, this includes an extra space for a minus sign. If the integer does not fit in the specified width, then WIDTH is ignored, and only the number of spaces needed to output the integer are used. To guarantee that only as many spaces are used as needed, specify a field width of 0. Setting the field width to 0 is especially useful when an integer is embedded within text, because no extraneous spaces will precede the integer when it is output:

```
-- assume TEXT_IO and needed instances of generic packages are visible
PUT ("Johnny is ");
PUT (ITEM => 8, WIDTH => 0);
PUT (" years old.");
```

These three PUT statements output

   Johnny is 8 years old.

If the width is not specified, the default width is used, resulting in an undesirable format such as the following:

   Johnny is   8 years old.

Within the INTEGER_IO package, the default for WIDTH is set to NUM'WIDTH. NUM is the integer type used to instantiate the INTEGER_IO package, and the attribute WIDTH (not to be confused with the formal parameter name) yields the minimum width that is sufficient to accommodate any value of type NUM.

In addition to the parameter WIDTH, PUT may be called with the parameter BASE, which specifies the number base. Any number base from 2 to 16 may be specified. Thus, based literals such as 16#5F#, 8#123#, and 2#101# may be output. When the base is not specified, the default value of 10 is used, and no base is indicated in the output. A base 10 number is never output as, for instance, 10#145#.

The following code demonstrates various ways that integer literals may be output:

```
-- assume needed instance of INTEGER_IO is visible
PUT (ITEM => 32); -- outputs 32 using defaults
PUT (ITEM => 25, BASE => 10);         -- outputs 25 (no base indicated)
                                      -- named notation used
PUT (104, 5);   -- outputs □□104, where □ represents a blank space
                -- positional notation used; 5 indicates width

PUT (ITEM => -44, BASE => 8);         -- outputs -8#54#

PUT (ITEM => 2#101_100#, BASE => 8);  -- outputs 8#54#
                                      -- (2#101100# converted to 8#54#)
```

```
PUT (ITEM => 25, WIDTH => 11, BASE => 2);    -- outputs □□□2#11001#
PUT (ITEM => 102, WIDTH => 1);                -- outputs 102
```

In this code, an open box, □, indicates a blank space. Note that the formal parameters used in the named notation are ITEM, WIDTH, and BASE. Parameters must be specified in this same order when using positional notation. Also note that when integer literals are output, neither the plus sign nor scientific notation is used.

As previously mentioned, the default width is NUM'WIDTH, and the default base is 10. These defaults are set by the variables DEFAULT_WIDTH and DEFAULT_BASE in the INTEGER_IO package. These defaults may be overridden for a given instantiation by user-specified defaults:

```
-- assume instance of INTEGER_IO package, INT_IO, is visible
INT_IO.DEFAULT_WIDTH := 10;         -- may need dot notation to avoid
INT_IO.DEFAULT_BASE := 2;           -- ambiguity
PUT (22);                            -- outputs □□2#10110#
PUT (22, WIDTH => 2, BASE => 10);    -- outputs 22 (defaults overridden)
INT_IO.DEFAULT_BASE := 8;
PUT (22);                            -- outputs □□□□□8#26#
```

These user-specified defaults are employed each time a PUT statement accepts the default width or base value; the defaults stay in effect until changed.

Let us now consider the PUT procedure used to output floating point numbers. This PUT procedure is contained in the generic FLOAT_IO package that is nested in the TEXT_IO package. Since this PUT procedure is placed within a generic package, its instance (instantiated copy) is only available when the FLOAT_IO package is instantiated with a floating point type parameter. Each instantiation of the FLOAT_IO package creates another overloaded instance of this PUT procedure.

When using a PUT procedure to output floating point numbers, one may optionally use parameters to specify the number of columns to the left of the decimal point, to the right of the decimal point, and for the exponent. (Unlike the PUT procedure for integers, there is no parameter that specifies the number base.) These optional parameters are frequently employed because without them, the default scientific notation is used. Scientific notation is normally avoided because, unless the numbers are very large or very small, it is difficult to read. The complete list of formal parameters for this PUT procedure is ITEM, FORE, AFT, and EXP. This order must be observed when positional notation is used.

The value of FORE determines the minimum number of columns allotted to the left of the decimal point. If the number of digits to the left of the decimal point is less than the allotted space, then leading blanks are used. If the number of digits to the left of the decimal point exceeds the allotted space, then the value of FORE is ignored and the required amount of space is taken. To ensure that the number of columns to the left of the decimal point is never more than required, set FORE to 0. Setting FORE to 0 is especially useful when a floating point number is embedded within text, because no extraneous spaces appear between the text and the number.

Note that when FORE is set to a value large enough to accommodate any numbers being output, columns of floating point numbers can be arranged with their decimal points aligned. Consider the following code:

```
with TEXT_IO; use TEXT_IO;
procedure ALIGN_DECIMAL_POINTS is
    package REAL_IO is new FLOAT_IO (FLOAT);
    use REAL_IO;
    FLT: FLOAT;
begin
    FLT := 1.23456;
    for INDEX in 1 .. 5 loop
       PUT (FLT, FORE => 5, AFT => 5, EXP => 0);
       NEW_LINE;
       FLT := FLT * 10.0;
    end loop;
end ALIGN_DECIMAL_POINTS;
```

This program outputs the following column of numbers with aligned decimal points:

```
    1.23456
   12.34560
  123.45600
 1234.56000
12345.60000
```

In the preceding program, the formal parameter AFT is set to 5. The value of AFT determines the exact number of digits to the right of the decimal point. When necessary, the right side of the field is padded with zeros (not blanks). If AFT is set to 0, one digit still appears after the decimal point, as required by the syntax for floating point numbers. When AFT specifies fewer digits to the right of the decimal point than contained by the number to be output, then the number is rounded off, not truncated.

The value of EXP determines the minimum number of spaces allotted for the exponent that follows the E in scientific notation. When such an exponent is used, one significant digit is always placed to the left of the decimal point, and a plus or minus sign always precedes the exponent. When EXP is 0, no exponent is used. If the exponent does not fit in the allotted space, then the value of EXP is ignored, and the required space is taken.

The following code demonstrates the various ways that floating point literals may be output:

```
-- assume needed instance of FLOAT_IO is visible
PUT (32.0);                                 -- outputs 3.2000000E+01
                                            -- default format is
                                            -- scientific notation

PUT ( ITEM  => 44.212,                      -- outputs ☐☐44.21200
      FORE  => 4,                           -- where ☐ is a blank
      AFT   => 5,
      EXP   => 0 );

PUT ( 137.1, FORE => 2, AFT => 2, EXP => 0);    -- outputs 137.10
                                                -- FORE ignored
                                                -- exponent not written

PUT ( -4.8, FORE => 0, AFT => 0, EXP => 0);     -- outputs -4.8

PUT (15.628, FORE => 3, AFT => 2, EXP => 0);    -- outputs ☐15.63
                                                -- rounds off

PUT ( -67.028, FORE => 4, AFT => 2, EXP => 2);  -- outputs ☐☐-6.70E+1

PUT ( 0.419, FORE => 3, AFT => 1, EXP => 2);    -- outputs ☐☐4.2E-1

PUT ( 87.011, FORE => 3, AFT => 2, EXP => 5);   -- outputs ☐☐8.70E+0001

PUT ( 931.871, FORE => 4, AFT => 1, EXP => 1);  -- outputs ☐☐☐9.3E+2
```

Just as the variables DEFAULT_WIDTH and DEFAULT_BASE can be reset when outputting integers, the variables DEFAULT_FORE, DEFAULT_AFT, and DEFAULT_EXP may also be reset:

```
DEFAULT_FORE := 0;
DEFAULT_AFT := 2;
DEFAULT_EXP := 0;
PUT (159.568);               -- outputs 159.57
```

An overloaded PUT procedure for outputting fixed point numbers is provided in the generic package FIXED_IO. This procedure is identical to the one in FLOAT_IO, except that the default parameter values differ. One result of this difference is that, by default, no exponents are used.

Now let us consider the PUT procedure used to output objects belonging to an enumeration type. This PUT procedure is contained in the generic ENUMERATION_IO package that is nested in the TEXT_IO package. Since this PUT procedure is placed within a generic package, its instance (instantiated copy) is only available when the ENUMERATION_IO package is instantiated with some enumeration type parameter. Each instantiation of the ENUMERATION_IO package creates another overloaded instance of this PUT procedure.

When using this PUT procedure to output objects of an enumeration type, one may optionally specify the minimum field width and whether upper- or lowercase letters are to be used. If the specified field width is greater than the length of the enumeration literal, then blank spaces are placed after the literal. If the specified width is less than the length of the enumeration literal, then the specified field width is ignored; as many spaces are taken as needed. The default width is 0, which means that only the exact space needed for each literal is used. The result is an enumeration literal without any trailing blanks. To specify upper- or lowercase, use the values UPPER_CASE or LOWER_CASE for the third parameter, whose formal parameter name is SET. (The complete list of formal parameters is ITEM, WIDTH, and SET. This order must be observed when positional notation is used.) Unless otherwise specified, enumeration literals are always output in uppercase letters. One cannot specify a mixture of upper- and lowercase letters. The following example demonstrates the various ways that a PUT procedure may output values of the predefined enumeration type BOOLEAN:

```
-- assume needed instance of ENUMERATION_IO is visible
PUT (FALSE);                                    -- outputs FALSE
PUT (ITEM => TRUE, WIDTH => 6);                 -- outputs TRUE□□
                                                -- (uses 6 columns)
PUT (ITEM => FALSE,                             -- outputs false (in lowercase)
    WIDTH => 5,
    SET => LOWER_CASE);
PUT (ITEM => TRUE, SET => UPPER_CASE);          -- outputs TRUE (in uppercase)
PUT (ITEM => TRUE, WIDTH => 1);                 -- outputs TRUE
```

Within the ENUMERATION_IO package, the variables DEFAULT_WIDTH and DEFAULT_SETTING contain the default values for WIDTH and SET. These default values may be overridden with user-specified defaults in the same way that the variables DEFAULT_WIDTH and DEFAULT_BASE can be overridden when outputting integers, or that the variables DEFAULT_FORE, DEFAULT_AFT, and DEFAULT_EXP can be overridden when outputting real numbers.

We have examined the overloaded PUT procedures for outputting characters, strings, integers, real numbers, and enumeration literals. The GET procedure is similarly overloaded for each of these data types.

GET Procedures

Whereas PUT procedures are used to output values, the GET procedures are used to input values. Unlike the PUT procedures whose forms differ for each type of object being output, the GET procedure only has two forms. One form has three procedures that, in turn, input characters, strings, or enumeration values. This form has only one parameter, ITEM, which receives the value of the object being input. Another form of GET has three procedures that, in turn, input integers, floating point numbers, or fixed point numbers. This form has two parameters. The first parameter, ITEM, has already been described. The second parameter, WIDTH, is optional and specifies the number of columns to examine for the object being input. The following example shows how these overloaded GET procedures are called:

```
with TEXT_IO; use TEXT_IO;
procedure OUTPUT is
   package INT_IO is new INTEGER_IO (INTEGER);
   package FLT_IO is new FLOAT_IO (FLOAT);
   package BOOL_IO is new ENUMERATION_IO (BOOLEAN);
   use INT_IO, FLT_IO, BOOL_IO;
   INT: INTEGER;
   FLT: FLOAT;
   BOOL: BOOLEAN;
   CHAR: CHARACTER;
   STR: STRING (1 .. 5);
begin
   GET (CHAR);                          -- input character value is assigned
                                        -- to CHAR
   GET (INT);                           -- inputs the next integer
   GET (STR);                           -- inputs the next 5 characters
   GET (ITEM => INT, WIDTH => 7);       -- examines the next 7 columns for
                                        -- the value of INT
   GET (ITEM => BOOL);                  -- input is case insensitive (i.e., FALSE,
                                        -- false, FaLsE are equivalent)
   GET (ITEM => FLT, WIDTH => 4);       -- examines the next 4 columns for
                                        -- the value of FLT
end OUTPUT;
```

A value of the second parameter, WIDTH, is usually not specified. When this parameter is not specified, a default value of 0 is used. When WIDTH is set to 0, unformatted input is accepted. In unformatted input, leading blanks are skipped until the input is located. The parameter WIDTH is only specified when input is restricted to specific columns. (We will see an example of this later in the chapter in the section on file I/O.)

Put_Line and Get_Line

The procedures PUT_LINE and GET_LINE perform line-oriented I/O of strings. PUT_LINE (which has a single formal parameter, ITEM), outputs a string and then advances to the next line. The procedure call

```
PUT_LINE ("omphaloskepsis");
```

is thus equivalent to

```
PUT ("omphaloskepsis");
NEW_LINE;
```

As mentioned, PUT_LINE is available only for outputting strings, not characters, integers, floating point numbers, or enumeration literals:

```
PUT_LINE ('A');    -- illegal; not defined for characters
PUT_LINE (7);      -- illegal; not defined for integers
PUT_LINE ("A");    -- OK
PUT_LINE ("7");    -- OK
```

The procedure GET_LINE is used to input a line of text. GET_LINE has two parameters. The first parameter (ITEM) is a string variable that is assigned the inputted line of text. The second parameter (LAST) returns the length of the inputted line. GET_LINE keeps reading characters and assigning them to the string variable, until either the end of the line is reached or the string variable is full. If the end of the line is reached, then one advances to the next line; otherwise, the next time GET is invoked, reading will continue from the same line. Consider the following program:

```
with TEXT_IO; use TEXT_IO;
procedure USING_GET_LINE is
    NAME: STRING (1 .. 20);
    NAME_LENGTH: NATURAL;
begin
    PUT_LINE ("Enter your name");

    GET_LINE (NAME, NAME_LENGTH); -- inputs a line of text

    PUT_LINE ( NAME (1 .. NAME_LENGTH) );
        -- outputs string slice containing the inputted line

end USING_GET_LINE;
```

If the user of this program enters the name "Anaximander", the string variable NAME is assigned this string value, and the variable NAME_LENGTH returns the length of the name, 11. This length is then used to output the string slice, NAME (1 .. NAME_LENGTH), containing "Anaximander". The remainder of the string, NAME (NAME_LENGTH + 1 .. NAME'LAST), is not padded with blanks but is left undefined.

Controlling Columns, Lines, and Pages

In addition to the procedures just discussed, the TEXT_IO package contains subprograms that specify formats using the familiar concepts of columns, lines, and pages. With these subprograms, one may advance to a line, column, or page; establish line and page lengths; and determine the current position on the screen.

Six procedures provide the capability for advancing to lines and columns: SET_COL, SET_LINE, NEW_LINE, NEW_PAGE, SKIP_LINE, and SKIP_PAGE. If a file is not specified as the first parameter, SET_COL and SET_LINE can only be used to control output. If a file is specified (as will be shown later), these procedures may control input or output. The procedures NEW_LINE and NEW_PAGE only control output, and the procedures SKIP_LINE and SKIP_PAGE only control input.

The procedure SET_COL advances from the current position to the specified column. For example, the following call to SET_COL advances to the 24th column:

```
SET_COL (24);
```

The parameter used by SET_COL belongs to the subtype POSITIVE_COUNT of the integer type COUNT, defined in the TEXT_IO package as follows:

```
type COUNT is range 0..implementation defined ; -- integer type definition
subtype POSITIVE_COUNT is COUNT range 1 .. COUNT'LAST;
```

Since parameters used by SET_COL belong to a base type, COUNT, which is incompatible with other integer types, such parameters might require type conversion:

```
with TEXT_IO; use TEXT_IO;
procedure DIAGONAL_STARS is -- creates a diagonal line of 40 stars
begin
    for TAB in 1 .. 40 loop
        SET_COL ( POSITIVE_COUNT (TAB) ); -- type conversion necessary
        PUT_LINE ("*");
    end loop;
end DIAGONAL_STARS;
```

Besides SET_COL, all the other subprograms in the TEXT_IO package that specify formatting in terms of columns and lines also require parameters belonging to COUNT or POSITIVE_COUNT.

The procedure SET_LINE operates like SET_COL, except that the current position advances to the specified line rather than to the specified column. For example, the following call to SET_LINE advances the position to the 10th line of the current page:

```
SET_LINE (10);
```

Both procedures SET_COL and SET_LINE can only be used to advance the current position. If the current position is beyond the target position, then one advances to the target position on the next line or page. For instance, if the current position is column 7, SET_COL (5) will not backspace two positions. Rather the position will be advanced to column 5 on the next line. If the current position is already at column 5, then SET_COL (5) does not change the position. Similarly, if the current position is line 15, SET_LINE (14) does not go back one line. Rather, the position advances to line 14 of the next page.

Whereas the parameter of SET_LINE specifies a particular line, the parameter of NEW_LINE specifies the number of lines to advance from the current position. NEW_LINE has a default parameter value of 1. Therefore, when NEW_LINE is called without any parameter, one advances to the beginning of the next line. If a parameter value is supplied, then the default of 1 is overridden, and one advances the specified number of lines from the current position:

```
NEW_LINE;      -- advances 1 line
NEW_LINE (3);  -- advances 3 lines
```

The procedure NEW_PAGE is like NEW_LINE, except that one advances to the beginning of a new page instead of to a new line:

```
NEW_PAGE; -- advances to beginning of next page
```

Unlike NEW_LINE, however, NEW_PAGE has no parameters; one may advance only one page at a time.

The procedures SKIP_LINE and SKIP_PAGE behave like NEW_LINE and NEW_PAGE, respectively. The difference is that NEW_LINE and NEW_PAGE control an output device, whereas SKIP_LINE and SKIP_PAGE control an input device.

Two procedures are available that specify line and page lengths: SET_LINE_LENGTH and SET_PAGE_LENGTH. The line and page lengths are usually set to correspond to the size of a particular terminal display. For example, the following two procedure calls set a page to a maximum of 40 columns (length of each line), 24 lines (length of the page):

```
SET_LINE_LENGTH (40);  -- 40-column maximum
SET_PAGE_LENGTH (24);  -- 24-line maximum
```

Whenever output reaches the 40th column, the display automatically advances to the next line. Whenever output reaches the end of the 24th line, the display automatically advances to the next page.

If the line or page length is not explicitly set by the programmer, then the default is not to establish any maximum. In other words, the column and page lengths are unbounded. To specify explicitly an unbounded line or page length, call SET_LINE_LENGTH or SET_PAGE_LENGTH with a parameter value of 0. Better yet, use the predefined constant, UNBOUNDED (contained in the TEXT_IO package), which is set to 0:

```
SET_LINE_LENGTH (UNBOUNDED);   -- no maximum line length
SET_PAGE_LENGTH (UNBOUNDED);   -- no maximum page length
```

Three functions are available for reporting the current position: COL, LINE, and PAGE. The function COL returns the column number of the current position; LINE returns the line number of the current position; and PAGE returns the page number of the current position. If a file is not specified as the first parameter, these functions report the current position of the output. If a file is specified, these functions may report the current position of the input or output.

Finally, two functions are available that return the current maximum line length and maximum page length: LINE_LENGTH and PAGE_LENGTH. These functions only report information about the output. A value of 0 indicates that no maximum length was specified.

The following code shows how some of the preceding subprograms are used to arrange output by column, line, and page:

```
-- assume TEXT_IO is visible
-- sets screen size
SET_LINE_LENGTH (80);
SET_PAGE_LENGTH (24);

NEW_PAGE; -- line 1, column 1 of new page

SET_COL (31); -- line 1, column 31

PUT ("WISDOM OF THE AGES"); -- begins at line 1, column 31

NEW_LINE (2); -- advances to line 3, column 1

PUT ("Don't let your karma run over your dogma.");
    -- begins at line 3, column 1

SET_LINE (5); -- line 5, column 1

PUT ("You can lead a horse to water, but a pencil must be lead.");
    -- begins at line 5, column 1

NEW_LINE; -- advances to line 6, column 1

PUT_LINE ("Time flies like an arrow, but fruit flies like bananas.");
    -- begins at line 6, column 1

PUT ("Every bird can build a nest, but not everyone can lay an egg");
    -- begins at line 7, column 1

SET_LINE (1); -- line 1, column 1 of next page
```

File I/O

Each of the preceding subprograms that handles I/O to and from a standard I/O device has an overloaded form that handles I/O to and from a file. These overloaded forms only differ from the preceding subprograms by having an extra parameter. This extra parameter, FILE, which appears as the first parameter, names the file to be manipulated. For example, the following procedures manipulate the file called WISDOM:

```
-- assume TEXT_IO is visible
SET_LINE (WISDOM, 3); -- advances to line 3, column 1 in WISDOM file

SET_COL (WISDOM, 5); -- advances to column 5, line 3

PUT (WISDOM, "Where there's a will, there's a won't.");
   -- begins at line 3, column 5

NEW_LINE (WISDOM, 2); -- advances 2 lines
```

The procedures SET_COL, SET_LINE, and the versions of GET with a width parameter are particularly useful when inputting data from specific fields. Suppose, for example, that integer values located at the following lines and columns need to be input from a file called STATS_FILE:

Line 2: Columns 2 to 3   HEIGHT
         Columns 4 to 6   WEIGHT
         Columns 8 to 10   IQ
Line 4: Columns 8 to 13   INCOME
         Columns 14 to 17 AGE

This file contains information about a person's height, weight, IQ, income, and age, expressed as integer values. HEIGHT is in line 2, columns 2 to 3; WEIGHT is in line 2, columns 4 to 6; and so on. The following code reads each of these integer values from the file STATS_FILE:

```
-- assume TEXT_IO is visible
-- assume the current position is line 1, column 1
SKIP_LINE (STATS_FILE);           -- skips to line 2
SET_COL ( STATS_FILE, 2);         -- advances to column 2, line 2
GET ( STATS_FILE, HEIGHT, 2);     -- inputs height in columns 2 to 3
GET ( STATS_FILE, WEIGHT, 3);     -- inputs weight in columns 4 to 6
GET ( STATS_FILE, IQ);            -- inputs IQ in columns 8 to 10;
   -- since spaces separate this value, the width is omitted
SET_LINE ( STATS_FILE, 4);        -- advances to line 4
SET_COL ( STATS_FILE, 8);         -- advances to column 8, line 4
GET ( STATS_FILE, INCOME, 6);     -- inputs income in columns 8 to 13
GET ( STATS_FILE, AGE, 4);        -- inputs age in columns 14 to 17
```

Since STATS_FILE is an input file, the procedure SKIP_LINE is used instead of its cousin NEW_LINE. The procedures SET_COL and SET_LINE, however, operate on both input and output files (when a file is provided as a parameter).

Now that we have seen how information can be input from and output to a file, let us consider how files are created. Before file I/O can be performed, the file must be declared and created. Files are declared by using the predefined limited private type FILE_TYPE, contained in the TEXT_IO package. Files are created by using the procedure CREATE, also contained in the TEXT_IO package.

The following program declares and creates the file WISDOM, and then uses this file to store words of wisdom entered from the keyboard:

```
with TEXT_IO; use TEXT_IO;
procedure FILE_IO_WITH_TEXT_IO is
    WISDOM: FILE_TYPE;                          -- declares the file
    LINE: STRING (1..80);
    LINE_LENGTH: NATURAL;
begin
    CREATE (WISDOM, OUT_FILE, "Wisdom.Text");   -- creates a file
        -- WISDOM is the internal Ada file name
        -- "Wisdom.Text" is the external system file name

    PUT_LINE ("Enter your words of wisdom (up to 80 characters).");
    PUT_LINE ("Enter ""DONE"" when you are finished.");
    GET_LINE (LINE, LINE_LENGTH);
    while LINE (1 .. LINE_LENGTH) /= "DONE" loop
        PUT_LINE ( WISDOM, LINE (1 .. LINE_LENGTH) ); -- writes to file
        GET_LINE (LINE, LINE_LENGTH); -- reads from terminal
    end loop;

    CLOSE (WISDOM); -- closes file
end FILE_IO_WITH_TEXT_IO;
```

The file WISDOM is first declared to belong to FILE_TYPE. Procedure CREATE is then used to create this file physically on a disk. Procedure CREATE is declared in the TEXT_IO package as follows:

```
procedure CREATE ( FILE: in out FILE_TYPE;
                   MODE: in FILE_MODE := OUT_FILE;
                   NAME: in STRING := "";
                   FORM: in STRING := "" );
```

Procedure CREATE has four formal parameters, three with default values. The first formal parameter, FILE, is passed the name of the file to be created.

The second formal parameter, MODE, belongs to the type FILE_MODE, which is defined in the TEXT_IO package as follows:

```
type FILE_MODE is (IN_FILE, OUT_FILE);
```

The value IN_FILE declares the file to be in read-only mode. That is, a program may read from the file but not write to the file. The value OUT_FILE declares a write-only mode. A program may write to the file but not read from it. A file may only be in one mode at a time. The parameter MODE has the default value of OUT_FILE. When procedure CREATE is invoked, if this default value is overridden to IN_FILE, then an exception will be raised at runtime. This is because, when a file is first created, no items exist in the file to be read.

The third formal parameter, NAME, is passed the external system name of the file. This name differs from the internal file name passed to the parameter FILE. The internal file name is a valid Ada name that is used within an Ada program to reference the file. In contrast, the external name is the name by which the file is known to the outside world. For instance, the external name is used by the operating system to perform the actual physical I/O operations. There are no standard naming conventions for external names. On some systems, the file name includes a file extension following a dot: "Wisdom.Text". On other systems, a file name may appear as "&WISDOM::IO", and so on. The value of NAME, whatever form it takes on a particular system, is written as a string. This external file name is associated with the internal file name by the CREATE procedure.

In the procedure CREATE, NAME is given a default value of a null (empty) string. The external system name is thus optional. When an external name is not supplied (or is supplied as a null string), the file is created as a temporary file that exists only as long as the program is executing. This is unlike permanent files, which remain in existence for programs to reference, as needed.

The fourth formal parameter of CREATE, FORM, is required by some systems to supply special information about the file. This information might include a maximum file size, a read or write password, and so on. Consult the reference manual for your compiler to determine what, if any, values must be supplied for this parameter. The parameter FORM, like NAME, is given a default value of a null string.

Now that we understand how files are declared and created, let us return to the previous program, FILE_IO_WITH_TEXT_IO. Once the file WISDOM is created, the user is repeatedly prompted for words of wisdom. These words are output to the WISDOM file until the user enters "DONE". On some systems, a special character, such as control-Z, indicates the end of the file. On such systems, the program may use the predefined function END_OF_FILE instead of the special word "DONE":

while not END_OF_FILE **loop** . . .
-- uses the predefined BOOLEAN function to test for the end of file

Usually, END_OF_FILE is used when reading files, because this function often does not work well with interactive I/O devices. When properly working, the function END_OF_FILE returns the value TRUE when the end of file is reached; otherwise, it returns the value FALSE. Since the user is inputting items from the keyboard (the assumed standard input device), no file name is required after the function name END_OF_FILE. Similar functions, END_OF_LINE and END_OF_PAGE, are also provided by the TEXT_IO package.

Once the user of the program FILE_IO_WITH_TEXT_IO is done entering words of WISDOM and enters "DONE", the WISDOM file is closed with the procedure CLOSE. This procedure informs the operating system that the file is not currently needed by the program, and the association between the internal and external file names is broken. All open files should eventually be closed. Unlike some languages, Ada is not required to close all files automatically when the program ends. On some systems, if a file is not closed with the procedure CLOSE, data may be lost.

Once a file with an external name is created, the file is permanent. Unless it is deleted, this file can be manipulated by different programs at different times. For example, after the previous program creates the file WISDOM, another program may later read the words of wisdom contained in this file, as follows:

```
with TEXT_IO; use TEXT_IO;
procedure READ_EXISTING_FILE_WITH_TEXT_IO is
    INSIGHT: FILE_TYPE;
    ENLIGHTENMENT: STRING (1 .. 80);
    ENLIGHTENMENT_LENGTH: NATURAL;
begin
    OPEN (INSIGHT, IN_FILE, "Wisdom.Text"); -- opens existing file
    PUT_LINE ("WISDOM OF THE AGES"); -- outputs to terminal, not to file
    NEW_LINE;

    while not END_OF_FILE (INSIGHT) loop
        GET_LINE ( INSIGHT, ENLIGHTENMENT,
            ENLIGHTENMENT_LENGTH);
            -- inputs from file
        PUT_LINE ( ENLIGHTENMENT (1 .. ENLIGHTENMENT_LENGTH));
            -- outputs to terminal
    end loop;

    CLOSE (INSIGHT);
end READ_EXISTING_FILE_WITH_TEXT_IO;
```

Since the file containing words of wisdom already exists, this program opens the file, using the procedure OPEN, instead of creating it. Whereas the program that created the file "Wisdom.Text" gave it the internal name WISDOM, this program gives it the internal name INSIGHT. Like the procedure CREATE, OPEN associates a file's internal name with its external name. In general, the internal name associated with the external name of a file may be changed each time a program is run or even during a single execution of a program by closing the file and then reopening it with a different internal name.

The procedure OPEN is declared in the TEXT_IO package, as follows:

```
procedure OPEN (FILE:   in out FILE_TYPE;
                MODE: in FILE_MODE;
                NAME: in STRING;
                FORM: in STRING := "" );
```

The procedure OPEN uses the same parameters as CREATE, except that MODE and NAME do not have default values. These values must therefore be supplied. Files may either be opened in the read-only mode, IN_FILE, or in the write-only mode, OUT_FILE. In our example, since we are reading the words of wisdom from the file, the file is opened with the parameter value of IN_FILE.

Only existing files may be opened. If an attempt is made to open a file that does not exist, a NAME_ERROR is raised. Most systems, however, allow a file that already exists to be created. In such cases, CREATE opens the file. (The Ada Language Reference Manual is vague on this point, but this is common practice.)

Let us return to the program READ_EXISTING_FILE_WITH_TEXT_IO. When the file INSIGHT is opened, the current position is the beginning of the file. Each time the GET_LINE procedure is invoked, the next line is read from the file. The file is thus traversed sequentially, from beginning to end. To reference a particular item, one must search each item in the file in order, until the desired item is found or the end of the file is reached. Such files that may only be traversed sequentially are known as sequential files. The TEXT_IO package only supplies resources to handle sequential files. Another kind of file, known as a direct access (random access) file, is supported by the DIRECT_IO package. The direct access file will be discussed subsequently.

Whenever a file is opened, it must be either in a read-only mode, IN_FILE, or in a write-only mode, OUT_FILE. To change the mode within a program, one may close the file and then reopen it with a different mode value:

```
-- this code changes mode from IN_FILE to OUT_FILE
OPEN (INSIGHT, IN_FILE, "Wisdom.Text");
   ...
CLOSE (INSIGHT);
   ...
-- overwrites contents of file; does not append data to end of file
OPEN (INSIGHT, OUT_FILE, "Wisdom.Text");
```

Remember that each time the file is opened, one returns to the beginning of the file. The contents of an existing file are thus overwritten. Ada does not support a subprogram to append data to a file.

As an alternative to closing and then reopening a file, one may return to the beginning of the file and optionally reset its mode by calling the RESET procedure:

```
OPEN (INSIGHT, IN_FILE, "Wisdom.Text");   -- opens file in read-only mode
   ...
RESET (INSIGHT, OUT_FILE);   -- returns to beginning of file
                             -- resets mode to write-only (OUT_FILE)
```

There are two overloaded versions of RESET. The preceding version, which uses two parameters, returns to the beginning of the file and resets the mode value. The alternative version only has one parameter, the name of the file. This alternative version just returns to the beginning of the file without changing the mode value:

```
RESET (INSIGHT);   -- returns to the beginning of file without
                   -- changing the mode
```

Before ending our discussion of the TEXT_IO package, let us briefly mention a few other subprograms that are used for file manipulation. More complete descriptions may be found in the Ada Language Reference Manual.

The procedure DELETE is used to delete a file:

```
DELETE (INSIGHT); -- deletes the INSIGHT file
```

A file may only be deleted if it is open. Once a file is deleted, for all practical purposes, it ceases to exist.

Three functions—MODE, NAME, and FORM—are used to query the properties of a file. The function MODE returns the mode of the file. For files created with the TEXT_IO package, the value of MODE is either IN_FILE or OUT_FILE. The functions NAME and FORM return strings that contain the external system name of the file and the form of the file.

The function IS_OPEN returns the value TRUE or FALSE, depending on whether the specified file is open:

```
-- if the file is not open, then opens it
if not IS_OPEN (INSIGHT) then
    OPEN (INSIGHT, OUT_FILE, "Wisdom.Text");
end if;
```

Six subprograms are supplied that relate to the default destinations for input or output: SET_INPUT, SET_OUTPUT, STANDARD_INPUT, STANDARD_OUTPUT, CURRENT_INPUT, and CURRENT_OUTPUT. The procedure SET_INPUT establishes the default source of input, and the procedure SET_OUTPUT establishes the default destination of output. The functions STANDARD_INPUT and STANDARD_OUTPUT return the FILE_TYPE value of the standard I/O device. The functions CURRENT_INPUT and CURRENT_OUTPUT return the FILE_TYPE value of the current default source of input and the current default destination of output. The use of SET_OUTPUT and STANDARD_OUTPUT is illustrated in the following code:

```
-- assume TEXT_IO is visible
PUT ("Green");                    -- outputs string to standard output device
SET_OUTPUT (COLORS);
PUT ("Red");                      -- outputs to file COLORS
SET_OUTPUT (STANDARD_OUTPUT);
-- resets the default destination of output to the standard device
PUT ("Blue");                     -- outputs to standard output device
```

Unlike the file COLORS, STANDARD_INPUT and STANDARD_OUTPUT cannot be opened, closed, reset, or deleted.

Instead of reading from and writing to an external file, one may also read from and write to an internal character string. This service is provided by overloaded PUT and GET procedures that are located in the generic packages INTEGER_IO, FLOAT_IO, FIXED_IO, and ENUMERATION_IO. In the following code, for example, PUT procedures output an integer value, then a floating point value, then a Boolean value to an eight character string, OUTPUT:

```
with TEXT_IO; use TEXT_IO;
procedure INTERNAL_IO is
    package INT_IO is new INTEGER_IO (INTEGER);
    package FLT_IO is new FLOAT_IO (FLOAT);
    package BOOL_IO is new ENUMERATION_IO (BOOLEAN);
    use INT_IO, FLT_IO, BOOL_IO;
    OUTPUT: STRING (1 .. 8);
begin
    PUT (TO => OUTPUT, ITEM => 7, BASE => 2);
        -- writes an integer to the string
    PUT (OUTPUT);   -- outputs □□2#111# (the string)
                    -- □ represents a blank
    PUT (TO => OUTPUT, ITEM => 3.412, AFT => 1, EXP => 0);
        -- writes a floating point number to a string
    PUT (OUTPUT);   -- outputs □□□□□3.4 (the string)
    PUT (TO => OUTPUT, ITEM => TRUE, SET => LOWER_CASE);
        -- writes an enumeration literal to a string
    PUT (OUTPUT);   -- outputs true□□□□ (the string)
end INTERNAL_IO;
```

Note that instead of specifying the file that receives the output, these special versions of PUT specify the string that receives the output. These special versions do not provide the FORE and WIDTH parameters. The width is always the length of the string.

SEQUENTIAL_IO PACKAGE

The TEXT_IO package enables one to read, write, and manipulate sequential files containing human readable text. To output human readable text to a file, data such as numeric literals or enumeration literals must be converted (encoded) from their internal binary representations to character representations. Conversely, to input human readable numeric literals or enumeration literals from a file, they must be converted (coded) from their character representations to their internal binary representation. This coding and encoding are necessary if the files are to contain information that humans can read. Sometimes, however, the files do not need to be read by humans; they are only meant to be read by programs. In such cases, data can be efficiently input and output as a pattern of bits without any need for coding or encoding. The SEQUENTIAL_IO package provides this service. When this package is used, data can be input or output with no (or minimal) conversion.

The SEQUENTIAL_IO package allows a sequence of values belonging to the same type to be transferred to or from a file. This type may be a scalar type or a composite type (but not a limited private type). The following program, for instance, outputs records of type PRODUCT_TYPE to the file INVENTORY_FILE:

```
with SEQUENTIAL_IO; -- must with SEQUENTIAL_IO
procedure SEQUENTIAL_IO_DEMO is

    type PRODUCT_TYPE is
       record
          ID: STRING (1..5);
          QUANTITY: INTEGER range 0 .. 1_000;
       end record;

    package PRODUCT_IO is new SEQUENTIAL_IO (PRODUCT_TYPE);
       -- since SEQUENTIAL_IO is a generic package, it must be instantiated
    use PRODUCT_IO;

    INVENTORY_FILE: FILE_TYPE; -- this is PRODUCT_IO.FILE_TYPE

    BEST_SELLING_COMPUTER: PRODUCT_TYPE := ( ID       =>  "FV20D",
                                             QUANTITY =>  789 );
    BEST_SELLING_MOUSE: PRODUCT_TYPE :=    ( ID       =>  "19BRR",
                                             QUANTITY =>  223 );
    PRODUCT: PRODUCT_TYPE;

begin
    CREATE (FILE => INVENTORY_FILE, NAME => "Inventory.List");
       -- takes default (and required) MODE value of OUT_FILE
```

WRITE (FILE => INVENTORY_FILE, ITEM => BEST_SELLING_COMPUTER);
-- named notation

WRITE (INVENTORY_FILE, BEST_SELLING_MOUSE);
-- positional notation

RESET (FILE => INVENTORY_FILE, MODE => IN_FILE);
-- goes back to beginning of file and resets mode to IN_FILE

READ (FILE => INVENTORY_FILE, ITEM => PRODUCT);
-- reads BEST_SELLING_COMPUTER and gives this value to PRODUCT

CLOSE (FILE => INVENTORY_FILE);

end SEQUENTIAL_IO_DEMO;

As shown in this example, the package SEQUENTIAL_IO offers many of the same services as TEXT_IO. (See Appendix F of this book for a complete specification of the SEQUENTIAL_IO package.) Both packages provide distinct versions of the predefined types FILE_TYPE and FILE_MODE. Both packages also contain distinct versions of the subprograms CREATE, OPEN, CLOSE, DELETE, RESET, MODE, NAME, FORM, IS_OPEN, and END_OF_FILE. However, there are differences between the two packages. Unlike the TEXT_IO package, the SEQUENTIAL_IO package does not contain subprograms that format I/O or manipulate a file by columns, lines, and pages. Also, unlike the TEXT_IO package, the SEQUENTIAL_IO package is a generic package. Therefore, to perform sequential I/O on objects of a type, such as PRODUCT_TYPE, one must first instantiate the SEQUENTIAL_IO package with this type. Finally, unlike the TEXT_IO package, which performs I/O using the procedures PUT and GET, the SEQUENTIAL_IO package performs I/O using the procedures READ and WRITE.

As mentioned, each time the SEQUENTIAL_IO package is needed, it must be instantiated with a particular type. The previous example instantiates the SEQUENTIAL_IO package to perform I/O on objects of the type PRODUCT_TYPE:

package PRODUCT_IO **is new** SEQUENTIAL_IO (PRODUCT_TYPE);

As a result of this instantiation, every file, such as INVENTORY_FILE, belonging to PRODUCT_IO.FILE_TYPE may only contain values of type PRODUCT_TYPE.

Suppose that another instantiation of the SEQUENTIAL_IO package is performed using type BOOLEAN:

package BOOLEAN_IO **is new** SEQUENTIAL_IO (BOOLEAN);

Boolean objects may now be sent to any file of type BOOLEAN_IO.FILE_TYPE. As the following code illustrates, BOOLEAN_IO.FILE_TYPE and PRODUCT_IO.FILE_TYPE are distinct file types:

```
declare
    BOOLEAN_FILE: BOOLEAN_IO.FILE_TYPE;
    INVENTORY_FILE: PRODUCT_IO.FILE_TYPE;
begin
    CREATE (BOOLEAN_FILE, "Boolean.File");
    CREATE (INVENTORY_FILE, "Inventory.File");

    WRITE (BOOLEAN_FILE, TRUE);
    WRITE (INVENTORY_FILE, PRODUCT);
        -- PRODUCT defined in SEQUENTIAL_IO_DEMO
    WRITE (BOOLEAN_FILE, PRODUCT);    -- error
        -- may only output Boolean values
    WRITE (INVENTORY_FILE, FALSE);   -- error
        -- may only output PRODUCT_TYPE values
end;
```

File BOOLEAN_FILE may only contain values of type BOOLEAN, and file INVENTORY_FILE may only contain values of type PRODUCT_TYPE.

In general, a file created with the SEQUENTIAL_IO package may only be used to input and output values belonging to a single type. This restriction can be a problem when different kinds of data need to be placed in the same file. For instance, suppose that a sequential file is needed to store two different sets of information about men, depending on whether a man is a bachelor or is married. If the man is a bachelor, then information is needed on whether he is a misogynist or a misogamist. This information can be conveniently stored in a record:

```
type BACHELOR is
    record
        MISOGYNIST: BOOLEAN;
        MISOGAMIST: BOOLEAN;
    end record;
```

If the man is married, then the only information needed is the number of years that he has been married:

```
type MARRIED_MAN is
    record
        YEARS_MARRIED: INTEGER range 0 .. 100;
    end record;
```

Unfortunately, both these record types, BACHELOR and MARRIED_MAN, cannot be output to the same file. However, this problem can be circumvented by combining both record types into a single variant record type:

```
type MARITAL_STATUS_TYPE is (MARRIED, BACHELOR);

type MALE (MARITAL_STATUS: MARITAL_STATUS_TYPE := BACHELOR) is
    record
```

```
        case MARITAL_STATUS is
           when MARRIED =>
              YEARS_MARRIED: INTEGER range 0 .. 100;
           when BACHELOR =>
              MISOGYNIST: BOOLEAN;
              MISOGAMIST: BOOLEAN;
        end case;
     end record;
```

By instantiating the SEQUENTIAL_IO package with type MALE, one may perform file I/O on records belonging to this type:

```
package MEN_IO is new SEQUENTIAL_IO (MALE);
```

Some implementations of Ada only permit this instantiation if the discriminant, MARITAL_STATUS, is given a default value. By instantiating the SEQUENTIAL_IO package with type MALE, one may perform file I/O on records such as the following, which belong to this type:

```
-- data for a bachelor
PROGRAMMER: MALE   (  MARITAL_STATUS   =>   BACHELOR,
                      MISOGYNIST       =>   TRUE,
                      MISOGAMIST       =>   TRUE );

-- data for a married man
POLE_VAULTER: MALE (  MARITAL_STATUS   =>   MARRIED,
                      YEARS_MARRIED    =>   37 );
```

DIRECT_IO PACKAGE

The DIRECT_IO package is used to perform I/O on direct access (random access) files. (See Appendix G of this book for the complete specification of package DIRECT_IO.) A direct access file does not need to be traversed sequentially. One may jump around between the various items in the file. To reference a particular item in a direct access file, an index value may be specified. The first item in a direct access file has the index value of 1; the second item, the value 2; the third item, the value 3; and so on. It is also possible to perform file I/O sequentially without specifying the index value. When this option is taken, programs using the DIRECT_IO package appear very similar to programs using the SEQUENTIAL_IO package. For example, rewriting the SEQUENTIAL_IO_DEMO program (which appeared at the beginning of the preceding section) using DIRECT_IO results in the following program:

```
with DIRECT_IO;
procedure DIRECT_IO_DEMO is
```

```ada
      type PRODUCT_TYPE is
        record
          ID: STRING (1..5);
          QUANTITY: INTEGER range 0 .. 1_000;
        end record;

      package PRODUCT_IO is new DIRECT_IO (PRODUCT_TYPE);
          -- since DIRECT_IO is a generic package, it must be instantiated
      use PRODUCT_IO;

      INVENTORY_FILE: FILE_TYPE; -- this FILE_TYPE is defined in PRODUCT_IO
      BEST_SELLING_COMPUTER: PRODUCT_TYPE := ( ID       => "FV20D",
                                               QUANTITY => 789 );
      BEST_SELLING_MOUSE: PRODUCT_TYPE :=    ( ID       => "19BRR",
                                               QUANTITY => 223 );
      PRODUCT: PRODUCT_TYPE;

   begin
      CREATE ( FILE => INVENTORY_FILE,
               MODE => INOUT_FILE, -- MODE set for both reading and writing
               NAME => "Inventory.List" );

      WRITE (INVENTORY_FILE, BEST_SELLING_COMPUTER);
      WRITE (INVENTORY_FILE, BEST_SELLING_MOUSE);

      RESET (FILE => INVENTORY_FILE);
          -- goes back to beginning of file; mode does not change

      READ (INVENTORY_FILE, PRODUCT);
          -- reads BEST_SELLING_COMPUTER and gives this value to PRODUCT

      CLOSE (INVENTORY_FILE);
   end DIRECT_IO_DEMO;
```

As shown in this example, the DIRECT_IO package is, in many ways, similar to the SEQUENTIAL_IO package. Both packages are generic packages that provide the types FILE_TYPE and FILE_MODE. In addition, both packages provide the subprograms CREATE, OPEN, CLOSE, DELETE, RESET, MODE, NAME, FORM, IS_OPEN, READ, WRITE, and END_OF_FILE. Finally, both packages are used to input and output data that is not human readable text.

The DIRECT_IO_DEMO procedure does not specify an index value when it reads from or writes to the file and, therefore, uses read and write procedures identical to the ones in the SEQUENTIAL_IO package. When indexes are used, different overloaded versions of READ and WRITE are required. Note that the value of the file mode is INOUT_FILE. This value, which is only provided in the DIRECT_IO package, means that the file is in a read and write mode. In other words, direct access files assigned the mode INOUT_FILE can be written to and read from, without being closed or reset. This mode is the default file mode for the version of the CREATE procedure in the DIRECT_IO package.

As with sequential files, whenever a read or a write is performed on a direct access file, the file index is automatically incremented. As the following code illustrates, one may therefore alternate between reading from and writing to items of a file:

```
READ (INVENTORY_FILE, PRODUCT);      -- reads item n
WRITE (INVENTORY_FILE, PRODUCT);     -- writes to item n + 1, which now
                                     -- contains value of item n
READ (INVENTORY_FILE, PRODUCT);      -- reads item n + 2
WRITE (INVENTORY_FILE, PRODUCT);     -- writes to item n + 3, which now
                                     -- contains value of item n + 2
```

In addition to the READ and WRITE procedures just shown, which have two parameters, the DIRECT_IO package contains READ and WRITE procedures with three parameters. The third parameter specifies the index value of the item:

```
READ (INVENTORY_FILE, PRODUCT, 25);  -- reads the 25th item and writes
WRITE (INVENTORY_FILE, PRODUCT, 17); -- its value to the 17th item

READ ( FILE => INVENTORY_FILE,  -- invokes READ using named notation
       ITEM => PRODUCT,
       FROM => 6 );

WRITE ( FILE => INVENTORY_FILE, -- invokes WRITE using named notation
        ITEM => PRODUCT,
        TO => 8 );
```

The formal parameters FROM in procedure READ and TO in procedure WRITE are passed the index value of the item in the file that is to be read from or written to. This index value belongs to type COUNT. When a direct access file is empty, the index value is 0.

To understand better the use of index values in direct access files, consider a direct access file of records that contains information about books. The first record component stores the title of the book, and the second component stores the name of the book's author. The following package contains the procedure SEARCH, which uses the index values of the records to locate a book with a particular title:

```
package BINARY_SEARCH is

    subtype BOOK_TITLE is STRING (1..20);
    subtype BOOK_AUTHOR is STRING (1 .. 12);

    type BOOK_TYPE is
        record
            TITLE: BOOK_TITLE;
            AUTHOR: BOOK_AUTHOR;
        end record;

    procedure SEARCH ( FILE_NAME: in STRING;
                       TARGET_BOOK: in BOOK_TITLE );

end BINARY_SEARCH;
```

```ada
with TEXT_IO, DIRECT_IO; use TEXT_IO;
package body BINARY_SEARCH is
   package BOOK_IO is new DIRECT_IO (BOOK_TYPE);
   use BOOK_IO;

   procedure SEARCH ( FILE_NAME: in STRING;
                      TARGET_BOOK: in BOOK_ TITLE ) is

      BOOK_FILE: BOOK_IO.FILE_TYPE;
      BOOK: BOOK_TYPE;
      LOWER_BOUND: BOOK_IO.COUNT := 1;
      UPPER_BOUND: BOOK_IO.COUNT;
      MIDPOINT: BOOK_IO.COUNT;

   begin
      OPEN (BOOK_FILE, IN_FILE, FILE_NAME);
      UPPER_BOUND := SIZE (BOOK_FILE);

      loop
         if UPPER_BOUND < LOWER_BOUND then
            -- book not found
            PUT_LINE ("Not found");
            return;
         end if;

         MIDPOINT := (LOWER_BOUND + UPPER_BOUND) / 2;
         -- integer division

         READ (BOOK_FILE, BOOK, MIDPOINT);

         if BOOK.TITLE = TARGET_BOOK then
            -- book found
            PUT_LINE ("Author is " & BOOK.AUTHOR);
            return;
         end if;

         -- continues the search
         if BOOK.TITLE > TARGET_BOOK then
            -- selects first half of file
            UPPER_BOUND := MIDPOINT - 1;
         else
            -- selects second half of file
            LOWER_BOUND := MIDPOINT + 1;
         end if;

      end loop;
   end SEARCH;
end BINARY_SEARCH;
```

A program unit that mentions the package BINARY_SEARCH in its **with** and **use** clauses may invoke the procedure SEARCH as follows:

```ada
SEARCH ( FILE_NAME   => "Psychology.books",
         TARGET_BOOK => "The Primal Sigh    " );
```

When SEARCH is invoked, it searches the file "Psychology.books" for the book with the title *The Primal Sigh*. The kind of search used, a binary search, is efficient but can only work if the books are listed in alphabetical order by title. Briefly, this binary search examines the middle item in the file. If this middle item is not the desired item, then a check is made whether the desired item comes before or after this middle item. If, for example, the desired item comes before the middle item, then only the first half of the file is considered and the process repeats. The item in the middle of the first half of the file is checked. If this item is not the desired item, then a check is made whether the desired item comes before or after it. The process keeps repeating until the desired item is found or until it is determined that the item is not contained in the file.

Note that the procedure SEARCH invokes the function SIZE. This function, defined in DIRECT_IO, returns the size of the file (the number of items in the file). The value returned belongs to type COUNT.

We will conclude this section with two other subprograms contained in package DIRECT_IO: SET_INDEX and INDEX. SET_INDEX is a procedure that sets the index to a specified value (which may lie beyond the end of the file):

```
SET_INDEX (BOOK_FILE, 43);            -- sets index to 43rd book
SET_INDEX (FILE => BOOK_FILE, TO => 21);   -- named notation
```

INDEX is a function that returns the current index value of a direct access file:

```
CURRENT_BOOK := INDEX ( FILE => BOOK_FILE);   -- current index
   --assume CURRENT_BOOK of base type COUNT
```

IO_EXCEPTIONS PACKAGE

Package IO_EXCEPTIONS is a predefined library package that contains the exceptions that may be raised during I/O operations. All three I/O package specifications—TEXT_IO, SEQUENTIAL_IO, and DIRECT_IO—mention package IO_EXCEPTIONS in their **with** clauses. The specification of package IO_EXCEPTIONS contains the declarations of eight exceptions: STATUS_ERROR, MODE_ERROR, NAME_ERROR, USE_ERROR, DEVICE_ERROR, END_ERROR, DATA_ERROR, and LAYOUT_ERROR. We will briefly discuss these exceptions. Full descriptions may be found in the Ada Language Reference Manual.

Before discussing the individual exceptions, note that a program unit that mentions TEXT_IO, SEQUENTIAL_IO, or DIRECT_IO in its **with** clause automatically has available the exceptions listed in the IO_EXCEPTIONS package. This seems to violate the rule presented in Chapter 8 about packages not being able to reference indirectly the resources of other packages. In other words, if program P **with**s TEXT_IO, which in turn **with**s IO_EXCEPTIONS, program P cannot, on that basis alone, reference the resources of IO_EXCEPTIONS. The only reason program P can reference the exceptions defined in IO_EXCEPTIONS is because these exceptions are renamed in the package specifications for TEXT_IO (as well as in SEQUENTIAL_IO and DIRECT_IO):

STATUS_ERROR : **exception renames** IO_EXCEPTIONS.STATUS_ERROR;
MODE_ERROR : **exception renames** IO_EXCEPTIONS.MODE_ERROR;
NAME_ERROR : **exception renames** IO_EXCEPTIONS.NAME_ERROR;
. . .

Since this renaming occurs in the visible part of the I/O packages (their specifications), the alternative names—STATUS_ERROR, MODE_ERROR, NAME_ERROR, and so on—are made visible to external program units that reference these I/O packages. Renaming can thus alter the scope of the items being renamed, making them available to program units to which they would otherwise not be available.

Let us now briefly consider the conditions that raise the predefined I/O exceptions. STATUS_ERROR is raised whenever one attempts to manipulate an open file in a manner only appropriate to a closed file, or vice versa. For example, STATUS_ERROR is raised whenever one attempts to reset the mode of a file that is closed or attempts to open a file that is already open.

MODE_ERROR is raised whenever an attempted I/O operation is incompatible with the file's current mode. For example, this error is raised whenever one attempts to write to a file whose current mode is IN_FILE.

NAME_ERROR is raised when calling CREATE or OPEN with an invalid external file name. The external file name may be invalid because it is in the wrong form for a given computer system. Alternatively, the name may be invalid because an external file with this name does not exist.

USE_ERROR is raised whenever an I/O operation is attempted on a file where such an operation is not supported. For example, if the printer is declared as a file (as is often done), then one cannot open this file in a read mode.

DEVICE_ERROR is raised whenever an I/O operation cannot be carried out because of some failure affecting the I/O device.

END_ERROR is raised whenever an attempt is made to read past the end of a file. This error is very common.

DATA_ERROR is raised whenever input is in the wrong form or contains a value that is out of range.

LAYOUT_ERROR is raised whenever the formatting operations supplied by the TEXT_IO package are illegally used. The LAYOUT_ERROR is only renamed in the TEXT_IO package.

REFERENCING UNPRINTABLE CHARACTERS

The enumeration type CHARACTER, contained in the predefined package STANDARD, consists of 128 characters belonging to the character set of the American Standard Code for Information Interchange (ASCII). Out of these 128 characters, 95 can be referenced as literals by being placed in a pair of single quotes: 'A', '8', '!', and so on (assuming that a particular computer can enter all the printable ASCII characters). The other 33 characters, called control characters, cannot be referenced as literals. Control characters function as line feeds, carriage returns, line terminators, page terminators, and so on. These control characters, as well as any of the other 95 characters, may be referenced by using the VAL attribute. For instance, the control character for a line feed can be referenced as CHARACTER'VAL(10) because the line feed is at position 10 in the enumeration type CHARACTER. (The underlying numeric representation of the characters, their ASCII code, coincides with the position of the characters.) This notation, however, is unclear and error prone; unless one has memorized the ASCII code, one cannot discern which character is being referenced. To allow programmers to reference these control characters in a more natural fashion, the package ASCII is included within the package STANDARD (see Appendix C). The ASCII package assigns constant names to many of the ASCII characters. The constant names for the control characters are two- or three-letter mnemonics. For example, to reference the carriage return, one merely writes ASCII.CR. To reference the line feed, one writes ASCII.LF. These character constants may be concatenated with other characters or strings. Consider the following PUT statement, where BEL is the constant name for bell:

    PUT ("Dinner is ready!" & ASCII.BEL);
    -- outputs the message and rings the bell (which on some terminals sounds
    -- more like a swamp sow with its tail caught in the door)

Besides allowing the control characters to be easily referenced, the ASCII package enables one to reference ASCII characters that might not be available on a particular keyboard. For instance, if a keyboard is missing the character tilde, '~', one may reference this symbol with the constant ASCII.TILDE.

Since the package ASCII is embedded in the package STANDARD, it is automatically available to every program unit; no **with** ASCII clause can be employed. To avoid dot notation, however, one may employ the clause, **use** ASCII. By employing the **use** clause, one may reference the ASCII characters by simply writing their constant names: LF, CR, BEL, and so on.

As those well versed in other computer languages will testify, Ada is not particularly innovative when it comes to I/O. The next chapter on tasking, however, is a different story. As we will see, tasking—the concurrent execution of units of code—is handled in an innovative manner.

EXERCISES

1. Perform the necessary instantiations of the generic I/O packages to output objects of the following types:

   type CLOUDS **is** (CIRRUS, CIRROSTRATUS, CIRROCUMULUS, ALTOSTRATUS, ALTOCUMULUS, STRATOCUMULUS, NIMBOSTRATUS, CUMULUS, CUMULONIMBUS, STRATUS);
   type MORE_CLOUDS **is new** CLOUDS;
   type HOURS **is range** 0 .. 23;
   type MY_FLOAT **is new** FLOAT;

2. Assuming that the needed instance of the INTEGER_IO package is visible, what will each PUT statement output? (Show the correct format of this output.)

   PUT (ITEM => 15);
   PUT (ITEM => 15, BASE => 2);
   PUT (ITEM => 7_250, WIDTH => 2);
   PUT (ITEM => 2#1101#, BASE => 16);
   PUT (ITEM => 30, WIDTH => 9, BASE => 16);

3. Assuming that the needed instance of the FLOAT_IO package is visible, what will each PUT statement output? (Show the correct format of this output.)

   PUT (ITEM => 15.0);
   PUT (ITEM => 25.6, FORE => 3, AFT => 2, EXP => 0);
   PUT (ITEM => 123.4, FORE => 2, AFT => 2, EXP => 0);
   PUT (ITEM => 175.8, FORE => 0, AFT => 0, EXP => 0);
   PUT (ITEM => 25.79, FORE => 4, AFT => 1, EXP => 0);
   PUT (ITEM => -50.16, FORE => 5, AFT => 1, EXP => 2);
   PUT (ITEM => 0.096, FORE => 0, AFT => 1, EXP => 3);
   PUT (ITEM => 2_974.12, FORE => 4, AFT =>2, EXP => 1);

4. Assuming that the needed instance of the ENUMERATION_IO package is visible, what will each PUT statement output? (Show the correct format of this output.)

   PUT (ITEM => TRUE);
   PUT (ITEM => TRUE, WIDTH => 1);
   PUT (ITEM => FALSE, WIDTH => 9);
   PUT (ITEM => TRUE, SET => LOWER_CASE);
   PUT (ITEM => FALSE, WIDTH => 7, SET => UPPER_CASE);

5. Use the procedures SET_COL, SET_LINE, SKIP_LINE, and the versions of GET with a width parameter, to input integer values from the following specified fields:

Line 3:	Columns	5 to 7	WEIGHT
	Columns	8 to 9	HEIGHT
	Columns	10 to 12	AGE
Line 5:	Columns	2 to 4	IQ
	Columns	7 to 11	INCOME

6. Write a program that uses the TEXT_IO package to write the values of the following enumeration type to a file:

   type AIRPLANE_PARTS **is** (RADAR, COCKPIT, ENGINE, ENGINE_POD, PYLON, WING, VERTICAL_STABILIZER, RUDDER, TABS, ELEVATOR, HORIZONTAL_STABILIZER, FLAPS, SPOILERS, AILERON, THRUST_REVERSER);

   Write another program to read this file and output each of the enumeration literals in a column on the screen.

7. Rewrite the program in exercise 6 using the SEQUENTIAL_IO package instead of the TEXT_IO package. Directly examine the contents of the file and compare what you see with the contents of the file created with the program from exercise 6.

8. Rewrite the program in exercise 6 using the DIRECT_IO package instead of the TEXT_IO package. Directly examine the contents of the file and compare with the contents of the file created with the program from exercises 6 and 7.

Chapter 15

TASKING

The programs presented in the preceding chapters sequentially perform one activity after another. In Ada, one can also write programs that perform more than one activity concurrently (during the same period of time). This concurrent processing is called tasking. The units of code that run concurrently are called tasks.

There are two methods of concurrent processing: overlapped concurrency and interleaved concurrency. On computers with multiple processors, overlapped concurrency can be used. In overlapped concurrency, several tasks execute simultaneously, each on their own processor. On computers with a single processor, interleaved concurrency is used so that each task, in turn, is given a moment of processing time. This jumping around from task to task is performed so rapidly that an illusion is created that all tasks are running simultaneously. Whether overlapped or interleaved concurrency is used, from the programmer's perspective, the effect is the same. The programmer should think of each task as running simultaneously.

Tasks may thus be used when various activities need to be performed during the same period of time. For instance, in a program that controls a space station, one task might monitor the life support system, another might monitor solar activity, another might monitor the orientation of the space station, and so on. In addition, tasks may be used to simulate (model) events in the real world that occur at the same time. Tasks may also be used to increase execution speed, especially when the computer has multiple processors.

The topic of Ada tasking is very involved. Entire books have been devoted to the subject. It is beyond the scope of this book to give such an exhaustive discussion of tasking. Rather, this chapter stresses the features of Ada tasks; it does not discuss all of the complex issues surrounding the use of these features to solve real problems.

We begin this chapter by considering tasks that do not interface with each other. Next we consider tasks that do interface. Such tasks may or may not transfer data. We first explore tasks that do not transfer data, then tasks that do transfer data. The next two sections of this chapter cover the selective wait, and conditional entry calls and timed entry calls. These constructs permit greater control of task interaction. We then explore task attributes, entry families, and a useful pragma for prioritizing tasks. Next, we discuss task types, followed by a section on task interference, which is a common problem with concurrent processing. A solution to this problem is presented. Dynamically created tasks are then briefly covered, followed by a real-world tasking example.

TASKS THAT DO NOT INTERFACE

Concurrent processing is commonly used by the "computer" between our ears. Without too much mental strain, most of us can, for instance, chew gum, listen to the radio, and drive a car at the same time. Suppose that we attempt to have a computer simulate these activities by invoking the procedures CHEW_GUM, LISTEN_TO_RADIO, and DRIVE_TO_MOTHER:

```
procedure NOON_ACTIVITY is
begin
    CHEW_GUM;
    LISTEN_TO_RADIO;
    DRIVE_TO_MOTHER;
end NOON_ACTIVITY;
```

NOON_ACTIVITY is not as efficient as we are because the three procedures are performed sequentially, not concurrently. First the procedure CHEW_GUM is executed, followed by LISTEN_TO_RADIO, followed by DRIVE_TO_MOTHER. In order to execute all three procedures concurrently, we must use tasks:

```
procedure NOON_ACTIVITY is
    task EXERCISE_JAW; -- task specification
    task body EXERCISE_JAW is -- task body
    begin
        CHEW_GUM;
    end EXERCISE_JAW;
```

```
task EXPERIENCE_MUSIC; -- task specification
task body EXPERIENCE_MUSIC is -- task body
begin
    LISTEN_TO_RADIO;
end EXPERIENCE_MUSIC;

task VISIT_MOM; -- task specification
task body VISIT_MOM is -- task body
begin
    DRIVE_TO_MOTHER;
end VISIT_MOM;

begin -- NOON_ACTIVITY
    null; -- must always have at least one executable statement
end NOON_ACTIVITY;
```

Note that three tasks—EXERCISE_JAW, EXPERIENCE_MUSIC, and VISIT_MOM—are embedded within the declarative part of the procedure NOON_ACTIVITY. Tasks must always be embedded in the declarative part of other units; they cannot be separate compilation units. (A task body, however, may be separately compiled as a subunit.) The unit in which tasks are embedded is referred to as the "master unit" (or "environment task"). The tasks are said to "depend" on the master unit.

Also note that the three procedures are each invoked from within a task. The procedure CHEW_GUM is invoked from within the task EXERCISE_JAW; the procedure LISTEN_TO_RADIO is invoked from within the task EXPERIENCE_MUSIC; and the procedure DRIVE_TO_MOTHER is invoked from within the task VISIT_MOM.

Each of the three tasks contained within NOON_ACTIVITY has a specification and a body. The specification consists of the keyword **task**, followed by the task name. (As we will discuss momentarily, tasks that interface with each other require a different form of specification.) The task body begins with the keywords **task body**, followed by the task name and the keyword **is**. Optional declarations are placed between the keywords **is** and **begin**. (There are no declarations in the tasks of the example.) Executable code is placed between the keywords **begin** and **end**. The keyword **end** is optionally followed by the task name. Tasks that don't interface thus have the following form:

```
task task name; -- specification
task body task name is -- body
    declarations
begin
    statements
end task name;
```

Let us now examine how the procedure NOON_ACTIVITY works. First, the three dependent tasks—EXERCISE_JAW, EXPERIENCE_MUSIC, and

VISIT_MOM—are elaborated in the declarative part of the procedure NOON_ACTIVITY. Then, as soon as NOON_ACTIVITY starts executing (starting with the keyword **begin**), all three tasks are activated concurrently. (On a computer with a single processor, of course, one of these three tasks must receive the first "slice" of processing time. Which task receives this first slice is not defined by the Ada language.) Each task invokes one of the procedures: CHEW_GUM, LISTEN_TO_RADIO, or DRIVE_TO_MOTHER. As each of these procedures finishes executing, so does the task that invoked them. When the three tasks finish executing, so does the procedure NOON_ACTIVITY, in which they are embedded.

Note that the three tasks in the example do not interface, that is, they do not exchange data or synchronize. ("Synchronize" means to meet at a predetermined point in the code.) Rather, each of these tasks operates independently of the other two tasks.

There is an alternative way of writing procedure NOON_ACTIVITY. Any of the procedures contained within the three tasks can instead be placed in the statement part of NOON_ACTIVITY, as follows:

```
procedure NOON_ACTIVITY is
    task EXERCISE_JAW; -- task specification
    task body EXERCISE_JAW is -- task body
    begin
        CHEW_GUM;
    end EXERCISE_JAW;

    task EXPERIENCE_MUSIC; -- task specification
    task body EXPERIENCE_MUSIC is -- task body
    begin
        LISTEN_TO_RADIO;
    end EXPERIENCE_MUSIC;
begin -- NOON_ACTIVITY
    DRIVE_TO_MOTHER;
end NOON_ACTIVITY;
```

In this alternative, the task VISIT_MOM is omitted, and the procedure, DRIVE_TO_MOTHER, which is invoked by this task, is instead placed in the statement part of NOON_ACTIVITY. Either of the other two procedures could be alternatively placed in NOON_ACTIVITY. Any difference in performance between these alternative ways of writing NOON_ACTIVITY is unspecified by the Ada standards. Note that in this alternative, NOON_ACTIVITY functions as an environment task that executes DRIVE_TO_MOTHER. NOON_ACTIVITY is not finished executing when DRIVE_TO_MOTHER is finished executing, unless its dependent tasks, EXERCISE_JAW and EXPERIENCE_MUSIC, are also finished executing.

TASKS THAT INTERFACE WITHOUT TRANSFERRING DATA

In the preceding section, we discussed tasks that do not interface. Now let us consider tasks that interface without transferring data. These tasks are used when only synchronization is required. Sometimes the activities of two tasks must be synchronized so that one task does not get too far behind or ahead of the other task. Consider the following example:

```
procedure VISIT_MOTHER is

    task MAKE_MOM_HAPPY is -- task specification
        entry EAT_HER_FOOD;
    end MAKE_MOM_HAPPY;

    task body MAKE_MOM_HAPPY is -- task body
    begin
        accept EAT_HER_FOOD do
            CHEW_AND_SWALLOW;
        end EAT_HER_FOOD;
    end MAKE_MOM_HAPPY;

    task TIME_WITH_MOM; -- task specification
    task body TIME_WITH_MOM is -- task body
    begin
        MAKE_MOM_HAPPY.EAT_HER_FOOD;
    end TIME_WITH_MOM;

begin -- VISIT_MOTHER
    null;
end VISIT_MOTHER;
```

In this example, the procedure VISIT_MOTHER contains two tasks: MAKE_MOM_HAPPY and TIME_WITH_MOM. Note that the task specification of MAKE_MOM_HAPPY, unlike that of TIME_WITH_MOM, contains an **entry** clause. The general form of a task specification that contains an **entry** clause is as follows:

```
task task name is
    entry entry name (parameter definitions );
end task name;
```

This specification begins with the keyword **task**, followed by the task name and the keyword **is**. The specification ends with the keyword **end**, followed optionally by the task name. Two kinds of items may be placed in such a specification: certain pragmas (one of which will be discussed at the end of this chapter) and **entry** clauses. An **entry** clause contains the keyword **entry**, the entry name, and optional parameter definitions.

An **entry** clause is used for synchronization and, optionally, for transferring data between tasks. The task MAKE_MOM_HAPPY contains a single **entry** clause:

```
entry EAT_HER_FOOD;
```

Since no parameters follow the entry identifier EAT_HER_FOOD, this **entry** clause is used only for synchronization, not for transferring data.

The **entry** clause associates an entry identifier in the task specification with one or more entry points inside the task body. These entry points, indicated by **accept** statements, are the actual points in the code where tasks synchronize and transfer data. Thus, for each **entry** clause in a task specification, one or more associated **accept** statements must appear in the corresponding task body.

In procedure VISIT_MOTHER, the **entry** clause EAT_HER_FOOD is associated with the **accept** statement having the same identifier:

```
accept EAT_HER_FOOD do
    CHEW_AND_SWALLOW;
end EAT_HER_FOOD;
```

An **accept** statement has the following form:

accept *entry identifier* (*parameter definitions*) **do**
    statements
end *entry identifier;*

The **accept** statement begins with the keyword **accept**, followed by the entry identifier (including any parameters), and the keyword **do**. It ends with the keyword **end**, followed by an optional entry identifier. Executable statements are placed between the keywords **do** and **end**.

Now that we have discussed the structure of a task that interfaces with another task, we will describe how two tasks interface. In order for two tasks to interface, one task must call the other task. The task that does the calling is known as the calling task. The task that is called is known as the acceptor task. The **entry** clauses in the specification of the acceptor task provide interface information needed by other tasks to call the acceptor task. This interface information includes the entry identifiers and the optional parameter definitions, which specify how data are transferred.

Tasks are called in much the same way that procedures are called, except that the calling task must specify both the task identifier and the entry identifier. In the procedure VISIT_MOTHER, the task TIME_WITH_MOM is the calling task, and MAKE_MOM_HAPPY is the acceptor task. TIME_WITH_MOM calls MAKE_MOM_HAPPY as follows:

```
MAKE_MOM_HAPPY.EAT_HER_FOOD;
```

The call consists of the task identifier MAKE_MOM_HAPPY, followed by a dot, followed by the entry identifier EAT_HER_FOOD. Dot notation cannot be avoided by employing a **use** clause, because tasks may not be mentioned in a **use** clause. There is, however, a mechanism for avoiding dot notation. Within a calling task, a task entry can be renamed as a procedure:

```
task body TIME_WITH_MOM is -- body of calling task
    procedure PLEASE_MOTHER renames
        MAKE_MOM_HAPPY.EAT_HER_FOOD;
        -- rename an entry as a procedure
begin
    PLEASE_MOTHER; -- task entry called as a procedure
end TIME_WITH_MOM;
```

By renaming a task entry as a procedure, the task entry can optionally be called as a procedure. The procedure identifier does not hide the task entry identifier; the task entry may still be called as before, using dot notation.

When an entry of a task is called, one of the task's associated **accept** statements is executed when that point in the code is reached. When the **accept** statement is executed, the group of statements contained within it is executed. This group of statements specifies the actions to be performed as the tasks are interfacing. In the acceptor task MAKE_MOM_HAPPY, the **accept** statement EAT_HER_FOOD only specifies one action to be performed: CHEW_AND_SWALLOW.

The **accept** statement can only appear in a task body; it can never appear, for instance, in the statement part of a procedure. Thus, the executable statement of the task TIME_WITH_MOM can be placed in the statement part of the procedure VISIT_MOTHER. However, the executable statements of the task MAKE_MOM_HAPPY cannot be placed in this procedure because they include an **accept** statement:

```
...
begin -- procedure VISIT_MOTHER
    accept EAT_HER_FOOD do       -- error, accept statement cannot be
        CHEW_AND_SWALLOW;        -- placed in a procedure
    end EAT_HER_FOOD;
end VISIT_MOTHER;
```

Now let us consider how the procedure VISIT_MOTHER works. After the declarations of the procedure are elaborated and execution begins, the two tasks, MAKE_MOM_HAPPY and TIME_WITH_MOM, are activated. The task TIME_WITH_MOM calls the acceptor task MAKE_MOM_HAPPY. Depending on the execution speed of each task, three possible situations can result. First, the acceptor task might be prepared to accept a call before a call is made. Second, a call might be made before the acceptor task is prepared to accept it. Third, a call might be made at the same moment that the acceptor task is prepared to accept it.

Consider the first situation, where the acceptor task is prepared to accept a call before a call is made. In this situation, the acceptor task waits until a call is eventually made. In terms of our example, the acceptor task,

MAKE_MOM_HAPPY, reaches its **accept** statement before the calling task, TIME_WITH_MOM, calls the associated task entry. MAKE_MOM_HAPPY then waits for a call to be made. When TIME_WITH_MOM finally makes the entry call, MAKE_MOM_HAPPY.EAT_HER_FOOD, the wait of MAKE_MOM_HAPPY is over, and the two tasks "rendezvous."

The term "rendezvous" refers to the meeting of two tasks. During a rendezvous, the two tasks synchronize and optionally transfer data. (In the example, no data transfer takes place.) During the rendezvous, the acceptor task executes all the statements within its **accept** statement while the calling task is suspended. When all the statements within the **accept** statement are done executing, the rendezvous is finished. The tasks are once again free to go their separate merry ways.

Since the calling task is suspended until the **accept** statement finishes executing, the number of statements in the **accept** statement should be kept to a minimum. Statements that do not need to be executed during a rendezvous should be placed outside of the **accept** statement, so that the calling task is not suspended longer than necessary.

In terms of our example, when the calling task TIME_WITH_MOM finally makes the entry call MAKE_MOM_HAPPY.EAT_HER_FOOD, MAKE_MOM_HAPPY executes the one statement within its **accept** statement: CHEW_AND_SWALLOW. TIME_WITH_MOM waits until CHEW_AND_SWALLOW is done executing, at which time the rendezvous is finished. When the rendezvous is finished, the tasks MAKE_MOM_HAPPY and TIME_WITH_MOM disassociate and continue executing independently. Figure 15.1 shows the rendezvous process when an acceptor task is prepared to accept a call before the call is made.

Let us now consider the second situation that may result when one task calls another task: a call might be made before the acceptor task is prepared to accept it. In this situation, the calling task waits until its call is eventually accepted.

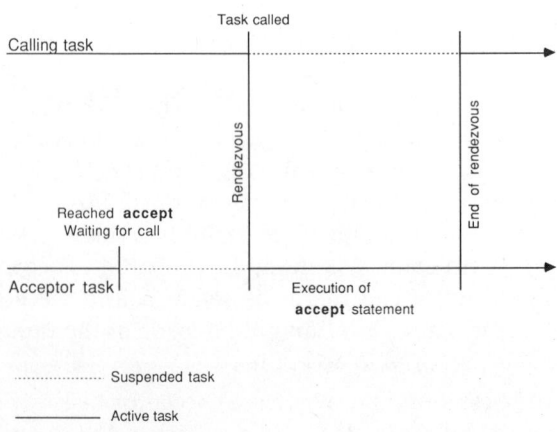

Figure 15.1 The rendezvous

Applying this situation to the example, the calling task, TIME_WITH_MOM, makes the entry call MAKE_MOM_HAPPY.EAT_HER_FOOD before the acceptor task, MAKE_MOM_HAPPY, reaches the associated accept statement. TIME_WITH_MOM waits until MAKE_MOM_HAPPY reaches the accept statement and accepts its call. When MAKE_MOM_HAPPY accepts the call, a rendezvous is initiated.

In the third situation, a call is made at the same moment that the acceptor task is prepared to accept it. In this situation, a rendezvous is immediately initiated; neither task waits. This situation is rare. Since each task progresses at its own rate, it is unlikely for a task to reach its **accept** statement the moment its associated entry is called.

Note that, in the preceding example, the task MAKE_MOM_HAPPY is called only once, and its **accept** statement is reached only once. Suppose, however, that MAKE_MOM_HAPPY is called twice:

```
procedure VISIT_MOTHER is

   task MAKE_MOM_HAPPY is
     entry EAT_HER_FOOD;
   end MAKE_MOM_HAPPY;
   task body MAKE_MOM_HAPPY is
   begin
     accept EAT_HER_FOOD do -- error; called twice, but reached once
        CHEW_AND_SWALLOW;
     end EAT_HER_FOOD;
   end MAKE_MOM_HAPPY;

   task TIME_WITH_MOM;
   task body TIME_WITH_MOM is
   begin
     MAKE_MOM_HAPPY.EAT_HER_FOOD; -- calls MAKE_MOM_HAPPY
   end TIME_WITH_MOM;

begin -- VISIT_MOTHER
   MAKE_MOM_HAPPY.EAT_HER_FOOD; -- calls MAKE_MOM_HAPPY
end VISIT_MOTHER;
```

This example illustrates a tasking error that arises because MAKE_MOM_HAPPY reaches its **accept** statement only once yet is called twice: once from the task body TIME_WITH_MOM and once from the statement part of the procedure VISIT_MOTHER. Let us see how this error arises. Suppose that the task TIME_WITH_MOM first calls MAKE_MOM_HAPPY. In this case, if VISIT_MOTHER makes its call while TIME_WITH_MOM and MAKE_MOM_HAPPY are in a rendezvous, then it must wait. Only two tasks can participate in a rendezvous. After the rendezvous is finished, the task MAKE_MOM_HAPPY terminates. The predefined TASKING_ERROR is raised because VISIT_MOTHER is now waiting to rendezvous with a task that has terminated.

It is perfectly legitimate for a task entry to be called twice. However, to avoid a tasking error, the body of the acceptor task must be written so that the associated **accept** statement is also reached twice. This may be accomplished, for instance, by looping over the **accept** statement twice or by simply writing the **accept** statement twice:

```
task MAKE_MOM_HAPPY is
  entry EAT_HER_FOOD;
end MAKE_MOM_HAPPY;

task body MAKE_MOM_HAPPY is
begin
    accept EAT_HER_FOOD do
        CHEW_AND_SWALLOW;
    end EAT_HER_FOOD;

    accept EAT_HER_FOOD do
        CHEW_AND_SWALLOW;
    end EAT_HER_FOOD;

end MAKE_MOM_HAPPY;
```

The single task entry, EAT_HER_FOOD, is associated with the two **accept** statements within the task body. The first task entry call is accepted by the first **accept** statement, and the second task entry call is accepted by the second **accept** statement. (Tasks that contain more than one **accept** statement will be discussed in the next section.)

Now that we have seen how a tasking exception can be raised, let us briefly see how exception handlers can be used to handle such an exception. In Chapter 11, we showed how exception handlers may be placed in block statements, subprograms, and packages. Exception handlers may also be placed in a task body:

```
task body TIME_WITH_MOM is
begin
    MAKE_MOM_HAPPY.EAT_HER_FOOD; -- call MAKE_MOM_HAPPY
exception
    when TASKING_ERROR => ASK_FOR_SECONDS;
end TIME_WITH_MOM;
```

In this example, whenever a TASKING_ERROR is raised, the exception handler invokes the procedure ASK_FOR_SECONDS. If the task is running and an exception is raised that is not handled by this exception handler, then the task automatically terminates; the exception does not propagate as it does for block statements, subprograms, and packages. This behavior, however, only applies to exceptions that are raised as tasks are executing and if no rendezvous is in progress.

A full description of how exceptions are propagated by tasks is beyond the scope of this book. The following brief description is for the advanced reader. If a rendezvous is in progress and the exception is not handled in the **accept** statement of the acceptor task, then the exception propagates to the point immediately following the **accept** statement. The exception also propagates to the task that last called the acceptor task. Exceptions may propagate in other ways. If an exception is raised in the declarative part of a task body, then the task terminates and the exception, TASKING_ERROR, propagates to the unit from which the task was activated. For descriptions of additional ways that exceptions can be propagated, consult the Ada Language Reference Manual.

As we have seen in a previous example, a task entry can be called multiple times. In such situations, the acceptor task may not be able to accept all the entry calls as they are made. Thus a backlog of entry calls may form. This backlog of entry calls is stored in a queue for that task entry. Each task entry has its own entry queue. When the acceptor task is ready to accept a call to an entry, it accepts the calls in the entry queue on a first in first out (FIFO) basis. A task whose call is in an entry queue is suspended until its call is accepted and the rendezvous is finished. (By the way, an acceptor task may use the COUNT attribute to inquire about the number of entry calls that have been placed in an entry queue. This attribute appends to the name of a task entry and may only reside within the acceptor task body.)

TASKS THAT INTERFACE AND TRANSFER DATA

Now that we have discussed tasks that rendezvous without transferring data, we will explore tasks that rendezvous and transfer data:

```
task GAS_STATION_ATTENDANT is -- task specification
    entry SERVICE_ISLAND (CAR: CAR_TYPE);
end GAS_STATION_ATTENDANT;

task body GAS_STATION_ATTENDANT is -- task body
begin
    loop
        accept SERVICE_ISLAND (CAR: CAR_TYPE ) do
            FILL_WITH_GAS (CAR);
        end SERVICE_ISLAND;
    end loop;
end GAS_STATION_ATTENDANT;
```

Speaking loosely, the task GAS_STATION_ATTENDANT waits for a car to arrive at the service island. When a car arrives, it is filled with gas, and the "gas station attendant" waits for the next car to arrive. Since an infinite loop is used, this process continues nonstop, 24 hours a day, 7 days a week, with no time off.

More specifically, here is how this task works. When GAS_STATION_ATTENDANT runs, the infinite loop in the task body is entered, and the **accept** statement SERVICE_ISLAND is reached. The task waits until the associated task entry SERVICE_ISLAND is called by an external unit. Note that the task entry has a parameter definition: CAR is declared to be a formal **in** parameter of type CAR_TYPE, which we assume has been previously defined. (Parameter modes for tasks are like those for procedures: when the parameter mode is omitted, an **in** parameter is assumed.) Since this task entry has a formal **in** parameter, CAR, the external calling unit must include an actual parameter in its call, which is passed to this formal parameter. It is through such parameter passing that data are transferred between tasks:

   GAS_STATION_ATTENDANT.SERVICE_ISLAND (MY_CAR);

When the rendezvous is initiated, the calling task passes the value of the parameter MY_CAR to the **accept** statement, SERVICE_ISLAND, within the acceptor task. The **accept** statement then invokes the procedure FILL_WITH_GAS with this parameter value. After the procedure FILL_WITH_GAS is done executing, the rendezvous is finished.

Note that the data transfer that occurs in this example is from the calling task to the acceptor task. Data may also be transferred from the acceptor task to the calling task. This is accomplished just as it is for procedures—by using **out** or **in out** parameter modes.

Consider an **accept** statement that has an **in** parameter and an **out** parameter:

   accept PARAMETER_MODES (IN_PARAM: **in** POSITIVE;
                           OUT_PARAM: **out** CHARACTER) **do**
      if IN_PARAM **in** CHARACTER'POS ('A') .. CHARACTER'POS ('Z') **then**
         OUT_PARAM := CHARACTER'VAL (IN_PARAM);
      else
         OUT_PARAM := ' ';
      end if;
   end PARAMETER_MODES;

When the **accept** statement is executed, the actual parameter value in the entry call is passed to IN_PARAM. This value is then used by the **if** statement within the **accept** statement. If the value of IN_PARAM lies within the range of 65 to 90 inclusive (which are the positions of the uppercase letters in the ASCII character set), then OUT_PARAM is set to the character at that position, else OUT_PARAM is set to a blank character. After the statements in the **accept** statement are done executing, the result stored in OUT_PARAM is then passed back to the calling task, and the rendezvous ends.

Another way that task entry calls are similar to procedure calls is that they both may use positional or named notation. Thus, assuming that the previous **accept** statement is in the body of task T (which is not shown), the following task entry calls are equivalent:

T.PARAMETER_MODES (65, CHAR);   -- (assume CHAR is a character
                                -- variable)
    -- positional notation

T.PARAMETER_MODES (IN_PARAM => 65, OUT_PARAM => CHAR);
    -- named notation

So far every task presented has contained, at most, one **entry** clause. As the following example shows, tasks may contain multiple entries:

task GAS_STATION_ATTENDANT **is** -- task specification
    entry SERVICE_ISLAND (CAR: CAR_TYPE);
    entry GARAGE (CAR: CAR_TYPE);
end GAS_STATION_ATTENDANT;

task body GAS_STATION_ATTENDANT **is** -- task body
begin
    loop
        accept SERVICE_ISLAND (CAR: CAR_TYPE) **do**
            FILL_WITH_GAS (CAR);
        end SERVICE_ISLAND;
        accept GARAGE (CAR: CAR_TYPE) **do**
            FIX (CAR);
        end GARAGE;
    end loop;
end GAS_STATION_ATTENDANT;

The two task entries, SERVICE_ISLAND and GARAGE, each has a formal parameter of type CAR_TYPE. Again, speaking loosely, the gas station attendant waits for a car to arrive at the service island. When a car arrives, it is filled with gas. The attendant then waits for a car to enter the garage. When a car enters the garage, it is fixed. The process then repeats: the attendant waits for a car to arrive at the service island, then for a car to enter the garage, and so on. This is no way to run a gas station. The attendant insists on going back and forth between the service island and the garage, regardless of the number of cars waiting for each kind of service. For example, after a car enters the service island and is filled with gas, the attendant then waits for a car to enter the garage. The attendant keeps waiting even if a long line of cars forms at the service island. (This task is modeled after my neighborhood gas station.)

More specifically, the code works as follows. Once the infinite loop in the task body is entered and the first **accept** statement, SERVICE_ISLAND, is reached, the task waits until the corresponding task entry is called. When a call is made, a rendezvous occurs, and the **accept** statement then invokes the procedure FILL_WITH_GAS. After the procedure is done executing, the rendezvous is finished, and the second **accept** statement, GARAGE, is reached. The task waits until the GARAGE task entry is called. When a call is made, a rendezvous occurs, and the **accept** statement then invokes the procedure FIX. When FIX is done executing, the rendezvous is finished, and the loop returns us to the **accept** statement for SERVICE_ISLAND, where the process repeats.

In order to write a more reasonable version of task GAS_STATION_ATTENDANT, a **select** statement can be used.

THE SELECTIVE WAIT

The **select** statement permits nonsequential execution of code. There are three basic kinds of **select** statements: the selective wait, conditional entry calls, and timed entry calls. The selective wait is used by acceptor tasks to control how they accept entry calls. There are several variations of the selective wait. Conditional and timed entry calls are used by calling tasks to control how they call task entries. These two forms of the **select** statement will be covered in the next section. The kind of **select** statement that we need to improve task GAS_STATION_ATTENDANT is a variation of the selective wait, which has the following form:

```
select
    accept statement
or
    accept statement
    . . .
or
    accept statement
end select;
```

The **select** statement begins with the keyword **select** and ends with the keywords **end select**. Within this variation of the **select** statement are multiple **accept** statements, each separated by an **or**. This **select** statement selects any of the **accept** statements whose associated entry has been called. It does not wait for a particular entry call if other entries have been called. Applying this variation of the **select** statement to the previous version of GAS_STATION_ATTENDANT, we obtain the following:

```
task GAS_STATION_ATTENDANT is -- task specification
    entry SERVICE_ISLAND (CAR: CAR_TYPE);
    entry GARAGE (CAR: CAR_TYPE);
end GAS_STATION_ATTENDANT;
```

```
task body GAS_STATION_ATTENDANT is -- task body
begin
    loop
        select -- a version of the selective wait
            accept SERVICE_ISLAND (CAR: CAR_TYPE) do
                FILL_WITH_GAS (CAR);
            end SERVICE_ISLAND;
        or
            accept GARAGE (CAR: CAR_TYPE) do
                FIX (CAR);
            end GARAGE;
        end select;
    end loop;
end GAS_STATION_ATTENDANT;
```

Again, speaking loosely, if a car arrives at the service island, and no car is at the garage, then the gas station attendant fills the car with gas. Conversely, if a car is at the garage, and no car is at the service island, then the attendant fixes the car. If a car is waiting at both the service island and the garage, then the attendant arbitrarily selects one car or the other to service. If no car is either at the service island or the garage, then the attendant waits for the first car to arrive.

More specifically, once the **select** statement within the infinite loop is reached, the acceptor task accepts whichever task entry was called. If both task entries were called, Ada does not specify which entry is selected. If neither entry was called, the acceptor task waits for whichever entry is called first.

One of the problems with the last version of GAS_STATION_ATTENDANT is that we are assuming that gas is always available. As everyone knows, this is not the case. The next version of the task, which uses another variation of the selective wait, deals with this problem by placing a **when** clause before the **accept** statement for SERVICE_ISLAND:

```
task GAS_STATION_ATTENDANT is -- task specification
    entry SERVICE_ISLAND (CAR: CAR_TYPE);
    entry GARAGE (CAR: CAR_TYPE);
end GAS_STATION_ATTENDANT;

task body GAS_STATION_ATTENDANT is -- task body
begin
    loop
        select
            when GAS_AVAILABLE =>
                accept SERVICE_ISLAND (CAR: CAR_TYPE) do -- guarded
                    FILL_WITH_GAS (CAR);
                end SERVICE_ISLAND;
```

```
        or
            accept GARAGE (CAR: CAR_TYPE) do -- unguarded
                FIX (CAR);
            end GARAGE;
        end select;
    end loop;
end GAS_STATION_ATTENDANT;
```

An **accept** statement preceded by a **when** clause is said to be "guarded." In other words, the **when** clause acts as a "guard," permitting or not permitting the acceptor task to reach the **accept** statement. The **when** clause consists of the keyword **when**, followed by a Boolean expression, and an arrow. If the Boolean expression has the value TRUE, then the guard permits the **accept** statement to be reached. In such cases, the alternative containing the **accept** statement is "open" and is a possible candidate for a rendezvous. If the Boolean expression has the value FALSE, then the alternative containing the **accept** statement is "closed" and cannot be considered for a rendezvous. In the example, the guard contains the Boolean function GAS_AVAILABLE. If GAS_AVAILABLE is TRUE, then the select alternative is open, and the **accept** statement for SERVICE_ISLAND can be considered for a rendezvous, just as if the **when** clause were not present. If GAS_AVAILABLE is FALSE, then this alternative is closed, and the **accept** statement for SERVICE_ISLAND cannot be considered for a rendezvous (although the entry within a closed alternative may still be called by other tasks).

When gas is available, this version of GAS_STATION_ATTENDANT behaves just like the previous version. The gas station attendant either accepts a car at the service station or at the garage, depending on which request is made first. If both requests are made, then one request is arbitrarily selected. If neither request is made, then the attendant waits.

Suppose, however, that gas is not available. In this case, only cars entering the garage are considered. If no car enters the garage, the gas station attendant just waits; no attempt is made to take a car at the service island.

Care must be taken when all of the alternatives in a **select** statement are guarded. Consider, for example, the following version of GAS_STATION_ATTENDANT:

```
task GAS_STATION_ATTENDANT is -- task specification
    entry SERVICE_ISLAND (CAR: CAR_TYPE);
    entry GARAGE (CAR: CAR_TYPE);
end GAS_STATION_ATTENDANT;

task body GAS_STATION_ATTENDANT is -- task body
begin
    loop
        select -- program error might be raised
            when GAS_AVAILABLE =>
```

```
      accept SERVICE_ISLAND (CAR: CAR_TYPE) do -- guarded
        FILL_WITH_GAS (CAR);
      end SERVICE_ISLAND;
    or
      when GARAGE_AVAILABLE =>
        accept GARAGE (CAR: CAR_TYPE) do -- guarded
          FIX (CAR);
        end GARAGE;
    end select;
  end loop;
end GAS_STATION_ATTENDANT;
```

Each **accept** statement in this example is guarded. When the **select** statement is entered, each guard is evaluated, and only open alternatives are considered. If there are no open alternatives (all the guards are false), then the predefined exception, PROGRAM_ERROR, is raised. In the example, therefore, one must be sure that the Boolean functions, GAS_AVAILABLE and GARAGE_AVAILABLE, can never both be false. If this cannot be guaranteed, then the danger of an error being raised can be avoided by using an **else** clause within the **select** statement. The following example is yet another variation of the selective wait:

```
task GAS_STATION_ATTENDANT is -- task specification
    entry SERVICE_ISLAND (CAR: CAR_TYPE);
    entry GARAGE (CAR: CAR_TYPE);
end GAS_STATION_ATTENDANT;

task body GAS_STATION_ATTENDANT is -- task body
begin
  loop
    select -- selective wait
      when GAS_AVAILABLE =>
        accept SERVICE_ISLAND (CAR: CAR_TYPE) do -- guarded
          FILL_WITH_GAS (CAR);
        end SERVICE_ISLAND;
    or
      when GARAGE_AVAILABLE =>
        accept GARAGE (CAR: CAR_TYPE) do -- guarded
          FIX (CAR);
        end GARAGE;
    else
      SLEEP;
    end select;
  end loop;
end GAS_STATION_ATTENDANT;
```

In this example, the **select** statement contains three alternatives, which are separated by the keywords **or** and **else**. The first two alternatives are guarded as before. The third alternative, however, is preceded by the keyword **else**.

Instead of containing an **accept** statement, this alternative contains a call to the procedure SLEEP. The third alternative is only selected when one of the other two alternatives cannot be selected. These other alternatives cannot be selected either when they are closed or when they are open but their associated task entries have not been called.

Speaking loosely again, the gas station attendant first checks to see if gas is available and if the garage is available. If neither is available, then the attendant sleeps. If, however, gas is available and/or the garage is available, then before considering sleep, the attendant checks whether any cars are waiting for whatever service is available. If a car is waiting for an available service, then instead of sleeping, the attendant services the car. Finally, if one or both services are available but no cars are waiting to be serviced, then the attendant sleeps; he does not wait for an available service to be requested. Note that by using the **else** clause, the attendant never waits.

In the examples shown so far, when an acceptor task arrives at a rendezvous point before the calling task, it either waits indefinitely for a calling task to make a call, or it shows ultimate impatience by refusing to wait for even a moment. There is an alternative to these two extremes. A programmer may specify how long an acceptor task must wait. This variation of the selective wait uses the keyword **delay**:

```
task GAS_STATION_ATTENDANT is -- task specification
    entry SERVICE_ISLAND (CAR: CAR_TYPE);
    entry GARAGE (CAR: CAR_TYPE);
end GAS_STATION_ATTENDANT;

task body GAS_STATION_ATTENDANT is -- task body
begin
    loop
        select -- selective wait
            accept SERVICE_ISLAND (CAR: CAR_TYPE) do
                FILL_WITH_GAS (CAR);
            end SERVICE_ISLAND;
        or
            accept GARAGE (CAR: CAR_TYPE) do
                FIX (CAR);
            end GARAGE;
        or
            delay 3_600.0; -- wait 1 hour before sleeping
            SLEEP;
        end select;
    end loop;
end GAS_STATION_ATTENDANT;
```

In this example, when the **select** statement is reached, the gas station attendant checks whether a car is at the service island or at the garage. If neither service is requested, the attendant waits up to 1 hour. If a car arrives before the hour is up, then the attendant provides it with the requested service. If the hour expires without a car arriving, the attendant stops waiting and sleeps.

This code does not behave as one would expect by just examining it. When the **select** statement is reached, if no calls have been made to the task entries SERVICE_ISLAND or GARAGE, then the task waits up to the amount of time specified in the **delay** statement. Recall from Chapter 4 that the **delay** statement delays the execution of code for a specified number of seconds. However, when the **delay** statement is used in a **select** statement, the result is surprising. In the preceding code, for instance, instead of unconditionally waiting 1 hour (3600 seconds), the **delay** statement acts as a timer that is interrupted the moment a unit calls one of the task entries in the **select** statement. Suppose, for example, that after 50 minutes have passed, a task calls the GARAGE task entry. As soon as this call is made, the task GAS_STATION_ATTENDANT stops the timer, accepts the call, and the rendezvous is initiated. After the rendezvous is finished, the call to the procedure SLEEP is not made, and the **select** statement is exited. The call to SLEEP is only made if a full hour elapses without any task calling the task entries within the **select** statement.

Instead of a **delay** statement, a **terminate** statement may also be placed within the **or** clause of a **select** statement:

```
task GAS_STATION_ATTENDANT is -- task specification
    entry SERVICE_ISLAND (CAR: CAR_TYPE);
    entry GARAGE (CAR: CAR_TYPE);
end GAS_STATION_ATTENDANT;

task body GAS_STATION_ATTENDANT is -- task body
begin
    loop
        select -- selective wait
            accept SERVICE_ISLAND (CAR: CAR_TYPE) do
                FILL_WITH_GAS (CAR);
            end SERVICE_ISLAND;
        or
            accept GARAGE (CAR: CAR_TYPE) do
                FIX (CAR);
            end GARAGE;
        or -- no service required, so terminate task
            terminate;
        end select;
    end loop;
end GAS_STATION_ATTENDANT;
```

In this example, if no call has been made to the SERVICE_ISLAND or GARAGE task entries, then the task GAS_STATION_ATTENDANT terminates. This task is terminated with the **terminate** statement, which just consists of the keyword **terminate**. The **terminate** statement may be guarded, although this is infrequently done. When the **terminate** statement is used, a task does not simply quit in "midstream"; it terminates only when there are no calls in its task entry queues that are waiting to be accepted. This is in sharp contrast to the **abort** statement (not a form of the selective wait).

Unlike the **terminate** statement, the **abort** statement usually brings task execution to a screeching halt. The **abort** statement should only be used in emergencies when one must "slam on the brakes," because the aborted task may leave incomplete and perhaps corrupted results in its wake.

The **abort** statement consists of the keyword **abort**, followed by a list of tasks to be aborted:

```
abort GAS_STATION_ATTENDANT;
```

The exact behavior of the **abort** statement depends on the activity taking place at the time. Usually the tasks listed after the keyword **abort** are quickly aborted; however, they may not be the only program units that are aborted. All tasks that depend on the aborted tasks are aborted as well, in addition to all the active subprograms that the aborted tasks invoked.

We have seen variations of the selective wait that have the following special **select** alternatives: an **else** clause, a **delay** statement, or a **terminate** statement. Three rules apply when using these special alternatives. First, no more than one of these special alternatives may be contained in a single **select** statement. The **terminate** alternative, for example, may not appear in the same **select** statement with a **delay** alternative or an **else** clause. Second, a **select** statement cannot solely consist of a special alternative; it must include at least one **accept** statement. Third, these special alternatives are selected only when none of the other alternatives can be selected.

CONDITIONAL ENTRY CALLS AND TIMED ENTRY CALLS

So far we have seen how a form of the **select** statement, called the selective wait, can be used within the acceptor task. Now we will discuss two other forms of the **select** statement, which may only appear in the calling task: the conditional entry call and the timed entry call. Let us first examine the conditional entry call. The following example simulates the behavior of the impatient motorist who leaves one gas station in search of another if service is not immediately provided:

```
select -- conditional entry call
    GAS_STATION_ATTENDANT.SERVICE_ISLAND (MY_CAR);
else
    TRY_ANOTHER_GAS_STATION;
end select;
```

This code first attempts to call the task entry SERVICE_ISLAND, in task GAS_STATION_ATTENDANT. If the call is not immediately accepted by the task, then the **else** clause is executed, which activates the procedure TRY_ANOTHER_GAS_STATION.

Let us now consider the timed entry call. The motorist in the following example is not quite as impatient as the motorist in the preceding example. This motorist waits 5 minutes before leaving one gas station in search of another.

```
select -- timed entry call
    GAS_STATION_ATTENDANT.SERVICE_ISLAND (MY_CAR);
or
    delay 300.0; -- wait 5 minutes
    TRY_ANOTHER_GAS_STATION;
end select;
```

The code calls the task entry SERVICE_ISLAND. If the call is not immediately accepted by the task GAS_STATION_ATTENDANT, then a **delay** statement that acts as a 5 minute (300 second) timer is activated. If the task accepts the entry call before the 5 minutes are over, then the timer is abruptly halted, and a rendezvous takes place. After the rendezvous is finished, the **select** statement is exited. On the other hand, if the entry call is not accepted within 5 minutes, then the entry call is removed from the SERVICE_ISLAND entry queue, and the procedure TRY_ANOTHER_GAS_STATION is executed. After the procedure is finished executing, the **select** statement is exited.

TASK ATTRIBUTES

There are several attributes that relate to tasks. We have already mentioned the COUNT attribute, which tells us how many entry calls are waiting in an entry queue. Other useful attributes that relate to tasks are TERMINATE and CALLABLE. Both these attributes append to task names.

To understand these attributes, let us consider the three states of a task: running, completed, or terminated. (There is actually a fourth state, abnormal, that arises when the **abort** command is issued.) A task is running when it is actively performing its duties. A task is completed when it has reached its final **end** statement but other tasks that depend on it (i.e., contained within it) are still running. A task is terminated when it reaches its final **end** statement and no tasks that depend on it are running.

Keeping these definitions in mind, the attribute P'TERMINATE, where P is the task name, is TRUE or FALSE depending on whether task P has terminated. The attribute P'CALLABLE is TRUE or FALSE depending on whether task P is callable. A task is callable only if it is running. If an attempt is made to call a task that has either completed or terminated, then the TASKING_ERROR exception is raised. Therefore, when in doubt about the state of a task, use the CALLABLE attribute before attempting to call the task:

```
if GAS_STATION_ATTENDANT'CALLABLE then
    GAS_STATION_ATTENDANT.GARAGE (MY_CAR);
else -- cannot call task because it completed or terminated
    FIX_CAR_MYSELF;
end if;
```

In this calling unit, the attribute is used to determine whether the task GAS_STATION_ATTENDANT is callable. If this task is running and therefore callable, then a call is made to the GARAGE entry of this task. If this task is not callable, then the procedure FIX_CAR_MYSELF is invoked. Note that we cannot safely replace GAS_STATION_ATTENDANT'CALLABLE with **not** GAS_STATION_ATTENDANT'TERMINATE. The replacement cannot be safely made because of the possibility of completed tasks. Even though a completed task has not terminated, it cannot be called.

ENTRY FAMILIES

Entry families resemble one-dimensional arrays. Recall from Chapter 5 that in one-dimensional arrays, a single identifier can refer to many related objects. Similarly, by using entry families, a single entry identifier can refer to many related entries. The following task specification shows the need for entry families:

```
task MULTIPLE_ENTRIES is
    entry POINT_1 (ON: in BOOLEAN);
    entry POINT_2 (ON: in BOOLEAN);
    entry POINT_3 (ON: in BOOLEAN);
    entry POINT_4 (ON: in BOOLEAN);
    entry POINT_5 (ON: in BOOLEAN);
    entry EMERGENCY;
    entry NO_EMERGENCY;
end MULTIPLE_ENTRIES;
```

This task specification contains two kinds of related entries. There are entry points 1 to 5 that have Boolean **in** parameters, and entries that deal with emergencies. These two kinds of entries may be written more concisely by using two entry families, each family representing a group of related entries:

```
task MULTIPLE_ENTRIES is
    entry POINT (1 .. 5) (ON: in BOOLEAN);
        -- entry family of 5 entries each with a Boolean parameter
    entry EMERGENCY (BOOLEAN);
        -- entry family of 2 entries each with no parameters
end MULTIPLE_ENTRIES;
```

The entry family POINT has integer index values that range from 1 to 5 and a formal parameter of type BOOLEAN. The entry family EMERGENCY has Boolean index values that range from FALSE to TRUE, and no parameters. Given this task specification, the body of the task may provide **accept** statements such as the following:

```
accept POINT (3) (ON: in BOOLEAN);-- third member of entry family
accept EMERGENCY (TRUE);-- second member of entry family
```

External tasks can then call entries in these entry families as follows:

```
MULTIPLE_ENTRIES.POINT (3) (ON => TRUE);
    -- call the third member of entry family with a parameter of TRUE
MULTIPLE_ENTRIES.EMERGENCY (TRUE);
    -- call the second member of entry family (without any parameter)
```

Do not confuse the entry family index with the entry parameter. In the first task entry call, the value TRUE is an entry parameter that is needed whether or not entry families are used. The number 3 is the entry family index. In the second task entry call, the value TRUE is not an entry parameter but an entry family index. The index values for this entry family range from FALSE to TRUE, so the index value of TRUE selects the second member of the entry family.

PRAGMA PRIORITY

There are only two kinds of items that may be placed in a task specification: **entry** clauses and certain pragmas, such as the **pragma** PRIORITY. We have already discussed **entry** clauses. We will now cover perhaps the most useful pragma that relates to tasks: **pragma** PRIORITY. Recall that a pragma is a compiler directive. **Pragma** PRIORITY directs the compiler to prioritize tasks from the least important to the most important.

Prioritizing tasks can be useful when the number of active tasks exceeds the number of available processors. In such situations, the processors must somehow be allocated to the tasks. By prioritizing tasks, the programmer controls the allocation of available processors so that a task with a higher priority is always selected over a task with a lower priority.

A task is assigned a priority by placing the **pragma** PRIORITY in its specification. The keyword **pragma** is followed by the word PRIORITY, then by an integer priority number enclosed in parentheses. In the following task specifications, IMPORTANT and NOT_SO_IMPORTANT are assigned the priority levels of 9 and 1, respectively:

```
task IMPORTANT is
    pragma PRIORITY (9);
    entry MONITOR_PATIENT;
end IMPORTANT;

task NOT_SO_IMPORTANT is
    pragma PRIORITY (1);
    entry HEAT_COFFEE;
end NOT_SO_IMPORTANT;
```

Note that a larger integer value denotes a higher priority level. (This integer value actually belongs to an integer subtype, PRIORITY, which is defined in the package SYSTEM.) The number of priority levels allowed is implementation dependent. Also note that task priorities are static, that is, they cannot be changed as a program is running.

TASK TYPES

It was pointed out in Chapter 3 that an exotic type exists called a task type. All tasks belong to a task type. However, the tasks presented so far in this chapter are not explicitly declared to belong to any task type. As a result, these tasks are one of a kind, each implicitly belonging to a different anonymous task type. (This is analogous to arrays that implicitly belong to an anonymous array type, as discussed in Chapter 5.)

Syntactically, task type declarations appear just like the previous task specifications in this chapter, except that the keyword **type** follows the keyword **task**:

```
task type RESOURCE is  -- task type declaration
    entry SEIZE;
    entry RELEASE;
end RESOURCE;
```

The task body corresponding to a task type declaration is the same as that of tasks that are not declared as task types.

Once a task type is specified, objects that are particular tasks can then be declared to belong to this task type:

```
LASER_PRINTER, DOT_MATRIX: RESOURCE; -- declares two tasks
```

Both tasks, LASER_PRINTER and DOT_MATRIX, are declared to belong to the same task type, RESOURCE. This means that both these tasks have identical characteristics. One such characteristic is that both tasks have the same task entries. (By the way, this is why one must use dot notation when calling a task. The tasks LASER_PRINTER and DOT_MATRIX have the same task entries, SEIZE and RELEASE. Therefore, dot notation, which includes the task name, is the only way the entries can be distinguished.) Another shared characteristic is that both tasks perform the same processing but do so independently. Also, both tasks declare the same variables and constants, although these variables and constants are not actually shared between the tasks. Each task, in other words, has its own copy of these variables and constants. Therefore, whenever two or more copies of the identical task are needed, instead of writing each task separately, simply define a single task type, and declare as many tasks as needed to belong to this type.

Task types are limited private types (see Chapter 8). Thus, task objects cannot be assigned or compared to one another. However, task objects can be used as subprogram parameters, and an array or record of task objects may be declared:

```
task type MESSAGE_TYPE;
type MESSAGE_ARRAY is array (1..2) of MESSAGE_TYPE;
MESSAGE: MESSAGE_ARRAY; -- an array of tasks
procedure OUTPUT (UNIT: in MESSAGE_TYPE);
```

TASK INTERFERENCE

Writing Ada programs that use tasks can be tricky. There are many pitfalls and unexpected side effects. One of the more common pitfalls is task interference. Task interference may occur when two or more tasks concurrently use the same resource, such as a screen, printer, or disk drive. In the following example, two tasks interfere with each other as they concurrently output the same message to the screen:

```
with TEXT_IO; use TEXT_IO;
procedure PRINT is
   task type MESSAGE_TYPE;
   COPY_1, COPY_2: MESSAGE_TYPE;
   task body MESSAGE_TYPE is
   begin
      PUT ("...now that we have gigantic computers, programming has " &
         "become an equally gigantic problem. -- E.W. Dijkstra");
      NEW_LINE;
   end MESSAGE_TYPE;
begin -- both tasks, COPY_1 and COPY_2, are activated here
   null;
end PRINT;
```

COPY_1 and COPY_2 are declared to be tasks of type MESSAGE_TYPE. Both these tasks concurrently output the same message when they are activated. As with previous examples, the tasks are activated when the keyword **begin** is reached.

Try running this code and see what happens. On most computer systems, when the same resource is shared, the tasks interfere with each other. Thus instead of outputting two consecutive copies of the message, the copies are intertwined, resulting in garbage. A few letters of one copy are output, then a few letters from the other copy, and so on.

This problem of task interference can be solved by the following task type, which is taken from the Ada Language Reference Manual :

```
task type RESOURCE is
    entry SEIZE;
    entry RELEASE;
end RESOURCE;
```

The two entry points, SEIZE and RELEASE, are called by other tasks in order to seize or release a resource such as the screen, printer, or disk drive. This prevents other tasks from using the same resource at the same time. Thus, when a task needs to use a resource, it seizes control of it by calling the task entry SEIZE. When it is done with the resource, it releases control by calling the task entry RELEASE. The resource is then once again available for other tasks to seize. Task interference is therefore avoided because a task cannot seize control of a resource unless the task that previously used the resource has relinquished control.

Assume that SCREEN is declared to be a task of type RESOURCE. A task can then seize the screen by calling SCREEN.SEIZE and can release the screen by calling SCREEN.RELEASE. After incorporating these calls, the task body of MESSAGE_TYPE, which was in procedure PRINT, appears as follows:

```
separate (PRINT)
task body MESSAGE_TYPE is
begin
    SCREEN.SEIZE; -- seizes control of the screen
    PUT ("...now that we have gigantic computers, programming has " &
        "become an equally gigantic problem. -- E.W. Dijkstra");
    NEW_LINE;
    SCREEN.RELEASE; -- releases control of the screen
end MESSAGE_TYPE;
```

Note that this task body has been made into a separate compilation unit called a subunit. Subunits were discussed in Chapters 7 and 10.

Now that we have explained how the task type RESOURCE can be used to eliminate task interference, let us examine how it works. The following package contains the specification and body of RESOURCE, which is taken, with minor modifications, from the Ada Language Reference Manual:

```
package RESOURCE_HANDLER is
    task type RESOURCE is -- task type specification
        entry SEIZE;
        entry RELEASE;
    end RESOURCE;
end RESOURCE_HANDLER;

package body RESOURCE_HANDLER is
    task body RESOURCE is -- task body
        IN_USE: BOOLEAN := FALSE;
    begin
        loop
            select
                when not IN_USE =>
                    accept SEIZE do
                        IN_USE := TRUE;
                    end SEIZE;
            or
                accept RELEASE do
                    IN_USE := FALSE;
                end RELEASE;
            or
                terminate;
            end select;
        end loop;
    end RESOURCE;
end RESOURCE_HANDLER;
```

Note that we placed the task type specification in the package specification and the task body in the package body. (It is also legal to place the entire task in the package body, but the task is then hidden from external units.)

The task body of RESOURCE begins by initializing the Boolean variable IN_USE to FALSE. When the **select** statement is reached, the alternative containing the guarded **accept** statement, SEIZE, is therefore open. A rendezvous is thus made with whichever task first calls the corresponding task entry. Suppose that tasks A and B (not shown) both try to seize the same resource and that task A calls the task entry SEIZE before task B. During the rendezvous with task A, IN_USE is set to TRUE, the rendezvous ends, and the loop returns us to the beginning of the **select** statement. Since IN_USE is now set to TRUE, the select alternative containing the entry SEIZE is closed. Thus, RESOURCE waits for a call to the entry RELEASE, which is the only entry call that it can accept. The **terminate** alternative is not selected because not all the entry queues are empty. The SEIZE queue contains an entry call that, by this time, was probably made by the slower task B. Once task A finishes outputting its message and calls the task entry RELEASE, IN_USE is set to FALSE. The loop again returns us to the beginning of the **select** statement. This time a rendezvous is made with task B. After task B finishes outputting its message and calls the entry RELEASE, the loop returns us once again to the beginning of the **select** statement. This time, since there are no calls waiting in either entry queue, the **terminate** alternative is selected.

Let us now update the PRINT procedure to use the RESOURCE_HANDLER package. In order to use this package, the procedure PRINT must mention this package in its **with** clause:

```
with TEXT_IO, RESOURCE_HANDLER;
use TEXT_IO, RESOURCE_HANDLER;
procedure PRINT is
    SCREEN: RESOURCE;
    task type MESSAGE_TYPE;
    COPY_1, COPY_2: MESSAGE_TYPE;
    task body MESSAGE_TYPE is separate; -- body stub
begin -- SCREEN, COPY_1, and COPY_2 are activated here
    null;
end PRINT;
```

Once the package RESOURCE_HANDLER is made available, the task SCREEN is then declared to be of type RESOURCE. Note that since the task body of MESSAGE_TYPE was made into a subunit in a previous example, it no longer resides in the declarative part of procedure PRINT but is replaced by a body stub. Also note that as soon as the keyword **begin** is reached, all three tasks—SCREEN, COPY_1, and COPY_2—are activated. If the package RESOURCE_HANDLER contained the task SCREEN instead of the task type RESOURCE, then SCREEN would become active during package initialization, that is, when the **begin** keyword was reached in the package body. (For packages that do not explicitly contain an initialization part, one that contains the **null** statement is assumed to exist.) Such a situation will be shown in the last example of this chapter.

DYNAMICALLY CREATED TASKS

In all the examples given so far, tasks have been created statically. However, tasks may also be created dynamically. In other words, while a program is executing, tasks can be created (and disposed of) as they are needed. Dynamically created tasks are thus especially useful when the number of tasks needed for a particular application depends on runtime conditions and therefore cannot be known in advance. The topic of dynamically created tasks is an advanced one that is only briefly introduced in this section.

Dynamically created tasks are brought into existence like other dynamically created objects—by using access types. The following version of the PRINT procedure dynamically allocates the task SCREEN. The other two tasks, COPY_1 and COPY_2, are statically created as before:

```
with TEXT_IO, RESOURCE_HANDLER;
use TEXT_IO, RESOURCE_HANDLER;
procedure PRINT is
    type SCREEN_TASK is access RESOURCE; -- access type
    SCREEN: SCREEN_TASK := new RESOURCE;   -- task SCREEN
                                           -- activated here
    task type MESSAGE_TYPE;
    COPY_1, COPY_2: MESSAGE_TYPE;
    task body MESSAGE is separate; -- body stub
begin -- COPY_1 and COPY_2 activated here
    null;
end PRINT;
```

Note that the task type RESOURCE is used in the declaration of the access type SCREEN_TASK. The task SCREEN is activated when it is created using an allocator. Thus the task SCREEN is activated while the procedure PRINT is being elaborated. When elaboration is finished and PRINT begins to execute (when the **begin** is reached), tasks COPY_1 and COPY_2 are then activated.

REAL-WORLD EXAMPLE

Before ending this chapter, we shall consider a real-world example of how Ada tasks may be used. This program is considerably more complex than the other programs in this chapter. For illustrative purposes, this program has been kept relatively short; however, it could easily be expanded into a full-fledged program with real application.

This tasking example is part of a simple communication system between sensors and a computerized controller in a factory. There are two kinds of sensors: bar code readers, and object detectors for determining the presence of a factory part (any piece of hardware produced in a factory). The bar code readers report when a factory part with a bar code passes their line of sight. The object detectors simply signal the presence of a factory part. (In the code that follows, this object detector is referred to as the PART_PRESENT_SWITCH.) The controller receives information from these two sensors and takes appropriate action.

The controller needs two kinds of information from these sensors: the location of the sensor reporting its findings (indicated by a number from 0 to 999), and, in the case of the bar code readers, the value of the bar code that is read (indicated by a number from 0 to 9999). This information is transmitted to the controller as simple ASCII characters. Our tasking example, therefore, is part of the communication system that takes ASCII data from the communication line, verifies and formats the data into packets, and makes it available to the controller.

In actual factory environments, communication lines are often "noisy" and serve multiple purposes. In such environments, it makes sense to send data in formatted packets. This is because a formatted packet contains a fixed amount of data with a specific physical layout; therefore, data corruption is easy to detect. In our communication system, if noise in the lines corrupts any data, then the affected packet is discarded. Only valid packets are decoded and offered to the controller.

To implement this communication system between sensors and a controller, we use four tasks: DRIVER, RECEIVER, TRANSLATOR, and CONTROLLER. DRIVER, which serves as the main program, is declared as a procedure. This procedure is an environment task from which the dependent tasks are activated. (All Ada programs are, in this sense, tasks.)

RECEIVER is the task that monitors the communication line for streams of incoming ASCII characters. In our communication system, the arrival of data for a packet is announced with a special control character: the ASCII character SOH (Start Of Header) or control-A. Following this control character are the data to be placed in a packet, consisting of exactly 10 printable characters. If fewer than 10 characters arrive, RECEIVER discards the data. When a packet is discarded, RECEIVER starts over again and waits for the beginning of data for a new packet. When 10 new characters arrive following SOH, RECEIVER collects them and builds a packet of information. When a packet is correctly built, RECEIVER makes it available to TRANSLATOR. (If a new packet arrives before an old packet is taken by TRANSLATOR, then the old packet is overwritten.) RECEIVER only knows the physical format of a packet; it knows nothing about the logical content of a packet. The logical content is the concern of TRANSLATOR.

TRANSLATOR waits for a packet to be built by RECEIVER. When TRANSLATOR then gets the packet, it decodes the packet and validates its contents. Validation includes determining which device (bar code reader or object detector) sent the packet and validating the contents of the message. Invalid packets are discarded. Valid packets are made available to CONTROLLER. TRANSLATOR waits for CONTROLLER to accept the packet before getting the next packet from RECEIVER.

CONTROLLER takes packets of information from TRANSLATOR and makes decisions based on this information. In an actual factory, a controller might "decide" to speed up the assembly line, reroute factory parts, and so on. In our example, however, the controller is a "dummy" that merely prints messages to the screen.

The code for this tasking example is presented in the following order: DRIVER, followed by the specifications and bodies of RECEIVER, TRANSLATOR, and CONTROLLER:

Tasking 411

```
with TEXT_IO, TRANSLATOR, RECEIVER;
procedure DRIVER is
    BUFFER: STRING (1 .. 80);
    LENGTH: NATURAL;
begin
    while not TEXT_IO.END_OF_FILE loop
        TEXT_IO.GET_LINE (BUFFER, LENGTH);
        RECEIVER.RECEIVE_PACKETS.GET_CHARACTER (ASCII.SOH);
        for K in 1 .. LENGTH loop
            RECEIVER.GET_CHARACTER (BUFFER (K));
        end loop;
    end loop;
end DRIVER;
```

```
package RECEIVER is
    PACKET_LENGTH: constant := 10;
    subtype PACKET_DATA_TYPE is STRING (1 .. PACKET_LENGTH);
    task RECEIVE_PACKETS is
        entry GET_CHARACTER (C: in CHARACTER);
        -- GET_CHARACTER may be bound to a hardware interrupt (see
        -- Chapter 16)
        entry GET_PACKET (PACKET_DATA: out PACKET_DATA_TYPE);
    end RECEIVE_PACKETS;
end RECEIVER;
```

```
package body RECEIVER is
    subtype PRINTING_CHARS is CHARACTER range ' ' .. '~';
    task body RECEIVE_PACKETS is
        PACKET_BODY: PACKET_DATA_TYPE;
        PACKET_ELEMENT: CHARACTER;
        PACKET_READY: BOOLEAN := FALSE;
    begin
        loop
            select
                -- ensures that if a packet is ready AND someone is waiting for
                -- it, that they will get it
                when not PACKET_READY or GET_PACKET'COUNT = 0 =>
                    accept GET_CHARACTER (C: in CHARACTER) do
                        PACKET_ELEMENT := C;
                    end GET_CHARACTER;
                    -- if this starts a new packet
                    while PACKET_ELEMENT = ASCII.SOH loop
                        -- get packet body
                        for K in 1 .. PACKET_LENGTH loop
                            accept GET_CHARACTER (C: in CHARACTER) do
                                PACKET_ELEMENT := C;
                            end GET_CHARACTER;
                            -- stop if illegal character
                            exit when PACKET_ELEMENT not in
                                PRINTING_CHARS;
                            PACKET_BODY (K) := PACKET_ELEMENT;
                        end loop;
```

```
                        -- if the last character received was valid, the packet
                        -- is ready to go
                        PACKET_READY := PACKET_ELEMENT in
                            PRINTING_CHARS;
                    end loop;
            or
                -- wait until a packet is ready
                when PACKET_READY =>
                    accept GET_PACKET (PACKET_DATA: out
                        PACKET_DATA_TYPE) do
                            PACKET_DATA := PACKET_BODY;
                    end GET_PACKET;
                    PACKET_READY := FALSE;
            end select;
        end loop;
    end RECEIVE_PACKETS;
end RECEIVER;
```

```
package TRANSLATOR is
    task TRANSLATE;
end TRANSLATOR;
```

```
with RECEIVER, CONTROLLER;
package body TRANSLATOR is
    task body TRANSLATE is
        PACKET: RECEIVER.PACKET_DATA_TYPE;
        BAR_CODE: constant CHARACTER := 'B';
        PART_PRESENT_SWITCH: constant CHARACTER := 'P';
        KIND_FIELD: constant := 1;
        subtype LOCATION_FIELD is POSITIVE range 3 .. 5;
        subtype CODE_FIELD is POSITIVE range 7 ..
            RECEIVER.PACKET_LENGTH;
        LOCATION: CONTROLLER.TRACK_LOCATION;
        BARCODE: CONTROLLER.BARCODE_TYPE;
    begin
        loop
            begin -- a block without declarations
                -- waits for a packet from RECEIVER
                RECEIVER.RECEIVE_PACKETS.GET_PACKET (PACKET);
                -- decode packet data
                case PACKET (KIND_FIELD) is
                    when BAR_CODE =>
                        LOCATION := CONTROLLER.TRACK_LOCATION'VALUE
                            (PACKET (LOCATION_FIELD));
                        BARCODE := CONTROLLER.BARCODE_TYPE'VALUE
                            (PACKET (CODE_FIELD));
                        -- waits for controller to accept data
                        CONTROLLER.MONITOR_PLANT.UNIT_LOCATION
                            (LOCATION, BARCODE);
```

```ada
            when PART_PRESENT_SWITCH =>
               LOCATION := CONTROLLER.TRACK_LOCATION'VALUE
                  (PACKET (LOCATION_FIELD));
               -- waits for controller to accept data
               CONTROLLER.MONITOR_PLANT.PART_PRESENT
                  (LOCATION);
            when others =>
               null; -- bad or unused packet type; ignore it
         end case;
      exception
         when CONSTRAINT_ERROR | NUMERIC ERROR =>
            null; -- bad packet; ignore it
      end;
      end loop;
   end TRANSLATE;
end TRANSLATOR;
```

```ada
package CONTROLLER is
   type BARCODE_TYPE is range 0 .. 9999;
   type TRACK_LOCATION is range 0 .. 999;
   task MONITOR_PLANT is
      entry UNIT_LOCATION ( READER: TRACK_LOCATION;
                            UNIT_NUMBER: BARCODE_TYPE);
      entry PART_PRESENT (POSITION: TRACK_LOCATION);
   end MONITOR_PLANT;
end CONTROLLER;
```

```ada
with TEXT_IO;
package body CONTROLLER is
   task body MONITOR_PLANT is
   begin
      loop
         select
            accept UNIT_LOCATION (READER: TRACK_LOCATION;
                         UNIT_NUMBER: BARCODE_TYPE) do
               TEXT_IO.PUT_LINE ("Unit number " &
                         BARCODE_TYPE'IMAGE (UNIT_NUMBER) &
                         " spotted at location " &
                         TRACK_LOCATION'IMAGE (READER) & '.');
            end UNIT_LOCATION;
         or
            accept PART_PRESENT (POSITION: TRACK_LOCATION) do
               TEXT_IO.PUT_LINE ("Part present " & " at location " &
                         TRACK_LOCATION'IMAGE (POSITION) & '.');
            end PART_PRESENT;
         end select;
      end loop;
   end MONITOR_PLANT;
end CONTROLLER;
```

This program is too long for a line-by-line analysis, but a few important points will be discussed. Data flows from RECEIVER to TRANSLATOR to CONTROLLER. This, however, does not mean that RECEIVER calls TRANSLATOR, which calls CONTROLLER. The tasks RECEIVER and CONTROLLER are "passive" acceptor tasks. They just respond to calls from other tasks. The task TRANSLATOR, however, is an "active" calling task. It only calls other tasks. These tasks are set up in this way to reduce the risk of the critical tasks, RECEIVER and CONTROLLER, from getting suspended. Either a calling task or an acceptor task may get suspended. If a calling task calls another task that is not ready to rendezvous, then the calling task is suspended. If an acceptor task reaches a **select** statement and no calls have been made to its entries, then the acceptor task is suspended. Although in both situations a task is suspended, there is an important difference. The difference is that a calling task can only wait for one event—for the called task to accept its call. In contrast, an acceptor task can wait for potentially hundreds of events—for any task to call any one of its many entries in a **select** statement.

Keeping this distinction in mind, CONTROLLER is written as an acceptor task, because it must be able to respond to many events; it cannot afford to wait for any one event. CONTROLLER must always be prepared to receive communication packets and to respond as necessary. RECEIVER is also an acceptor task because it too must be able to respond to many events. RECEIVER must continually be prepared to receive a stream of characters over the communication line. If RECEIVER, for instance, were written as a calling task, there would always be the danger of it getting hung up waiting for its call to be accepted. As a result, RECEIVER would be unable to service a possible flood of incoming data. In contrast to RECEIVER and CONTROLLER, TRANSLATOR is a calling task. Some task has to do the waiting, and TRANSLATOR is designed to wait. If, for example, RECEIVER and CONTROLLER are operating at different speeds and neither can afford to wait for the other, then there is no problem. TRANSLATOR acts as a go-between and waits for each of them. This is not a problem because TRANSLATOR is designed with nothing better to do.

Let us now consider a few of the less obvious portions of the code. One such portion includes the guards that RECEIVER places on its entries. Recall that when a task reaches a **select** statement and there is more than one open alternative with another task waiting to rendezvous, Ada does not define which alternative to take. It is even possible for a particular implementation to never select GET_PACKET if characters are coming in fast and furiously. In such a case, TRANSLATOR would be starved for information, because its request to get a packet would not be fulfilled. The guards are used to provide fairness in the selection process, ensuring that GET_PACKET will be selected if a packet is ready <u>and</u> TRANSLATOR is waiting for it. If no packet is ready, the system must select GET_CHARACTER. If a packet is ready but TRANSLATOR is not waiting for it, then, in the event of a simultaneous arrival of a character and a packet request, the system may choose as it pleases. In all cases, the amount of processing required by RECEIVER is kept to a minimum to keep the response time fast.

While these tasks form a complete Ada program, if you attempt running this program, there are some caveats. First, note that none of the tasks allow for termination. Thus there is no Ada-defined way to shut the system down. Most interactive systems will abort the tasks if you use the normal method of terminating runaway processes. Second, note that TEXT_IO used for concurrent access to the same device is system dependent; DRIVER and CONTROLLER may not work together as written on some systems. If you have problems running this program on your system, try routing controller output to a file other than STANDARD_OUTPUT.

This chapter has introduced the complex topic of tasking. The next chapter will also introduce an advanced topic: low-level programming.

EXERCISES

1. What is a task entry? How do task entries relate to the **accept** statement?

2. Explain the Ada rendezvous. When do the calling task and the acceptor task wait?

3. a. Consider the following declarations:

   ```
   type DIRECTION_TYPE is (UP, DOWN, RIGHT, LEFT);
   subtype X_RANGE is INTEGER range 0..1023; -- modify as needed
   subtype Y_RANGE is INTEGER range 0..1023; -- modify as needed
   type COORDINATE_TYPE is
      record
         X: X_RANGE;
         Y: Y_RANGE;
      end record;
   COORDINATE: COORDINATE_TYPE;
   ```

   Given the above declarations and the following **accept** statement, write a program that concurrently updates the position of an object and monitors a keyboard for requests to move the object UP, DOWN, RIGHT, or LEFT.

   ```
   accept ADVANCE (DIRECTION: in DIRECTION_TYPE) do
      case DIRECTION is
         when UP =>
            COORDINATE.Y := COORDINATE.Y + 1;
         when DOWN =>
            COORDINATE.Y := COORDINATE.Y - 1;
   ```

```
          when RIGHT =>
              COORDINATE.X := COORDINATE.X + 1;
          when LEFT =>
              COORDINATE.X := COORDINATE.X - 1;
       end case;
       UPDATE_POSITION (COORDINATE);
   end ADVANCE;
```

Note: If your computer does not easily support graphics, do not worry about the body of procedure UPDATE_POSITION. Just get your program to compile.

    b. Write an exception handler to handle situations where X or Y go out of range. Place this exception handler in the program unit that calls the task entry ADVANCE.

4. Explain what the following code within a body of an acceptor task might accomplish:

```
   select
       accept GET_SCREEN_INPUT (ITEM: CHARACTER);
   or
       delay 900.0;
       LOG_OFF;
   end select;
```

5. How will the preceding **select** statement behave if the second alternative containing the **delay** statement is replaced by an else clause?

```
   select
       accept GET_SCREEN_INPUT (ITEM: CHARACTER);
   else
       LOG_OFF;
   end select;
```

6. What is illegal about each of the following program units?

    a.
```
       with P;
       procedure MAIN is
          task T;
          task body T is
          begin
              MAIN.A;
          end T;
       begin
          accept A do
              P;
          end A;
       end MAIN;
```

b. **with** P;
   procedure MAIN **is**
      task T2;
      task body T2 **is**
      begin
         accept E1 **do**
            P;
         end E1;
      end T2;
      task T1;
      task body T1 **is**
      begin
         T2.E1;
      end T1;
   begin
      null;
   end MAIN;

c. **with** P1, P2;
   procedure MAIN **is**
      task T3 **is**
         entry E1;
         entry E2;
      end T3;
      task body T3 **is**
      begin
         select
            accept E1 **do**
               P1;
            end E1;
         or
            accept E2 **do**
               P2;
            end E2;
         end select;
      end T3;
      task T1;
      task body T1 **is**
      begin
         T3.E1;
      end T1;
      task T2;
      task body T2 **is**
      begin
         T3.E2;
      end T2;
   begin
      null;
   end MAIN;

7. Classify each of the following **select** statements as either a selective wait, a timed entry call, or a conditional entry call. (Assume T is a task, E is an entry, and P, P1, and P2 are procedures.)

   a. **select**
          T.E;
      else
          P;
      end select;

   b. **select**
          T.E;
      or
          delay 60.0;
          P;
      end select;

   c. **select**
          accept A do
              P1;
          end A;
      or
          delay 60.0;
          P2;
      end select;

   d. **select**
          accept A do
              P;
          end A;
      or
          terminate;
      end select;

8. What is incorrect with each of these selective wait statements?

   a. **select**
          accept E1 do
              P1;
          end E1;
      or
          accept E2 do
              P2;
          end E2;
      or
          delay 10.5;
          P3;
      else
          P4;
      end select;

b. **select**
    terminate;
  end select;

c. **select**
    accept E1 **do**
      P1;
    end E1;
  or
    accept E2 **do**
      P2;
    end E2;
  or
    delay 3600.0;
    P3;
  or
    terminate;
  end select;

d. UPDATE (DAY);   -- update DAY to a value from MONDAY to
                   -- SUNDAY
  select
    when DAY **in** MONDAY .. WEDNESDAY =>
      accept E1 **do**
        P1;
      end E1;
  or
    when DAY = SATURDAY =>
      accept E2 **do**
        P2;
      end E2;
  end select;

e. **select**
    accept E1 **do**
      P1;
    end E1;
  else
    accept E2 **do**
      P2;
    end E2;
  end select;

9. Which <u>one</u> of the following task specifications is illegal?

  a. **task** CLEANING;

  b. **task** CLEANING **is**
      entry VACUUM;
      entry MOP;
      entry DUST;
    end CLEANING;

c. **task** MUSIC **is**
       entry STATION (1 .. 50) (ON: BOOLEAN);
   end MUSIC;

d. **task** MUSIC **is**
       type MUSIC_TYPE **is** (COUNTRY, CLASSICAL, JAZZ, POP);
       entry STATION (MUSIC: MUSIC_TYPE);
   end MUSIC;

Chapter 16

LOW-LEVEL PROGRAMMING

As we have seen throughout this book, Ada encourages programmers to think in an abstract, high-level manner. Issues about where data are stored in memory or how the data are physically represented are usually of no concern. However, in applications that require direct interfacing with the underlying hardware, attention to such low-level details may be unavoidable. Interfacing with the hardware means communicating with it. The program and the hardware give each other commands and return messages in response to these commands. This communication is often channeled through specific fields of bits within fixed memory locations.

The hardware with which a program interfaces might be the computer that is executing the program or an external piece of equipment. Programs interface with many different kinds of external equipment. A program, for instance, may control the radar on an aircraft, monitor the fuel injection system of an automobile, or direct a compact disk to play a preprogrammed sequence of recordings. Such systems are known as embedded systems because the computer or processor that executes the program is contained within a larger system. Processors have even been embedded in running shoes to keep track of the number of miles that a runner travels and the number of calories that have been burned.

To interface with hardware, a program may need to reference directly certain fields of bits within a specified location in computer memory. It is through these fields of bits that information is exchanged between the program and the hardware. Programming at this bit level is known as low-level programming.

Low-level programming also includes hardware interrupts, machine specific instructions, addresses, and so on. In general, low-level programming means getting down to the "bare iron" of the machine.

Low-level programming is usually done in assembly code, because many high-level languages provide little support for low-level programming. This is not true, however, with Ada. Since Ada was designed with embedded systems in mind, Ada has low-level programming capabilities. In Ada, for example, a programmer can specify the location and internal representation of data.

To perform low-level programming, the programmer is not obliged to discard Ada's high-level abstractions and think only in terms of bits and bytes. Rather, Ada allows the programmer to describe low-level operations on bits and bytes in terms of high-level abstractions. As a result, not only is code more understandable; it is also more portable. The hardware-dependent portion of the code can be localized and then used by the remaining code to interface with the hardware in an abstract, hardware-independent manner.

Another low-level feature of Ada that supports portability is the package SYSTEM (see Appendix D of this book). Every Ada compiler has its own version of this package. This package contains named numbers, constants, types, and subtypes that specify characteristics of the particular computer that executes the Ada programs. Although the values of these items are system dependent, their names and meaning are not. When rehosting code to a different computer, therefore, the identifiers for these named numbers and types retain their meaning and do not need to be changed. For example, the package SYSTEM contains the predefined named numbers MIN_INT and MAX_INT. These numbers hold the smallest and largest integer values that can be represented by a particular system. Thus, on any system, the following declaration will provide the largest range of values allowed in an integer type declaration:

type GREATEST_INTEGER_RANGE **is range** MIN_INT .. MAX_INT;

The particular values of MIN_INT and MAX_INT vary from system to system. However, the meaning of MIN_INT and MAX_INT stays the same, and this declaration remains portable. We will mention other items contained in the package SYSTEM as they are used in this chapter.

Much of the information in this chapter is contained in Chapter 13 of the Ada Language Reference Manual, which describes the low-level programming features of Ada. Many of these features are implementation dependent; they can be implemented and handled in different ways.

To find out how a feature is handled by your particular compiler, consult Appendix F of your compiler reference manual. Appendix F, which must be included in every reference manual, describes all the implementation-dependent characteristics of a given compiler. In addition, Appendix F contains the specification of the package SYSTEM and lists implementation-dependent pragmas and attributes.

When possible, we will not assume any particular implementation of Ada, but instead, will provide a general overview of the ways that Ada supports low-level programming. This chapter begins with representation attributes and representation clauses that deal with data representation. Representation attributes report how data are represented in the computer, and representation clauses control how data are represented. Next, a pragma that allows composite objects to be packed will be explored, followed by a discussion of unchecked conversion. The chapter concludes with an explanation of how Ada may interface with programs written in other languages.

REPRESENTATION ATTRIBUTES

Representation attributes provide information about the low-level characteristics of objects, types, and program units. We will discuss six of these attributes: ADDRESS, SIZE, STORAGE_SIZE, POSITION, FIRST_BIT, and LAST_BIT.

Attribute ADDRESS

The ADDRESS attribute reports where in computer memory an object, program unit, label, or task entry is stored. For example, if P is an integer variable or constant, the expression P'ADDRESS gives the address where P is stored. If P is a procedure, function, package, or task, then P'ADDRESS gives the address where the machine code for the body of this unit of code begins.

The address value returned by this attribute belongs to type ADDRESS, which is defined in the package SYSTEM. Type ADDRESS is usually, but not necessarily, some positive integer type. The examples presented in this chapter will assume that this is the case.

Attribute SIZE

The SIZE attribute applies to an object, type, or subtype (including a private object or type). When SIZE applies to an object, it yields the number of bits that are allocated to store the object. For example, if P is a variable or constant that is stored in a 32-bit word, then P'SIZE yields the value 32. If SIZE is applied to a type or subtype, then it yields the minimum number of bits that are needed to hold any possible value of this type or subtype. For instance, on a 16-bit computer, INTEGER'SIZE often yields 16. This means that at least 16 bits are needed to hold any possible value of type INTEGER. On a different system, of course, INTEGER'SIZE may yield a different value.

Attribute STORAGE_SIZE

The STORAGE_SIZE attribute gives information about available storage for access types or tasks. If P is an access type, then P'STORAGE_SIZE reports the number of storage units that are reserved for storing dynamically allocated variables accessed by pointers of type P. If P is a task, then P'STORAGE_SIZE reports the number of storage units that are reserved for the activation of task P. If P is a task type, then P'STORAGE_SIZE reports the number of storage units that are reserved for the activation of each task belonging to the task type P.

Note that storage size is defined in terms of storage units. A storage unit is the smallest unit of memory that is addressable (that can be referenced by a single address value). The size of storage units may vary, depending on a particular system. A storage unit might be an 8-bit byte, a 16-bit word, a 32-bit word, and so on. To determine the size, as measured in numbers of bits, reference the named number STORAGE_UNIT, which is contained in the package SYSTEM. On computers, for example, where bytes consisting of 8 bits are addressable, the value for STORAGE_UNIT is 8. As mentioned in the beginning of this chapter, items such as STORAGE_UNIT, provided by the package SYSTEM, allow code to be more portable and general. Even though the value of STORAGE_UNIT varies from one system to another, the meaning of STORAGE_UNIT stays the same.

Attributes POSITION, FIRST_BIT, and LAST_BIT

Attributes POSITION, FIRST_BIT, and LAST_BIT apply to record components. These attributes give information about the physical layout of the components within a record. Consider the following declarations:

```
type RECORD_TYPE is
    record
        CHAR: CHARACTER;
        BOOL: BOOLEAN;
    end record;
R: RECORD_TYPE;
```

If we assume that a storage unit is an 8-bit byte, the components of this record might be physically laid out as shown in Figure 16.1. The attribute POSITION yields the number of storage units (in this case, bytes) that a record component is offset from the beginning of the record. Since CHAR begins in byte 1, it is not offset at all from the beginning of the record. Thus, R.CHAR'POSITION yields the value of 0. Since BOOL begins in byte 2, it is

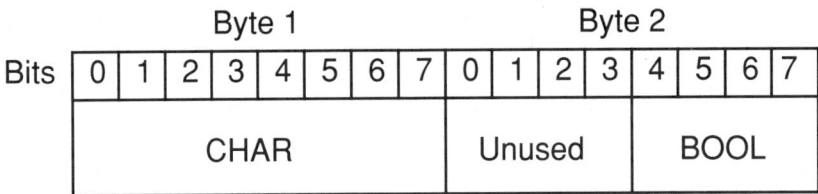

Figure 16.1 Record format

offset by 1 byte from the beginning of the record. Thus, R.BOOL'POSITION yields the value of 1.

The attribute FIRST_BIT yields the number of bits that the first bit of a record component is offset from the beginning of the storage unit in which it is contained. Thus, the expression R.CHAR'FIRST_BIT yields 0, and R.BOOL'FIRST_BIT yields 4.

Finally, the attribute LAST_BIT yields the number of bits that the last bit of a record component is offset from the beginning of the storage unit that contains the first bit of the record component. Thus, R.CHAR'LAST_BIT yields 7, and R.BOOL'LAST_BIT also yields 7.

We have only discussed 6 out of the 12 representation attributes. The other 6 attributes all deal with the representation of numeric types. Readers interested in these other attributes should refer to the Ada Language Reference Manual.

REPRESENTATION CLAUSES

Whereas representation attributes passively report on the low-level features of items, representation clauses actively control such low-level features. Representation clauses are placed in a package specification or in the declarative part of a unit of code. There are four kinds of representation clauses: length clauses, enumeration clauses, record representation clauses, and address clauses.

Length Clauses

Length clauses establish the amount of storage space allocated for objects of a specified type. As shown in the following example, length clauses use the SIZE attribute previously discussed:

```
type DIRECTION is (UP, DOWN, LEFT, RIGHT);
for DIRECTION'SIZE use 2;
    -- allocates, at most, 2 bits for each object of type DIRECTION
```

The length clause begins with the keyword **for**, followed by the name of a type, a tick mark ('), and the attribute SIZE. Next comes the keyword **use**, followed by the maximum number of bits used to store objects of this type. In this example, the length clause forbids more than 2 bits to be used to store an object of type DIRECTION. Two bits are adequate to store the four literals in DIRECTION. For example, the bits 00 could represent UP; 01, DOWN; 10, LEFT; and 11, RIGHT. We could allocate more bits for objects of type DIRECTION but not fewer bits. There is no way to store four different objects using only 1 bit. The following length clause is therefore illegal:

>   **for** DIRECTION'SIZE **use** 1;
>   -- illegal; 1 bit cannot hold four different literals

Furthermore, just because a length clause requests enough space for all the objects of a type, there is no guarantee that a given compiler will be able to honor the request. When a compiler, for whatever reason, cannot honor the request, an error is reported. Thus a length clause may not be portable; it may be accepted by one compiler and rejected by another compiler.

Enumeration Clauses

Enumeration clauses allow a programmer to specify the underlying internal representation of enumeration literals. With languages such as FORTRAN that do not support enumeration types, programmers often define integer objects in place of enumeration literals. For example, without using enumeration types, six kinds of errors can be represented by declaring six different integer objects: NO_ERROR, INFORMATIONAL, WARNING, ERROR, FATAL_ERROR, and SYSTEM_ERROR. The programmer can then associate each of these objects with a particular integer value. NO_ERROR can be assigned the value of 0; INFORMATIONAL, the value of 1; and so on. In Ada, however, the programmer can just declare an enumeration type to represent all six kinds of errors:

>   **type** ERROR_TYPE **is** (NO_ERROR, INFORMATIONAL, WARNING, ERROR, FATAL_ERROR, SYSTEM_ERROR);

Unless otherwise directed, the compiler figures out a representation scheme for this enumeration type. Compilers will undoubtedly associate the enumeration literals with the values 0, 1, 2, 3, and so on, because these values correspond to the position of the literals within the type declaration. Compilers, however, are free to choose any representation scheme.

Note that the compiler does more than simply associate each literal of the enumeration type with an integer value. The compiler also enforces the data abstraction of enumeration literals by treating them as read-only values and by making sure that they can only mix with objects of the same type. Thus, the compiler does not allow an integer value to be assigned to FATAL_ERROR, nor does the compiler allow FATAL_ERROR to be used in a mathematical expression such as 2 * FATAL_ERROR + 1.

In most applications, then, the programmer allows the compiler to represent internally enumeration literals as it sees fit. However, in low-level programming, the programmer may want to represent internally enumeration literals with a particular set of integer values. For instance, suppose that a piece of hardware returns, in a 4-bit field, the six kinds of errors listed in ERROR_TYPE. Each kind of error is represented by a pattern of 4 bits:

0000	no error
0001	informational
0011	warning
0100	error
1100	fatal error
1111	system error

To associate these bit patterns with the enumeration literals, we can use an enumeration clause:

type ERROR_TYPE **is** (NO_ERROR, INFORMATIONAL, WARNING, ERROR, FATAL_ERROR, SYSTEM_ERROR);

-- enumeration clause
for ERROR_TYPE **use** (NO_ERROR   =>   2#0000#,
                            INFORMATIONAL   =>   2#0001#,
                            WARNING   =>   2#0011#,
                            ERROR   =>   2#0100#,
                            FATAL_ERROR   =>   2#1100#,
                            SYSTEM_ERROR   =>   2#1111#);

The enumeration clause consists of the keyword **for**; the name of a previously declared enumeration type; the keyword **use**; and a list of enumeration literals, together with their associated integer representations. These integer representations must be of type universal integer, and they must be static. The associations between the enumeration literals and their integer representations are specified as an aggregate. Our example uses named notation, but positional notation can also be used:

for ERROR_TYPE **use** (0, 1, 3, 4, 12, 15); -- positional notation

In addition to using positional notation, this version uses base 10 aggregate values instead of base 2 values. Base 2 is often used, however, so that the bit patterns can easily be discerned. Note that the values in the aggregate are listed in ascending order. This order is required. The order of enumeration literals in their type declaration must match the order of their numeric representations. Note also that the numeric representations are not sequential. This is common.

Before continuing, we should point out that the numeric representation specified for each enumeration literal does not affect the value returned by the attribute POS. Thus, ERROR_TYPE'POS(SYSTEM_ERROR) yields 5 because SYSTEM_ERROR is the fifth item (starting from 0) listed in the enumeration type. The fact that SYSTEM_ERROR is internally represented by the integer 15 is irrelevant. [However, the compiler will have to work harder to evaluate ERROR_TYPE'POS(SYSTEM_ERROR) whenever SYSTEM_ERROR is not internally represented by this same value, 5.]

As shown in the preceding example, instead of continually thinking in terms of bits and bytes, we can use an enumeration clause to represent bit patterns in terms of enumeration literals. We can then use enumeration literals without thinking about their low-level representation. For instance, the bit pattern representing a system error can be referenced by the value SYSTEM_ERROR. This is yet another example where bit-level details are described in abstract terms.

Now let us consider a situation where the preceding error messages have a second, alternative representation. There is a clever method for giving two different representations to the same set of enumeration literals. This method employs a derived type, which is given a different representation from its parent type:

```
package ALTERNATIVE_REPRESENTATIONS is

    type FORM_A is (NO_ERROR, INFORMATIONAL, WARNING, ERROR,
                    FATAL_ERROR, SYSTEM_ERROR );
    type FORM_B is new FORM_A; -- derived type

private

    for FORM_A use
      ( NO_ERROR            =>   2#0000#,
        INFORMATIONAL       =>   2#0001#,
        WARNING             =>   2#0011#,
        ERROR               =>   2#0100#,
        FATAL_ERROR         =>   2#1100#,
        SYSTEM_ERROR        =>   2#1111# );

    for FORM_B use
      ( NO_ERROR            =>   2#0001#,
        INFORMATIONAL       =>   2#0011#,
        WARNING             =>   2#0101#,
        ERROR               =>   2#0111#,
        FATAL_ERROR         =>   2#1001#,
        SYSTEM_ERROR        =>   2#1011# );

end ALTERNATIVE_REPRESENTATIONS;
```

This package specification first defines the enumeration type FORM_A. Next is defined the derived type FORM_B, whose parent type is FORM_A. These type declarations are followed by the enumeration clauses, which are placed in the private part of the package. These enumeration clauses define the two different representations of the error messages. The derived type is given one representation, and its parent type is given another representation. This is only allowed if the derived type is declared <u>before</u> its parent type is assigned a representation.

It may seem strange that the representation clauses are placed in the private part of the package specification, since this specification does not declare any private types. This placement is not required but is done to remind users of the package not to be concerned with how these enumeration types are internally represented. Information about the internal representation is provided for the compiler's benefit.

Since type FORM_B is derived from FORM_A, type conversion may be used to convert an object from one type to the other. When an object is converted to a different type, it takes on a different representation, as shown in the following code:

```
with ALTERNATIVE_REPRESENTATIONS;
use ALTERNATIVE_REPRESENTATIONS;
procedure CONVERT is
    STATUS_B: FORM_B := ERROR; -- bit representation 0111
    STATUS_A: FORM_A;
begin
    STATUS_A := FORM_A (STATUS_B);
        -- bit representation 0111 converted to 0100
end CONVERT;
```

The object STATUS_B of type FORM_B is initialized to the value ERROR. STATUS_B is therefore internally represented by the value 2#0111#. When STATUS_B is converted to type FORM_A, the internal representation of its value, ERROR, is also converted. The internal representation of ERROR is therefore changed from 2#0111# to 2#0100#.

Record Representation Clauses

When directly interfacing with hardware, the programmer must sometimes format blocks of data into fields of bits containing different information. Each block of data may be represented by a record, and each field of bits may be represented as a component of this record. A record representation clause can then be used to associate each record component with the specific location of its bit field in the block of data.

Consider, for example, a computer-controlled machine that creates extreme temperatures and pressures inside of a sealed container. Suppose that the designer of this machine specifies a 32-bit interface consisting of two 16-bit computer words. Each word is divided into fields of bits. The values of the bits that make up a bit field represent specific information about the container. Suppose that there are four bit fields, which, in turn, provide information about the kind of container that is used, the temperature created within the container, the pressure created within the container, and the angle of the container. These four bit fields might be formatted as shown in Figure 16.2.

We are assuming that a storage unit is a 16-bit word and that the bits are numbered from left to right, beginning with 0. The first 16-bit word (word 0) contains information about the container and the temperature within the container. The CONTAINER field is located in bits 0 to 2 of word 0. Suppose that the designer of this interface has assigned the following meanings to these bit patterns in the CONTAINER field:

    001   container is a steel pod
    010   container is a ceramic chamber
    100   container is a carbon cylinder

Only the three bit patterns listed have a defined meaning, although five other bit patterns (000, 011, 101, 110, and 111) are possible. Selecting a subset of possible bit patterns is a common practice.

The next field, TEMPERATURE, is located in bits 3 to 15 of word 0. This 13-bit field gives the temperature inside the container. Let us assume that TEMPERATURE can be represented as an integer number.

The next 16-bit word (word 1) contains information about the pressure and angle of the container. PRESSURE occupies a 9-bit field, and ANGLE occupies a 7-bit field. Let us assume that PRESSURE can be represented as an integer number. ANGLE contains information about the orientation of the container. Suppose that the following meanings have been assigned to the bit patterns in the ANGLE field:

    0000010   container orientation is perpendicular
    0001000   container orientation is parallel
    0100000   container orientation is skew

Again note that only a subset of all possible bit patterns has an assigned meaning.

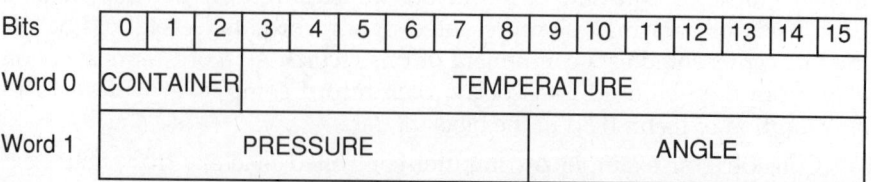

Figure 16.2   Format of two-word interface

Let us begin representing the block of data in this 32-bit interface by writing the hardware-independent code, which expresses these bit fields as abstract objects. We will then write the hardware-dependent code, which deals with the actual location of the bit fields within the block of data.

The first step in writing the hardware-independent code is to define the data types associated with each field. The CONTAINER field contains information about whether the container is a steel pod, a ceramic chamber, or a carbon cylinder. We can represent this information as an enumeration type:

type CONTAINER_TYPE **is** (STEEL_POD, CERAMIC_CHAMBER, CARBON_CYLINDER);

Note that the enumeration literals follow the same order as their numeric representations: 001, 010, 100. As mentioned in the section on enumeration clauses, this order must be observed.

The TEMPERATURE field occupies 13 bits. Assuming that no limits are placed on values of TEMPERATURE, we can define an integer type with a range from 0 to the largest number that can fit in 13 bits ($2^{13}-1$):

type TEMPERATURE_RANGE **is range** 0 .. 2 ** 13 - 1;

Similarly, for the PRESSURE field, which occupies 9 bits, we can define an integer type with a range from 0 to the largest number that can fit in 9 bits (2^9-1):

type PRESSURE_RANGE **is range** 0 .. 2 ** 9 - 1;

Finally, we can represent the information about the container's ANGLE field by using an enumeration type:

type ORIENTATION **is** (PERPENDICULAR, PARALLEL, SKEW);

Now that we have defined the data types for all the bit fields, the next step is to represent these fields as components of a record type:

type INTERFACE_FORMAT **is**
  record
    CONTAINER: CONTAINER_TYPE;
    TEMPERATURE: TEMPERATURE_RANGE;
    PRESSURE: PRESSURE_RANGE;
    ANGLE: ORIENTATION;
  end record;

The block of data is thus represented abstractly as a record, and each bit field in the block of data is represented abstractly as a component of the record.

All of the declarations used so far are abstract and hardware independent. We must next write the hardware-dependent code, which associates each record component of INTERFACE_FORMAT with the actual locations of the bit fields:

```
-- hardware-dependent code
-- length clauses
for TEMPERATURE_RANGE'SIZE use 13;
for PRESSURE_RANGE'SIZE use 9;

-- enumeration clauses
for CONTAINER_TYPE use ( STEEL_POD          => 2#001#,
                         CERAMIC_CHAMBER    => 2#010#,
                         CARBON_CYLINDER    => 2#100# );

for ORIENTATION use    ( PERPENDICULAR      => 2#0000010#,
                         PARALLEL           => 2#0001000#,
                         SKEW               => 2#0100000# );

-- record representation clause
for INTERFACE_FORMAT use
    record at mod 2;                    -- align at even address
        CONTAINER at 0 range 0..2;      -- word 0, bits 0 to 2
        TEMPERATURE at 0 range 3..15;   -- word 0, bits 3 to 15
        PRESSURE at 1 range 0..8;       -- word 1, bits 0 to 8
        ANGLE at 1 range 9..15;         -- word 1, bits 9 to 15
    end record;
```

The first two clauses are length clauses that allocate the appropriate number of bits for objects of type TEMPERATURE_RANGE and PRESSURE_RANGE. The second two clauses are enumeration clauses for the enumeration types CONTAINER_TYPE and ORIENTATION. These enumeration clauses associate each enumeration literal with its integer representation. Nothing is introduced in these first four clauses that was not covered in the previous sections on length clauses and enumeration clauses. The fifth clause, however, is our first example of a record representation clause. This clause specifies the bit locations of each component of the previously declared record type INTERFACE_FORMAT. The clause also specifies how records of this type are to be aligned in memory. The clause begins with the keyword **for**, followed by the name of the record type and the keywords **use record**. Next comes the optional record alignment clause. A particular alignment may make it easier for a computer to reference the record components. Our alignment clause,

   at mod 2;

aligns the beginning of a record of type INTERFACE_FORMAT to an even address, that is, to an address that is a multiple of 2. If we are using a computer where each address corresponds to a computer word, then this alignment clause aligns the record to a double word boundary. Other values besides 2 can be used in this clause. For instance, the clause **at mod** 4 places the record at an address that is a multiple of 4. Thus, if we are using a computer where each address corresponds to a byte and where 4 bytes constitute a single word, then this alignment clause aligns the record to a single word boundary.

Between this optional alignment clause and the keywords **end record** are specifications for the record components. These specifications establish the physical locations of each component within the record. Consider, for example, the first component specification:

CONTAINER **at** 0 **range** 0 .. 2;

The record component CONTAINER is specified to begin at the first storage unit of the record (word 0) and to span bit positions 0 to 2. TEMPERATURE is contained in the same storage unit (word 0) and spans the bit positions 3 to 15:

TEMPERATURE **at** 0 **range** 3..15;

The other two components, PRESSURE and ANGLE, are contained in the second storage unit of the record (word 1). PRESSURE spans bits 0 to 8 of this second word, and ANGLE spans bits 9 to 15.

Anyone who has worked with hardware knows that the numbering of bit positions varies between manufacturers. The Ada standards, therefore, do not specify how bits must be ordered within the record representation clause. Some implementations of Ada number the bits from left to right, as shown in Figure 16.2. Other implementations number the bits from right to left. Although the Ada standards do not specify how to order the bits, the standards do specify that the bits must be numbered starting with 0, not 1.

Another aspect of record representation clauses that is not specified by the Ada standards is whether a record component can span multiple storage units. To find out if this is allowed by your compiler, and if so, how this is accomplished, refer to Appendix F in your compiler's reference manual.

Address Clauses

The address clause allows programmers to specify the address of an object, the starting address of a unit of code, or the address of a hardware interrupt (a signal that interrupts processing). This capability is typically used to reference fixed locations in memory that serve particular hardware functions.

Suppose that we wish to store an integer variable X at the location 16#01F2#. This may be accomplished as follows:

```
X: INTEGER;
for X use at 16#01F2#; -- places X at this memory location
```

The address clause consists of the keyword **for**, followed by the name of the object, the keywords **use at**, and the address where the object is to be located.

The starting address of a procedure may likewise be specified:

```
procedure P;
for P use at 8#360#; -- starting address of procedure P
```

This address clause instructs the compiler to place the machine code for procedure P at the specified beginning location.

In addition to specifying the address of objects and units of code, address clauses can be used to specify the location of hardware interrupts. A hardware interrupt is typically a signal received at a fixed location in memory. This signal instructs the computer to interrupt temporarily current processing and take some special action, such as inputting or outputting certain information or attending to some external piece of equipment. The unit of code that responds to an interrupt is called an interrupt handler. In Ada, interrupt handlers are naturally implemented as tasks. (Tasks were covered in Chapter 15.)

The following task is an interrupt handler that keeps a running score of hits and misses. The score, which is stored at a fixed location, is incremented or decremented, depending on two different hardware interrupts:

```
task RUNNING_SCORE is
    entry HIT;
    entry MISS;
    for HIT use at 8#010#;
    for MISS use at 8#020#;
end RUNNING_SCORE;

task body RUNNING_SCORE is
    SCORE: INTEGER := 0;
    for SCORE use at 8#500#;
begin
    loop
        select
            accept HIT do
                SCORE := SCORE + 1; -- increments SCORE when
                                    -- interrupt at 8#010#
            end HIT;
        or
            accept MISS do
                SCORE := SCORE - 1; -- decrements SCORE when
                                    -- interrupt at 8#020#
```

```
        end MISS;
      end select;
    end loop;
end RUNNING_SCORE;
```

This task has two entries: HIT and MISS. Immediately following these entries are the address clauses that specify the location of the interrupts. The address clauses associate HIT with a hardware interrupt at address 8#010# and MISS with a hardware interrupt at 8#020#. As a result of the first association, whenever an interrupt occurs at 8#010#, the task entry HIT is called and its associated **accept** statement in the task body increments SCORE. Whenever an interrupt occurs at 8#020#, the task entry MISS is called and its associated **accept** statement decrements SCORE. Note that SCORE is stored at the fixed location 8#500#. Also note that when a task entry, such as HIT or MISS, is associated with a hardware interrupt, regular calls can still be made to this task entry.

As a note to the advanced reader, if control information is passed along with an interrupt, it is passed as one or more **in** parameters. Only **in** parameters are allowed. Also, the address clauses may not associate more than one entry with a given address (although a compiler may not catch this error).

PRAGMA PACK

The pragma PACK requests the compiler to represent a composite type (an array or record type) in a packed (compressed) form. Consider, for example, a Boolean array type:

type BOOLEAN_ARRAY **is array** (1..16) **of** BOOLEAN;
pragma PACK (BOOLEAN_ARRAY);

The amount of storage allocated to store arrays of type BOOLEAN_ARRAY varies from compiler to compiler. One compiler might store each Boolean component of the array in a single word. Another compiler might store each Boolean value in a single byte or in a single bit. The pragma PACK requests the compiler to store objects of the composite type using as few bits as possible. Some compilers may honor the request and "squeeze" the array components together. Other compilers may choose to ignore this request. Unlike the representation clauses, if pragma PACK is requested and the compiler does not honor the request, no error will be reported.

UNCHECKED CONVERSION

Unchecked conversion copies a sequence of bits from an object of one type to an object of another type. During this process, the sequence of bits remains unaltered. Only the type of object that this sequence represents is changed. Unchecked conversion thus allows us to override Ada's ban against assigning one data type to another. This process is different from the explicit type conversions that we have previously encountered. When, for instance, the integer 3 is explicitly converted to a floating point number, FLOAT(3), the bit pattern is altered to reflect the new interpretation.

To use unchecked conversion, one must instantiate the predefined generic function UNCHECKED_CONVERSION. This generic function is an independent library unit, which is not contained in a package. The program unit that references UNCHECKED_CONVERSION must therefore mention it in a **with** clause. UNCHECKED_CONVERSION cannot be placed in a **use** clause since its only "resources"—the function name and its formal generic and nongeneric parameters—are already directly visible. The **use** clause can only be applied to nongeneric library packages.

The specification of UNCHECKED_CONVERSION appears as follows:

```
generic
    type SOURCE is limited private; -- generic parameters
    type TARGET is limited private;
function UNCHECKED_CONVERSION ( S: SOURCE ) return TARGET;
```

There are two formal generic parameters: SOURCE and TARGET. Thus, to instantiate this generic function, two parameters must be provided: one for the source type, the other for the target type. The function created by instantiating this generic is invoked with a parameter value of type SOURCE. This function returns the same sequence of bits as the parameter value of type SOURCE but as a representation of a value of type TARGET.

Let us now consider an example that uses UNCHECKED_CONVERSION. Suppose that the interface to some piece of hardware requires us to view the same sequence of bits as both a 16-bit integer and also as a bit string (an array of 16 Boolean values):

```
with UNCHECKED_CONVERSION;
procedure DEMO is
    type BOOLEAN_ARRAY is array (1 .. 16) of BOOLEAN;
    pragma PACK (BOOLEAN_ARRAY);
    BIT_STRING: BOOLEAN_ARRAY; -- assume 16-bit bit string
    INT: INTEGER; -- assume 16-bit integer

    function TO_BIT_STRING is new -- represents integer as a bit string
        UNCHECKED_CONVERSION ( SOURCE => INTEGER,
            TARGET => BOOLEAN_ARRAY );
```

```
begin
    INT := 2#0010_1101_1110_1111#;
    BIT_STRING := TO_BIT_STRING ( INT ); -- returns a bit string
    ...
end DEMO;
```

After the unchecked conversion is performed, each component of BIT_STRING is a Boolean variable stored as a single bit. The value of each component of BIT_STRING is FALSE or TRUE, depending on whether the corresponding bit in INT is 0 or 1.

In this example, INT and BIT_STRING are assumed to be the same size. When the source object and target object differ in size, some compilers will truncate the longer object, others will report an error, and so on. To find out what your compiler will do, refer to Appendix F in your compiler's reference manual.

Unchecked conversion should only be used when necessary, because it can result in erroneous code. The compiler takes no responsibility making sure that the bit pattern of the target object makes sense. This is the responsibility of the programmer.

LANGUAGE INTERFACES

Some implementations of Ada support the pragma INTERFACE, which allows Ada programs to interface with programs written in other languages. These other languages may include other high-level languages such as FORTRAN and Pascal, or low-level assembly languages. The pragma INTERFACE may be placed in a package specification or in the declarative part of a program unit. The following example shows how the pragma INTERFACE allows Ada to use three trigonometric functions that are implemented in FORTRAN:

```
package FORTRAN_FUNCTIONS is
    function SIN (X: FLOAT) return FLOAT;
    function COS (X: FLOAT) return FLOAT;
    function TAN (X: FLOAT) return FLOAT;
    pragma INTERFACE (FORTRAN, SIN);
    pragma INTERFACE (FORTRAN, COS);
    pragma INTERFACE (FORTRAN, TAN);
end FORTRAN_FUNCTIONS;
```

The first three declarations in this package are FORTRAN function specifications, written using Ada syntax. For each of these function specifications, a pragma INTERFACE follows. The bodies of these functions consist of the FORTRAN code. Therefore, this package does not need a body.

Pragma INTERFACE has two parameters. The first parameter specifies the name of the language with which Ada is to interface. The second parameter specifies the particular subprogram written in this other language. The pragma instructs the compiler to invoke the specified subprogram using the calling conventions of this other language.

Any Ada program that mentions package FORTRAN_FUNCTIONS in its **with** clause may invoke these FORTRAN functions just as if they were implemented in Ada. Many compilers, however, place certain restrictions on how the pragma INTERFACE may be used. Once again, refer to Appendix F of your computer's reference manual for details.

In addition to interfacing with other computer languages, some implementations of Ada allow for machine code insertions. How these insertions are made varies from compiler to compiler. If you are interested in this capability, refer to Appendix F of your compiler's reference manual and to the predefined package MACHINE_CODE. This package contains type declarations for machine language instructions. Also refer to Chapter 13 of the Ada Language Reference Manual for a general description.

EXERCISES

1. Explain the difference between MIN_INT and INTEGER'FIRST, and between MAX_INT and INTEGER'LAST.

2. Explain the differences between SYSTEM.ADDRESS, discussed in this chapter, and access types, discussed in Chapter 12.

3. Write code that stores a character variable CHAR at address 8#167#.

4. Consider the following declarations:
   ```
   type R is
      record
         A: TYPE_A;
         B: TYPE_B;
         C: TYPE_C;
      end record;
   X: R;
   ```
   Suppose that this record is stored in a 32-bit word as follows (where bits are numbered from left to right):

A	bits 0 to 11
B	bits 12 to 15
C	bits 24 to 31

Assuming that the storage unit is an 8-bit byte, what are the values of the following representation attributes?

X.A'POSITION   X.A'FIRST_BIT   X.A'LAST_BIT
X.B'POSITION   X.B'FIRST_BIT   X.B'LAST_BIT
X.C'POSITION   X.C'FIRST_BIT   X.C'LAST_BIT

5. What is the minimum number of bits needed to store the values of the following enumeration type?

   type B_FLAT_MAJOR **is** (B_FLAT, C, D, E_FLAT, F, G, A);

   Write a length clause to establish the amount of storage space allocated for objects of type B_FLAT_MAJOR.

6. Use an enumeration clause to associate each of the following bit patterns with the enumeration literals of the following type:

   type SIGNAL **is** (RED, YELLOW, GREEN);

   001   red
   011   yellow
   111   green

7. Give the enumeration literals of SIGNAL, in exercise 6, the following second representation:

   010   red
   110   yellow
   111   green

   Once the enumeration literals of SIGNAL are given two different representations, write code to convert an object of type SIGNAL from one representation to the other.

8. Explain why the following enumeration clause cannot be used to associate the specified bit patterns with the enumeration literals of type STATUS:

   type STATUS **is** (OK, NOT_OK, UNKNOWN);
   for STATUS **use** (OK   =>   2#0101#,
                            NOT_OK   =>   2#0011#,
                            UNKNOWN   =>   2#1000#);

9. Reconsider the computer-controlled machine, presented in this chapter, that is capable of creating high temperatures and pressures within a sealed container. Suppose that the 32-bit interface to this machine is changed as follows:

Word 0	CONTAINER	bits 0 to 2
	unused	bits 3 to 7
	ANGLE	bits 8 to 14
	unused	bit 15
Word 1	TEMPERATURE	bits 0 to 9
	PRESSURE	bits 10 to 15

Rewrite the machine-dependent code to reflect this change.

10. Write a program that uses the generic UNCHECKED_CONVERSION function to represent an integer as a string. How does this differ from the use of the overloaded PUT procedure, discussed in Chapter 14, which outputs an integer value to a string?

Appendixes

Appendixes A through H are reprinted from the *Reference Manual for the Ada Programming Language* (ANSI/MIL-STD-1815A-1983). All references in these appendixes are to the manual rather than to this book.

APPENDIX A. PREDEFINED LANGUAGE ATTRIBUTES

This appendix contains a complete list of the predefined language attributes.

P'ADDRESS   For a prefix P that denotes an object, a program unit, a label, or an entry:

Yields the address of the first of the storage units allocated to P. For a subprogram, package, task unit, or label, this value refers to the machine code associated with the corresponding body or statement. For an entry for which an address clause has been given, the value refers to the corresponding hardware interrupt. The value of this attribute is of the type ADDRESS defined in the package SYSTEM. (See 13.7.2.)

P'AFT   For a prefix P that denotes a fixed point subtype:

Yields the number of decimal digits needed after the point to accommodate the precision of the subtype P, unless the delta of the subtype P is greater than 0.1, in which case the attribute yields the value one. (P'AFT is the smallest positive integer N for which (10**N)*P'DELTA is greater than or equal to one.) The value of this attribute is of the type *universal_integer*. (See 3.5.10.)

P'BASE   For a prefix P that denotes a type or subtype:

This attribute denotes the base type of P. It is only allowed as the prefix of the name of another attribute: for example, P'BASE'FIRST. (See 3.3.3.)

441

P'CALLABLE   For a prefix P that is appropriate for a task type:

Yields the value FALSE when the execution of the task P is either completed or terminated, or when the task is abnormal; yields the value TRUE otherwise. The value of this attribute is of the predefined type BOOLEAN. (See 9.9.)

P'CONSTRAINED   For a prefix P that denotes an object of a type with discriminants:

Yields the value TRUE if a discriminant constraint applies to the object P, or if the object is a constant (including a formal parameter or generic formal parameter of mode **in**); yields the value FALSE otherwise. If P is a generic formal parameter of mode **in out**, or if P is a formal parameter of mode **in out** or **out** and the type mark given in the corresponding parameter specification denotes an unconstrained type with discriminants, then the value of this attribute is obtained from that of the corresponding actual parameter. The value of this attribute is of the predefined type BOOLEAN. (See 3.7.4.)

P'CONSTRAINED   For a prefix P that denotes a private type or subtype:

Yields the value FALSE if P denotes an unconstrained nonformal private type with discriminants; also yields the value FALSE if P denotes a generic formal private type and the associated actual subtype is either an unconstrained type with discriminants or an unconstrained array type; yields the value TRUE otherwise. The value of this attribute is of the predefined type BOOLEAN. (See 7.4.2.)

P'COUNT   For a prefix P that denotes an entry of a task unit:

Yields the number of entry calls presently queued on the entry (if the attribute is evaluated within an accept statement for the entry P, the count does not include the calling task). The value of this attribute is of the type *universal_integer*. (See 9.9.)

P'DELTA   For a prefix P that denotes a fixed point subtype:

Yields the value of the delta specified in the fixed accuracy definition for the subtype P. The value of this attribute is of the type *universal_real*. (See 3.5.10.)

P'DIGITS   For a prefix P that denotes a floating point subtype:

Yields the number of decimal digits in the decimal mantissa of model numbers of the subtype P. (This attribute yields the number D of section 3.5.7.) The value of this attribute is of the type *universal_integer*. (See 3.5.8.)

P'EMAX   For a prefix P that denotes a floating point subtype:

Yields the largest exponent value in the binary canonical form of model numbers of the subtype P. (This attribute yields the product $4*B$ of section 3.5.7.) The value of this attribute is of the type *universal_integer*. (See 3.5.8.)

P'EPSILON   For a prefix P that denotes a floating point subtype:

Yields the absolute value of the difference between the model number 1.0 and the next model number above, for the subtype P. The value of this attribute is of the type *universal_real*. (See 3.5.8.)

P'FIRST   For a prefix P that denotes a scalar type, or a subtype of a scalar type:

                  Yields the lower bound of P. The value of this attribute has the same type as
                  P. (See 3.5.)

P'FIRST   For a prefix P that is appropriate for an array type, or that denotes a constrained array subtype:

                  Yields the lower bound of the first index range. The value of this attribute
                  has the same type as this lower bound. (See 3.6.2 and 3.8.2.)

P'FIRST(N)   For a prefix P that is appropriate for an array type, or that denotes a constrained array subtype:

                  Yields the lower bound of the N-th index range. The value of this attribute
                  has the same type as this lower bound. The argument N must be a static
                  expression of type *universal_integer*. The value of N must be positive
                  (nonzero) and no greater than the dimensionality of the array. (See 3.6.2 and
                  3.8.2.)

P'FIRST_BIT   For a prefix P that denotes a component of a record object:

                  Yields the offset, from the start of the first of the storage units occupied by
                  the component, of the first bit occupied by the component. This offset is
                  measured in bits. The value of this attribute is of the type *universal_integer*.
                  (See 13.7.2.)

P'FORE   For a prefix P that denotes a fixed point subtype:

                  Yields the minimum number of characters needed for the integer part of the
                  decimal representation of any value of the subtype P, assuming that the
                  representation does not include an exponent, but includes a one-character
                  prefix that is either a minus sign or a space. (This minimum number does not
                  include superfluous zeros or underlines, and is at least two.) The value of
                  this attribute is of the type *universal_integer*. (See 3.5.10.)

P'IMAGE   For a prefix P that denotes a discrete type or subtype:

                  This attribute is a function with a single parameter. The actual parameter X
                  must be a value of the base type of P. The result type is the predefined type
                  STRING. The result is the *image* of the value of X, that is, a sequence of
                  characters representing the value in display form. The image of an integer
                  value is the corresponding decimal literal; without underlines, leading
                  zeros, exponent, or trailing spaces; but with a one character prefix that is
                  either a minus sign or a space.

                  The image of an enumeration value is either the corresponding identifier in
                  upper case or the corresponding character literal (including the two
                  apostrophes); neither leading nor trailing spaces are included. The image of
                  a character other than a graphic character is implementation-defined. (See
                  3.5.5.)

P'LARGE   For a prefix P that denotes a real subtype:

                  The attribute yields the largest positive model number of the subtype P. The
                  value of this attribute is of the type *universal_real*. (See 3.5.8 and 3.5.10.)

P'LAST   For a prefix P that denotes a scalar type, or a subtype of a scalar type:

                  Yields the upper bound of P. The value of this attribute has the same type as
                  P. (See 3.5.)

P'LAST	For a prefix P that is appropriate for an array type, or that denotes a c strained array subtype:
	Yields the upper bound of the first index range. The value of this attrib has the same type as this upper bound. (See 3.6.2 and 3.8.2.)
P'LAST(N)	For a prefix P that is appropriate for an array type, or that denotes a constrained array subtype:
	Yields the upper bound of the N-th index range. The value of this attribute has the same type as this upper bound. The argument N must be a static expression of type *universal_integer*. The value of N must be positive (nonzero) and no greater than the dimensionality of the array. (See 3.6.2 and 3.8.2.)
P'LAST_BIT	For a prefix P that denotes a component of a record object:
	Yields the offset, from the start of the first of the storage units occupied by the component, of the last bit occupied by the component. This offset is measured in bits. The value of this attribute is of the type *universal_integer*. (See 13.7.2.)
P'LENGTH	For a prefix P that is appropriate for an array type, or that denotes a constrained array subtype:
	Yields the number of values of the first index range (zero for a null range). The value of this attribute is of the type *universal_integer*. (See 3.6.2.)
P'LENGTH(N)	For a prefix P that is appropriate for an array type, or that denotes a constrained array subtype:
	Yields the number of values of the N-th index range (zero for a null range). The value of this attribute is of the type *universal_integer*. The argument N must be a static expression of type *universal_integer*. The value of N must be positive (nonzero) and no greater than the dimensionality of the array. (See 3.6.2 and 3.8.2.)
P'MACHINE_EMAX	For a prefix P that denotes a floating point type or subtype:
	Yields the largest value of *exponent* for the machine representation of the base type of P. The value of this attribute is of the type *universal_integer*. (See 13.7.3.)
P'MACHINE_EMIN	For a prefix P that denotes a floating point type or subtype:
	Yields the smallest (most negative) value of *exponent* for the machine representation of the base type of P. The value of this attribute is of the type *universal_integer*. (See 13.7.3.)
P'MACHINE_MANTISSA	For a prefix P that denotes a floating point type or subtype:
	Yields the number of digits in the *mantissa* for the machine representation of the base type of P (the digits are extended digits in the range 0 to P'MACHINE_RADIX - 1). The value of this attribute is of the type *universal_integer*. (See 13.7.3.)

P'MACHINE_OVERFLOWS For a prefix P that denotes a real type or subtype:

Yields the value TRUE if every predefined operation on values of the base type of P either provides a correct result, or raises the exception NUMERIC_ERROR in overflow situations; yields the value FALSE otherwise. The value of this attribute is of the predefined type BOOLEAN. (See 13.7.3.)

P'MACHINE_RADIX For a prefix P that denotes a floating point type or subtype:

Yields the value of the *radix* used by the machine representation of the base type of P. The value of this attribute is of the type *universal_integer*. (See 13.7.3.)

P'MACHINE_ROUNDS For a prefix P that denotes a real type or subtype:

Yields the value TRUE if every predefined arithmetic operation on values of the base type of P either returns an exact result or performs rounding; yields the value FALSE otherwise. The value of this attribute is of the predefined type BOOLEAN. (See 13.7.3.)

P'MANTISSA For a prefix P that denotes a real subtype:

Yields the number of binary digits in the binary mantissa of model numbers of the subtype P. (This attribute yields the number B of section 3.5.7 for a floating point type, or of section 3.5.9 for a fixed point type.) The value of this attribute is of the type *universal_integer*. (See 3.5.8 and 3.5.10.)

P'POS For a prefix P that denotes a discrete type or subtype:

This attribute is a function with a single parameter. The actual parameter X must be a value of the base type of P. The result type is the type *universal_integer*. The result is the position number of the value of the actual parameter. (See 3.5.5.)

P'POSITION For a prefix P that denotes a component of a record object:

Yields the offset, from the start of the first storage unit occupied by the record, of the first of the storage units occupied by the component. This offset is measured in storage units. The value of this attribute is of the type *universal_integer*. (See 13.7.2.)

P'PRED For a prefix P that denotes a discrete type or subtype:

This attribute is a function with a single parameter. The actual parameter X must be a value of the base type of P. The result type is the base type of P. The result is the value whose position number is one less than that of X. The exception CONSTRAINT_ERROR is raised if X equals P'BASE'FIRST. (See 3.5.5.)

P'RANGE For a prefix P that is appropriate for an array type, or that denotes a constrained array subtype:

Yields the first index range of P, that is, the range P'FIRST .. P'LAST. (See 3.6.2.)

P'RANGE(N)   For a prefix P that is appropriate for an array type, or that denotes a constrained array subtype:

Yields the N-th index range of P, that is, the range P'FIRST(N) .. P'LAST(N). (See 3.6.2.)

P'SAFE_EMAX   For a prefix P that denotes a floating point type or subtype:

Yields the largest exponent value in the binary canonical form of safe numbers of the base type of P. (This attribute yields the number E of section 3.5.7.) The value of this attribute is of the type *universal_integer*. (See 3.5.8.)

P'SAFE_LARGE   For a prefix P that denotes a real type or subtype:

Yields the largest positive safe number of the base type of P. The value of this attribute is of the type *universal_real*. (See 3.5.8 and 3.5.10.)

P'SAFE_SMALL   For a prefix P that denotes a real type or subtype:

Yields the smallest positive (nonzero) safe number of the base type of P. The value of this attribute is of the type *universal_real*. (See 3.5.8 and 3.5.10.)

P'SIZE   For a prefix P that denotes an object:

Yields the number of bits allocated to hold the object. The value of this attribute is of the type *universal_integer*. (See 13.7.2.)

P'SIZE   For a prefix P that denotes any type or subtype:

Yields the minimum number of bits that is needed by the implementation to hold any possible object of the type or subtype P. The value of this attribute is of the type *universal_integer*. (See 13.7.2.)

P'SMALL   For a prefix P that denotes a real subtype:

Yields the smallest positive (nonzero) model number of the subtype P. The value of this attribute is of the type *universal_real*. (See 3.5.8 and 3.5.10.)

P'STORAGE_SIZE   For a prefix P that denotes an access type or subtype:

Yields the total number of storage units reserved for the collection associated with the base type of P. The value of this attribute is of the type *universal_integer*. (See 13.7.2.)

P'STORAGE_SIZE   For a prefix P that denotes a task type or a task object:

Yields the number of storage units reserved for each activation of a task of the type P or for the activation of the task object P. The value of this attribute is of the type *universal_integer*. (See 13.7.2.)

P'SUCC   For a prefix P that denotes a discrete type or subtype:

This attribute is a function with a single parameter. The actual parameter X must be a value of the base type of P. The result type is the base type of P. The result is the value whose position number is one greater than that of X. The exception CONSTRAINT_ERROR is raised if X equals P'BASE'LAST. (See 3.5.5.)

Appendixes **447**

P'TERMINATED   For a prefix P that is appropriate for a task type:

Yields the value TRUE if the task P is terminated; yields the value FALSE otherwise. The value of this attribute is of the predefined type BOOLEAN. (See 9.9.)

P'VAL   For a prefix P that denotes a discrete type or subtype:

This attribute is a special function with a single parameter X which can be of any integer type. The result type is the base type of P. The result is the value whose position number is the *universal_integer* value corresponding to X. The exception CONSTRAINT_ERROR is raised if the *universal_integer* value corresponding to X is not in the range P'POS (P'BASE'FIRST) .. P'POS (P'BASE'LAST). (See 3.5.5.)

P'VALUE   For a prefix P that denotes a discrete type or subtype:

This attribute is a function with a single parameter. The actual parameter X must be a value of the predefined type STRING. The result type is the base type of P. Any leading and any trailing spaces of the sequence of characters that corresponds to X are ignored.

For an enumeration type, if the sequence of characters has the syntax of an enumeration literal and if this literal exists for the base type of P, the result is the corresponding enumeration value. For an integer type, if the sequence of characters has the syntax of an integer literal, with an optional single leading character that is a plus or minus sign, and if there is a corresponding value in the base type of P, the result is this value. In any other case, the exception CONSTRAINT_ERROR is raised. (See 3.5.5.)

P'WIDTH   For a prefix P that denotes a discrete subtype:

Yields the maximum image length over all values of the subtype P (the *image* is the sequence of characters returned by the attribute IMAGE). The value of this attribute is of the type *universal_integer*. (See 3.5.5.)

APPENDIX B. PREDEFINED LANGUAGE PRAGMAS

This appendix contains a complete list of the predefined language pragmas.

Pragma	Meaning
CONTROLLED	Takes the simple name of an access type as the single argument. This pragma is only allowed immediately within the declarative part or package specification that contains the declaration of the access type; the declaration must occur before the pragma. This pragma is not allowed for a derived type. This pragma specifies that automatic storage reclamation must not be performed for objects designated by values of the access type, except upon leaving the innermost block statement, subprogram body, or task body that encloses the access type declaration, or after leaving the main program (see 4.8).
ELABORATE	Takes one or more simple names denoting library units as arguments. This pragma is only allowed immediately after the context clause of a compilation unit (before the subsequent library unit or secondary unit). Each argument must be the simple name of a library unit mentioned by the context clause. This pragma specifies that the corresponding library unit body must be elaborated before the given compilation unit. If the given compilation unit is a subunit, the library unit body must be elaborated before the body of the ancestor library unit of the subunit (see 10.5).
INLINE	Takes one or more names as arguments; each name is either the name of a subprogram or the name of a generic subprogram. This pragma is only allowed at the place of a declarative item in a declarative part or package specification, or after a library unit in a compilation, but before any subsequent compilation unit. This pragma specifies that the subprogram bodies should be expanded inline at each call whenever possible; in the case of a generic subprogram, the pragma applies to calls of its instantiations (see 6.3.2).
INTERFACE	Takes a language name and a subprogram name as arguments. This pragma is allowed at the place of a declarative item, and must apply in this case to a subprogram declared by an earlier declarative item of the same declarative part or package specification. This pragma is also allowed for a library unit; in this case the pragma must appear after the subprogram declaration, and before any subsequent compilation unit. This pragma specifies the other language (and thereby the calling conventions) and informs the compiler that an object module will be supplied for the corresponding subprogram (see 13.9).
LIST	Takes one of the identifiers ON or OFF as the single argument. This pragma is allowed anywhere a pragma is allowed. It specifies that listing of the compilation is to be continued or suspended until a LIST pragma with the opposite argument is given within the same compilation. The pragma itself is always listed if the compiler is producing a listing.
MEMORY_SIZE	Takes a numeric literal as the single argument. This pragma is only allowed at the start of a compilation, before the first compilation unit (if any) of the compilation. The effect of this pragma is to use the value of the specified numeric literal for the definition of the named number MEMORY_SIZE (see 13.7).

OPTIMIZE	Takes one of the identifiers TIME or SPACE as the single argument. This pragma is only allowed within a declarative part and it applies to the block or body enclosing the declarative part. It specifies whether time or space is the primary optimization criterion.
PACK	Takes the simple name of a record or array type as the single argument. The allowed positions for this pragma, and the restrictions on the named type, are governed by the same rules as for a representation clause. The pragma specifies that storage minimization should be the main criterion when selecting the representation of the given type (see 13.1).
PAGE	This pragma has no argument, and is allowed anywhere a pragma is allowed. It specifies that the program text which follows the pragma should start on a new page (if the compiler is currently producing a listing).
PRIORITY	Takes a static expression of the predefined integer subtype PRIORITY as the single argument. This pragma is only allowed within the specification of a task unit or immediately within the outermost declarative part of a main program. It specifies the priority of the task (or tasks of the task type) or the priority of the main program (see 9.8).
SHARED	Takes the simple name of a variable as the single argument. This pragma is allowed only for a variable declared by an object declaration and whose type is a scalar or access type; the variable declaration and the pragma must both occur (in this order) immediately within the same declarative part or package specification. This pragma specifies that every read or update of the variable is a synchronization point for that variable. An implementation must restrict the objects for which this pragma is allowed to objects for which each of direct reading and direct updating is implemented as an indivisible operation (see 9.11).
STORAGE_UNIT	Takes a numeric literal as the single argument. This pragma is only allowed at the start of a compilation, before the first compilation unit (if any) of the compilation. The effect of this pragma is to use the value of the specified numeric literal for the definition of the named number STORAGE_UNIT (see 13.7).
SUPPRESS	Takes as arguments the identifier of a check and optionally also the name of either an object, a type or subtype, a subprogram, a task unit, or a generic unit. This pragma is only allowed either immediately within a declarative part or immediately within a package specification. In the latter case, the only allowed form is with a name that denotes an entity (or several overloaded subprograms) declared immediately within the package specification. The permission to omit the given check extends from the place of the pragma to the end of the declarative region associated with the innermost enclosing block statement or program unit. For a pragma given in a package specification, the permission extends to the end of the scope of the named entity.

If the pragma includes a name, the permission to omit the given check is further restricted: it is given only for operations on the named object or on all objects of the base type of a named type or subtype; for calls of a named subprogram; for activations of tasks of the named task type; or for instantiations of the given generic unit (see 11.7). |
| SYSTEM_NAME | Takes an enumeration literal as the single argument. This pragma is only allowed at the start of a compilation, before the first compilation unit (if any) of the compilation. The effect of this pragma is to use the enumeration literal with the specified identifier for the definition of the constant SYSTEM_NAME. This pragma is only allowed if the specified identifier corresponds to one of the literals of the type NAME declared in the package SYSTEM (see 13.7). |

APPENDIX C. STANDARD PACKAGE

The appendix contains the specification of the package STANDARD, which includes the predefined types and their operations. These types and operations are automatically available to all program units. The operations are shown as comments since they are implicitly declared.

```
package STANDARD is

  type BOOLEAN is (FALSE, TRUE);

  -- The predefined relational operators for this type are as follows:

  -- function "="   (LEFT, RIGHT : BOOLEAN) return BOOLEAN;
  -- function "/="  (LEFT, RIGHT : BOOLEAN) return BOOLEAN;
  -- function "<"   (LEFT, RIGHT : BOOLEAN) return BOOLEAN;
  -- function "<="  (LEFT, RIGHT : BOOLEAN) return BOOLEAN;
  -- function ">"   (LEFT, RIGHT : BOOLEAN) return BOOLEAN;
  -- function ">="  (LEFT, RIGHT : BOOLEAN) return BOOLEAN;

  -- The predefined logical operators and the predefined logical negation operator are as follows:

  -- function "and" (LEFT, RIGHT : BOOLEAN) return BOOLEAN;
  -- function "or"  (LEFT, RIGHT : BOOLEAN) return BOOLEAN;
  -- function "xor" (LEFT, RIGHT : BOOLEAN) return BOOLEAN;

  -- function "not" (RIGHT : BOOLEAN) return BOOLEAN;


  -- The universal type universal_integer is predefined.

  type INTEGER is implementation_defined;

  -- The predefined operators for this type are as follows:

  -- function "="   (LEFT, RIGHT : INTEGER) return BOOLEAN;
  -- function "/="  (LEFT, RIGHT : INTEGER) return BOOLEAN;
  -- function "<"   (LEFT, RIGHT : INTEGER) return BOOLEAN;
  -- function "<="  (LEFT, RIGHT : INTEGER) return BOOLEAN;
  -- function ">"   (LEFT, RIGHT : INTEGER) return BOOLEAN;
  -- function ">="  (LEFT, RIGHT : INTEGER) return BOOLEAN;

  -- function "+"   (RIGHT : INTEGER) return INTEGER;
  -- function "-"   (RIGHT : INTEGER) return INTEGER;
  -- function "abs" (RIGHT : INTEGER) return INTEGER;
```

```
-- function "+"    (LEFT, RIGHT : INTEGER) return INTEGER;
-- function "-"    (LEFT, RIGHT : INTEGER) return INTEGER;
-- function "*"    (LEFT, RIGHT : INTEGER) return INTEGER;
-- function "/"    (LEFT, RIGHT : INTEGER) return INTEGER;
-- function "rem"  (LEFT, RIGHT : INTEGER) return INTEGER;
-- function "mod"  (LEFT, RIGHT : INTEGER) return INTEGER;

-- function "**"   (LEFT : INTEGER; RIGHT : INTEGER) return INTEGER;
```

-- An implementation may provide additional predefined integer types. It is recommended that the
-- names of such additional types end with INTEGER as in SHORT_INTEGER or LONG_INTEGER.
-- The specification of each operator for the type *universal_integer*, or for any additional
-- predefined integer type, is obtained by replacing INTEGER by the name of the type in the
-- specification of the corresponding operator of the type INTEGER, except for the right operand
-- of the exponentiating operator.

-- The universal type *universal_real* is predefined.

type FLOAT is *implementation_defined*;

-- The predefined operators for this type are as follows:

```
-- function "="    (LEFT, RIGHT : FLOAT) return BOOLEAN;
-- function "/="   (LEFT, RIGHT : FLOAT) return BOOLEAN;
-- function "<"    (LEFT, RIGHT : FLOAT) return BOOLEAN;
-- function "<="   (LEFT, RIGHT : FLOAT) return BOOLEAN;
-- function ">"    (LEFT, RIGHT : FLOAT) return BOOLEAN;
-- function ">="   (LEFT, RIGHT : FLOAT) return BOOLEAN;

-- function "+"    (RIGHT : FLOAT) return FLOAT;
-- function "-"    (RIGHT : FLOAT) return FLOAT;
-- function "abs"  (RIGHT : FLOAT) return FLOAT;

-- function "+"    (LEFT, RIGHT : FLOAT) return FLOAT;
-- function "-"    (LEFT, RIGHT : FLOAT) return FLOAT;
-- function "*"    (LEFT, RIGHT : FLOAT) return FLOAT;
-- function "/"    (LEFT, RIGHT : FLOAT) return FLOAT;

-- function "**"   (LEFT : FLOAT; RIGHT : INTEGER) return FLOAT;
```

-- An implementation may provide additional predefined floating point types. It is recom-
-- mended that the names of such additional types end with FLOAT as in SHORT_FLOAT or
-- LONG_FLOAT. The specification of each operator for the type *universal_real*, or for any
-- additional predefined floating point type, is obtained by replacing FLOAT by the name of the
-- type in the specification of the corresponding operator of the type FLOAT.

-- In addition, the following operators are predefined for universal types:

```
-- function "*"   (LEFT : universal_integer; RIGHT : universal_real)    return universal_real;
-- function "*"   (LEFT : universal_real;    RIGHT : universal_integer) return universal_real;
-- function "/"   (LEFT : universal_real;    RIGHT : universal_integer) return universal_real;
```

-- The type *universal_fixed* is predefined. The only operators declared for this type are

```
-- function "*"   (LEFT : any_fixed_point_type; RIGHT : any_fixed_point_type) return universal_fixed;
-- function "/"   (LEFT : any_fixed_point_type; RIGHT : any_fixed_point_type) return universal_fixed;
```

-- The following characters form the standard ASCII character set. Character literals cor-
-- responding to control characters are not identifiers; they are indicated in italics in this definition.

```
type CHARACTER is

    ( nul,   soh,   stx,   etx,   eot,   enq,   ack,   bel,
      bs,    ht,    lf,    vt,    ff,    cr,    so,    si,
      dle,   dc1,   dc2,   dc3,   dc4,   nak,   syn,   etb,
      can,   em,    sub,   esc,   fs,    gs,    rs,    us,

      ' ',   '!',   '"',   '#',   '$',   '%',   '&',   ''',
      '(',   ')',   '*',   '+',   ',',   '-',   '.',   '/',
      '0',   '1',   '2',   '3',   '4',   '5',   '6',   '7',
      '8',   '9',   ':',   ';',   '<',   '=',   '>',   '?',

      '@',   'A',   'B',   'C',   'D',   'E',   'F',   'G',
      'H',   'I',   'J',   'K',   'L',   'M',   'N',   'O',
      'P',   'Q',   'R',   'S',   'T',   'U',   'V',   'W',
      'X',   'Y',   'Z',   '[',   '\',   ']',   '^',   '_',

      '`',   'a',   'b',   'c',   'd',   'e',   'f',   'g',
      'h',   'i',   'j',   'k',   'l',   'm',   'n',   'o',
      'p',   'q',   'r',   's',   't',   'u',   'v',   'w',
      'x',   'y',   'z',   '{',   '|',   '}',   '~',   del );

for CHARACTER use  --  128 ASCII character set without holes
    (0, 1, 2, 3, 4, 5, ..., 125, 126, 127);

-- The predefined operators for the type CHARACTER are the same as for any enumeration type.

package ASCII is
    -- Control characters:

    NUL  : constant CHARACTER := nul;     SOH  : constant CHARACTER := soh;
    STX  : constant CHARACTER := stx;     ETX  : constant CHARACTER := etx;
    EOT  : constant CHARACTER := eot;     ENQ  : constant CHARACTER := enq;
    ACK  : constant CHARACTER := ack;     BEL  : constant CHARACTER := bel;
    BS   : constant CHARACTER := bs;      HT   : constant CHARACTER := ht;
    LF   : constant CHARACTER := lf;      VT   : constant CHARACTER := vt;
    FF   : constant CHARACTER := ff;      CR   : constant CHARACTER := cr;
    SO   : constant CHARACTER := so;      SI   : constant CHARACTER := si;
    DLE  : constant CHARACTER := dle;     DC1  : constant CHARACTER := dc1;
    DC2  : constant CHARACTER := dc2;     DC3  : constant CHARACTER := dc3;
    DC4  : constant CHARACTER := dc4;     NAK  : constant CHARACTER := nak;
    SYN  : constant CHARACTER := syn;     ETB  : constant CHARACTER := etb;
    CAN  : constant CHARACTER := can;     EM   : constant CHARACTER := em;
    SUB  : constant CHARACTER := sub;     ESC  : constant CHARACTER := esc;
    FS   : constant CHARACTER := fs;      GS   : constant CHARACTER := gs;
    RS   : constant CHARACTER := rs;      US   : constant CHARACTER := us;
    DEL  : constant CHARACTER := del;

    -- Other characters:

    EXCLAM     : constant CHARACTER := '!';   QUOTATION  : constant CHARACTER := '"';
    SHARP      : constant CHARACTER := '#';   DOLLAR     : constant CHARACTER := '$';
    PERCENT    : constant CHARACTER := '%';   AMPERSAND  : constant CHARACTER := '&';
    COLON      : constant CHARACTER := ':';   SEMICOLON  : constant CHARACTER := ';';
    QUERY      : constant CHARACTER := '?';   AT_SIGN    : constant CHARACTER := '@';
    L_BRACKET  : constant CHARACTER := '[';   BACK_SLASH : constant CHARACTER := '\';
    R_BRACKET  : constant CHARACTER := ']';   CIRCUMFLEX : constant CHARACTER := '^';
    UNDERLINE  : constant CHARACTER := '_';   GRAVE      : constant CHARACTER := '`';
    L_BRACE    : constant CHARACTER := '{';   BAR        : constant CHARACTER := '|';
    R_BRACE    : constant CHARACTER := '}';   TILDE      : constant CHARACTER := '~';
```

-- Lower case letters:

LC_A : **constant** CHARACTER := 'a';
...
LC_Z : **constant** CHARACTER := 'z';

end ASCII;

-- Predefined subtypes:

subtype NATURAL **is** INTEGER **range** 0 .. INTEGER'LAST;
subtype POSITIVE **is** INTEGER **range** 1 .. INTEGER'LAST;

-- Predefined string type:

type STRING **is array**(POSITIVE **range** <>) **of** CHARACTER;

pragma PACK(STRING);

-- The predefined operators for this type are as follows:

```
-- function "="  (LEFT, RIGHT : STRING) return BOOLEAN;
-- function "/=" (LEFT, RIGHT : STRING) return BOOLEAN;
-- function "<"  (LEFT, RIGHT : STRING) return BOOLEAN;
-- function "<=" (LEFT, RIGHT : STRING) return BOOLEAN;
-- function ">"  (LEFT, RIGHT : STRING) return BOOLEAN;
-- function ">=" (LEFT, RIGHT : STRING) return BOOLEAN;

-- function "&"  (LEFT : STRING;     RIGHT : STRING)    return STRING;
-- function "&"  (LEFT : CHARACTER;  RIGHT : STRING)    return STRING;
-- function "&"  (LEFT : STRING;     RIGHT : CHARACTER) return STRING;
-- function "&"  (LEFT : CHARACTER;  RIGHT : CHARACTER) return STRING;
```

type DURATION **is delta** *implementation_defined* **range** *implementation_defined*;

-- The predefined operators for the type DURATION are the same as for any fixed point type.

-- The predefined exceptions:

```
CONSTRAINT_ERROR : exception;
NUMERIC_ERROR    : exception;
PROGRAM_ERROR    : exception;
STORAGE_ERROR    : exception;
TASKING_ERROR    : exception;
```

end STANDARD;

APPENDIX D. SYSTEM PACKAGE

This appendix contains the specification of the package SYSTEM. The package SYSTEM contains the definitions of computer-dependent characteristics. The details of this package are provided in Appendix F of the reference manual included with every Ada compiler.

```
package SYSTEM is
    type ADDRESS    is implementation_defined;
    type NAME       is implementation_defined_enumeration_type;

    SYSTEM_NAME     : constant NAME := implementation_defined;

    STORAGE_UNIT    : constant := implementation_defined;
    MEMORY_SIZE     : constant := implementation_defined;

    -- System-Dependent Named Numbers:

    MIN_INT         : constant := implementation_defined;
    MAX_INT         : constant := implementation_defined;
    MAX_DIGITS      : constant := implementation_defined;
    MAX_MANTISSA    : constant := implementation_defined;
    FINE_DELTA      : constant := implementation_defined;
    TICK            : constant := implementation_defined;

    -- Other System-Dependent Declarations

    subtype PRIORITY is INTEGER range implementation_defined;

    ...
end SYSTEM;
```

APPENDIX E. TEXT_IO PACKAGE

This appendix contains the specification of the package TEXT_IO.

```ada
with IO_EXCEPTIONS;
package TEXT_IO is

   type FILE_TYPE is limited private;

   type FILE_MODE is (IN_FILE, OUT_FILE);

   type COUNT is range 0 .. implementation_defined;
   subtype POSITIVE_COUNT is COUNT range 1 .. COUNT'LAST;
   UNBOUNDED : constant COUNT := 0; -- line and page length

   subtype FIELD       is INTEGER range 0 .. implementation_defined;
   subtype NUMBER_BASE is INTEGER range 2 .. 16;

   type TYPE_SET is (LOWER_CASE, UPPER_CASE);

   -- File Management

   procedure CREATE ( FILE : in out FILE_TYPE;
                      MODE : in FILE_MODE := OUT_FILE;
                      NAME : in STRING    := "";
                      FORM : in STRING    := "");

   procedure OPEN   ( FILE : in out FILE_TYPE;
                      MODE : in FILE_MODE;
                      NAME : in STRING;
                      FORM : in STRING := "");

   procedure CLOSE  (FILE : in out FILE_TYPE);
   procedure DELETE (FILE : in out FILE_TYPE);
   procedure RESET  (FILE : in out FILE_TYPE; MODE : in FILE_MODE);
   procedure RESET  (FILE : in out FILE_TYPE);

   function MODE (FILE : in FILE_TYPE) return FILE_MODE ;
   function NAME (FILE : in FILE_TYPE) return STRING;
   function FORM (FILE : in FILE_TYPE) return STRING;

   function IS_OPEN(FILE : in FILE_TYPE) return BOOLEAN;

   -- Control of default input and output files

   procedure SET_INPUT  (FILE : in FILE_TYPE);
   procedure SET_OUTPUT (FILE : in FILE_TYPE);


   function STANDARD_INPUT   return FILE_TYPE;
   function STANDARD_OUTPUT  return FILE_TYPE;

   function CURRENT_INPUT    return FILE_TYPE;
   function CURRENT_OUTPUT   return FILE_TYPE;
```

-- Specification of line and page lengths

procedure SET_LINE_LENGTH   (FILE : in FILE_TYPE; TO : in COUNT);
procedure SET_LINE_LENGTH   (TO : in COUNT);

procedure SET_PAGE_LENGTH   (FILE : in FILE_TYPE; TO : in COUNT);
procedure SET_PAGE_LENGTH   (TO : in COUNT);

function LINE_LENGTH (FILE : in FILE_TYPE) return COUNT;
function LINE_LENGTH   return COUNT;

function PAGE_LENGTH (FILE : in FILE_TYPE) return COUNT;
function PAGE_LENGTH   return COUNT;

-- Column, Line, and Page Control

procedure NEW_LINE   (FILE : in FILE_TYPE; SPACING : in POSITIVE_COUNT := 1);
procedure NEW_LINE   (SPACING : in POSITIVE_COUNT := 1);

procedure SKIP_LINE   (FILE : in FILE_TYPE; SPACING : in POSITIVE_COUNT := 1);
procedure SKIP_LINE   (SPACING : in POSITIVE_COUNT := 1);

function END_OF_LINE (FILE : in FILE_TYPE) return BOOLEAN;
function END_OF_LINE   return BOOLEAN;

procedure NEW_PAGE   (FILE : in FILE_TYPE);
procedure NEW_PAGE;

procedure SKIP_PAGE   (FILE : in FILE_TYPE);
procedure SKIP_PAGE;

function END_OF_PAGE (FILE : in FILE_TYPE) return BOOLEAN;
function END_OF_PAGE   return BOOLEAN;

function END_OF_FILE (FILE : in FILE_TYPE) return BOOLEAN;
function END_OF_FILE   return BOOLEAN;

procedure SET_COL (FILE : in FILE_TYPE; TO : in POSITIVE_COUNT);
procedure SET_COL (TO   : in POSITIVE_COUNT);

procedure SET_LINE (FILE : in FILE_TYPE; TO : in POSITIVE_COUNT);
procedure SET_LINE (TO   : in POSITIVE_COUNT);

function COL (FILE : in FILE_TYPE) return POSITIVE_COUNT;
function COL   return POSITIVE_COUNT;

function LINE (FILE : in FILE_TYPE) return POSITIVE_COUNT;
function LINE return POSITIVE_COUNT;

function PAGE (FILE : in FILE_TYPE) return POSITIVE_COUNT;
function PAGE return POSITIVE_COUNT;

-- Character Input-Output

procedure GET(FILE : in   FILE_TYPE; ITEM : out CHARACTER);
procedure GET(ITEM : out CHARACTER);
procedure PUT(FILE : in   FILE_TYPE; ITEM : in CHARACTER);
procedure PUT(ITEM : in   CHARACTER);

```
-- String Input-Output

procedure  GET(FILE    : in   FILE_TYPE; ITEM : out STRING);
procedure  GET(ITEM    : out  STRING);
procedure  PUT(FILE    : in   FILE_TYPE; ITEM : in STRING);
procedure  PUT(ITEM    : in   STRING);

procedure  GET_LINE(FILE : in   FILE_TYPE; ITEM : out STRING; LAST : out NATURAL);
procedure  GET_LINE(ITEM : out  STRING; LAST : out NATURAL);
procedure  PUT_LINE(FILE : in   FILE_TYPE; ITEM : in STRING);
procedure  PUT_LINE(ITEM : in   STRING);

-- Generic package for Input-Output of Integer Types

generic
   type NUM is range <>;
package INTEGER_IO is

   DEFAULT_WIDTH  : FIELD := NUM'WIDTH;
   DEFAULT_BASE   : NUMBER_BASE := 10;

   procedure GET(FILE    : in   FILE_TYPE; ITEM : out NUM; WIDTH : in FIELD := 0);
   procedure GET(ITEM    : out  NUM; WIDTH : in FIELD := 0);

   procedure PUT(FILE    : in FILE_TYPE;
                 ITEM    : in NUM;
                 WIDTH   : in FIELD := DEFAULT_WIDTH;
                 BASE    : in NUMBER_BASE := DEFAULT_BASE);
   procedure PUT(ITEM    : in NUM;
                 WIDTH   : in FIELD := DEFAULT_WIDTH;
                 BASE    : in NUMBER_BASE := DEFAULT_BASE);

   procedure GET(FROM  : in   STRING; ITEM : out NUM; LAST : out POSITIVE);
   procedure PUT(TO    : out  STRING;
                 ITEM  : in NUM;
                 BASE  : in NUMBER_BASE := DEFAULT_BASE);

end INTEGER_IO;

-- Generic packages for Input-Output of Real Types

generic
   type NUM is digits <>;
package FLOAT_IO is

   DEFAULT_FORE  : FIELD := 2;
   DEFAULT_AFT   : FIELD := NUM'DIGITS-1;
   DEFAULT_EXP   : FIELD := 3;

   procedure GET(FILE : in FILE_TYPE; ITEM : out NUM; WIDTH : in FIELD := 0);
   procedure GET(ITEM : out NUM; WIDTH : in FIELD := 0);

   procedure PUT(FILE  : in FILE_TYPE;
                 ITEM  : in NUM;
                 FORE  : in FIELD := DEFAULT_FORE;
                 AFT   : in FIELD := DEFAULT_AFT;
                 EXP   : in FIELD := DEFAULT_EXP);
   procedure PUT(ITEM  : in NUM;
                 FORE  : in FIELD := DEFAULT_FORE;
                 AFT   : in FIELD := DEFAULT_AFT;
                 EXP   : in FIELD := DEFAULT_EXP);

   procedure GET(FROM  : in STRING; ITEM : out NUM; LAST : out POSITIVE);
   procedure PUT(TO    : out STRING;
                 ITEM  : in NUM;
                 AFT   : in FIELD := DEFAULT_AFT;
                 EXP   : in FIELD := DEFAULT_EXP);
end FLOAT_IO;
```

```
generic
  type NUM is delta <>;
package FIXED_IO is

  DEFAULT_FORE    : FIELD := NUM'FORE;
  DEFAULT_AFT     : FIELD := NUM'AFT;
  DEFAULT_EXP     : FIELD := 0;

  procedure GET(FILE  : in FILE_TYPE; ITEM : out NUM; WIDTH : in FIELD := 0);
  procedure GET(ITEM  : out NUM; WIDTH : in FIELD := 0);

  procedure PUT(FILE  : in FILE_TYPE;
                ITEM  : in NUM;
                FORE  : in FIELD := DEFAULT_FORE;
                AFT   : in FIELD := DEFAULT_AFT;
                EXP   : in FIELD := DEFAULT_EXP);
  procedure PUT(ITEM  : in NUM;
                FORE  : in FIELD := DEFAULT_FORE;
                AFT   : in FIELD := DEFAULT_AFT;
                EXP   : in FIELD := DEFAULT_EXP);

  procedure GET(FROM  : in  STRING; ITEM : out NUM; LAST : out POSITIVE);
  procedure PUT(TO    : out STRING;
                ITEM  : in NUM;
                AFT   : in FIELD := DEFAULT_AFT;
                EXP   : in FIELD := DEFAULT_EXP);

end FIXED_IO;

-- Generic package for Input-Output of Enumeration Types

generic
  type ENUM is (<>);
package ENUMERATION_IO is

  DEFAULT_WIDTH   : FIELD := 0;
  DEFAULT_SETTING : TYPE_SET := UPPER_CASE;

  procedure GET(FILE  : in FILE_TYPE; ITEM : out ENUM);
  procedure GET(ITEM  : out ENUM);

  procedure PUT(FILE  : in FILE_TYPE;
                ITEM  : in ENUM;
                WIDTH : in FIELD    := DEFAULT_WIDTH;
                SET   : in TYPE_SET := DEFAULT_SETTING);
  procedure PUT(ITEM  : in ENUM;
                WIDTH : in FIELD    := DEFAULT_WIDTH;
                SET   : in TYPE_SET := DEFAULT_SETTING);

  procedure GET(FROM  : in  STRING; ITEM : out ENUM; LAST : out POSITIVE);
  procedure PUT(TO    : out STRING;
                ITEM  : in ENUM;
                SET   : in TYPE_SET := DEFAULT_SETTING);
end ENUMERATION_IO;

-- Exceptions

STATUS_ERROR  : exception renames IO_EXCEPTIONS.STATUS_ERROR;
MODE_ERROR    : exception renames IO_EXCEPTIONS.MODE_ERROR;
NAME_ERROR    : exception renames IO_EXCEPTIONS.NAME_ERROR;
USE_ERROR     : exception renames IO_EXCEPTIONS.USE_ERROR;
DEVICE_ERROR  : exception renames IO_EXCEPTIONS.DEVICE_ERROR;
END_ERROR     : exception renames IO_EXCEPTIONS.END_ERROR;
DATA_ERROR    : exception renames IO_EXCEPTIONS.DATA_ERROR;
LAYOUT_ERROR  : exception renames IO_EXCEPTIONS.LAYOUT_ERROR;

private
  -- implementation-dependent
end TEXT_IO;
```

APPENDIX F. SEQUENTIAL_IO PACKAGE

This appendix contains the specification of the package SEQUENTIAL_IO.

```ada
with IO_EXCEPTIONS;
generic
   type ELEMENT_TYPE is private;
package SEQUENTIAL_IO is

   type FILE_TYPE is limited private;

   type FILE_MODE is (IN_FILE, OUT_FILE);


   -- File management

   procedure CREATE (FILE : in out FILE_TYPE;
                     MODE : in FILE_MODE := OUT_FILE;
                     NAME : in STRING := "";
                     FORM : in STRING := "");

   procedure OPEN   (FILE : in out FILE_TYPE;
                     MODE : in FILE_MODE;
                     NAME : in STRING;
                     FORM : in STRING := "");

   procedure CLOSE  (FILE : in out FILE_TYPE);
   procedure DELETE (FILE : in out FILE_TYPE);
   procedure RESET  (FILE : in out FILE_TYPE; MODE : in FILE_MODE);
   procedure RESET  (FILE : in out FILE_TYPE);

   function MODE    (FILE : in FILE_TYPE) return FILE_MODE;
   function NAME    (FILE : in FILE_TYPE) return STRING;
   function FORM    (FILE : in FILE_TYPE) return STRING;

   function IS_OPEN (FILE : in FILE_TYPE) return BOOLEAN;

   -- Input and output operations

   procedure READ  (FILE : in FILE_TYPE; ITEM : out ELEMENT_TYPE);
   procedure WRITE (FILE : in FILE_TYPE; ITEM : in  ELEMENT_TYPE);

   function END_OF_FILE(FILE : in FILE_TYPE) return BOOLEAN;

   -- Exceptions

   STATUS_ERROR : exception renames IO_EXCEPTIONS.STATUS_ERROR;
   MODE_ERROR   : exception renames IO_EXCEPTIONS.MODE_ERROR;
   NAME_ERROR   : exception renames IO_EXCEPTIONS.NAME_ERROR;
   USE_ERROR    : exception renames IO_EXCEPTIONS.USE_ERROR;
   DEVICE_ERROR : exception renames IO_EXCEPTIONS.DEVICE_ERROR;
   END_ERROR    : exception renames IO_EXCEPTIONS.END_ERROR;
   DATA_ERROR   : exception renames IO_EXCEPTIONS.DATA_ERROR;

private
   -- implementation-dependent
end SEQUENTIAL_IO;
```

APPENDIX G. DIRECT_IO PACKAGE

This appendix contains the specification of the package DIRECT_IO.

```
with IO_EXCEPTIONS;
generic
   type ELEMENT_TYPE is private;
package DIRECT_IO is

   type FILE_TYPE   is limited private;

   type     FILE_MODE is (IN_FILE, INOUT_FILE, OUT_FILE);
   type     COUNT        is range 0 .. implementation_defined;
   subtype  POSITIVE_COUNT is COUNT range 1 .. COUNT'LAST;


   -- File management

   procedure CREATE ( FILE   : in out FILE_TYPE;
                      MODE   : in FILE_MODE := INOUT_FILE;
                      NAME   : in STRING := "";
                      FORM   : in STRING := "");

   procedure OPEN   ( FILE   : in out FILE_TYPE;
                      MODE   : in FILE_MODE;
                      NAME   : in STRING;
                      FORM   : in STRING := "");

   procedure CLOSE  (FILE : in out FILE_TYPE);
   procedure DELETE (FILE : in out FILE_TYPE);
   procedure RESET  (FILE : in out FILE_TYPE; MODE : in FILE_MODE);
   procedure RESET  (FILE : in out FILE_TYPE);

   function MODE    (FILE : in FILE_TYPE) return FILE_MODE;
   function NAME    (FILE : in FILE_TYPE) return STRING;
   function FORM    (FILE : in FILE_TYPE) return STRING;

   function IS_OPEN (FILE : in FILE_TYPE) return BOOLEAN;
```

-- Input and output operations

procedure READ (FILE : **in** FILE_TYPE; ITEM : **out** ELEMENT_TYPE; FROM : POSITIVE_COUNT);
procedure READ (FILE : **in** FILE_TYPE; ITEM : **out** ELEMENT_TYPE);

procedure WRITE (FILE : **in** FILE_TYPE; ITEM : **in** ELEMENT_TYPE; TO : POSITIVE_COUNT);
procedure WRITE (FILE : **in** FILE_TYPE; ITEM : **in** ELEMENT_TYPE);

procedure SET_INDEX(FILE : **in** FILE_TYPE; TO : **in** POSITIVE_COUNT);

function INDEX (FILE : **in** FILE_TYPE) **return** POSITIVE_COUNT;
function SIZE (FILE : **in** FILE_TYPE) **return** COUNT;

function END_OF_FILE (FILE : **in** FILE_TYPE) **return** BOOLEAN;

-- Exceptions

STATUS_ERROR : **exception renames** IO_EXCEPTIONS.STATUS_ERROR;
MODE_ERROR   : **exception renames** IO_EXCEPTIONS.MODE_ERROR;
NAME_ERROR   : **exception renames** IO_EXCEPTIONS.NAME_ERROR;
USE_ERROR   : **exception renames** IO_EXCEPTIONS.USE_ERROR;
DEVICE_ERROR : **exception renames** IO_EXCEPTIONS.DEVICE_ERROR;
END_ERROR   : **exception renames** IO_EXCEPTIONS.END_ERROR;
DATA_ERROR   : **exception renames** IO_EXCEPTIONS.DATA_ERROR;

private
  -- implementation-dependent
end DIRECT_IO;

APPENDIX H. KEYWORDS

This appendix contains a complete list of Ada keywords. Keywords, also known as reserved words, have a predefined meaning and cannot be declared as identifiers. For readability, all keywords appearing in this book are in lowercase boldface letters.

abort	declare	generic	of	select
abs	delay	goto	or	separate
accept	delta		others	subtype
access	digits	if	out	
all	do	in		task
and		is	package	terminate
array			pragma	then
at	else		private	type
	elsif	limited	procedure	
	end	loop		
begin	entry		raise	use
body	exception		range	
	exit	mod	record	when
			rem	while
		new	renames	with
case	for	not	return	
constant	function	null	reverse	xor

INDEX

A

abort statement, 400
abs operator, 33 to 36, 52
acceptor task, 386
accept statement, 386 to 390, 403
access
    keyword, 301
    type, 18, 31, 299, 409
    value, *see* pointer
accuracy constraint, 337
actual parameter, 163, 164, 235, 238
Ada compiler system, 271
Ada library, 15, 197, 271
Ada Lovelace, 3
Ada LRM, 9, 10
Ada runtime environment, 278, 283, 284
ADDRESS attribute, 224, 423
address clause, 433
ADDRESS type, 423
AFT parameter, 352, 353, 367

aggregate, *see* array, aggregate; record, aggregate
AJPO, 5
all keyword, 304, 308
allocator, 299, 303, 409
Analytical Engine, 3
and operator, 39, 40, 113
and then, 41, 65
anonymous array, *see* array, anonymous
anonymous exception, *see* exception, anonymous
anonymous task type, 404
ANSI/MIL-STD-1815A, 3
arithmetic operators, *see* operators, arithmetic
array, 17, 91
    aggregate, 95, 100 to 103
    anonymous, 103, 148
    assignment, 103, 104, 120
    attributes, 115
    component, 91 to 93

concatenation, 109 to 111, 119, 377
constant, 99
dynamic, 105
index, 91 to 94
initialization, 95, 100
literal, *see* array, aggregate
of arrays, 114
of records, 135
of tasks, 405
one-dimensional, 92
operations, 119
slice, 109, 119
two-dimensional, 99
type, 93
type conversion, 120
unconstrained, 106, 184
ASCII characters, 37, 377
ASCII package, 377
assignment, *see also* array, assignment; record, assignment
operator, 26, 33
statement, 26, 33
at mod, 432
attribute, 19, 46
    ADDRESS, 224, 423
    CALLABLE, 401, 402
    CONSTRAINED, 143, 144
    COUNT, 391, 401
    FIRST, 46 to 48, 115 to 117
    FIRST_BIT, 424
    IMAGE, 46 to 49, 111
    LAST, 46 to 48, 115 to 117
    LAST_BIT, 424
    LENGTH, 115 to 117
    POS, 46 to 49, 332, 428
    POSITION, 424
    PRED, 46 to 48
    RANGE, 115 to 119
    SIZE, 423, 425, 426
    STORAGE_SIZE, 424
    SUCC, 46 to 48
    TERMINATE, 401, 402
    VAL, 46, 48, 49, 377
    VALUE, 46 to 49
    WIDTH, 350 to 352, 355

B

Babbage, Charles, 3
bar, *see* vertical bar
based
    literal, 28, 29
    number, 28
BASE parameter, 350 to 352
base type, 42, 334
begin keyword, 11
binary number, 28, 29, 351
binary operator, *see* operators, binary
binary search, 375
block
    identifier, 159, 160
    statement, 32, 106, 157, 158, 279
body, 264, *see also* function, body; procedure, body; package, body
Boolean
    constant, 38
    expression, 38, 39, 41
    literal, 29
    type, 38, 82
    variable, 38
    vector, 113
bottom-up design, 206

C

CALLABLE attribute, 401, 402
calling task, 386
case statement, 65
character
    constant, 38
    control, 377
    literal, 29

Index   469

type, 37
variable, 37, 38
circular dependency, 272, 273
closed alternative, 396
CLOSE procedure, 364, 365, 369, 372
COL function, 360
comments, 9, 30
compilation
   dependency, 267
   order, 268
   unit, 263
completeness checks, 205, 273
composite type, 17, 31, *see also* array; record
concatenation, *see* array, concatenation
concurrent processing, 381
conditional entry call, 394, 400
consistency checks, 205, 272
constant, 71
CONSTRAINED attribute, 143, 144
constrained record, *see* record, constrained
CONSTRAINT_ERROR exception, 278, 287
context specification, 10, 14, 197
control character, *see* character, control
control structures, 16, 57
conversion between types, *see* type conversion
COUNT attribute, 391, 401
COUNT type, 358, 373, 375
CREATE procedure, 362, 363, 365, 369, 372, 376
CURRENT_INPUT function, 366
CURRENT_OUTPUT function, 366

D

dangling pointer, 300
data abstraction, 3, 4, 106

DATA_ERROR exception, 375, 376
declarative part, 157, 264
   of function, 165
   of procedure, 11, 162
declared variable, 299
declare keyword, 158
DEFAULT_BASE variable, 352
default discriminant value, 142, 371
default parameter value, 13, 172
DEFAULT_SETTING variable, 355
DEFAULT_WIDTH variable, 352, 355
deferred constant, 223
delay statement, 77, 398 to 401
DELETE procedure, 366, 369, 372
delimiter, 25
delta keyword, 340
derived type, 334
designing in Ada, 205
developing Ada programs, 272
DEVICE_ERROR exception, 375, 376
digits keyword, 337
direct access file, 365, 371
DIRECT_IO package, 347, 365, 371, 375
directly visible, 15, 161, 197, 207, 209, 215
discrete range, 45
discrete type, 31
discriminant, 137 to 139
DOD, 1 to 3, 5
do keyword, 386
dot notation
   to access package resources, 15, 197, 208, 210, 212, 213, 218
   to call task, 386
   to resolve ambiguity, 208, 209, 248
   to select hidden identifiers, 80, 160
   to select record component, 130
dynamically allocated variable, 299, 300
dynamically created task, 408

E

elaboration, 11, 32, 203, 214, 215
else clause
   in **if** statement, 58, 59, 62
   in **select** statement, 397, 398, 400
elsif clause, 59, 63
embedded package, 214
embedded system, 2, 15, 421
END_ERROR exception, 375, 376
end keyword, 10, 11
END_OF_FILE function, 363, 369, 372
END_OF_LINE function, 363
END_OF_PAGE function, 363
entry
   clause, 385, 386
   family, 402
   queue, 391
enumeration
   clause, 426, 432
   constant, 37
   formatted I/O, 355, 356
   literal, 36, 37, 39
   order, 37, 39, 48
   type, 31, 36
   variable, 37
ENUMERATION_IO package, 62, 249, 354, 355
environment task, 383, 384, 410
erroneous program, 32, 167, 168, 304, 437
exception, 20, 277
   anonymous, 286, 287
   CONSTRAINT_ERROR, 278, 287
   DATA_ERROR, 375, 376
   DEVICE_ERROR, 375, 376
   END_ERROR, 375, 376
   identifier, 282
   LAYOUT_ERROR, 375, 376
   MODE_ERROR, 375, 376
   NAME_ERROR, 365, 375, 376
   NUMERIC_ERROR, 278, 287
   predefined, 278
   PROGRAM_ERROR, 278, 397
   propagation, 283, 390, 391
   raising, 283, 285
   STATUS_ERROR, 375, 376
   STORAGE_ERROR, 278
   suppression, 291
   TASKING_ERROR, 278, 389 to 391, 402
   USE_ERROR, 375, 376
   user-defined, 281
exception handler, 4, 20, 277, 279
   in block, 279
   in package, 287, 288
   in subprogram, 282
   in task, 390
exception keyword, 279
exclusive or, 40
exit statement, 17, 72, 73, 81, 85
exit when, 73, 81
EXP parameter, 352, 353

F

FALSE value, 29, 38
FIFO, 391
file, 349
   CLOSE, 364, 365, 369, 372
   CREATE, 362, 363, 365, 369, 372, 376
   DELETE, 366, 369, 372
   END_OF_FILE, 363, 369, 372
   FORM, 363, 366, 369, 372
   INDEX, 375
   IS_OPEN, 366, 369, 372
   MODE, 362, 365, 366, 369, 372
   NAME, 363, 365, 366, 369, 372
   OPEN, 364, 365, 369, 372, 376
   READ, 369, 372, 373
   RESET, 365, 366, 369, 372
   SIZE, 375
   WRITE, 369, 372, 373
file I/O, 360

Index   **471**

FILE_MODE type, 362, 369, 372
FILE parameter, 361 to 363
FILE_TYPE type, 362, 366, 369, 372
FIRST attribute, 46 to 48, 115 to 117
FIRST_BIT attribute, 424
FIXED_IO package, 249, 347, 354
fixed point
 constraint, 340
 formatted I/O, 354, 356
 number, 31
 type, 339
 universal, *see* universal type, fixed
floating point
 constant, 35, 36
 expression, *see* real, expression
 formatted I/O, 352 to 354, 356
 literal, *see* real, literal
 named number, *see* real, named number
 number, 31
 operations, *see* real, operations
 type, 35
 type definition, 335, 336
 universal, *see* universal type, real
 variable, 35, 36
FLOAT_IO package, 62, 249, 347, 352
FLOAT type, 35
FORE parameter, 352, 353
for loop, 14, 44, 72, 76
formal parameter, 163, 164, 235, 238
formatted I/O, 349
FORM function, 366, 369, 372
FORM parameter, 363
FORTRAN, 14, 20, 76, 83, 85, 426, 437
for use, 426, 427, 432
FROM parameter, 373
function, 17, 18, 157, 164, 263, 264, 266
 body, 164, 165
 specification, 164

G

generic, 11, 19, 235, 263, 265, 266
 function, 236
 instantiation, 11, 19, 62, 235
 object parameter, 247
 package, 245
 procedure, 241
 subprogram parameter, 250
 type parameter, 239, 245
GET_LINE procedure, 356, 365
GET procedure, 12, 348, 349, 355, 361, 367
goto statement**,** 4, 17, 84, 281
guard, 396, 397, 414

H

hardware interrupt, 434, 435
hexadecimal number, 28, 351
hierarchy of operation, *see* order of operation
HOLWG, 2

I

identifier, 9, 23
if statement**,** 57
IMAGE, attribute, 46 to 49, 111
implicit conversion of universal type, 341
implicit subtype, 43
incomplete type declaration, 312, 313
indentation of code, 10
INDEX function, 375
IN_FILE value, 362, 365, 366, 376
infix notation, 181, 211, 213, 214

information hiding, 3, 4, *see also* private part
inheriting operations, 337 to 339
initialization part of package, 203, 288
in operator, 41
INOUT_FILE value, 372
in out parameter
　for generic, 249
　for subprogram, 163, 164, 167, 169 to 171
　for task entry, 392
in parameter
　for generic, 249
　for subprogram, 165, 167, 169, 170
　for task entry, 392
insertion sort, 257 to 260
instantiation, *see* generic, instantiation
integer, 11
　constant, 32, 33
　expression, 32, 33
　formatted I/O, 350 to 352, 356, 361
　literal, 27, 329
　named number, 329
　operations, *see* arithmetic operators
　type, 31, 32
　type definition, 335, 336
　universal, *see* universal type, integer
　variable, 32, 33
INTEGER_IO package, 11, 62, 249, 250, 347, 350, 352
INTERFACE pragma, 437, 438
interleaved concurrency, 381
interrupt handler, 434
interrupts, *see* hardware interrupt
IO_EXCEPTIONS package, 347, 375
Ironman, 3
is keyword, 10, 11
IS_OPEN function, 366, 369, 372

K

keywords, 9

L

label, 85
language interface, 437
LAST attribute, 46 to 48, 115 to 117
LAST_BIT attribute, 424
LAST parameter, 357
LAYOUT_ERROR exception, 375, 376
LENGTH attribute, 115 to 117
length clause, 425, 432
lexical elements, 23
library unit, 177, 263, *see also* primary unit
LIFO, 201, 246
limited keyword, 224
limited private type, 224
LINE function, 360
LINE_LENGTH function, 360
linked list, 309
literal, 26
　expression, 83, 94, 331, 332
logical operators, *see* operators, logical
LONG_FLOAT type, 335
LONG_INTEGER type, 250, 331, 335, 336
loop, 17, 72
　counter, 77 to 80
　for, *see* **for** loop
　identifier, 80, 81
　while, *see* **while** loop
LOWER_CASE value, 355
low-level programming, 20, 421

M

machine code insertion, 438
MACHINE_CODE package, 438
main program, 10, 17
margin of error, 340
master unit, 383
MAX_INT, 331, 422
membership test, 41, 42, 44, 45
MIN_INT, 331, 422
mixed notation
    in array aggregate, 97
    in record aggregate, 131, 132
    in subprogram call, 171
MODE_ERROR exception, 375, 376
MODE function, 366, 369, 372
MODE parameter, 362, 365
mod operator, 33 to 36
modularity, 3, 4
module, 205
modulo, *see* **mod** operator

N

named notation
    in array aggregate, 95, 96, 100 to 103, 113
    in discriminant constraint, 139
    in enumeration clause, 427
    in generic instantiation, 239
    in record aggregate, 131, 135
    in subprogram call, 171, 174
    in task entry call, 393
named number, 329, 331, 332
NAME_ERROR exception, 365, 375, 376
NAME function, 366, 369, 372
NAME parameter, 363, 365
NATURAL subtype, 46, 250
nested loop, 80 to 82
nested record, 134, 135

new keyword
    as allocator, 303
    in derived type, 334
NEW_LINE procedure, 12, 13, 358, 359, 361
NEW_PAGE procedure, 358, 359
not in operator, 42
not operator, 39, 40, 113
null pointer, 302
null statement, 32, 70, 139
null string, 109
number declaration, 329 to 331
NUMERIC_ERROR exception, 278, 287

O

object-oriented design, 206
octal number, 28, 351
of keyword, 93
open alternative, 396, 397, 414
OPEN procedure, 364, 365, 369, 372, 376
operators
    arithmetic, 50
    binary, 34
    logical, 39, 40, 113, 114, 119
    order of operations, 50
    relational, 38, 39, 52, 111, 112, 121
    short circuit, *see* **and then**; **or else**
    unary, 34
OPTIMIZE pragma, 240, 241
order of operation, 50
or else, 41
or operator, 39, 40, 113
others
    in array aggregate, 96 to 98
    in **case** statement, 66 to 70
    in discriminated record type, 140
    in exception handler, 280, 286, 287
    in record aggregate, 131

OUT_FILE value, 362, 365, 366
out parameter
   for generic, 249
   for subprogram, 167, 168, 170, 171
   for task entry, 392
overlapped concurrency, 381
overloading, 4
   enumeration literals, 84
   operators, 13, 180 to 183, 225
   subprograms, 13, 178

P

package, 14, 15, 19, 195, 263, 265, 287, 288
   body, 19, 198, 266
   specification, 19, 196, 198, 266
PACK pragma, 435
PAGE function, 360
PAGE_LENGTH function, 360
parameter modes, 167, *see also* **in out** parameter; **in** parameter; **out** parameter
parent type, 334
Pascal, 3, 9, 14, 17, 75, 166, 235, 437
pointer, 18, 299, 300
   constant, 307
portability, 331, 335, 336, 422
POS attribute, 46 to 49, 332, 428
positional notation
   in array aggregate, 95, 96, 100 to 103
   in enumeration clause, 427
   in generic instantiation, 239
   in record aggregate, 131, 135
   in subprogram call, 171, 174
   in task entry call, 393
POSITION attribute, 424
POSITIVE_COUNT subtype, 358
POSITIVE subtype, 46, 250
pragma, 240
   INTERFACE, 437, 438

OPTIMIZE, 240, 241
PACK, 435
PRIORITY, 403
SUPRESS, 292
PRED attribute, 46 to 48
predefined subtype, 46
primary unit, 263, 264
PRIORITY pragma, 403
PRIORITY subtype, 404
private keyword, 219
private part, 198, 219
private type, 31, 218
procedure, 17, 18, 157, 162, 263, 264, 266, 282
   body, 11, 162, 266
   specification, 11, 162, 266
PROGRAM_ERROR exception, 278, 397
propagation of exception, *see* exception, propagation
PUT_LINE procedure, 12, 14, 356
PUT procedure, 13, 14, 348, 349
   for character, 349, 350
   for enumeration type, 354, 355
   for floating point, 352 to 354
   for integer, 350 to 352
   for output to string, 367, 368
   for string, 349, 350

Q

qualification, 84, 96, 180, 303

R

raise statement, 283, 285, 287
raising an exception, *see* exception, raising

Index **475**

random access file, *see* direct access file
RANGE attribute, 115 to 119
range constraint, 42
range keyword, 42
READ procedure, 369, 372, 373
real
   expression, 36
   literal, 28, 329
   named number, 329, 330
   operations, 36
   type, 31
   universal, *see* universal type, real
recompilation, 205, 223, 263, 270
record, 17, 129
   aggregate, 130 to 132
   alignment clause, 432, 433
   assignment, 133
   component, 130
   constant, 133
   constrained, 139, 143, 144
   discriminant, *see* discriminant
   literal, *see* record, aggregate
   of tasks, 405
   representation clause, 429
   unconstrained, 142 to 144
   variant, 136, 370, 371
recursion, *see* recursion, *see also* 184
relational operator, *see* operators, relational
rem operator, 33 to 36
renaming, 213, 214, 218, 376, 387
rendezvous, *see* task, rendezvous
repeat until loop, 17, 75
representation attribute, 423
representation clause, 425
reserved words, *see* keywords
RESET procedure, 365, 366, 369, 372
return statement, 164, 165, 278
reverse keyword, 82, 83
runtime error, 277

S

scalar type, 30
scientific notation, 27, 29, 201, 352, 353
scope, 160, 161, 376
secondary unit, 263, 264
selective wait, 394
selector, *see* vertical bar
select statement, 394, 395, 414
semicolon, 9, 10
separate keyword, 175, 176, 267
sequential files, 365
SEQUENTIAL_IO package, 347, 368, 375
SET_COL procedure, 323, 358, 359, 361
SET_INDEX procedure, 375
SET_INPUT procedure, 366
SET_LINE_LENGTH procedure, 359
SET_LINE procedure, 358, 359, 361
SET_OUTPUT procedure, 366, 367
SET_PAGE_LENGTH procedure, 359
SET parameter, 355
short circuit operators, *see* **and then**; **or else**
SHORT_FLOAT type, 335
SHORT_INTEGER type, 250, 335
SIGAda, 5
simple **loop**, 72
SIZE attribute, 423, 425, 426
SIZE function, 375
SKIP_LINE procedure, 358, 359, 361
SKIP_PAGE procedure, 358, 359
slice, *see* array, slice
software crisis, 1, 2
SPACE value, 240
stack, 201, 202, 225 to 227, 246 to 248, 288, 289
STANDARD_INPUT function, 366, 367
STANDARD_OUTPUT function, 366, 367

STANDARD package, 31, 37, 38, 46, 107, 112, 182, 250, 278, 335, 377
statement part, 157, 264
 of function, 165
 of package, *see* initialization part of package
 of procedure, 11, 162
static, 70, 71
STATUS_ERROR exception, 375, 376
Steelman, 3
step value, 83
STORAGE_ERROR exception, 278
STORAGE_SIZE attribute, 424
STORAGE_UNIT, 424
Strawman, 2
string, 9, 107
 aggregate, *see* string, literal
 constant, 108, 112
 literal, 29, 108, 112
 slice, 109
 user-defined, 112
 variable, 107, 108
strong typing, 3, 4, 12, 44, 332
structured control, 4
subprogram, 17, 157, 158, 263, *see also* procedure; function
subprogram library unit, 177
subtype, 42, 334
subunit, 174, 265, 266, 268, 269
 package body, 267
 subprogram body, 175, 176, 269
 task body, 383, 406
SUCC attribute, 46 to 48
suppressing exceptions, *see* exception, suppression
SUPPRESS pragma, 292
synchronize, *see* task, synchronization
SYSTEM package, 331, 404, 422 to 424

T

task, 20, 381
 attributes, 401
 calls, 386
 interference, 405
 rendezvous, 20, 388, 389
 specification, 383, 385
 synchronization, 384, 385
 termination, 389
 type, 31, 404
TASKING_ERROR exception, 278, 389 to 391, 402
temporary file, 363
TERMINATE attribute, 401, 402
terminate statement, 399, 400
TEXT_IO package, 14, 249, 348, 368, 375
then clause, 57, 58
timed entry call, 394, 400
TIME value, 240
Tinman, 2, 3
TO parameter, 373
top-down design, 205, 206
TRUE value, 29, 38
truth table, 39
type conversion, 49, 120, 334
types, 18

U

unary operator, *see* operators, unary
UNBOUNDED constant, 359, 360
UNCHECKED_CONVERSION, 436
UNCHECKED_DEALLOCATION, 304
unconstrained array, *see* array, unconstrained
unconstrained record, *see* record, unconstrained
underscore, 24, 25, 27, 28

universal type, 329
  fixed, 340
  integer, 329, 330, 332, 333
  real, 329 to 331, 333
unprintable character, 377
UPPER_CASE value, 355
use at, 434
use clause, 10, 15, 178, 197, 206, 210, 386, 387
USE_ERROR exception, 375, 376

V

VAL attribute, 46, 48, 49, 377
VALUE attribute, 46 to 49
variable, 11
variant record, *see* record, variant
vertical bar, 25
  in array aggregate, 97
  in **case** statement, 68
  in exception handler, 280
  in record aggregate, 131
visibility, 161, *see also* scope

W

when clause
  in **case** statement, 66 to 70
  in discriminated record, 139, 140
  in exception handler, 280, 285, 287
  in **select** statement, 395, 396
when others, *see* **others**
while loop, 72, 73, 76
WIDTH attribute, 351
WIDTH parameter, 350 to 352, 355, 356
with clause, 10, 14, 177, 197, 206, 268, 269
Woodenman, 2
WRITE, procedure, 369, 372, 373

X

xor operator, 39, 40, 51, 52, 113